Franklin County, Tennessee

Marriages

1838 – 1874

Byron and Barbara Sistler

JANAWAY PUBLISHING, INC.
2013

Franklin County, Tennessee, Marriages 1838-1874

Copyright © 1985 by Byron Sistler

Originally printed, Nashville, 1985

Reprinted
by

Janaway Publishing, Inc.
732 Kelsey Ct.
Santa Maria, California 93454
(805) 925-1038
www.JanawayPublishing.com

2006, 2013

Permission to reproduce in any form
must be secured from the publisher.

ISBN: 978-1-59641-049-7

Made in the United States of America

FRANKLIN COUNTY, TN MARRIAGES

1838-1874

Where two dates appear on an entry, the first one is the date license was issued, the second (in parentheses) the date marriage was solemnized. If only one date, it can mean (1) the date of execution was the same as the date of license issuance, or (2) execution of the marriage was not reported to the courthouse, or (3) the clerk failed to note in the marriage book that the license was returned.

Ordinarily, if there was any evidence the license was not returned we would so indicate in the entry. Sometimes the book would reveal definitely that a certain marriage did not take place, and in such instances we would make note of that in our entry.

We transcribed these marriage records directly from a microfilmed copy of the original county marriage books, so error, where it occurs, will usually be ours. However, it should be remembered that entries in the books themselves were copied from the licenses by clerks, and it is obvious from examining the pages that many of them were not prepared with great care. Sometimes, for example, the date of execution will appear in the book as a date prior to license issuance. In such cases, as well as where we had to guess in deciphering the handwriting, a question mark or "sic" is inserted on the entry.

Byron Sistler
Barbara Sistler

Nashville, TN
March, 1985

Abanathy, William to Cynthia Human 8-17-1872 (8-18-1872)
Acklin, Alexander S. to Jemima Oliver 1-11-1849
Acklin, James V. to Sarah Rollins 9-9-1839
Acklin, Syler to Creasy Parks 11-12-1868 (no return)
Acklin, Wm. H. to E. P. Fletcher 12-6-1847 (12-7-1847)
Acree, John S. to Anna Lambert 4-6-1867 (4-7-1867)
Adams, James H. to M. J. Walls 8-6-1872 (8-8-1872)
Adams, Jessee to Anna McCall 10-2-1843
Adams, John A. to Laura Runnels 2-16-1856 (2-17-1856)
Adams, John W. to Sarah J. Perry 4-10-1852
Adams, Pinkney to America Jones 12-20-1860
Adams, William to Martha A. Heathcoat 12-13-1852 (12-14-1852)
Adcock, J. W. to M. J. Crabtree 12-14-1867 (no return)
Adcock, William to Eliza Crowden 1-30-1850 (1-31-1850)
Adcock, Wiseman to Hannah Dial 4-8-1844
Addington, David to Malinda J. Cox 6-1-1842 (6-2-1842)
Addington, Jason to Elizabeth Taylor 11-13-1842
Adkins, G. W. to N. M. Smith 2-10-1840 (no return)
Aikin, Michiel to Polly Reed 8-23-1849 (8-28-1849)
Ake, John M. to Bethany Stephens 6-30-1847
Ake, John M. to Nicy Rose 10-12-1844
Alexander, Elijah to Lyda Frost 8-18-1859 (8-19-1859)
Alexander, Jordan to Margret Guinn 4-10-1854
Allen, Alex to Eliza (Miss) Bean 3-2-1869 (no return)
Allen, George W. to Martha Elen Lee 7-15-1847 (7-16-1847)
Allen, J. H. to Rebecca Lawson 2-13-1866 (2-15-1866)
Allen, Jessee to Cathrine Long 8-29-1842 (8-31-1842)
Allen, Pinkney to Susan Bryant 12-18-1873 (12-19-1873)
Allen, Stephen to Sarah Jett 2-14-1851 (no return)
Allen, W. P. to Nannie V. Hacher 11-23-1872 (10?-10-1873)
Allen, Wm. T. to Lizzie Backwell 4-11-1866 (no return)
Alley, James to Nancy A. Brown 5-4-1838 (5-6-1838)
Allison, Joseph to Eliza Thompson 9-5-1854 (9-10-1854)
Allred, H. to Missouri Little 1-15-1867 (1-16-1867)
Alman, John W. to Martha Allen 1-11-1855
Alspaugh, Henry P. S. to Nancy R. Reeves 9-3-1853 (9-4-1853)
Amond, James H. to Susan Vaughan 12-27-1856 (12-28-1856)
Anderson, A. J. S. to Martha J. Tarwaters 11-31-1858
Anderson, A. J. to Mary Westmer 7-20-1867 (7-21-1867)
Anderson, Alfred H. to Margret Finney 11-5-1855 (11-11-1855)
Anderson, Andrew B. to Adaline Dickenson 4-17-1841 (4-18-1841)
Anderson, B. F. to Elizabeth Neville 8-21-1867 (8-22-1867)
Anderson, David L. to Mary E. Woods 9-16-1867
Anderson, David to Dicy Dial 8-1-1867 (8-4-1867)
Anderson, E. D. to Laura L. Miller 1-13-1872 (no return)
Anderson, George W. to Mary Jane Baggett 1-6-1866 (no return)
Anderson, George to Samantha Smith 7-15-1853 (7-18-1853)
Anderson, Hiram to Sarah Hill 5-13-1850
Anderson, J. R. to Sarah A. Bruce 12-14-1870 (no return)
Anderson, J. W. to M. E. (Miss) Barnes 5-19-1869 (5-20-1869)
Anderson, Jacob M. to Nancy E. Bratton 9-11-1855
Anderson, James H. to Cathrine Hammonds 5-31-1869 (no return)
Anderson, James M. to Nancy Jane Buchanan 10-20-1846
Anderson, James to Malinda Green 12-31-1868 (no return)
Anderson, John F. to Mary Stephens 8-27-1854
Anderson, John to E. F. Reagin 1-7-1840
Anderson, John to Elizabeth Winford 1-7-1869 (no return)
Anderson, Lewis to Charlotta Moore 12-15-1840 (12-17-1840)
Anderson, M. A. to Julia Callaway 12-31-1843 (no return)
Anderson, Milton to Lizzie Miller 5-28-1866 (5-29-1866)
Anderson, Minor to Kiziah Hopper 9-14-1839 (9-15-1839)
Anderson, N. F. to Marinda E. George 9-14-1865 (no return)
Anderson, T. D. W. to Sarah F. Little 10-7-1866
Anderson, Thomas D. W. to Elender Ferrell 4-21-1858 (no return)
Anderson, Thomas to Elizabeth Duncan 5-6-1852 (5-7-1852)
Anderson, W. M. to M. A. Shavers 7-23-1874 (no return)
Anderton, William T. to Amanda Spears 5-3-1873 (no return)
Andrews, A. J. to Martha J. Tarwaters 11-3-1858 (no return)
Andrews, R. C. to Levina Baker 2-12-1842
Angel, John J. to Azubah M. Taft 9-20-1847 (9-21-1847)
Anthony, N. S. to Nannie C. Osborn 3-10-1874 (3-12-1874)
Anthony, Stanford to Sarah Holder 9-12-1843
Arledge, Clement to Eliza M. Roseborough 1-20-1853
Arledge, Coleman to Ann Campbell 11-3-1851 (11-4-1851)
Arledge, Thomas to Mary (Miss) Lefeber 12-9-1869

Arledge, Tillman to Ellen Mason 7-10-1855
Arledge, Tillman to Martha Green 10-29-1842 (10-30-1842)
Armstrong, Daniel B. to Mary Cook 10-15-1844
Armstrong, David to Mary J. Miles 9-25-1854 (no return)
Armstrong, J. E. to Martha Armstrong 9-4-1868 (no return)
Armstrong, John W. to A. C. (Miss) Baker 1-19-1869 (1-21-1869)
Armstrong, William to Susanah Willis 3-16-1842
Arnett, J. D. to Mattie Moore 1-1-1872 (1-3-1872)
Arnett, Wm. R. to Elizabeth Hatchett 1-3-1853 (1-4-1853)
Arnold, J. L. to Sallie Davis 10-6-1874 (no return)
Arnold, J. T. to Elizabeth Yarborough 9-22-1866 (no return)
Arnold, James W. to Lucinda Ladd 6-17-1872
Arnold, Jeremiah to Elizabeth Stubblefield 1-31-1839
Arnold, John to Milethia Wells 9-?-1855
Arnold, Joseph M. to Sarah Fergerson 10-7-1855
Arnold, Ralph to Mourning Knuckles 7-27-1847 (8-3-1847)
Ashbrook, Daniel to Sarah Ann Green 11-26-1849
Asher, Lexington to Martha Seargent 1-15-1853 (1-18-1853)
Ashley, Daniel to Polly Suthard 4-16-1844 (4-25-1844)
Ashley, Edward to Mary A. Williams 8-1-1842
Ashley, Elias to Rebecca H. Bradford 4-7-1848
Ashley, James M. to Lucinda Steel 9-9-1871 (no return)
Ashley, John H. to Eliza Gilliam 9-1-1843 (no return)
Ashley, Jourdan to Sophia Bradford 7-19-1841 (7-23-1841)
Ashley, Michael to Lucinda Winkler 12-7-1852 (12-8-1852)
Atkins, R. S. to Bettie Ray 1-12-1870
Austell, C. B. to Ellen Seargeant 12-11-1858 (1-1-1859)
Austell, Joseph to Susan Williams 3-20-1873
Austen, S. B. to Margrett Boman 3-3-1867
Austin, James to Henrietta Rogers 2-3-1872 (2-5-1872)
Austin, Washington to Mary Gipson 12-20-1845
Awalt, Jacob P. to Rebecca P. Morgan 1-2-1839 (no return)
Awalt, John to Mickey Brimage 7-18-1846 (7-19-1846)
Awalt, Joshua F. to Susan Brown 10-4-1858 (no return)
Awalt, Wm. C. to Susan M. Bean 9-20-1854 (9-21-1854)
Ayers, Levi Q. to Virginia P. Hutchins 12-29-1851 (12-30-1851)
Ayers, Richard S. to Laura Hope 9-5-1874 (9-6-1874)
Ayres, Wm. H. to Dulana Tate 8-28-1852 (9-10-1852)
Bagget, Abram to Nancy Runnels 7-19-1838
Baggett, A. C. to Mary J. Bradberry 9-14-1852 (9-15-1852)
Baggett, Abel G. to Nancy Beckum 1-19-1847
Baggett, Abram to Elizabeth Guess 10-26-1844 (10-27-1844)
Baggett, James B. to Nancy F. Harrison 10-1-1849 (no return)
Baggett, Moses A. to Missouri C. Majors 11-27-1848 (11-29-1848)
Baggett, Thomas H. to Margret J. Smith 10-6-1856 (10-10-1856)
Baggett, W. R. to Martha L. Frame 10-13-1859
Bagley, James to D. A. Morris 6-17-1867 (no return)
Baker, D. P. to M. L. Branch 12-6-1865 (12-7-1865)
Baker, David to Rose Ann Awalt 3-2-1854
Baker, E. P. to Mary J. Wilson 9-2-1868 (9-3-1868)
Baker, Elijah to Ann E. Smith 2-10-1844 (no return)
Baker, G. L. to Mary Durham 11-26-1874 (11-27-1874)
Baker, George T. to Elizabeth Swann 7-1-1848 (7-2-1848)
Baker, J. J. to Mary J. F. Buckner 12-11-1871 (12-4-1871)
Baker, John to Cynthia Frame 3-11-1844 (3-14-1844)
Baker, Rufus to Emma J. Thompson 11-23-1867 (11-25-1867)
Baker, Samuel to Elizabeth Partin 2-12-1852
Baker, William to Fereby E. Swann 11 7 1857 (no return)
Baker, Wm. L. to Mary E. Webb 10-7-1873 (no return)
Bales, Ruben W. to Mary A. Frame 2-16-1843
Ballard, Henry M. to Jemima Burgess 5-5-1838 (5-6-1838)
Ballard, William to Cynthia A. Tipps 8-29-1860 (8-30-1860)
Banks, David to Sarah A. Lasater 1-23-1852 (1-25-1852)
Banks, G. E. to Miss Mattie Johnston 1-10-1870 (12?-10-1870)
Banks, G. G. to Elizabeth Philips 2-24-1859
Banks, J. J. to Miss Joicy Banks 1-7-1869
Banks, James A. to Louisa J. Mitchell 10-14-1854 (10-15-1854)
Banks, James R. to Emeline Collins 11-4-1856
Banks, John F. L. to Nancy C. Banks 12-2-1850
Banks, John W. to Lurany R. Nixon 12-23-1874
Banks, John to Magret Gipson 2-9-1846
Banks, Jordan to Sarah Long 8-24-1843
Banks, Joseph to Mary Stamps 6-24-1858 (no return)
Banks, Jourdan to Rachiel Barnes 12-31-1838
Banks, Solomon to Matilda Runnels 7-31-1850 (8-4-1850)

Banks?, William R. to Caroline Mitchell 12-12-1845 (12-14-1845)
Barbee, A. W. to Rachel Cole 5-17-1849 (5-18-1849)
Barber, John G. to Sarah E. Williams 1-9-1856 (1-10-1856)
Barley, Joseph W. to Margrett R. Parker 1-31?-1860 (1-21?-1860)
Barnes, Berry to Harriett Hooser 12-15-1839
Barnes, Bird to Mary Jane Moody 9-26-1866 (9-21?-1866)
Barnes, Charley to Mary Pace 9-1-1858
Barnes, Cyrus to Piety A. Swann 2-28-1843
Barnes, Dennis to Deliley King 12-22-1841
Barnes, Dennis to Nancy A. Pelham 11-27-1865 (no return)
Barnes, George W. to Malinda J. Newman 8-31-1855 (9-3-1855)
Barnes, George to Margret Pelham 5-23-1859
Barnes, George to Nancy Brewer 11-22-1869 (no return)
Barnes, George to Symantha Short 5-21-1867 (5-22-1867)
Barnes, Jessee to Ann Moody 1-17-1867
Barnes, John to L. J. Holiway 10-4-1872 (10-25-1872)
Barnes, Jonas to Caroline Hays 5-18-1849 (5-20-1849)
Barnes, Jonas to Mary Overton 5-19-1860 (5-20-1860)
Barnes, Jonas to Nancy C. Sansom 10-4-1865 (10-6-1865)
Barnes, Joseph to Malinda Hill 2-3-1849 (2-4-1849)
Barnes, Peter to Nancy Jane Gainer 7-2-1849
Barnes, Richard to Elizabeth Thompson 12-28-1847
Barnes, William H. to Maggie Home 8-21-1872 (no return)
Barnet?, Samuel to Sarah Hill 8-20-1856
Barnett, H. to S. A. Hendly 8-2-1867
Barnett, James W. to Sarah Spray 10-25-1856 (10-26-1856)
Barnett, James to Mary E. Lenton 3-6-1865 (3-7-1865)
Barney, Bennett C. to Margrett E. Hutton 5-28-1856
Bartles, Francis A. to Sarah Jane Dravit 8-17-1865
Bass, Giles W. to Susan Keith 10-12-1839 (no return)
Bass, H. C. to Mahala Smith 2-18-1840 (no return)
Bass, John H. to M. E. Darwin 10-21-1867 (10-24-1867)
Bass, John M. to Matilda Hammer 12-19-1867 (no return)
Bass, William F. to Althenia Russell 10-27-1870
Bass, William R. to Mary Smith 6-20-1849
Bates, Daniel M. to Mary Hays 2-13-1849
Bates, R. T. to Nancy Shoo 1-18-1868 (1-19-1868)
Bates, Ulysees to M. O. Hunt 8-10-1868 (8-11-1868)
Battle, J. A. to Fannie Womack 4-21-1871 (no return)
Baxter, J. K. P. to Millie Stephens 1-19-1859
Baxter, John H. to Cathrine Sewell 5-10-1854 (5-12-1854)
Baxter, Squire B. to Elendor Sewell 6-15-1850
Baxter, Wm. P. to Sarah A. Atchley 10-11-1851
Baytes, D. M. to Sarah Holden 3-18-1841 (no return)
Bean, C. C. to Martha Sanders 6-7-1857
Bean, C. H. to Mary J. Travis 10-18-1856 (10-19-1856)
Bean, E. R. to C. Johnson 11-24-1869 (no return)
Bean, Ezekael M. to Eliza E. Marshall 8-19-1854 (8-22-1854)
Bean, Jacob M. to Nancy Bowling 5-11-1840
Bean, James M. to Rebecca Ann Arnold 6-7-1857
Bean, Obediah to Margaret Gipson 3-24-1853
Bean, Obidiah to Nancy A. Miller 8-22-1857
Bean, William to Annie Weaver 1-28-1843 (1-29-1843)
Beard, Isham H. to Ruthy Tinsley 9-20-1846 (9-21-1846)
Beaver, James R. to N. J. Brown 9-11-1871
Beaver, Jessee to Betsey Carr 11-1-1838
Beck, William M. to Sarah Williams 9-7-1855 (9-9-1855)
Becknell, D. K. to Callie Brown 9-4-1865 (9-5-1865)
Becknell, Stephen to Mollie Gilbert 12-5-1873 (no return)
Bell, Jas. F. to Sarah A. Rone 12-17-1867 (no return)
Bell, John C. to Susanah J. McCord 6-21-1845 (5-20-1846)
Belle, Orville to Rebecca Oliver 12-21-1853 (12-22-1853)
Bennett, A. C. to Virginia Wilson 3-2-1868 (3-3-1868)
Bennett, Francis M. to Frances McKelvey 11-24-1857 (11-26-1857)
Bennett, George to Mary Womack 5-3-1851
Bennett, Giles A. to Elizabeth C. Lynch 1-4-1846 (1-14-1846)
Bennett, H. R. to Clarisa Keaton 9-20-1838 (9-?-1838)
Bennett, Harmon to Mary A. Rose 9-12-1865 (no return)
Bennett, Isaac B. to Elizabeth Hutcherson 3-27-1852 (3-28-1852)
Bennett, James to Dosha Decherd 12-8-1852
Bennett, James to Mary Swann 1-8-1852
Bennett, John M. to Maria Borum 2-15-1844
Bennett, John to Martha A. Adams 10-6-1853 (10-7-1853)
Bennett, L. G. to Ibby Dial 7-27-1847 (7-30-1847)
Bennett, Simon W. to Elizabeth Finney 1-18-1854
Bennett, Wm. to Mary A. Williams 8-9-1852 (8-11-1852)
Bennette, John K. to Lavenia Parks 9-24-1873 (9-25-1873)
Bennette, Thomas to Manerva (Miss) Bryant 1-14-1874 (1-15-1874)
Berford, K. H. to Evey L. Awalt 10-28-1843 (11-7-1843)
Berry, John to America Anderson 6-7-1839 (8-4-1839)
Berry, John to Mary J. Bass 6-5-1852
Berry, John to Rachiel Garner 8-23-1858
Berry, Ross B. to Nancy Baxter 2-15-1855
Berry, W. G. to Stacy Shelton 9-30-1867
Berryhill, Joe to Mary Delzell 12-17-1874 (12-19-1874)
Berryhill, Lewis to Sarah Mahafee 2-27-1863 (3-1-1863)
Berryhill, Linsfield to Mary A. Wilks 1-17-1854
Berryhill, Robert A. to Sarah A. Conn 8-2-1852
Beshier, Lorenzo to Mary E. Worth 9-16-1873 (9-18-1873)
Best, S. to M. A. Nance 4-17-1866 (4-18-1866)
Bethel, W. D. to Elizabeth Hammons 5-19-1859
Bevel, Henry D. to Mary F. Silvertooth 11-7-1874 (11-8-1874)
Bevil, John to Issabella m. Baggett 1-9-1854
Bibbons, Joseph to Martha Pratt 2-19-1853 (2-20-1853)
Bice, Elijah to Polly Ann Lee 8-16-1847 (8-17-1847)
Bice, Elijah to Sarah C. Sisk 8-31-1865 (9-15-1865)
Bickerson, William to Lizzie McPherson 3-1-1872
Bickley, J. T. to Joe Wiseman 9-28-1870
Bickley, W. L. to Mary J. Turner 4-24-1860
Bingham, H. A. to Sally Gossage 2-26-1840
Birdsong, John H. to Martha E. Johnson 10-16-1848
Bishop, John L. to Sarah Farmer 6-6-1855
Bishop, John to Amanda M. Reynolds 10-2-1873
Bishop, William to Sarah E. Crawford 10-10-1871
Bishop, William to Sarah Knuckles 1-22-1846
Bishop, Wm. E. to N. E. Neal 1-12-1871 (1-11?-1871)
Bishop, Wm. H. to Nancy M. Swearingame 12-2-1874 (12-6-1874)
Bishop, Wm. to Elizabeth Payne 11-7-1865 (11-24-1865)
Bishop, Wm. to Ellen Finney 3-27-1868 (3-29-1868)
Bishop, Wm. to Sallie Hill 9-30-1867
Black, J. F. to E. H. Poe 12-23-1867 (12-26-1867)
Black, John F. to Mary Sarton 1-14-1839 (1-17-1839)
Black, Patton M. to Frances L. Denson 11-1-1848 (11-2-1848)
Black, Samuel to Sophia Decherd 6-28-1853
Black, William P. to Susan Hendricks 1-7-1868 (no return)
Blackman, G. W. to Elizabeth G. Vibbet 1-12-1861 (1-13-1861)
Blackwell, A. P. to F. E. Moseley 3-13-1872 (no return)
Blackwell, C. W. to V. C. Marberry 4-30-1867
Blackwell, Joel to Sarah E. Graham 1-24-1843
Blackwood, Hugh to Mary V. Farris 12-26-1850
Blackwood, Johnsy to Margret F. Blackwood 4-29-1839
Blackwood, William to Elizabeth Banks 12-26-1849 (12-27-1849)
Blackwood, Wm. J. to Mary Ann Knight 1-17-1852 (no return)
Blair, C. F. to Mattie J. Duncan 12-19-1866 (12-20-1866)
Blair, J. L. W. to Fanny W. Rowe 3-1-1865 (3-2-1865)
Blakemore, John to Nancy Allen 7-12-1860
Blakley, John W. to Cathrine H. Preuet 4-17-1872 (no return)
Blanton, Charles L. to Jane S. Vanzant 11-25-1842
Blanton, Charles L. to Lucy J. Moseley 5-30-1850 (no return)
Blanton, Henson G. to Cornelius E. Vanzant 9-16-1844 (9-17-1844)
Blanton, John S. to Lucy C. Wakefield 6-19-1852 (6-24-1852)
Bledsoe, A. S. to M. J. Anderson 6-6-1867
Bledsoe, James to Lizzie Hannah 3-16-1865
Bledsoe, James to Rebecca Call 9-12-1851
Bledsoe, Wm. J. to Armentha Allen 12-21-1849 (12-22-1849)
Boatman, Wm. to A. M. Harris 9-26-1865 (10-3-1865)
Bobo, Elisha to Mary A. Horton 11-21-1842 (11-29-1842)
Bobo, John E. to Phoebe A. Jackson 11-27-1855
Boesman, George to Mary Ann Stewart 2-15-1846
Boggs, John O. to Elizabeth Darnell 1-8-1855
Boggs, S. J. to Mahala A. Boren 10-30-1867
Bogle, Jos. B. to Emma E. Mann 1-22-1874
Bohana, Hosea to Elizabeth Hill 2-21-1866 (no return)
Bohanan, W. E. to Nancy Ann Smith 2-25-1867 (3-4-1867)
Bohannan, Charles H. to Amanda J. Wallace 8-28-1874 (8-29-1874)
Boice, William C. to Lucinda Brannon 7-26-1838
Bolin, C. L. to N. J. Patterson 8-25-1868 (8-26-1868)
Bolin, H. C. to Viney Smith 2-12-1866 (no return)
Bolin, Joseph to Mary Smith 1-11-1858 (1-16-1858)
Bolin, Melton to Sarah A. Knight 5-1-1865 (no return)

Bolin, William H. H. to Cathrine Shelton 5-10-1858
Bomer, Wm. to Elmyra A. Beck 11-7-1855
Booth, C. A. to Margret A. Pyland 11-12-1870 (11-16-1870)
Booth, John W. to Louisa J. Payne 2-24-1872 (2-25-1872)
Boothman, E. to Mary Nichols 3-10-1868 (no return)
Boren, Danl. to Nancy McClure 7-10-1872 (7-11-1872)
Bostic, Chesley B. to Frances Griffin 12-13-1842 (12-10?-1842)
Bostick, B. R. to M. M. Bennett 9-16-1866 (9-18-1866)
Bostick, Benj. to S. A. Buckner 1-15-1870 (1-16-1870)
Bostick, Chesley B. to Susan S. Stovall 5-7-1852 (5-9-1852)
Bostick, F. G. to Polly Partin 12-15-1865 (no return)
Bostick, Jno. H.R. to Jane E. Winfro 9-25-1848 (9-26-1848)
Bostick, Nathan to Caroline Stovall 7-17-1841 (7-18-1841)
Boswell, John to Martha L. Clark 12-30-1874 (no return)
Bowdon, James C. to Ann A. Green 12-24-1847
Bowen, L. C. to S. F. Bush 12-18-1871
Bowers, G. W. to Martha J. Williams 5-9-1865 (5-11-1865)
Bowers, J. H. to Mary A. Kiningham 5-30-1866 (5-?-1866)
Bowers, Samuel to Julia A. Francis 7-22-1851
Bowers, Solomon to Martha Ann Allen 12-17-1846 (12-18-1846)
Bowling, James W. to Nancy L. Wakefield 1-17-1859 (1-18-1859)
Bowling, Samuel P. to Laura V. Enochs 5-10-1873 (5-14-1873)
Bowman, Edward S. to Letha Jane Alexander 4-7-1841 (no return)
Bowman, William to Hannah Isbel 8-8-1839 (9-15-1839)
Boyce, J. B. to L. J. (Miss) Duncan 1-12-1869 (no return)
Boyd, J. R. to M. J. Garrett 11-30-1847 (no return)
Bradberry, M. A. to Sarah Graves 6-10-1866 (no return)
Bradford, A. W. to C. M. Bradford 8-31-1859 (no return)
Bradford, A. W. to Celia m. Bradford 8-31-1859 (no return)
Bradford, Alford to Cathrine Robertson 5-15-1850 (no return)
Bradford, Arther to Martha Gifford 5-1-1853
Bradford, Elijah to Sarah Robinson 9-12-1844 (9-15-1844)
Bradford, Ephriam to Sarah Craig 12-4-1860
Bradford, J. R. to Nancy J. Clark 8-24-1860 (8-26-1860)
Bradford, Jessee to Mariah Harington 5-6-1858 (no return)
Bradford, John to Louisa M. Wilson 3-2-1850 (no return)
Bradford, Obediah to Sarah Jane Arnold 7-11-1873 (7-13-1873)
Bradford, Thomas to Isbel Miller 9-21-1843 (9-24-1843)
Bradford, William M. to Susan F. Henderson 2-16-1848
Bradfort, Anthony to Susan Guin 7-15-1850
Bradley, Moses to Nancy Brown 4-2-1853 (4-4-1853)
Bradshaw, W. A. to Eliza E. Russell 12-31-1860 (1-1-1861)
Bragg, Benj. to Mary J. Langston 1-16-1858 (1-17-1858)
Bragg, J. W. to Mollie J. West 11-30-1871 (no return)
Brakefield, I. N. to Darcus Russell 9-27-1847
Brakefield, W. T. to Isabel Mattenlee 12-2-1859 (no return)
Brakefield, W. W. to R. E. West 7-13-1872 (7-14-1872)
Brakefield, Willis S. to Sarah B. Adams 1-14-1852
Braly, Walter to Lottie Ann Faris 4-3-1851 (4-4-1851)
Bramet?, Samuel to Sarah Hill (no dates)
Bramlett, H. H. to M. Pless 2-10-1870 (no return)
Bramley, James to Terressa Parnell 9-22-1847 (9-23-1847)
Branch, D. G. to Leah Hardy 4-2-1870 (no return)
Branch, W. A. to Anna J. Ivey 6-1-1872 (no return)
Branch, W. A. to Louisa Jane Sisk 7-13-1840 (7-?-1840)
Brandon, B. B. to Rachiel Ables 5-27-1861 (5-28-1861)
Brandon, John L. to Elizabeth Bean 10-19-1874 (no return)
Brandon, John W. to Eliza Jane Rich 4-10-1841 (4-11-1841)
Brandon, Wm. B. to Nancy C. Parks 9-18-1855
Brannan, Albert to Martha Partin 3-19-1846
Brannan, Geo. W. to Mary A. Lee 2-11-1856 (2-15-1856)
Brannan, Robert to Elizabeth Swann 8-11-1852 (8-12-1852)
Brannan, William B. to Mary Ann Chapman 5-29-1846
Brannon, James C. to Martha Jane Nichols 8-8-1846 (8-14-1846)
Brannon, John M. to Mary A. Rogers 10-7-1839 (10-8-1839)
Brannon, Williamson to C. Cherry 2-26-1840 (no return)
Bratton, J. R. to Tenner E. Heniford 11-29-1870 (12-1-1870)
Bratton, James M. to Charlotte T. Knight 8-29-1860 (8-30-1860)
Bratton, Joseph M. to N. A. H. Borem 1-18-1845 (1-22-1845)
Bratton, Joseph M. to Sarah Bennett 1-5-1849
Brazelton, Abram to Margrett Noah 12-22-1857 (12-23-1857)
Brazelton, Andrew Jackson to Frances C. England 10-22-1839
Brazelton, Green to Mary Ann Sharp 2-27-1845
Brazelton, Green to Mary Holland 3-16-1843 (3-17-1843)
Brazelton, Jacob H. to Samira Thurman 1-7-1842

Brazelton, John G. to Ann Bledsoe 1-10-1839
Brazelton, W. G. to Mary J. Brazier 12-9-1868 (no return)
Brazelton, William W. to Charlott P. Sims 12-16-1841 (no return)
Brazelton, William W. to Mary E. Buchanan 11-18-1847
Brazelton, William jr. to Manervia Faris 9-23-1846 (no return)
Brazelton, William to Ann F. Faris 1-8-1851 (no return)
Brazelton, Wm. to Hester A. R. Kirkendol 6-4-1868 (6-29-1868)
Brazier, James W. to M. J. Brown 11-3-1868
Brazier, Sion S. to Mary L. Baker 11-22-1841
Breeden, Archibald M. to Mary Ann Heaston 9-2-1845 (9-?-1845)
Breeden, W. A. to Nancy Ann Anderson 11-4-1860 (11-8-1860)
Brensfield, John A. to Rebecca Johnson 5-28-1859
Brewer, C. B. to M. C. (Miss) Watson 4-29-1869
Brewer, Erasmus G. to Margrett Lynch 7-15-1846
Brewer, George to Frances Goff 10-24-1865 (10-25-1865)
Brewer, George to Rebecca Davis 12-28-1859 (2-29-1860)
Brewer, J. L. to Rebecca Brewer 2-11-1870 (no return)
Brewer, James to Julia Roberts 5-29-1874 (5-31-1874)
Brewer, P. W. to Sarah M. Keath 2-1-1858 (2-5-1858)
Brewer, Wm. to Jane Hill 8-20-1867 (8-22-1867)
Briant, Jessee to Elizabeth Gamble 5-6-1851
Bridges, Elisha to Sena Vanzant 12-12-1844
Bridges, G. H. to E. R. McCord 1-1-1859 (no return)
Bridges, Isaac to M. J. Smith 2-18-1839
Bridges, Jacob J. to Elizabeth Cosents 12-1-1857 (no return)
Bridges, John O. to Olivia Hatchett 9-19-1867
Bridges, Manville H. to Elizabeth McCord 1-1-1859 (no return)
Bridges, Oliver H. to Mary A. Nuckles 1-4-1840
Bridges, R. J. to M. E. Poston 4-23-1867
Bridges, Russell B. to Mary Ann Morgan 10-22-1856 (no return)
Bridges, Samuel to Rachiel Martin 8-11-1842
Bridgeway, John H. to Mary A. Cole 4-9-1842 (no return)
Brimage, John to Mary A. R. Tripp 11-9-1852
Brinkley, James to Susan Hill 11-6-1872 (no return)
Brinsfield, Wm. to Mary Jane Miles 12-4-1856 (12-10-1856)
Brisco, John to Martha Scoggins 8-27-1843
Brittain, W. W. to E. F. Lyon 12-13-1871
Bromage, Alexander to Charity Winkler 9-1-1852
Brooks, Fredrick to Mollie Shelby 9-19-1870 (9-20-1870)
Brooks, H. P. to Mary A. Sanders 1-17-1872
Brooks, John S. to Rachiel C. Weaver 1-29-1866 (1-30-1866)
Brooks, Moses Y. to Lidia Wilson 2-18-1858 (no return)
Brougham, John to Martha Roda 6-2-1859
Brown, G. A. to Josephene C. Orr 12-10-1874 (no return)
Brown, Geo. W. to Delila P. Revis 2-15-1872
Brown, George W. to Sarah S. E. Hise 1-17-1866
Brown, Hiram to Martha A. Curle 12-15-1842
Brown, J. E. to Elizabeth Sisk 5-31-1860 (6-3-1860)
Brown, J. F. to M. L. Smith 4-19-1867 (4-21-1867)
Brown, J. L. to Elizabeth Garner 5-26-1860 (5-27-1860)
Brown, Jessee E. to Jennie E. Wood 11-5-1873
Brown, John A. L. to Cyrena Jones 11-28-1846 (11-30-1846)
Brown, John A. to Caroline Weaver 7-2-1870 (7-4-1870)
Brown, John W. to Elizabeth Burrough 12-25-1849 (no return)
Brown, John to Mary Ann Jones 10-27-1838
Brown, Joseph to Martha Roberson 9-20-1850 (9-21-1850)
Brown, Joshua to Sarah Shasteen 8-10-1870 (no return)
Brown, Josiah C. to Cynthia L. Morris 8-30-1855
Brown, Marion to Mary Bowens 2-20-1854 (2-25-1854)
Brown, Mathew J. S. to Elvira Epps 9-14-1854
Brown, Nathaniel J. to Nancy A. Cook 1-7-1850 (1-9-1850)
Brown, Peter to Rebecca Dunbar 1-1-1840
Brown, Rederick P. to C. A. Cobble 11-16-1870 (10-12-1870?)
Brown, Robert to Sarah Jane Lewis 8-29-1846 (8-30-1846)
Brown, William to Nancy Gilliam 6-23-1842
Brown, Wm. E. to Margrett Richardson 8-11-1874 (8-13-1874)
Brown, Wm. to Eliza Radigins 12-1-1858 (12-2-1858)
Bruce, J. L. to Mollie P. Wiseman 9-30-1868 (no return)
Bruce, John to Elizabeth Seargant 1-14-1869
Bryant, Ephram to Fannie Farris 9-18-1873 (9-15?-1873)
Bryant, J. C. to Mary Jetton 6-15-1871
Bryant, Robt. H. to Zay Chartan 8-27-1874 (no return)
Bryant, William Colton to Rebecca Ann Wilson 12-30-1845
Bryant, William J. to Mary C. Reeves 9-25-1851
Bryant, William to Martha Blakely 4-1-1838 (4-6-1838)

Bryant, William to Melinda B. Olliver 3-18-1839 (no return)
Buchanan, Benj. A. to Jane Ray 11-28-1872
Buchanan, Clay to Agness Peters 10-2-1873
Buchanan, David to Cathrine Presswood 9-18-1858 (9-19-1858)
Buchanan, John A. to Rebecca E. Womack 12-5-1872 (12-6-1872)
Buchanan, John to Elizabeth Anderton 1-4-1841 (1-5-1841)
Buchanan, John to Mary Hanks 12-1-1857
Buchanan, Wm. S. to Nancy Keith 8-1-1850
Buchanan, Wm. to Mary Clanton 4-23-1858 (no return)
Buckner, D. L. to Mary S. Justin 10-28-1873 (no return)
Buckner, Joe to Vina Lynch 12-12-1868 (no return)
Buckner, Presley R. to Mary Bostick 11-4-1856 (11-6-1856)
Buckner, Richmond T. to Nancy J. Perkins 12-11-1843 (12-12-1843)
Buckner, Richmond T. to Sarah A. Perkins 4-7-1849
Buckner, S. W. to Mary K. Brakefield 3-10-1874
Buckner, Wilson to Mary S. Bass 5-23-1872
Burk, Elmore to Bety Vaughn 9-29-1870
Burk, Thomas M. to Mary C. Lucas 10-15-1847
Burk, Wm. P. to Mary Denson 2-19-1857
Burkes, James to Amy Lucas 12-26-1839
Burkes, John to Martha Lucas 6-28-1839
Burkes, Martin C. to Sally Osborn 9-21-1838 (10-4-1838)
Burkes, Richard to Charlott Burkes 9-27-1838 (no return)
Burks, James to Mary Duncan 12-23-1871
Burks, John W. to Harriett Denson 9-21-1858 (9-22-1858)
Burks, Obadiah to Sarah Miller 12-16-1874 (12-20-1874)
Burks, William to Martha Clark 12-5-1860 (12-9-1860)
Burress, J. W. to Sally Parks 6-24-1873
Burris, Jacob to Mary Jane Branch 6-24-1839
Burrough, Jos. M. to Eliza A. Patrick 11-9-1859 (11-10-1859)
Burrough, Joseph M. to Elizabeth Estill 12-8-1840 (no return)
Burrough, Joseph M. to Sarah S. Price 4-25-1850
Burrow, Goodman to Rebecca Miller 3-18-1854 (3-19-1854)
Burt, Alford to Elizabeth Brasford 7-4-1840 (7-5-1840)
Burt, Alford to Lucinda Franklin 12-22-1848
Burt, Calvin C. to Nancy Parks 6-4-1854
Burt, Charles F. to Mary E. Eggleston 10-13-1856 (10-14-1856)
Burt, Gaston to Araminta M. Payne 7-30-1855 (7-31-1855)
Burt, J. H. to Lucretia Casteel 1-24-1866 (1-25-1866)
Burt, J. J. to Nancy Smith 10-29-1845 (11-19-1845)
Burt, Jos. G. to Nancy J. M. Hanley 8-23-1858
Burt, Joseph G. to Nancy J. m. Haislep 8-22-1857 (no return)
Burt, Willis to Elizabeth Rogers 2-4-1853 (2-8-1853)
Burt, Wm. to Rachiel E. Smith 9-6-1858 (9-8-1858)
Busby, John to Cynthia J. Cluck 5-22-1849
Busby, M. to M. (Miss) Brannon 12-15-1868 (12-18-1868)
Butler, Samuel to Peggy (Mrs.) Wilkins 2-28-1861 (3-4-1861)
Butner?, Robt. V. to Sarah R. Widener 1-2-1872 (1-3-1872)
Butterworth, John to A. R. Short 4-17-1872 (4-18-1872)
Buttrick, David to Josephene Cook 4-25-1865 (no return)
Bynum, David W. to Sarah Morris 6-26-1844 (6-27-1844)
Bynum, Isaac to Rabella Morris 7-28-1856 (7-29-1856)
Byrom, Asbury M. to Fanny E. Moris 11-25-1874
Byrom, Benjamin to Eliza Hays 10-18-1847 (10-19-1847)
Byrom, E. B. to Emeline Holder 11-23-1868
Byrom, Edwin B. to A. C. Jordan 1-9-1861 (1-10-1861)
Byrom, Geo. S. to Sallie E. McElvoy 2-23-1870 (2-24-1870)
Byrom, Green H. to Margret A. Rice 10-7-1854 (10-15-1854)
Byrom, H. F. to Margret Janes 11-1-1870 (no return)
Byrom, H. J. to T. E. Shasteen 12-22-1866
Byrom, H. L. to Elizabeth Jones 11-10-1869
Byrom, Henry L. to Winney Smith 10-24-1843 (10-25-1843)
Byrom, J. A. to Mary A. Dean 10-12-1869
Byrom, J. W. to T. J. Curle 4-11-1865 (4-13-1865)
Byrom, James R. to Synthia Jones 8-9-1842 (8-11-1842)
Byrom, Jas. H. P. to Arie E. Martin 12-28-1871
Byrom, John W. to Elizabeth Lewis 6-13-1868 (6-14-1868)
Byrom, Milton L. to Jane E. Blake 7-8-1856 (7-9-1856)
Byrom, Wm. H. to Nancy C. Byrom 6-4-1852
Byrum, John A. to Matilda H. Crick 12-3-1855 (12-5-1855)
Cadzon, Archibald D. to Agness B. Hurst 1-9-1873
Cagle, Joseph V. to M. E. Kennedy 1-21-1871 (no return)
Caldwell, Samuel to Eliza B. Thompson 1-10-1839 (1-11-1839)
Call, Caleb C. to Sopherias M. Lynch 9-1-1841 (9-3-1841)
Cambrel, James L. to Nancy Summers 4-6-1861

Cameron, John to Mary Coffrey 11-27-1854 (11-30-1854)
Camp, Anderson A. to Rebecca Partin 10-3-1855 (10-4-1855)
Camp, George L. to Martha Willhite 7-14-1842
Camp, Thomas S. to Rachael Herriford 3-7-1838 (no return)
Campbell, A. Z. to M. F. Pickeny 11-22-1873
Campbell, A. to Mary Noah 12-28-1840
Campbell, Archibald to Mary Noe 7-26-1840
Campbell, Armstead to Mary Louisa Faris 9-14-1846 (9-16-1846)
Campbell, Burrell to Martha Hill 11-9-1838 (no return)
Campbell, E. F. to M. M. Jones 9-23-1871 (no return)
Campbell, James to Virginia A. Moore 9-16-1848
Campbell, Joseph to Emeline Counts 11-2-1848
Campbell, Layton W. to Elizabeth May 1-30-1856
Campbell, Marion to Polly Ann Campbell 6-15-1858 (no return)
Campbell, Thomas to Rebecca C. Little 12-12-1849 (12-13-1849)
Cannady, Michael to Susan J. Long 10-3-1866 (no return)
Cannon, H. to Malinda Pellum 8-1-1865 (8-5-1865)
Cannon, Wm. W. to Elizabeth J. Nelson 3-4-1852 (3-5-1852)
Caperton, Ryan to Susan Williams 2-15-1840 (no return)
Caperton, Ryon to Elizabeth Webb 12-21-1846
Capshaw, William to Nancy Gunn 1-8-1840
Cardon, Henry J. to Elizabeth J. Seaton 12-21-1855 (12-23-1855)
Carlton, J. M. B. to A. E. Brazelton 3-23-1869
Carr, Harrison T. to Ann W. Estill 1-15-1856
Carrol, Jon O. to Niny Barnes 3-9-1849
Carroll, George W. to Mary Matthews 7-8-1843 (7-9-1843)
Carroll, Levi P. to Margrett S. Knight 10-18-1873 (10-19-1873)
Carroll, Minor to Lucinda Browning 9-26-1838
Carroll, William to Nancy Ludewell 6-25-1838 (no return)
Carroll, Z. N. to Mary J. Miller 9-7-1865
Carson, Robert to Martha Shaw 3-12-1849
Carson, W. L. R. to Miss S. E. Scivily 4-17-1869 (no return)
Carter, Hiram J. to Rachiel Gray 9-28-1872 (10-1-1872)
Carter, J. W. to Annie Moseley 11-2-1869 (11-4-1869)
Carter, Joseph W. to Mary L. Estill 11-18-1847
Carter, Joseph to Julia Henderson 9-20-1853
Carter, Joseph to Mary E. Francis 4-24-1851
Carter, Joseph to Nancy Stephens 10-19-1865 (no return)
Carter, Stephen B. to Mary J. Williams 12-31-1872
Carter, Stephen to Mary A. Luchan? 2-26-1849
Carter, Wm. W. to Susan A. Jinkins 4-8-1857 (4-9-1857) [*]
Case, Henry T. to Georgia A. White 2-10-1870 (no return)
Cashion, Temple J. to Dana Pitcock 11-25-1856 (no return)
Cashion, Wm. A. to Sarah C. Wiseman 12-23-1871 (no return)
Cashon, James to Mary Wade 1-3-1852 (1-4-1852)
Casteel, John W. to Eliza A. Liles 9-12-1853 (9-13-1853)
Castleberry, J. M. to Fannie Wiley 6-29-1872 (7-4-1872)
Catchings, A. J. to Elizabeth Parsons 3-21-1859 (3-28-1859)
Catchings, Benj. to Malisa Ann Rose 8-12-1844
Catchings, Meredith to Mahala Barnes 12-9-1853 (12-11-1853)
Catchings, Meredith to Tempy Singleton 11-21-1843
Catchings, S. A. to Mary Reynolds 12-11-1867 (12-12-1867)
Catchings, W. C. to Jane Sexton 11-16-1858 (11-17-1858)
Cates, M. M. to M. E. Cobb 9-25-1865 (no return)
Cates, Norman to Jane Williams 7-27-1841
Cates, Richard to Lucinda Williams 2-9-1848 (2-11-1848)
Cavin, Francis to Mahala Rail 10-14-1843
Cavin, Robt. to Malinda Jolly 2-22-1854 (2-23-1854)
Center, Phinnis W. to Matilda E. Farris 8-12-1874 (8-18-1874)
Chafin, Jas. H. to Charity A. Aldman 11-12-1858 (no return)
Chafin, John H. to Charity Ann Aldman 11-12-1858 (11-14-1858)
Chambers, Eli to Caroline Hendricks 8-11-1856 (8-14-1856)
Champion, Daniel to Margret A. Sewell 10-4-1856 (10-5-1856)
Champion, Daniel to Polly Champion 11-21-1845
Champion, Daniel, jr. to Louisa A. Young 7-18-1842 (7-20-1842)
Champion, J. R. to W. F. McKelby 3-25-1869 (no return)
Champion, Joseph to Mary Jane Sells 11-17-1870 (11-20-1870)
Champion, William to Adaline Jackson 10-23-1848 (10-24-1848)
Champion, Wm. to Margrett Mahathy 8-21-1869 (8-29-1869)
Chapman, Joseph N. to Nancy J. Moore 1-5-1852 (no return)
Chapman, T. A. to N. M. Roton 8-23-1865 (8-24-1865)
Chastain, Thos. W. to Jane Mathews 12-10-1857 (12-13-1857)
Chasteen, Andron to Sarah E. Helton 11-29-1858 (11-30-1858)
Chasteen, Chas. W. to Sophia Graves 9-27-1855
Chasteen, R. H. to Elizabeth Foster 12-20-1859 (12-23-1859)

Chavors, Wm. to Elizabeth Spray 2-2-1852 (2-5-1852)
Cheny, Benj. to Emiley E. Nugent 4-27-1854
Cherry, Benjamin to Rebecca Hopkins 3-2-1846
Cherry, Wm. L. to E. A. Martin 9-18-1873
Childers, West S. to Maria Muse 1-12-1839 (1-17-1839)
Chilton, Richard to Suffey Nuckles 4-2-1867 (4-3-1867)
Chilton, Robt. to Nancy Carroll 9-20-1844 (9-22-1844)
Chilton, Thomas L. to Mary M. Jones 10-19-1857 (10-20-1857)
Chilton, Wesley W. to Elizabeth R. Wiggin 11-18-1857 (11-26-1857)
Chitwood, Joel to Sarah Duncan 1-21-1843 (1-22-1843)
Chitwood, John to Elizabeth F. Rhew 7-31-1871 (8-2-1871)
Chitwood, John to Frances L. Martin 12-8-1838 (12-25-1838)
Christian, Allen to Rhoda Ann Sewell 7-9-1855 (8-9-1855)
Church, Henderson to Mary M. Neal 11-28-1859
Church, Henderson to Sophia C. Hice 8-9-1854
Church, Jacob to Nancy Ray 7-5-1865 (7-7-1865)
Church, John F. to Charlotte Linebaugh 9-15-1859 (9-18-1859)
Church, Samuel to Eve Weaver 1-6-1848 (1-9-1848)
Church, William to Eliza J. Neal 6-13-1867
Church, William to Ellen Wagner 5-14-1870 (5-16-1870)
Claborn, J. S. to R. B. Wilson 6-29-1874 (6-30-1874)
Clanton, Wesley to Mary Claxton 4-18-1858 (no return)
Clark, Benj. to Mary E. Sisk 12-18-1858 (12-22-1858)
Clark, Benjamin to Charlotta Koger 11-7-1868 (11-12-1868)
Clark, Boulin to T. K. Corn 10-14-1879 (10-15-1868?)
Clark, C. M. to Elizabeth Young 12-24-1873 (12-25-1873)
Clark, Ellick to Elizabeth Chinch 8-25-1846 (no return)
Clark, Henry to Mariah Morris 10-25-1855
Clark, John to Jane Crownover 9-26-1874 (9-27-1874)
Clark, John to Mary E. Sims 1-10-1844 (1-11-1844)
Clark, John to Nancy Sides 7-12-1869 (no return)
Clark, Jos. to Lucinda Gillaspie 10-6-1859
Clark, Thomas A. to Naoma A. Darrel 4-20-1858
Clark, Thomas A. to Naoma A. Darrell 4-20-1858 (no return)
Clark, Thos. to Sarah Bradford 9-25-1847 (9-26-1847)
Clark, Warren H. to Sarah Mason 12-25-1872 (12-26-1872)
Clark, Wilson H. to Bethenay Morris 3-22-1849
Claxton, Rush to America J. Nash 6-5-1858 (no return)
Clay, James M. to Nancy M. Lamb 6-9-1843
Clay, John R. to Elizabeth Haws 7-17-1848
Cleaveland, A. C. to E. (Miss) Barnes 7-8-1867
Cleavland, Moses to Frances Mullin 8-23-1858 (8-22?-1858)
Clemons, John to M. (Mrs.) Coggins 3-18-1871 (3-19-1871)
Clensman, Albert to Rena C. (Miss) Pelham 2-3-1874
Clepton, Ansel to Louisa Barnes 1-3-1859 (no return)
Cleveland, Champion C. to Malinda E. Moore 12-10-1857
Clevins, Atwood to Mary Oliver 1-13-1853 (1-18-1853)
Clifton, A. to Mary Garner 6-29-1859
Cluck, Wm. to Narcissa A. Donaldson 8-7-1858 (8-10-1858)
Coarton, James to Amanda Hendley 11-7-1865 (11-24-1865)
Cobb, George W. to Mary Arnold 1-12-1849
Cobb, J. K. to Sarah Hasty 2-9-1842 (2-10-1842)
Cobb, James P. to Susanah E. Darrow 8-29-1856
Cobble, A. W. to Nancy C. Morris 12-27-1865 (12-28-1865)
Cobble, Jackson H. to Mary J. Jones 5-7-1851 (5-8-1851)
Cobble, John to Louisa Branch 12-1-1860 (12-2-1860)
Cobble, John to Mary A. Smith 1-10-1857 (1-11-1857)
Cobble, William to Nancy Webb 7-19-1854 (7-23-1854)
Coburn, John to C. C. Dechord 11-23-1866 (no return)
Cochran, Charles P. to Elizabeth Estill 5-24-1855
Cody, John F. to Martha J. Garnett 4-10-1865
Coker, J. C. to Mary Richardson 3-5-1866
Coker, John to Elizabeth Comings 5-9-1849
Coker, Melmuth to Milly Gipsoni 1-1-1841
Coker, William to Jane Cumins 4-4-1843 (4-5-1843)
Coldwell, John to Sophia Knight 2-12-1868 (2-13-1868)
Coldwell, W. A. to N. A. Rogers 9-26-1867
Cole, James to Susan Graybill 11-14-1871 (11-16-1871)
Cole, Joshua P. to Rachiel J. Moore 10-12-1841
Cole, Samuel P. to Rosauna M. Baker 9-1-1841 (no return)
Cole, W. P. to M. C. Riddle 10-14-1869 (no return)
Cole, William to Mary Osborne 11-2-1852
Coleman, Baley to Cathrine Miler 7-14-1851
Coleman, Charles A. to Sarah M. Moseley 12-27-1852 (12-28-1852)
Collins, A. W. to S. L. Metcalf 2-26-1868
Collins, Alfred to Mary A. Campbell 9-9-1842 (9-12-1842)
Collins, Barbee to Louisa C. Wicks 1-22-1850 (1-24-1850)
Collins, James G. to Sarah P. Breeden 10-3-1840 (10-4-1840)
Collins, James H. to Caledonia Forshee 12-17-1871 (no return)
Collins, James H. to Sarah Garner 10-13-1873 (10-16-1873)
Collins, James to Lucinda E. Church 5-28-1852 (5-30-1852)
Collins, Jessee to Sarah Thomas 2-8-1851 (2-9-1851)
Collins, John to Canzada Pack 9-23-1867
Collins, John to Charlotte Nelson 3-2-1849
Collins, Josiah to Mary Pearson 9-6-1844
Collins, P. M. to Sarah Ann Garner 10-13-1873
Collins, Rice to Elizabeth Shaw 12-12-1870 (no return)
Collins, W. D. to A. E. Gipson 5-25-1874 (3?-31-1874)
Collins, William L. to Mary J. Bickley 12-3-1860 (12-11-1860)
Collins, Wm. J. to Eliza J. Myrick 10-13-1856 (10-14-1856)
Colton, E. H. to Caroline Crabtree 12-23-1868 (12-24-1868)
Colton, J. M. to S. S. Green 2-14-1870 (no return)
Colton, Lee to Anna B. Wright 8-6-1872 (no return)
Colyar, Arther S. to Agnes E. Estill 12-9-1847
Colyar, James S. to M. A. Provine 8-28-1840
Combs, J. J. to Mary E. McKelvey 10-28-1873
Combs, John A. to Margaret Goldin 12-12-1843 (no return)
Combs, Thomas to M. C. Anderson 11-8-1869 (no return)
Compton, John to Cathrine Awalt 10-3-1849 (10-4-1849)
Comstock, William to Ida Sherman 1-29-1867
Conaway, Daniel to Betsy Night 3-2-1845
Cone, Layfayette to Susan Wiseman 6-13-1865 (6-15-1865)
Conley, Daniel to Frances Keelin 4-2-1855 (4-9-1855)
Conn, R. G. to S. C. Knight 7-30-1868 (no return)
Connant, Joseph to A. J. Partin 12-3-1873 (12-4-1873)
Conner, D. A. to Mary Askins 2-4-1840
Cook, C. C. to R. C. Morris 2-9-1856 (2-10-1856)
Cook, Isaac to Polly A. Young 7-21-1842
Cook, Isaac to Sarah Hodge 7-11-1871 (no return)
Cook, James H. to Angeline Reed 3-5-1858 (3-7-1858)
Cook, Joseph C. to Martha Anderson 9-10-1838
Cook, Joseph to Elizabeth Roberson 1-10-1845
Cook, Noah to Ann Swain 8-12-1857
Coolen, Henry to Mary Lee Moore 6-12-1865 (6-13-1865)
Cooper, A. S. to Harriett E. Large 4-29-1861
Cooper, Cornelius to Jane Taylor 3-27-1841 (no return)
Cooper, Eli P. to Drucilla Stiles 6-8-1850
Cooper, James to Emeline Simpson 8-17-1849
Cooper, Laten to Sarah Prewit 1-20-1843 (1-22-1843)
Cooper, William to Margrett Windsor 3-19-1840 (3-18?-1840)
Cooper, William to Sallena Simpson 12-11-1848 (12-13-1848)
Coots, J. M. to Susan Herrington 6-2-1874 (6-3-1874)
Corcson, James Will to Mary J. Warren 6-17-1866 (no return)
Corin, James to Nancy McCarver 3-29-1856 (3-30-1856)
Corn, Benj. W. to Elizabeth A. Graham 3-19-1849 (3-20-1849)
Corn, George W. to Nancy C. Muse 8-22-1850
Corn, J. B. to T. T. Duncan 12-22-1868 (12-23-1868)
Corn, Jessee B. to Eliza W. Embrey 9-2-1858
Corn, Jessee B. to Sarah C. Wood 11-1-1853 (11-3-1853)
Corn, John A. to Sarah Corn 12-27-1845
Corn, John B. to Susan Warren 11-17-1853 (11-19-1853)
Corn, M. to Mary A. Corn 2-26-1870 (no return)
Corn, Payton S. to Terrissa K. Duncan 9-12-1850
Corn, R. S. to N. A. (Mrs.) Carter 2-14-1871
Corn, Richard S. to Adaline McNiel 10-29-1846 (10-?-1846)
Corn, Richard S. to Malissa Corn 3-28-1842 (3-31-1842)
Corn, William to Ede Hunt 8-3-1840 (8-6-1840)
Corn, Wm. H. to Winford Knight 7-25-1859 (7-28-1859)
Cornelius, William to Sarah Ingram 1-12-1846 (no return)
Corning, D. B. to L. E. Smith 3-10-1866
Couch, Newton to Susan Eveline Calloway 8-30-1866 (8-31-1866)
Coulson, N. H. to Ellen Sims 4-29-1839 (4-30-1839)
Counts, James to Nancy Stiles 4-22-1856
Counts, Jesse S. to Julia A. Arledge 12-20-1854 (12-21-1854)
Counts, Joh to Mary M. Bell 1-11-1847 (1-12-1847)
Courtney, Mathew to Hannah Carroll 3-19-1858 (3-20-1858)
Covey, William to Mary A. Swann 1-12-1857 (1-13-1857)
Cowan, Alford E. to Susan Newberry 10-12-1853 (10-13-1853)
Cowan, Henry to Elizabeth Franklin 9-28-1839 (9-29-1839)
Cowan, James P. to Nancy Stephens 3-4-1861 (3-5-1861)

Cowan, James W. to Jennie M. Williams 2-14-1872 (no return)
Cowan, N. S. to Josie B. Kelley 9-25-1867
Cowan, Robt. H. to Hannah Thurman? 12-19-1872 (no return)
Cowan, Ross B. to Mary Garrett 3-12-1857
Cowan, Ross B. to Mary H. Brazelton 12-8-1840 (no return)
Cowan, Samuel H. to Mary E. Moore 3-5-1840 (no return)
Cowan, W. H. to Julia A. Seargent 3-31-1868 (?-?-1868)
Cowan, William M. to Mary F. Bledsoe 3-11-1857
Cowan, William to Elizabeth Lewis 10-4-1842 (10-2?-1842)
Cowan, Wm. M. to S. C. Farris 2-14-1870 (no return)
Cowan, Wm. to Indianna Williams 11-6-1867 (11-7-1867)
Cowling, Joseph to Permelia Camp 1-13-1841 (1-?-1841)
Cox, A. M. to Susan E. Fowler 12-21-1865
Cox, James to Susan Wilson 4-1-1844 (no return)
Cox, John A. to Fannie Leounard 2-15-1867
Cox, Thomas to Rhoda A. Jones 9-21-1854
Cox, Wm. C. to Ellen H. Jestin 12-8-1853
Crabtree, A. L. to Eliza Holcomb 11-26-1866 (12-12-1866)
Crabtree, Benj. F. to Sarah E. Hugh 5-4-1866 (no return)
Crabtree, C. M. to Amanda M. Brown 5-22-1866 (no return)
Crabtree, George W. to America M. Holder 12-27-1873 (1-1-1873?)
Crabtree, George to Susanah Berry 7-8-1841
Crabtree, George to Susanah J. Suiter 8-12-1849
Crabtree, John M. to Nancy Gifford 12-25-1856
Crabtree, Martin to Mary Richards 6-18-1874
Crafford, James to Sarah Hensey? 3-26-1854
Craig, James to Elizabeth Garner 2-20-1843 (2-23-1843)
Crane, W. G. to Mollie M. Cole 9-22-1871
Crawford, A. T. to A. E. (Miss) Hall 3-20-1869 (3-21-1869)
Crawford, Alexander M. to Polly McClure 8-7-1841
Crawford, Henry to Catherine Denson 2-25-1860 (2-29-1860)
Crawford, Henry to Eliza Henshaw 10-29-1839
Crawford, John to Susan (Mrs.) Green 9-15-1869 (no return)
Crawley, James H. to Anna E. Oakley 5-14-1867
Creciate, Henry to Louisa A. Burnett 2-24-1872 (2-28-1872)
Crewgar, George to Ellen Corn 4-16-1866 (4-?-1866)
Crisman, Charles to Sevil Lewis 10-20-1853 (10-21-1853)
Crisman, William B. to Anna Alexander 7-31-1860
Cromwell, Napolian to Elizabeth J. Sharp 8-16-1843 (no return)
Crownover, Bengamin to Sarah Pane 5-15-1857
Crownover, Charles P. to Deboriah McBee 8-16-1846
Crownover, James C. to Elizabeth Roan 5-29-1856
Crownover, Jonathan to Feby Taylor 1-?-1842 (1-10-1842)
Crownover, Joseph to Mary J. Montgomery 9-11-1867
Crownover, William to Hannah Berry 3-19-1845
Crownover, William to Laura Montgomery 1-22-1874 (1-25-1874)
Crownover, Wm. to Malissa Kitchens 1-13-1872
Cruse, Redmon to S. E. Duboise 10-14-1869 (no return)
Crutcher, James M. to Susan M. Horton 11-8-1848 (11-9-1848)
Cullins, J. W. to Rebecca A. Adams 4-6-1867 (4-9-1867)
Culver, Flemming to Jane Isbell 11-30-1866
Culver, T. W. to Sarah Partlow 12-31-1872 (1-2-1873)
Culver, Thos. to Tennessee Nippers 6-28-1871
Cummings, A. B. to Sarah (Mrs.) Highamer 1-29-1861 (11?-29-1861)
Cummings, William to Elizabeth J. Boggs 8-19-1852 (8-25-1852)
Cunningham, Daniel to Ann Roberts 12-9-1865 (12-10-1865)
Cunningham, Jos. H. to Virginia S. Mooney 9-4-1851 (not executed)
Cunningham, T. C. to Sarah A. Coulson 12-31-1873 (1-1-1874)
Cunningham, Thomas to Sarah E. Farris 1-31-1861
Cunningham, Wilson to Mary Callahan 2-25-1871 (no return)
Curl, C. C. to Sarah Clark 3-18-1873 (6-29-1873)
Curle, W. J. to N. E. Shasteen 11-14-1866 (no return)
Curtis, John to Elizabeth Colyar 1-21-1842 (1-23-1842)
Curtis, P. R. to Mary E. Wilkerson 10-22-1873
Custer, Elbert W. to Louisa Adaline Caraway 10-19-1841
  (10-25-1841)
Dabs, Henry to Hannah Ford 3-4-1844 (3-6-1844)
Dalley, Abram to Easther Darwin 2-14-1873
Damrel, George B. to Elizabeth Nelson 1-19-1859
Damron, Edley to Ann Stoval 9-17-1872 (9-19-1872)
Damron, James to Susan Riddle 1-3-1868 (1-8-1868)
Damron, John W. to Elizabeth C. Metcalf 4-24-1855
Damron, John to Sarah A. Syler 10-27-1859 (no return)
Damron, John to Sarah Syler 10-27-1866 (10-28-1859?)
Damron, Joseph to Mary Neal 10-29-1870 (11-1-1870)

Damron, Thomas to Jane Blythe 6-12-1855 (6-13-1855)
Damron, William to Catherine Damron 5-10-1855
Daniel, Calloway to Matilda Vanzant 6-26-1851 (no return)
Daniel, Jesse to Sarah E. Ivey 7-19-1858 (7-21-1858)
Daniel, John L. to S. B. Hopkins 3-4-1843 (no return)
Daniel, R. A. to Caroline Smith 12-24-1845
Daniel, Solomon L. to Mary C. Holt 11-19-1873 (11-20-1875)
Daniel, Thomas to Mary Bartlett 2-4-1851 (2-6-1851)
Daniel, Thomas to Rebecca Putnam 2-2-1860 (no return)
Daniel, W. R. to T. C. Holt 9-23-1869
Dardis, W. T. to Mary E. Gray 2-23-1842 (no return)
Darell, A. P. to Louisa Ward 8-6-1839
Darivin, Francis M. to Nancy Singleton 2-11-1846 (2-12-1846)
Darnaby, Wm. A. to Elizabeth G. Sublett 3-10-1855 (3-11-1855)
Darnell, Joseph to Cordelia Jones 8-31-1867 (9-1-1867)
Darrell, A. B. to Louisa E. Brown 4-11-1844
Darrell, August P. to Martha J. McCoy 4-19-1854
Darwin, James M. to Eliza A. Oakley 7-15-1852 (7-16-1852)
Darwin, John P. to Rebecca A. Stroud 1-6-1851
Darwin, P. B. to M. A. Phillips 8-22-1868 (no return)
Darwin, Payton to Louisa J. Phillips 7-19-1873 (7-23-1873)
Darwin, Powell to Nancy Kennerly 1-14-1839 (no return)
Darwin, Robt. to Mary M. Knight 4-22-1847
Darwin, Thomas J. to Amanda M. McCollum 9-18-1850 (9-19-1850)
Darwin, W. P. to N? J. Besley 2-18-1868 (no return)
Daulton, James M. to Nancy C. Cole 11-14-1843 (11-16-1843)
Davenport, James M. C. to Mary Hasty 12-7-1844 (12-8-1844)
David, A. R. to Sarah L. Cowan 4-5-1847 (4-6-1847)
Davidson, Mathew B. to Virginia Hendley 3-2-1867 (3-4-1867)
Davis, A. to Lucinda Simpson 5-4-1866 (5-7-1866)
Davis, Alexander to E. Couch 11-25-1859 (no return)
Davis, D. J. to Sarah Wiggin 2-24-1859 (3-8-1859)
Davis, Ellott C. to Martha A. Nash 7-26-1855
Davis, George W. D. to Samntha E. Speck 9-5-1856 (9-9-1856)
Davis, James A. to Malinda Chavers 2-10-1858
Davis, James H. to Mary S. Garner 7-12-1842 (no return)
Davis, James W. to Jemima Gregory 9-3-1855 (9-?-1855)
Davis, John S. to Frances L. Burt 3-31-1842
Davis, John to Mary Robertson 9-12-1857 (9-13-1857)
Davis, John to Nancy Ashley 8-23-1855 (no return)
Davis, Jonathan H. to Pelitha A. Williams 5-21-1840
Davis, M. to Sallie A. Hill 2-26-1870 (no return)
Davis, Mc. H. to Lyddia J. Rice 2-16-1872 (2-18-1872)
Davis, N. L. to N. A. M. Brown 11-21-1865 (11-22-1865)
Davis, Nathan to Lucinda Grant 3-31-1855 (4-1-1855)
Davis, Oliver to M. J. Cavin 4-29-1860 (no return)
Davis, Robt. to Manerva J. Kitchens 8-6-1849 (8-9-1849)
Davis, Thos. M. to Eliza E. Kitchens 12-17-1853
Davis, Thos. to Emeline Gifford 2-21-1867 (no return)
Davis, W. H. to Mary Ann Farris 12-2-1874 (12-3-1874)
Davis, W. M. to P. E. Parks 2-1-1871 (no return)
Davis, Wesley to Rebecca Wilcher 8-13-1845 (no return)
Davis, William C. to Mary V. Kitchens 9-22-1857
Davis, William H. to Kate Marks 1-14-1873 (1-15-1873)
Davis, William R. to Eliza J. Ashley 10-31-1874 (11-2-1874)
Davis, William to Elizabeth Reagus 8-2-1853 (no return)
Davis, William to Nancy Darnaby 1-27-1841 (1-28-1841)
Davis, Williford to Frances C. Pyland 12-2-1857 (12-3-1857)
Davis, Wm. to Ardema Simpson 12-18-1859 (no return)
Davis, Wm. to Martha Weaver 8-6-1873
Davis, Wm. to Sarah Perry 8-24-1865 (9-15-1865)
Davison, James to Clarrissa Parks 12-22-1852 (12-23-1852)
Davison, James to Harriett Lakey 1-7-1841
Day, Geo. W. to Emily Hopkins 7-9-1842 (7-10-1842)
Days, Sylvester to Mary G. Arledge 4-2-1867
Dean, Fredrick T. to Jane Ray 8-6-1853 (8-8-1853)
Dean, Jerry to Telitha Ivey 7-20-1868 (no return)
Dean, Robert to E. C. Grant 12-23-1866 (no return)
Dean, Robt. to Sarah M. Ray 12-27-1859 (12-28-1859)
Deaton, George W. to Frances Sparks 4-10-1848
Deaton, James A. to Mary Chavors 9-30-1851 (10-2-1851)
Deaton, Simeone to Sivillia Stiles 12-22-1854 (12-24-1854)
Decher, William W. to Rhoda P. Franklin 12-23-1846 (12-24-1846)
Decherd, John H. to Jemima C. Estill 8-5-1851
Decherd, William I. to Elzira Lynch 8-20-1848

Decker, William to Sarah Guthery 12-24-1850 (12-25-1850)
Delzell, William to Nancy McKelvey 12-8-1852 (12-7?-1852)
Dending, John to Ann Prudee 3-8-1859 (no return)
Dennis, Henry to Mary A. Fletcher 9-13-1852 (9-19-1852)
Denson, John W. to M. E. Robertson 5-10-1860
Denson, W. T. to Frances E. Finch 9-14-1867 (9-15-1867)
Dent, James to Frances Liles 7-14-1844
Dermott, Robt. to Martha Warren 8-11-1866 (no return)
Deshields, Joel to Sharlotta T. Jolly 1-11-1851
Devim, William to Margrett Dumpley 2-26-1851
Dewitt, Wm. E. to R. A. Campbell 5-10-1860
Dial, Hasten to Emily Hill 6-29-1850
Dial, Isaac to Caroline Jones 9-3-1846
Dial, Jackson to Sarah Bennett 12-13-1853
Dial, Jacob D. to Sarah Simmons 7-17-1850 (7-18-1850)
Dial, James to Caldonia Tucker 3-21-1874
Dial, James to Polly Finney 7-3-1844 (7-5-1844)
Dickens, George S. to Mary A. Laughmiller 12-10-1873 (12-11-1873)
Dickey, Nathan H. to Margarett E. Campbell 4-27-1853 (4-28-1853)
Dickson, E. F. to M. J. Holder 9-9-1868 (9-10-1868)
Diel, Calvin D. to Mary McDaniel 1-10-1849
Diggom, John to Nancy Hutchinson 4-28-1853
Dishroom, G. I. to Amanda A. Farris 6-5-1867
Dixon, Ruben to Harriett Baites 1-17-1838
Dixon, W. H. to L. J. McClure 10-25-1854
Dodd, Joel to Margrett Smith 3-17-1850
Dodson, Newton to Louisa J. Mason 9-23-1850 (9-25-1850)
Dodson, Samuel to Eliza A. Posey 9-25-1857
Dolby, John to Elvira A. Farris 12-23-1852 (12-26-1852)
Dollins, John A. to Elizabeth Jones 1-11-1847 (no return)
Dollins, Thomas F. to Virginia C. Lasater 10-18-1848
Donaldson, James M. to Dosha Ann Trigg 9-2-1846 (?-?-1846)
Donaldson, Lewis to Mrtha Dampon 1-26-1865 (1-2?-1865)
Donaldson, R. S. to Missouri C. Etherly 12-10-1856 (12-11-1856)
Donaldson, Robt. S. to Cyntha T. Alspaugh 3-14-1871 (3-10?-1871)
Donaldson, Silas to Elizabeth Ashley 12-19-1849 (1-9-1850)
Donaldson, W. M. to N. S. Kilpatrick 4-22-1859 (4-24-1859)
Dorsey, G. W. to M. E. Boswell 9-18-1872 (no return)
Dossett, George W. to Martha Nugent 6-28-1858 (no return)
Dossett, Wm. to Nancy J. Gipson 7-6-1854 (7-9-1854)
Dotson, Andrew to Eliza Conaway 3-24-1873 (no return)
Dotson, Henderson to Lucinda A. Ashley 10-16-1865 (10-17-1865)
Dotson, John O. to Margret E. Leonard 10-24-1867
Dotson, John to Martha Crownover 12-17-1856 (12-18-1856)
Dotson, Rodney to Rachiel Parker 1-20-1843 (1-23-1843)
Dotson, Rufus to Mary E. Dotson 11-28-1871 (12-17-1871)
Dotson, Solomon to Malinda Money 2-26-1843
Dotson, William to Julia Ann Glaze 9-18-1847 (9-19-1847)
Dotson, Z. R. to Julia D. M. M. Bratton 12-28-1854 (12-10?-1854)
Dotson, Zachariah R. to Agnis Omings 4-26-1848 (4-27-1848)
Doty, Jas. to Sarah Hill 7-5-1871
Dougan, Timothy to Briggett Dorrell 10-21-1854 (10-24-1854)
Dougherty, John to Malinda Burt 8-18-1852 (8-19-1852)
Douglas, S. to Martha Ikard 12-30-1870 (no return)
Douglass, J. S. to Elizabeth Morris 4-11-1866 (no return)
Douglass, John A. to D. D. Laughinhouse 12-13-1854
Downum, James L. to Lucinda Vincent 3-17-1847 (3-21-1847)
Downum, John R. to Mary F. Parks 12-8-1846 (12-22-1846)
Downum, Richard S. to Julia Ann Daggett 7-16-1846
Downum, Sidney to Lucinda Farris 12-23-1858
Drake, John T. to Mary A. Newman 1-10-1854 (no return)
Driskell, Warner E. to Mary E. Metcalf 11-13-1852 (11-14-1852)
Driver, Henry A. to Mahala Gipson 1-23-1845 (1-26-1845)
Driver, Jordan to Dicy Vaughan 2-12-1840 (2-13-1840)
Duboise, Andrew to Mary E. Freeman? 3-27-1845 (no return)
Dubose, R. M. to Bessie Egleston 12-16-1873 (12-18-1873)
Duckworth, E. G. to Ulis Elps 9-23-1867 (9-26-1867)
Duckworth, J. W. to Gustia J. Huggins 12-5-1870 (12-7-1870)
Duckworth, Samuel to Luvina Devenport 5-15-189 (no return)
Duffer, Edward to Hiron Wilson 12-24-1849 (12-25-1849)
Dukes, Martin to Sarah E. Couburn 10-6-1873 (10-8-1873)
Dulin, H. H. to Martha A. Turman 5-30-1860
Duncan, Alexr. to Issabella McKelvey 12-11-1865 (12-14-1865)
Duncan, Andrew J. to Dicy Duncan 12-23-1839
Duncan, B. K. to Edney (Miss) Sharp 11-25-1869

Duncan, G. W. to M. E. Corn 10-7-1869 (no return)
Duncan, J. A. to Virginia Rose 7-2-1866 (7-5-1867?)
Duncan, John H. to Levina Simmons 1-18-1838
Duncan, John H. to Missouria Hart 12-22-1866 (12-23-1866)
Duncan, O. H. B. to Virginia A. Sharp 4-8-1843 (4-9-1843)
Durham, William jr. to Leatha J. Kennerly 1-4-1851 (1-5-1851)
Durn, William to Cathrine Sofey 4-5-1872
Dutton, Wiley to Eveline Rose 1-17-1843
Duvall, William R. to Lauvisa Shasteen 11-19-1874
Dyal, David to Susan Jones 4-27-1839 (4-28-1839)
Dyal, John to Hannah Guthree 3-24-1841 (no return)
Dyer, Josh to Susanah Smith 7-3-1858 (7-4-1858)
Eals, T. J. to Velia A. Cauffe 2-10-1861 (2-11-1861)
Earndalo, R. A. to Ellen Seargent 1-5-1859 (no return)
Easley, Lemuel to Frances Statom 12-1-1865 (no return)
Easley, William to Levina Shaffitt 1-20-1844
Easlick, Thos. A. to Eliza Jones 11-15-1859
Easterly, W. F. to N. E. Jones 6-3-1871 (6-7-1871)
Easterwood, John to Manerva Franklin 4-11-1870
Eaton, Alford to Mollie K. Carter 7-31-1867 (8-1-1867)
Eddie, Samuel D. to Celester Murphy 1-24-1868
Edmonson, A. E. to Susan F. Brown 12-8-1868
Edmonson, Wesley to Mollie Walker 10-8-1869
Edwards, Andrew to Glathy Banks 11-24-1857 (no return)
Edwards, James A. to Sarah Clifton 9-5-1866 (9-31?-1866)
Edwards, James L. to Elizabeth McClure 12-31-1840 (no return)
Edwards, John L. to Euphrasha E. Lasater 10-3-1850
Edwards, Wiley to Malinda Cavin 12-1-1857 (no return)
Edwards, Wiley to Milley Gamble 10-27-1843
Edwards, William A. to Sarah Banks 8-2-1855
Edwards, William C. to Frances Durham 9-17-1846
Edwards, William to Melvina Crownover 9-3-1850
Eggleston, William C. to Elizabeth C. Hickman 10-28-1857 (10-29-1857)
Elbords, Jonathan to Mary F. Green 9-13-1844
Elkin, Robt. to Nancy Colyar 1-1-1857
Elkins, A. R. to M. E. Bennett 7-25-1866 (no return)
Elkins, J. M. sr. to Lucretia Tate 1-8-1866 (no return)
Elkins, James M. to Sallie Buckner 12-18-1865 (12-19-1865)
Elliott, B. T. to M. (Miss) Rich 6-2-1874 (6-7-1874)
Elliott, Benjamin to Elizabeth Gover 12-18-1846
Elliott, Dawson B. to Mary R. Bradford 12-23-1849
Elliott, Francis M. to Fanny Sparks 7-28-1873 (7-12-1873)
Elliott, J. B. to M. C. Odear 12-2-1871 (12-3-1871)
Elliott, John B. to Mary Kirby 12-5-1856
Elliott, L. P. to Mary F. Bruce 3-21-1867
Elliott, William to Huldah Holder 11-7-1844 (11-17-1844)
Elliott, Wm. F. to Irena Logan 10-17-1844
Ellis, George to Jane Perry 4-15-1871
Ellis, John A. to Martha J. Hall 12-4-1871 (no return)
Ellis, John to Mary B. Adair 7-4-1838
Ellis, Joseph to Frances L. Smith 12-15-1855 (12-18-1855)
Ellis, Wm. R. to Hulda Hall 11-6-1871 (no return)
Ellison, Z. J. to Mary Hendley 5-2-1844
Embrey, Clifton R. to Mary Ann Sharp 3-5-1846 (3-6-1846)
Embrey, John K. to Julia A. Darrell 1-24-1843 (no return)
Embrey, M. D. to Elizabeth Wells 8-16-1869 (no return)
Embrey, M. D. to Virginia E. Modena 5-2-1860 (5-3-1860)
Embrey, W. S. to M. L. Hines 12-10-1870 (no return)
Embrey, Wiley S. to Nancy Meredith 12-1-1857 (no return)
Embrey, Willis S. to Jane Stamps 12-22-1847 (12-23-1847)
Embrick, John to Joanna Mattie 9-18-1871 (9-21-1871)
Emerson, B. H. to Elizabeth Meredith 11-10-1840
Emerson, Thomas to Mary Seargent 12-19-1839
England, James A. to Sarah J. Miller 11-30-1843
Englent, John to Cynthia A. Gillespie 10-3-1871 (no return)
Epps, Isham to Nancy E. Hendricks 12-24-1849 (12-25-1849)
Erwin, Hugh L. to Frances M. Lee 2-21-1854 (2-26-1854)
Eslick, J. D. to Edetha (Mrs.) Farris 10-11-1870 (no return)
Eslick, Thos. A. to Eliza Jones 11-15-1859 (no return)
Estill, Francis T. to Cathrine H. Garner 2-12-1846
Estill, Henry R. to E. E. Turney 3-2-1848
Estill, Isaac to Musadora Franklin 4-13-1853
Estill, James H. to Florinda Clements 2-12-1851 (2-13-1851)
Estill, Jefferson to Frances Staples 1-17-1843

Estill, William W. to Jane E. Brazelton 1-5-1852
Estill, William to Mary A. Cheny 2-13-1867 (no return)
Ethridge, George to M. Power 12-?-1858 (12-20-1858)
Ethridge, Hardy H. to Susan Mayes 3-2-1857 (3-3-1857)
Ethridge, James to Martha McClure 8-29-1864 (8-11-1864)
Ethridge, Jessee to Elizabeth Hill 8-24-1853 (8-25-1853)
Ethridge, John to Eliza McKee 3-19-1840
Ethridge, L. B. to Ellan Damron 4-18-1872 (no return)
Ethridge, L. B. to Nancy Bradley 10-14-1874 (10-15-1875?)
Evans, James C. to Nancy C. Byrom 11-13-1855 (11-15-1855)
Evans, James to Olly Tucker 10-4-1856 (10-5-1856)
Evans, William M. to Caroline Reagin 7-6-1849
Evans, Williams to Ann Weaver 11-19-1860 (11-21-1860)
Evans, Wm. M. to Marinda Houston 11-10-1852
Evans, Wm. M. to Mary Ann Deaton 2-14-1849
Fagg, John R. to Sarah F. Petty 10-26-1870 (no return)
Fagg, R. E. to Emma J. Bardy 11-28-1870 (11-30-1870)
Fagg, William B. to Martha Sublett 7-27-1843 (7-30-1843)
Fagg, Z. to Sarah J. Jones 3-21-1871 (3-23-1871)
Fanning, W. C. to Frances Taylor 2-15-1867 (no return)
Fares, Thomas H. to Nancy Gore 1-5-1842 (no return)
Faris, F. B. to Martha Henley 7-11-1838 (7-?-1838)
Faris, G. W. to Mary J. Young 12-28-1864 (12-29-1864)
Faris, Geo. W. to Ann J. Upton 9-17-1854 (9-18-1854)
Faris, George W. to Eliza Ann Tucker 4-14-1853
Faris, Hezekiah to Sarah Cunningham 4-25-1843 (4-26-1843)
Faris, James S. to Lucy J. Faris 12-20-1854 (12-21-1854)
Faris, James to Margret Caroll 10-3-1838 (no return)
Faris, Reuben S. to Nancy Riddle 3-16-1861? (with 1851)
Faris, Richard to Salina Lestor 2-14-1855 (2-15-1855)
Faris, Wm. D. to Ann Farris 3-30-1843
Farmer, Samuel M. to Rebecca J. Eskridge 11-14-1843 (11-21-1843)
Farmer, Welbourn L. to Eliza Foster 10-19-1844 (10-20-1844)
Farmer, Wm. B. to M. H. Stroud 12-24-1870 (12-25-1870)
Farnsworth, Alexander to Martha Brown 1-22-1869
Farris, Edward B. to Martha H. Dobson 11-12-1850 (11-13-1850)
Farris, Fedrick G. to Mary Ann Miller 3-26-1845 (3-23?-1845)
Farris, G. S. to Sarah F. Custer 3-8-1865
Farris, Geo. W. to C. A. Garner 5-1-1845
Farris, George W. to Margrett Barnes 3-18-1842 (3-20-1842)
Farris, H. L. to Eliza Jane Faris 2-15-1866
Farris, John H. to Phebe Shasteen 9-15-1865 (9-17-1865)
Farris, John S. to Sarah L. Hines 11-29-1839
Farris, John W. to Editha Janes 9-21-1859
Farris, Littleton to Margret E. Sims 7-30-1856 (no return)
Farris, Milton D. to Mary A. Sims 7-27-1840 (7-30-1840)
Farris, Richard C. to Mary E. Brown 1-30-1854 (1-31-1854)
Farris, Richard N. to Eliza Jane Blackwood 1-22-1844 (1-23-1844)
Farris, Ruben to L. H. Norris 11-2-1869 (11-3-1869)
Farris, Samuel K. to Cathrine Smith 10-24-1843 (10-25-1843)
Farris, T. B. to Fanny Phillips 12-4-1868 (no return)
Farris, T. C. to M. J. Crawford 12-20-1871
Farris, T. W. to L. J. Wade 10-3-1867
Farris, Thomas D. to Eveline Farris 2-18-1841 (no return)
Farris, William J. to Elizabeth Gamble 5-4-1841
Farris, William to Hannah Morris 6-29-1874
Farris, Wm. M. to Amanda M. Taylor 10-19-1867 (10-17?-1867)
Farris, Wm. to Josephene McCullock 9-26-1873
Fawner, James W. to Margrett Short 2-5-1847
Featherston, Clement to Litha J. Kennerly 1-20-1858 (no return)
Feemster, John B. to Sarah E. Reeves 4-8-1851
Fergerson, Stephen to Nancy Vandergriff 3-2-1851
Ferrell, Patrick to Margrett Jenkins 8-20-1849
Ferrell, Vincent B. to Roselinda Cashin 5-8-1843 (no return)
Filpot, Wm. to Amanda Hendley 9-9-1869 (no return)
Finch, Daniel to Nancy Wileman 11-24-1845 (no return)
Finch, John W. to Rebeca Wileman 2-16-1857 (no return)
Finch, Thomas to Ann Eliza Moffitt 12-16-1846 (12-17-1846)
Finch, Thos. H. to Amelia A. Hill 2-8-1854
Finney, A. J. to Mary A. Tankersley 12-24-1853 (12-25-1853)
Finney, A. J. to Sarah W. S. Rich 2-20-1869 (2-22-1869)
Finney, John to Eliza Orear 4-2-1847 (4-18-1847)
Finney, Nelson to Martha Dyal 1-15-189 (1-17-1839)
Finney, W. T. to Ellen Morris 11-3-1866 (no return)
Finney, William to Elizabeth Boyd 3-21-1861

Finney, Wm. R. to Sarah Runnels 8-14-1851
Fitzgerald, John to Mary Hill 8-4-1851
Fitzgeralds, Michael to Jane T. Swain 2-23-1857
Fitzgibbons, Thomas to Sarah C. Mederis 6-8-1872
Fitzpatrick, J. B. to Mag (Miss) Marks 11-20-1867
Fitzpatrick, James T. to Sarah J. Greer 10-11-1865 (10-12-1865)
Fitzpatrick, John W. to Mary M. Gambol 10-23-1867 (no return)
Flemming, Henry B. to Mary E. Farris 11-14-1870
Fletcher, Dean A. to Martha A. McGee 12-26-1854 (12-27-1854)
Fletcher, J. C. to M. C. Bowers 9-16-1867 (no return)
Fletcher, John J. to Mary A. Higginbotham 11-21-1854
    (not executed)
Fletcher, Wm. D. to Adelphia A. Tanner 8-6-1852 (8-8-1852)
Floyd, A. B. to Eliza Lindsey 3-20-1872 (3-21-1872)
Floyd, Williamson R. to Mariah Oliver 5-24-1856 (5-25-1856)
Fly, J. W. to E. A. Baker 9-28-1866 (no return)
Fogortey, Edward to Margret J. Malone 7-3-1858 (7-5-1858)
Folwell, G. E. to Florence M. Graves 8-1-1865 (8-2-1865)
Fontain, George to Susan Lasater 11-24-1865 (no return)
Forbes, F. M. to S. E. McBride 12-3-1870 (12-4-1870)
Ford, Joseph A. to Mary A. Hudgins 12-15-1858
Ford, Nicholas J. to Mary A. Sharp 8-21-1842
Ford, William M. to Mary G. Stewart 2-2-1874 (no return)
Foreman, Jessee C. to Amelia Dechard 2-21-1857 (2-25-1857)
Foster, A. J. B. to Julia Ann Sims 8-14-1848 (8-15-1848)
Foster, A. to M. J. Allison 2-15-1864 (2-16-1864)
Foster, Albert to N. J. Russol 1-6-1868 (1-7-1868)
Foster, J. H. to M. J. Hannah 2-29-1868 (3-1-1868)
Foster, James B. to Susan J. Thurman? 5-6-1840
Foster, Rufus C. to Nancy C. Lucas 2-11-1856 (no return)
Foster, Thaddeus to Angie Logan 7-4-1865 (7-5-1865)
Foster, Thomas to Tempy Jones 1-17-1839
Foster, Thos. to Ann Foster 9-24-1870
Foster, Thos. to H. E. Alspaugh 2-10-1868 (2-11-1868)
Foster, William to Nancy Nichols 8-15-1855 (no return)
Fowler, Thos. N. to Mary Ann Owens 8-5-1872 (no return)
Fox, Enoch D. to Mary A. Cooper 10-16-1853 (10-17-1853)
Fox, George to Rebecca Roberson 12-23-1845
Fox, John W. to Hannah Smith 10-9-1851 (10-14-1851)
Frame, James M. to Susan D. Tripp 4-6-1856 (no return)
Frame, John W. to Heneretta D. Lee 3-22-1854
Frame, Joseph to Elizabeth J. Roseborough 2-23-1852
Frame, William L. to Martha Franklin 1-31-1844 (2-1-1844)
Frame, William S. to Elizabeth Smith 10-26-1850 (no return)
Francis, George N. to Margret E. Suddarth 7-29-1851
Francis, Hugh to Catharine Buchanan 4-12-1838
Francis, J. P. to Ellen Elliott 8-3-1868 (no return)
Francis, John B. to Mary Gross 6-30-1842
Francis, Nathaniel T. to Mary E. Malone 9-3-1849
Francis, Stephen M. to Rosanna Gross 4-8-1841 (no return)
Francis, W. R. to Margret McIlheran 2-12-1840 (no return)
Francis, William A. to Caroline Jones 9-15-1846
Franklin, Anderson to J. B. Sisk 12-8-1873 (12-9-1873)
Franklin, Benj. W. to Martha E. Young 7-2-1852 (7-4-1852)
Franklin, Benjamin to Louisa Talley 12-29-1851 (no return)
Franklin, Coleman to Elizabeth L. Eskridge 11-11-1845
Franklin, David A. to Elizabeth A. Young 11-8-1849 (11-9-1849)
Franklin, James W. to Susan Dossey 4-19-1848 (4-21-1848)
Franklin, John B. to Mary A. Syler 11-15-1860
Franklin, Joshua to Malinda Hill 11-23-1846 (11-24-1846)
Franklin, Moses C. to Nancy C. Silvertooth 10-20-1851 (10-23-1851)
Franklin, William C. to Martha F. Strambler 11-19-1841
Franks, John to Nancy Christy 4-25-1846 (4-26-1846)
Fraure, Benjamin to Martha E. Mains? 9-7-1848
Frazier, Eli to Rhoda A. Minnix 10-26-1840 (no return)
Frazier, Samuel to Elizabeth Denson 1-21-1846 (1-22-1846)
Freeman, N. G. to Allice Orear 11-19-1870 (11-20-1871)
Friend, Efford to Louisa F. Dechard 9-11-1854 (9-12-1854)
Frizzell, Nathan to Emma H. Stamper 2-19-1857
Frost, John to Sarah Hurt 1-17-1851 (1-19-1851)
Fry, John to Elizabeth Atkins 6-30-1866 (7-4-1866)
Fulcher, Volentine to Mary McCarty 2-8-1838
Fullmore, A. J. to Sarah L. Damron 3-14-1853 (3-24-1853)
Fulmore, H. C. to Nancy C. Smith 1-30-1865 (2-1-1865)
Fuqua, John to Elizabeth A. Cowan 11-5-1857 (no return)

Furgarson, Lemuel to Mary J. Magbee 3-25-1867 (3-31-1867)
Furgeson, John to Sarah E. Malone 8-17-1865
Furman, William R. to Polly H. Beckley 3-6-1843 (3-12-1843)
Furney, Lewis to Mary Newman 1-7-1860 (1-8-1860)
Gadsey, Charles A. to Adaline A. Wagner 9-7-1853
Gainer, George to Levina Stephens 1-8-1843
Gaines, William B. to Lizzie Pearson 7-1-1871 (7-27-1871)
Gallaugher, Patrick to Amanda Davis 4-30-1858 (no return)
Gambel, Wiley to Martha Fergerson 2-7-1856
Gamble, Robert to Annie Summers 1-12-1866 (1-14-1866)
Gambol, Dennis to Hannah Stephens 9-21-1865 (9-24-1865)
Gambol, Dennis to Lucy West 10-24-1855
Gambol, Melledge to Elizabeth Perry 12-27-1849
Gambol, Robt. to Susan (Miss) Ballard 5-2-1874 (5-3-1874)
Gan, George W. to Mary J. Graves 9-7-1867 (9-8-1867)
Gann, James to Sarah E. Bell 7-19-1872
Gannaway, Thomas P. to Aura A. Bartlett 10-22-1851
Gantt, Jas. C. to Ruhama E. Ray 8-8-1860 (8-9-1860)
Gardner, James I. to Ellen Lipscomb 5-6-1871 (5-7-1871)
Gardner, Wm. P. to Mary J. Chilton 11-7-1850
Garner, A. B. to Fanny Wedington 9-20-1870 (no return)
Garner, Amos to Nancy Lynch 9-5-1846 (9-6-1846)
Garner, Andrew J. to Nancy Ann Prince 1-29-1872 (2-3-1872)
Garner, Andrew to Hetty Jackson 12-17-1872 (12-26-1872)
Garner, C. C. to M. A. Duddue 2-4-1874 (2-5-1871?)
Garner, Charles to Sarah Wileman 2-10-1858 (no return)
Garner, Elisha to Darcas Wilkerson 1-4-1870 (no return)
Garner, George W. to Susan Gipson 12-29-1851
Garner, George to Margrett Pearson 8-28-1871 (8-30-1871)
Garner, George to S. J. Collins 9-5-1867 (9-13-1868?)
Garner, Grifen to Mary Barnes 5-1-1852
Garner, Henry T. to S. E. Keith 8-10-1872 (8-15-1872)
Garner, J. C. to Mary C. Prior 3-20-1866
Garner, Jackson to Cathrine Long 1-8-1843
Garner, James B. to Lucy Embrey 4-8-1841
Garner, John to Jane Smith 10-17-1857 (10-18-1857)
Garner, John to M. J. (Miss) Kelley 4-24-1866 (no return)
Garner, John to Mary S. Garner 6-26-1873 (6-27-1873)
Garner, John to Nancy Gipson 8-1-1848 (8-2-1848)
Garner, Josiah C. to Lucinda Rose 11-19-1850
Garner, Larkin B. to Sarah Catchings 9-26-1841
Garner, Mansel to Nancy Walker 2-25-1847
Garner, Meredith to Franky A. Lynch 5-21-1867 (no return)
Garner, Merrier W. to Lelia T. Estill 1-6-1848
Garner, Morgan to Elizabeth Norman 4-26-1838 (no return)
Garner, Nathan W. to Mollie N. Tucker 10-1-1873 (10-2-1873)
Garner, Taylor to Sally Ann Lynch 4-4-1872
Garner, W. T. to Orpha M. Mitchell 1-12-1870 (12?-13-1870)
Garner, W. W. to Allice Porter 10-30-1867
Garner, William T. to Nancy A. Hendley 7-6-1874
Garner, William to Angeline Kelley 10-21-1857
Garner, William to Caraline Marlow 3-23-1858 (3-25-1858)
Garner, Wm. T. to Annie Underwood 11-6-1873
Garnett, Nathan N. to Sarah E. Borum 4-19-1856 (4-20-1856)
Garrett, A. M. to Sarah A. Gilliam 9-16-1840 (9-20-1840)
Garrett, William to Darcas Tarwater 10-10-1850 (10-12-1850)
Garvin, Thomas O. to Mary H. Farmer 3-2-1848
Gatlis, Newton J. to Sophia Lanham 8-27-1873
Gauff, H. to E. A. Nichols 11-30-1867 (no return)
Gault, H. M. to Mary E. Damron 8-14-1871 (no return)
George, Thomas D. W. to Sarah Ann McDaniel 4-18-1850
George, William to Barbary A. King 2-22-1842 (3-3-1842)
Gibson, H. G. to Cathrine Wagner 5-27-1873 (5-29-1873)
Gibson, Isaac to Ann Gilliam 9-20-1843 (9-21-1843)
Gibson, W. G. to Martha Gibson 1-11-1865 (1-12-1865)
Gifford, Jos. W. to Sarah L. Turley 7-21-1871
Gifford, Robert to Susanah Pratt 12-15-1851 (no return)
Gifford, Sampson to Nancy George 1-12-1870 (no return)
Gifford, Samuel to Mary Jane Bishop 6-14-1858
Gilbert, G. G. to E. J. (Mrs.) Cardon 1-22-1869 (no return)
Gilbert, J. G. to Sarah E. Tillitt 11-14-1866 (no return)
Gilbert, John A. to Nancy C. Taylor 11-4-1846 (11-5-1846)
Gilbert, William H. to Mary A. Jones 1-15-1842 (1-17-1842)
Gilbert, William T. to Lucy C. Bicknell 10-24-1872 (10-27-1872)
Gillaspie, George to Jane Hannah 3-7-1852 (3-8-1852)
Gillaspie, Henry to Susan Wiggin 1-11-1854 (not executed)
Gillaspie, James S. to Elizabeth A. Etherly 8-14-1858 (8-15-1858)
Gillaspie, Nathan to Judith Oakley 10-24-1859
Gillaspie, Tipton L. to Lurana A. Gillaspie 9-28-1854
Gillaspie, W. H. to Mary M. Staton 1-28-1865 (1-29-1865)
Gillbreth, Thomas to Keziah Odon 12-25-1848 (12-26-1848)
Gillespie, James H. to Paulina A. Gillespie 1-9-1856 (1-10-1856)
Gillespie, James W. to Sarah M. Bickley 5-7-1856
Gillespie, R. J. to Delitha Gipson 4-20-1872 (4-22-1872)
Gillespie, W. J. to Julia Rallston 1-18-1872 (no return)
Gilliam, Charley to Cathrine Sigo 1-21-1852
Gilliam, Harris to Jane F. Stephens 8-26-1852 (8-23?-1852)
Gilliam, Henry R. to Sarah Keel 6-2-1853
Gilliam, James to Mary A. Garrett 5-4-1842
Gilliam, John to Elizabeth Coker 9-18-1845
Gilliam, Minyard to Mary Smith 7-27-1857 (8-2-1857)
Gilliam, Samuel to M. A. Buckner 1-2-1869 (1-7-1869)
Gilliam, William H. to Elizabeth C. Garrett 5-23-1844 (5-25-1844)
Gilliam, William to Mary A. Banks 1-25-1858 (1-28-1858)
Gillmore, J. M. to S. C. Mangrum 6-21-1869 (6-10?-1869)
Gillmour, Hugh to Susan Binkley 3-24-1873 (3-27-1873)
Gipson, Allen to Margrett Garner 1-3-1855
Gipson, Amos to Vicca Long 4-8-1853
Gipson, Andrew to Elizabeth Hill 3-2-1849 (3-4-1849)
Gipson, B. D. to Martha Warren 12-9-1868
Gipson, B. D. to S. E. Armstrong 7-13-1872 (7-14-1872)
Gipson, Benjamin D. to Mary Jane Darnell 12-20-1845 (12-30-1845)
Gipson, David to Sarah Peery 1-8-1844
Gipson, David to Susan Goodman 11-13-1852 (no return)
Gipson, Franklin T. to Mary Ann Clifton 6-4-1858 (no return)
Gipson, George W. to Mary Duncan 11-7-1872 (11-9-1872)
Gipson, Jessee B. to Mary C. Coker 2-6-1866
Gipson, John L. to Mary J. Hill 1-15-1853
Gipson, John to Nancy Gilliam 9-24-1849 (9-25-1849)
Gipson, John to T. C. Holt 7-29-1869
Gipson, John to Virginia Ellen Reed 3-14-1872
Gipson, W. C. to Hattie Lynch 1-8-1866 (1-9-1866)
Gipson, William to Sarah Ruder 2-12-1847
Gist, William L. to Jane Montgomery 10-19-1848
Glass, Hiram to Delila Mash 7-25-1853 (7-26-1853)
Glover, James M. to Mary J. Noah 6-13-1857 (6-14-1857)
Godby, Thomas to Sarah A. Parry 2-8-1871 (no return)
Goff, James to Rachiel Carr 7-17-1851
Goff, Orange to Harriett Ballard 1-1-1872 (1-3-1872)
Golden, James to Cathrine Welch 8-22-1853 (8-23-1853)
Golden, Samuel to Milden Williams 12-27-1866 (no return)
Golliday, James to Malinda Long 4-10-1867
Gonce, Lemuel W. to Sarah Anderson 10-15-1848
Goodloe, Thomas J. to Ethalinda A. Stephens 12-18-1856
Goodman, Jacob to Rachiel Gray 9-21-1849
Goolsby, Charles V. to Sally Willerford 7-7-1838 (7-8-1838)
Goolsby, Kirby W. to Mahulda Banks 9-9-1842 (9-14-1842)
Goolsby, Thornton to Louisa Greenlee 6-18-1844
Gordon, Amanzey B. to Harriet March 9-10-1838 (9-11-1838)
Gordon, W. J. to Eliza Cemray 2-3-1874 (2-4-1874)
Gore, Daniel to Nancy McGowan 8-2-1844
Gore, Thomas to Louisa Gore 9-29-1851
Gossage, A. J. to Caroline Fitch 12-16-1843 (12-17-1843)
Gossage, Thos. J. to Mary E. Hessey 3-10-1868
Gossage, William to Rebecca (Miss) Smith 12-21-1842 (12-22-1842)
Gossage, William to Sally Fitch 2-12-1838 (2-15-1838)
Gossage, Wm. B. to Maud H. Mason 12-10-1873
Gouce, J. W. to Jennie Lovell 4-22-1870 (no return)
Gouce, Jno. W. to Jennie Lovell 4-22-1870 (5-1-1870)
Goulden, John to Sarah J. Nichols 11-18-1852
Gour, John to Sarah A. Hasket 7-7-1842
Gover, Samuel B. to Sarah A. Mathews 8-16-1853
Gowry, Georg to A. E. (Miss) Vaughn 12-29-1869 (12-31-1869)
Grady, William W. to Martha E. E. Mathews 1-8-1840
Graham, James R. to Rebecca Gilbert 4-4-1853 (4-18-1853)
Graham, Wm. to Nancy Crutchfield 12-2-1865 (12-4-1865)
Grant, H. G. W. to Roda H. Bobo 10-22-1840 (no return)
Grant, G. W. to Samira Garner 9-15-1844
Grant, James C. to Elizabeth Parks 9-16-1851 (no return)
Grant, John to Delilah Weaver 3-31-1866 (4-1-1866)

Grant, R. R. to Sarah E. Shasteen 9-14-1867
Grant, Thomas to Adaline Reynolds 7-25-1866 (no return)
Grant, Thomas to Margret J. Williams 4-13-1871 (4-15-1871)
Grant, William to Elizabeth Webb 12-5-1838
Graves, John F. to Sarah Chasteen 10-23-1858 (10-29-1858)
Graves, Thompson W. to Louisa J. Shasteen 11-16-1852
Gray, Brice P. to Josephene R. Johnston 11-17-1870
Gray, George L. to Bell Taylor 12-4-1860
Gray, Hayston to Esther Parks 1-1-1875 (1-4-1875)
Gray, J. W. to M. A. W. Jones 2-12-1872 (2-13-1872)
Gray, J. W. to S. M. Jones 2-24-1868 (2-25-1868)
Gray, John D. to Mary McDavid 4-11-1848 (4-12-1848)
Gray, Luke to Elvira Mahon 8-1-1850
Gray, R. A. to L. N. Wiseman 5-7-1866 (5-10-1866)
Green, Albert G. to Mary Jane Morris 10-29-1842 (11-3-1842)
Green, Dr. William S. to Amanda Buchanan 5-10-1838
Green, Felix to Susan Hatchett 1-11-1858 (no return)
Green, Francis M. to Ann C. Farris 1-30-1871 (no return)
Green, James T. to Matilda E. Brazelton 11-29-1871 (11-30-1871)
Green, John T. to Susan Hatchett 12-20-1846 (12-24-1846)
Green, Joseph to M. J. Adcock 2-6-1860 (2-8-1860)
Green, Littleton to J. F. Sims 7-24-1865 (7-20?-1865)
Green, Nathan, jr. to Elizabeth A. Hatton 1-18-1844
Green, Newton to Sarah Rich 2-7-1870
Green, P. M. to Fannie Cole 6-2-1869 (6-24-1869)
Green, P. M. to M. J. Cole 6-?-1869 (no return)
Green, Richard to Sally Stewart 12-30-1870 (no return)
Green, Robert to N. A. Adcock 7-6-1859 (7-7-1859)
Green, Robt. J. to Nancy W. Green 11-17-1840 (11-19-1840)
Green, S. J. to Mollie Hyder 7-29-1870 (no return)
Green, Silas M. to Sarah W. Horton 1-10-1848
Green, Stanton J. to Temperance P. Williams 10-10-1855 (10-11-1855)
Green, Thomas to Mary Ann Muse 5-11-1849 (5-13-1849)
Green, Thos. to Sarah J. S. Swearengame 4-9-1868 (no return)
Green, Wm. R. to Annie Bennett 3-16-1870
Green, Wm. R. to Rebecca Muse 4-21-1849 (no return)
Greenlee, Abel to Martha Brazier 2-24-1853 (3-3-1853)
Greenlee, Allen to Mary Baker 9-14-1852 (9-15-1852)
Greenlee, H. L. to Amanda McWhirter 10-8-1867 (no return)
Greenlee, Ruben to Eleanor Finney 12-24-1845
Greer, M. C. to Jane Barnes 1-31-1855
Greer, Noel to Mary Francis 11-7-1838 (11-8-1838)
Gregory, T. D. to Mary Simmons 1-22-1868
Grevany, Muer to T. W. Anderson 10-7-1859 (10-9-1859)
Grider, James to Nancy E. Pippin 2-21-1861
Grider, John to Mary Jane Mooney 6-28-1866 (7-1-1866)
Grier, Joseph to Lucy Holder 10-5-1854
Griffin, James F. to Matilda Cherry 4-14-1859 (no return)
Griffin, James P. to Eleanor Sublett 8-28-1845
Griffin, John to Margret Ray 4-26-1872 (no return)
Griffin, W. M. to Lucy A. Delzell 9-2-1859 (9-4-1859)
Griffith, William G. to Elizabeth Rice 6-17-1841 (no return)
Grills, Bird to Mary Boyd 11-8-1838
Grills, William J. to Parmelia Roseman 12-2-1843 (12-3-1843)
Grizard, J. Wiley to Lizzie Turman 4-5-1870 (no return)
Grooms, David to Elizabeth Hosier 2-10-1854
Gross, A. M. to Eliza Dotson 7-22-1867
Gross, D. S. to Martha Haskin 11-22-1870 (11-23-1870)
Gross, Isaac to Martha Posey 6-10-1856 (6-12-1856)
Gross, John to Martha Jane Francis 11-26-1846 (11-30-1846)
Gross, John to Martha McCord 1-16-1861
Gross, John to Semira Jones 11-9-1842 (11-10-1842)
Groves, Richmond A. to Melvina Limbaugh 12-28-1849 (12-30-1849)
Groves, Solomon S. to Margret E. Faris 8-17-1872 (no return)
Grubbs, Jessee M. to Martha A. Shaver 9-4-1872 (no return)
Guess, Hiram to Sarah Norman 10-20-1842
Guess, John to Margrett Russell 11-8-1842 (11-10-1842)
Guest, Alford to Margret Simpson 11-26-1867 (11-28-1867)
Guin, Daniel to Lucy B. Barnes 10-2-1853
Guinn, Champion to Rebecca Jackson 10-16-1841 (no return)
Guinn, Elisha to Nancy C. Franklin 12-28-1846
Guinn, James to Emeline Brinkley 5-31-1853
Guinn, Jasper to Elizabeth Stewart 10-24-1865 (10-26-1865)
Guinn, Jessee to Mary Bradford 8-13-1870 (8-14-1870)

Guinn, Lemuel to Cyntha Hill 4-27-1870 (no return)
Guinn, William to Susan Odear 4-25-1841
Gunn, G. H. to M. E. Keel 11-29-1870 (12-1-1870)
Gunn, Josias to Juda Majors 12-20-1838 (1-1-1839)
Gunn, Samuel to Cathrine Sherell 8-2-1841 (8-5-1841)
Gunn, William to Lucy Roleman 4-25-1871 (4-26-1871)
Gunn, William to Permelia Keal 12-11-1844 (no return)
Gunter, John to Elizabeth Hooper 7-7-1869 (no return)
Guthrie, Thomas to M. J. Rogers 4-16-1860 (no return)
Guthrie, Thos. M. to Martha J. Rogers 4-14-1860 (4-15-1860)
Guthrie, William to Margrett West 8-8-1850
Guthrie, William to Martha Jernegan 1-24-1868 (no return)
Guthry, John to Marinda Markum 8-6-1853
Guthry, Wm. to Mollie Swearengin 5-24-1871 (5-29-1871)
Gwinn, Newborn W. to Elizabeth H. Barnes 4-6-1842
Gwinn, Riley to M. J. Barnes 11-20-1865 (11-21-1865)
Habeck, Julias M. to Mary L. McNabb 2-5-1856
Haggard, A. L. to Sallie A. (Miss) Nichols 11-13-1867
Hagin, Robt. L. to Susie S. Woods 10-17-1872
Hail, John to Elizabeth Corn 9-9-1851
Haislep, Wm. L. to Louisa J. Adcock 5-8-1858 (no return)
Hale, Alexr. W. to Martha A. Modena 7-21-1851 (7-22-1851)
Hale, George W. to Laura Grizzard 1-26-1852 (1-29-1852)
Hale, Luke to Martha M. Faris 12-24-1851
Hall, Elijah H. to Eunice E. Baker 3-24-1874 (3-25-1874)
Hall, Geo. W.? to Virginia A. Powell 11-6-1866 (no return)
Hall, Harrison to Constance A. Qualls 8-19-1852
Hall, Henry to Nancy Darrell 1-13-1848
Hall, Isaac H. to C. E. McElroy 10-25-1859 (10-26-1859)
Hall, Isaac H. to Milly J. Glover 5-23-1857 (5-24-1857)
Hall, James to Cathrine Winkler 6-2-1841
Hall, Lewis B. to Mary J. Auden 8-19-1871 (no return)
Hall, Lewis H. to Sarah E. Franks 8-31-1865 (9-2-1865)
Hall, M. C. to M. C. Limbaugh 2-24-1874 (2-26-1874)
Hall, Richard to Narcissa Neal 2-18-1839 (no return)
Hall, Seth H. to Emeline Morgan 7-19-1854 (7-23-1854)
Hall, William M. to Ruthy C. Crutchfield 11-29-1873 (11-9?-1873)
Hally, Howell to Elizabeth Seaton 11-14-1839
Hally, Willim C. to Pamey Easley 10-5-1838 (10-11-1838)
Hambrick, Joseph to Bethana Wilson 10-22-1840 (no return)
Hamelton, James I. to Georgia A. Miller 1-9-1873
Hamer, Samuel to M. J. Counts 8-9-1869 (no return)
Hamilton, Grant T. to Nancy Davidson 12-9-1841
Hamilton, J. T. to Martha E. Knight 10-15-1867 (no return)
Hamilton, Jasper S. to Jane Austin 5-24-1855 (5-30-1855)
Hamilton, Newton A. to Nancy C. Trigg 3-28-1873 (9-24-1873)
Hamilton, Newton A. to Narcissa J. Stovall 5-2-1851 (5-4-1851)
Hammer, Joseph to Mary E. Brown 10-26-1847
Hammers, Jacob to Charity Joiner 10-15-1858 (10-17-1858)
Hammers, Jacob to Matilda Yarber 2-10-1861
Hammons, Wm. M. to Sarah E. Stewart 8-17-1870 (no return)
Hammontree, J. J. to F. E. Blake 3-13-1868 (3-16-1868)
Hamption, Henry G. to Malinda E. Buckner 7-3-1858 (7-6-1858)
Hampton, James to Ginnatha Gore 1-2-1845
Hampton, Jno. to M. E. Oakley 1-13-1868 (no return)
Hampton, Robt. S. to Martha A. Reynolds 11-30-1858 (12-2-1858)
Hancock, Adam to Mary Jane Ingram 12-13-1849
Hancock, Robert to Julia J. Sharp 4-16-1840
Handley, Albert G. to Margret C. Patrick 6-24-1850 (6-26-1850)
Handley, Robert C. to Bettie (Miss) Marks 1-26-1869
Handley, W. L. to M. F. Mathews 11-15-1865
Handley, Wm. L. to Sarah Mathews 9-12-1853 (9-13-1853)
Hanley, John to Susan Senter no date (with 1843)
Hannah, Daniel to Elizabeth Darwin 12-18-1869
Hannah, Isaac A. to Sarah Stewart 7-18-1851
Hannah, John G. to N. E. Englet 6-21-1870 (no return)
Hannah, Robt. to Elizabeth A. Wood 3-25-1858
Hannah, Samuel A. to Fanny Malcom 6-2-1866 (no return)
Hannah, Wm. B. to Martha Orear 12-3-1859
Hardee, J. W. to Ann Custer 12-22-1866 (no return)
Harden, Peter to Sarah C. Hefner 3-4-1859
Hardin, John to Polly Ann Harden 12-25-1850 (no return)
Hardin, Moses J. to Margret H. Morgan 3-16-1847 (3-17-1847)
Hardy, J. B. to S. A. Baggett 12-18-1869
Harig, Henry to Musadora Drake 9-30-1853

Harman, Hardeman to Josephine Bouldwin 5-31-1853 (no return)
Harmoning, John F. to Malissa E. Boren 9-23-1872 (no return)
Harny, Alford to Aurenia Haney 11-15-1856 (11-16-1856)
Harris, B. F. to Mary A. Keith 2-20-1871 (2-21-1871)
Harris, Brazilla F. to Permelia Colyar 2-17-1855 (2-18-1855)
Harris, John to S. Kennerly 12-17-1874 (12-20-1874)
Harris, Robert to T. H. (Miss) Jones 1-19-1870 (no return)
Harris, Samuel A. to Sarah McCord 10-24-1843 (11-7-1843)
Harris, Temple to Virginia C. Turney 3-24-1874 (no return)
Harris, W. A. to Susanah L. Black 8-8-1865 (9-8-1865)
Harris, William B. to Mary Carson 7-23-1844
Harris, Wm. to Nannie Kennerly 7-25-1866 (no return)
Harrison, B. W. to Sarah Holder 8-20-1859 (8-21-1859)
Harrison, James to Sallie A. Gipson 12-23-1867 (no return)
Harrison, Perry to Vic Haralson 9-5-1867
Harrison, Pleasant to Nancy Pelham 1-12-1871 (1-13-1871)
Harrison, Wm. C. to A. S. Hughs 9-24-1866 (no return)
Harrison, Wm. T. to Lucy Dotson 10-17-1872
Harvy, Patrick to Nancy A. Royalty 7-21-1850
Haskins, John M. to Jemima Perry 3-26-1841
Hassey, A. T. to Sallie B. Stroud 9-7-1867
Hasty, J. A. to M. A. Ready 2-7-1860 (no return)
Hasty, Wm. M. to N. C. Byrom 8-2-1865 (8-3-1865)
Hatchet, John T. to Mary M. Mason 1-21-1861 (1-22-1861)
Hatchett, James L. to Jane E. Larkin 3-21-1859 (no return)
Hatfield, C. L. to Jane Tucker 12-25-1865 (12-27-1865)
Haverse?, D. H. to Sarena Farmer 3-28-1846
Hawkins, Jack to Sarah Brakefield 11-15-1873 (11-16-1873)
Hawkins, Joseph M. to Annie Pattie 6-26-1858 (6-27-1858)
Hawkins, P. B. to Cathrine A. Brakefield 12-13-1855
Hawkins, P. B. to S. M. Sewell 2-6-1871 (no return)
Hawkins, Samuel M. to Sinna J. Brazelton 12-20-1855
Hawkins, Squire J. to Mariah E. Buckner 12-17-1851 (12-18-1851)
Hayde, Atwood to Martha A. Reeves 11-29-1849
Haynes, W. S. S. to Matilda Hendricks 8-15-1867 (9-15-1867)
Hays, Bayley to Caroline Riddle 6-7-1856 (no return)
Hays, Jordan to S. T. Kirby 7-12-1865
Hays, Samuel to Frankey Barnes 6-2-1849 (6-3-1849)
Hays, W. M. to Elizabeth Miles 12-24-1867
Hays, William to Elmster? Coker 6-9-1857
Hayter, Samuel to Elizabeth M. Finch 9-26-1846
Head, Jacob to Rachiel Young 8-11-1865 (8-22-1865)
Headden, A. G. to A. J. Knight 8-21-1865
Heath, Geo. P. to Mary Church 2-16-1839 (2-17-1839)
Heath, George P. to Mary Church 1-17-1839
Heath, George W. L. to Anna V. Hise 1-25-1851 (1-26-1851)
Heathcoat, George to H. A. Strawn 5-29-1871
Heathcoat, W. C. to M. A. Bennet 10-13-1869 (no return)
Heathcoat, William to Julia E. Tarbor 12-22-1852
Hefner, Geo. W. to C. S. Dickson 1-10-1866 (1-11-1866)
Hefner, John P. to Mary C. Black 10-12-1850 (10-13-1850)
Hefner, Morgan T. to Elizabeth Limbaugh 5-10-1854
Heiston, William P. to Sarah A. Potes 4-9-1846 (7-9-1846)
Helton, James W. to Sarah Jane Ivey 9-15-1869 (9-16-1869)
Helton, P. H. to Angeline Gipson 6-2-1847 (6-4-1847)
Helton, P. R. to Manerva F. Marshall 1-6-1872 (1-7-1872)
Henderson, Alford to Nannie Turney 11-14-1870
Henderson, B. S. to V. S. Spyker 10-25-1859
Henderson, Marcus M. to Hannah E. Porter 6-20-1850
Henderson, William F. to Martha J. Russey 11-17-1842 (11-16?-1842)
Hendley, David A. to Mary E. Cherry 12-5-1874 (12-6-1874)
Hendley, John H. to Tennessee Partin 3-21-1872
Hendley, John J. to Martha J. Gipson 5-6-1872 (5-8-1872)
Hendly, James to Margret Garner 12-25-1866
Hendon, Wm. to Susan Wiggin 5-3-1854 (5-4-1854)
Hendricks, Daniel to Barbary Reed 12-27-1858 (1-1-1859)
Hendricks, Henry to Mary C. Ray 8-18-1856 (8-19-1856)
Hendricks, William to Mary A. Tipps 10-20-1870
Hendrix, Douglass to Hulda Martin 10-?-1839 (no return)
Henley, Alexander to Nancy A. Bennett 1-21-1868 (1-23-1868)
Henshaw, Nathan to Sarah Burks 1-2-1855
Henson, Geo. W. to Mary A. Shultz 11-19-1847
Henson, George to Martha Wilkinson 12-21-1845
Henson, John to Nicey Mills 11-13-1865
Henson, Reubin F. to Sarah A. Scott 10-13-1850

Hessey, J. H. to Nancy Howell 12-24-1870 (no return)
Hester, John to Mary A. Gossage 4-1-1854 (no return)
Hester, Robt. P. to Mary B. Darrell 7-7-1853 (7-8-1853)
Hester, Robt. to Lutitia Stovall 7-2-1866 (no return)
Hethcoat, John A. to Mary Reed 12-14-1872 (12-15-1872)
Heurst?, Clinton A. to Tehpenis? Lipscomb 7-16-1838 (7-17-1838)
Heytt, David A. to Sophia Haning 12-12-1855 (no return)
Hicks, Andrew to Elizabeth J. Rice 9-5-1851 (9-7-1851)
Hicks, Wm. to Mary A. Kirkendol 3-23-1872 (3-24-1872)
Higden, William to Rebecca Enochs 8-21?-1849 (8-24-1849?)
Higginbotham, B. W. to Sarah A. Young 2-6-1858 (2-7-1858)
Higginbotham, Benj. W. to America H. Young 11-10-1856 (no return)
Higginbotham, Isaac R. to Jane Talley 8-6-1856 (8-7-1856)
Higginbotham, J. R. to Elizabeth Hardyman 3-19-1869 (3-23-1869)
Higgins, C. V. to Amelia Parker 2-10-1868
Hill, Allen to Nancy McKnight 8-24-1867
Hill, Allen to Tennessee Henley 4-20-1872
Hill, Anderson to Manerva Guinn 3-25-1841
Hill, Bailey to Harriett Gainer 7-14-1857 (7-16-1857)
Hill, Bailey to Malissa Kitchens 1-29-1845 (1-30-1845)
Hill, Bayly to Sarah Perry 2-17-1842 (2-20-1842)
Hill, Benjamin to Jane Jenkins 5-14-1853
Hill, C. C. to Jane Mallard 8-15-1856 (8-17-1856)
Hill, Cammel to Frances Winn 4-16-1851 (no return)
Hill, David J. to Jane Maise 12-25-1856 (12-26-1856)
Hill, Davy to Ury Guinn 3-13-1844 (3-16-1844)
Hill, Francis M. to Sarah Ann Gipson 12-18-1860 (12-14?-1860)
Hill, Franklin to Lucretia Jenkins 8-30-1849
Hill, George W. to Mary A. Muse 12-18-1844 (12-19-1844)
Hill, George to Angeline Dial 5-10-1871
Hill, George to Nancy Scott 1-20-1840
Hill, Giles to Polly Smith 1-27-1846 (1-29-1846)
Hill, Green to Malinda Long 3-10-1848 (3-12-1848)
Hill, Hardin to Mary Morill 10-9-1839 (no return)
Hill, Henry to Phebias M. Frame 1-1-1841 (1-3-1841)
Hill, Hoden to Pelina Cook 8-30-1845 (8-31-1845)
Hill, Huston to Mary Fitzgerald 8-?-1854 (8-1-1854)
Hill, Huston to Mary Hill 7-26-1854
Hill, Jackson to Margret Bean 8-22-1857
Hill, Jessee R. to Elizabeth Gipson 12-29-1849 (12-30-1849)
Hill, John S. to Martha Rogers 6-11-1851 (6-12-1851)
Hill, John to Ellen Hays 11-7-1865 (11-24-1865)
Hill, John to Margrett Young 3-5-1847 (3-7-1847)
Hill, John to Phebia Gipson 4-18-1850 (4-21-1850)
Hill, John to Sarah Gipson 3-22-1848
Hill, Joshua to Malinda Barnes 2-5-1849
Hill, Josiah to Nancy Greenlee 2-8-1849
Hill, Lewis to Cynthia Driver 9-14-1838 (9-26-1838)
Hill, Moses jr. to Nancy Baines 8-26-1847
Hill, Moses to Lucinda Banels? 3-18-1854
Hill, Moses to Vina McCarver 2-20-1841 (2-21-1841)
Hill, N. to Angeline Sitze 12-22-1870
Hill, Orin to Elizabeth Custer 10-27-1840
Hill, Pleasant to Julia D. Acklin 1-17-1850
Hill, Polk to Elenor J. Wade 7-12-1871 (7-13-1871)
Hill, Rich to Nancy K. Finch 1-4-1855
Hill, Richard to Martha N. Perry 10-29-1866 (11-?-1866)
Hill, Rolin to Telitha Hill 4-30-1873
Hill, Samuel to Elizabeth Pickle 12-24-1867
Hill, Samuel to Musadore Oakley 1-14-1857
Hill, Thomas J. to Mary Lasater 12-20-1855 (12-23-1855)
Hill, Thomas to Mary Duboice 7-24-1838
Hill, William R. to Partina Tabbith 1-8-1845 (1-9-1845)
Hill, William to Margrett Bryant 2-6-1839 (no return)
Hill, William to Nancy J. Wagner 3-5-1866
Hill, William to Sarah Muse 6-6-1850
Hill, Wm. G. to Martha M. Sansom 9-4-1865 (10-10-1865)
Hilliard, Gilliam to Elizabeth Tipton 8-30-1871 (no return)
Hilton, James A. to D. Hendley 12-7-1874 (12-8-1874)
Hilton, James to Elizabeth Baker 9-9-1852
Hilton, Samuel P. to Nancy Jones 1-17-1843 (no return)
Hilton, W. B. to N. E. (Miss) Simpson 1-18-1869 (no return)
Hime, James to S. R. E. Reynolds 12-14-1867
Hindman, J. P. to Eliza Wilson 5-31-1866 (no return)

Hines, A. J. to M. F. Montgomery 12-14-1872 (no return)
Hines, M. P. to Lucy S. Keith 11-20-1866 (11-21-1866)
Hines, Robert to Sarah Moore 8-3-1848 (no return)
Hines, Robt. C. to Martha A. Marshall 5-4-1865
Hines, Thomas T. to Kate Stroud 10-10-1874 (10-11-1874)
Hinkle, Samuel to Esther Covey 8-24-1850 (9-7-1850)
Hinkle, Samuel to Martha Ann Finch 10-5-1870
Hinshaw, William to Nancy Roberson 5-2-1844
Hinton, John P. to M. F. Embrey 11-15-1865
Hise, David to Ann Adam 9-19-1860 (9-23-1860)
Hise, Henry N. to Maria L. Moore 1-13-1838 (1-14-1838)
Hise, J. L. to Sarah Hockersmith 11-14-1868 (11-15-1868)
Hise, Jacob W. to Amanda Thompson 12-8-1840 (no return)
Hise, John E. to Rebecca Tipps 11-19-1842 (11-20-1842)
Hise, Thomas to Sarah L. Marshall 7-28-1856 (8-3-1856)
Hitch, W. H. to Esther Ann Trigg 1-14-1846 (1-15-1846)
Hockersmith, E. J. to Patsy Reagin 6-25-1859 (6-26-1859)
Hockersmith, Esquire to Lucy E. Hise 1-20-1866 (1-21-1866)
Hockersmith, G. G. M. to Mary E. Rollins 5-13-1871 (5-21-1871)
Hockersmith, George M. to Elizabeth Darwin 12-30-1847
Hockersmith, John to Delphia J. Reagin 1-21-1856
Hockersmith, W. R. to Rosana Hill 12-14-1867
Hodge, Charley to Eliza Miller 12-28-1870 (no return)
Hofman, Levi to Nancy Payne 1-14-1874 (1-24-1874)
Hoge, S. C. to Temmie Holland 11-19-1872 (no return)
Hoges, James A. to Martha Holder 3-19-1853 (3-24-1853)
Hoke, Martin to Rutha Smith 9-20-1870 (9-23-1870)
Holbert, William to M. E. Ewing 4-19-1860 (no return)
Holder, Andrew S. to Rebecca J. Brouglimans? 10-16-1856 (no return)
Holder, Benj. F. to Mary F. Sells 8-?-1870 (no return)
Holder, C. C. to Mary J. Farris 7-17-1858 (7-18-1858)
Holder, C. G. to Louisa Williams 12-23-1867 (no return)
Holder, Cornelius to Ary Noe 12-17-1847 (12-19-1847)
Holder, Dempsey to Sarah Jane Smyth 12-22-1847
Holder, Dennis to Lucinda Byrom 12-21-1853 (12-22-1853)
Holder, Dyer to Leaunah Francis 2-15?-1838 (2-20-1838)
Holder, Edam to Mary Ann Woods 10-28-1844
Holder, G. W. to E. Majors 9-3-1868
Holder, J. H. to Lucinda Holt 9-14-1871 (no return)
Holder, James A. to Mary E. A. Rutledge 7-17-1855
Holder, James to Lotta Henson 5-8-1874 (5-17-1874)
Holder, James to Susan Jackson 10-19-1866 (no return)
Holder, Jerry to Mary Ann Ford 1-30-1846 (2-1-1846)
Holder, John C. to Amandy E. Farris 3-12-1846
Holder, John M. to Elizabeth Anderson 9-21-1847 (9-27-1847)
Holder, John to Elizabeth Holder 9-2-1852
Holder, John to Lizzie Parham 8-11-1870 (no return)
Holder, Joseph jr. to Susan Williams 9-27-1840 (2-27-1840?)
Holder, Joshua to Christiana Floyd 12-21-1847
Holder, L. V. to Lethan Shasteen 3-26-1867
Holder, Lewis to Mariah Lakey 5-19-1841
Holder, Solomon to Eliza J. Looney 1-9-1841
Holder, W. F. to Emma Nally 8-29-1867 (no return)
Holder, W. F. to S. E. Holt 10-13-1869 (no return)
Holder, William D. to Mary A. Brown 8-25-1873
Holder, William to Caroline Bates 7-25-1840 (7-26-1840)
Holder, William to Cathrine Sumers 10-1-1848
Holder, William to Mahulda Holder 8-24-1843
Holder, Wilson to Rebecca Muse 1-14-1842 (1-16-1842)
Holiday, Robt. to Sophia Counts 9-3-1873
Holladay, William to Artemetia T. Wright 2-28-1856 (no return)
Holland, Hugh to Mary J. Moore 10-20-1857 (no return)
Holland, Hugh to Mary J. Moore 10-20-1859 (no return)
Holland, J. M. to M. E. Buckner 2-9-1871
Holland, Jos. M. to Sallie Buckner 2-21-1860 (no return)
Holland, Richard L. to M. E. Perkins 11-29-1853 (no return)
Holland, Robt. to Matt Howard 12-27-1866 (no return)
Holland, William M. to C. E. Harris 11-1-1870 (no return)
Holland, William to Eliza Moore 12-17-1856
Holman, James P. to Mattie Crenshaw 8-16-1870 (9-16-1870)
Holsonback, Jeptha to Sarah Malone 6-8-1852 (6-9-1852)
Holt, Enoch to Mary Foreman 12-7-1842 (12-8-1842)
Holt, J. H. to M. C. Muse 10-27-1856 (10-29-1856)
Holt, J. H. to Rebecca E. Morris 3-18-1862 (3-20-1862)

Holt, J. W. to M. J. Cook 12-17-1873 (12-18-1873)
Holt, Jacob to Lucinda Holder 9-26-1838 (9-27-1838)
Holt, Jacob to Mary Deerin 4-19-1866 (no return)
Holt, Jacob to Rosanah Rane 10-31-1857 (11-1-1857)
Holt, James H. to Gracy E. Brown 11-19-1873 (11-20-1873)
Holt, Jeremiah to Kesiah Ford 5-6-1859 (5-8-1859)
Holt, Richard C. to Mary Warren 12-22-1841 (12-23-1841)
Holt, Seborn to Sarah Simpson 1-10-1840
Homes, Pinkney G. to Mary A. Underwood 9-29-1857 (no return)
Honey, David to Elizabeth Cobble 10-13-1870
Honey, Eli to Martha Roberson 7-17-1865 (no return)
Hooser, George to Sarah Pelham 2-28-1870 (3-2-1870)
Hoosier, John to N. J. Morrow 8-4-1865 (8-10-1865)
Hoosier, Wm. to Jane Furgerson 8-4-1865 (8-7-1865)
Hopfold, Hugo to Carrie Fisher 7-15-1873 (7-28-1873)
Hopkins, George W. to Susan Roberson 9-11-1850 (9-12-1850)
Hopkins, James to Martha Robertson 7-31-1858 (8-1-1858)
Hopkins, Solomon J. to Mary Ann Tucker 8-13-1849
Hopper, Joseph S. to Elizabeth Hudson 11-9-1842 (11-10-1842)
Horn, Clarence to Clarra Sartin 9-25-1867
Horon, Robert to Sarah Turley 10-12-1844 (10-13-1844)
Horton, A. H. to Jennie Herring 8-17-1869 (no return)
Horton, Benj. W. to Sarah Young 11-22-1852
Horton, Elmore R. to Jane E. Estill 1-25-1856
Horton, F. M. to Margret Noah 4-?-1859
Horton, J. E. to Margrett Tate 1-20-1870
Horton, Jasper L. to Hannah Nuckles 10-6-1856 (10-7-1856)
Horton, John to Emeline Jones 12-22-1870 (no return)
Horton, N. M. to S. A. Hannah 11-15-1858 (11-16-1858)
Horton, Newton M. to Sallie A. Hannah 11-15-1858 (no return)
Horton, Newton to Sallie A. Hannah 11-15-1859 (no return)
Horton, Simeon W. to Martha J. Bowling 7-20-1843
Houghton, S. W. to Jennie Mullikin 12-6-1858 (12-7-1858)
Houghton, Seth W. to Roena R. Hutchins 11-2-1848 (no return)
Houston, Geo. L. to Rachiel M. Ripps 10-13-1846 (10-14-1846)
Houston, Louis to Mary A. Mayse 7-16-1872 (7-18-1872)
Houston, Thomas S. to Malinda Baker 10-12-1841
Houston, William to Sarah Colyar 12-24-1860
Howard, E. J. to M. E. Howk 11-25-1858
Howard, Edward E. S. to Marinda J. Elmore 11-4-1851 (no return)
Howard, John B. to Emeline Adkerson 10-12-1869 (no return)
Howard, John W. to Nancy Kennedy 10-30-1859 (no return)
Howard, Michael to H. A. Canady 8-4-1858 (no return)
Howard, Thomas J. to Mary A. Cantrell 6-24-1851
Howard, Thomas P. to Lutitia White 12-29-1855
Howard, Thomas to Mary Embrey 4-24-1845
Howell, J. M. to E. Warren 8-8-1868 (8-4?-1868)
Howell, John to Elizabeth Richardson 6-7-1855 (6-9-1855)
Howell, Joseph to Mary Mattenbee 2-1-1858 (no return)
Huddleston, Francis D. to Suffronia H. Bledsoe 12-14-1843
Huddleston, Isaac R. to Martha Thurman 12-4-1845 (12-5-1845)
Huddleston, J. T. to Mary A. Sewell 12-31-1868 (no return)
Hudgins, H. T. to Rebecca B. Muse 8-30-1866 (no return)
Hudgins, J. B. to Nancy A. Morris 12-23-1858
Hudgins, James A. to Elizabeth Fanning 9-7-1865 (10-8-1865)
Hudgins, John J. to Sarah M. Chambers 8-9-1859 (8-11-1859)
Hudgins, Jones A. to E. E. Holt 11-7-1867
Hudgins, P. L. to Elizabeth Nixon 9-19-1866 (no return)
Huffer, D. W. to Mary E. Shelton 1-23-1874 (1-25-1874)
Huffer, H. H. to Telitha J. Powell 5-27-1874
Hufman, Michael to Jane Farris 11-20-1849
Huggins, Hubbard H. to Fidella J. Lasater 10-14-1858 (10-4?-1858)
Hughes, H. P. to S. E. Hill 4-20-1870
Hughes, J. M. to S. E. Summerell 5-11-1872 (5-15-1872)
Hughes, James to Martha S. Wilkerson 2-23-1874 (2-26-1874)
Humphrey, Thos. J. to Mary E. Weaver 4-23-1859 (4-24-1859)
Hunger, Thomas M. H. to Elia J. Baker 2-14-1870 (no return)
Hunt, Anthony to Margrett A. Hale 5-6-1874 (no return)
Hunt, David to Lucinda Crowders 6-26-1851
Hunt, George W. to Precilla Jane Powell 3-21-1844
Hunt, Hayden to Elizabeth Gore 11-27-1849 (no return)
Hunt, Lancen to Mary Crowder 8-7-1841
Hunt, Rhalient to Lucy A. Roseborough 10-12-1853 (10-13-1853)
Hunt, Spencer to Jemima Wilhite 11-26-1844
Hunter, Thos. H. M. to Ellea J. Baker 2-14-1870

Hurley, Zachariah G. to Sarah W. Murrell 11-29-1848
Hurt, Peter T. to Martha A. England 4-23-1850
Hutcherson, Thomas to Rachael L. Frame 9-17-1857 (no return)
Hutchins, John M. to Mary Russey 1-5-1869 (no return)
Hutchinson, Thomas to Nancy Bice 7-30-1855 (8-1-1855)
Hutton, Benjamin to Elizabeth Branch 1-15-1859 (no return)
Hutton, Isaac to Martha A. Mitchell 8-18-1856 (8-19-1856)
Hutton, James B. to Mary Jane Mitchell 8-9-1856 (8-12-1856)
Hutton, Meredith to Mima Osborn 2-8-1849 (2-9-1849)
Hutton, William to Delia Thomas 5-31-1850
Hyder, A. L. to Mary A. Keith 9-21-1840 (9-22-1840)
Hyder, Adam L. to Cathrine Colyar 1-4-1848 (1-6-1848)
Hyndes, John M. to Amelia H. Patrick 11-21-1854
Ikard, E. H. to Martisha Duncan 1-1-1851 (1-2-1851)
Ikard, Elijah H. to Elizabeth O. Rowe 1-25-1843 (1-26-1843)
Ikard, J. M. to T. E. Gocher 6-11-1866 (no return)
Ingalls, J. F. to R. J. Bowers 3-3-1868
Inglass, G. M. to Ida Binkley 7-29-1869 (8-?-1869)
Ingram, Benj. J. to Cyntha A. Howe 9-27-1844 (9-30-1844)
Irby, J. W. to Josephine Neal 10-9-1858
Isbell, James to Mary Cooley 6-28-1871
Isbell, Levi to Margrett Loney 3-28-1844 (no return)
Ivey, Anderson A. to Sarah Tanner 10-26-1854 (10-29-1854)
Ivey, James to Mary C. Holt 5-30-1843 (5-31-1843)
Ivey, John H. to Omega C. Muse 12-27-1852 (12-30-1852)
Ivey, Nathan M. to Mary J. Curle 12-6-1857 (no return)
Ivey, S. J. to C. M. E. J. Buchanan 6-8-1857 (6-9-1857)
Ivey, Young A. to Eunice Ashley 9-26-1846 (9-27-1846)
Jacks, Wm. to S. J. Kennedy 1-31-1870 (2-3-1870)
Jackson, Albert to Olevia J. Stewart 11-4-1856
Jackson, Andrew to Barbary Van Swearing Shoup 7-30-1870 (8-2-1870)
Jackson, Dink to Mary Ann Rich 11-3-1871 (11-5-1871)
Jackson, Edward A. to Sarah Knight 7-7-1853
Jackson, Francis M. to Lucy D. Lynch 9-15-1853
Jackson, J. A. to S. E. Blades 11-16-1864
Jackson, James C. to Sarah E. Gilliam 8-18-1874 (8-28-1874)
Jackson, James W. to Elizabeth Tankersley 12-20-1852
Jackson, John to Judy A. m. Elliott 8-18-1866 (no return)
Jackson, John to Judy Ann Mexico Ellitt 8-18-1866 (no return)
Jackson, Lindsay to Anna Denton 8-24-1843
Jackson, P. P. to M. A. Blivins 8-3-1869 (no return)
Jackson, R. W. to Mary C. Arnold 5-17-1873 (5-18-1873)
Jackson, Richard to Elender Faris 5-25-1849
Jackson, S. M. to Jennie T. Farris 12-14-1870 (no return)
Jackson, Thomas J. to Mildred C. Acklin 3-29-1853
Jackson, Warren to Julia Walraven 3-3-1868 (no return)
Jackson, Warren to Louisa Senter 3-24-1844
Jackson, Wilson C. to Rebecca Garner 8-3-1854
Jacoway, John to Nancy Middleton 11-24-1844
Jacoway, W. W. to Mary Shook 12-19-1871
James, W. R. to Sarah A. Mitchell 11-20-1872
Janes, John to Elizabeth Willis 12-14-1840 (12-?-1840)
Janes, Robt. R. to Sarah A. R. Tarpley 1-4-1858 (1-5-1858)
Jarnagan, Asa to Mary J. Fitch 8-8-1866 (no return)
Jarnegan, Franklin to E. L. Shasteen 1-18-1867 (1-20-1867)
Jeans, John to Glathia T. Farris 1-24-1871 (1-23?-1871)
Jearnegan, Elijah to Sarah Holder 12-20-1852
Jefferson, John to Sarah A. Peril 1-13-1853 (1-14-1853)
Jenkins, James F. to Mary Bula Clements 12-6-1869 (12-7-1869)
Jenkins, William G. to Mary Green 3-7-1840 (no return)
Jenkins, Wm. H. to Anna J. Wilkerson 9-30-1868 (10-1-1868)
Jennings, W. B. to Julia Syler 9-23-1858 (no return)
Jennings, W. B. to Julia Syler 9-23-1859 (no return)
Jernegan, Isaac to Lucy Holder 8-19-1852
Jernegan, Saml. to M. E. Smith 12-7-1867 (12-9-1867)
Jett, Bayless to Linda Bledsoe 7-18-1859 (7-19-1859)
Jett, William to Sarah N. Williamson 8-5-1846 (8-6-1846)
Jetton, Isaac to Elizabeth Williams 8-10-1848
Jetton, Joel to Malinda J. Reid 7-20-1859 (7-24-1859)
Jetton, Landon C. to Jane Seaton 11-19-1851 (no return)
Jetton, Thos. J. to Mary Prince 8-17-1870 (no return)
Jetton, Wiley to Lucinda Kemp 10-25-1852 (no return)
Jetton, Wm. M. to Sarah J. Williams 2-22-1849 (2-?-1849)
Jiles, Hezekiah to Lorena Osborn 12-24-1841 (12-27-1841)

Johnson, A. H. to Martha Anderson 7-20-1852
Johnson, Alford H. to Rebecca Finch 12-18-1845
Johnson, Charles A. to Ada A. Trimble 7-23-1873 (7-24-1873)
Johnson, Duke to Sarah Coots 7-25-1874 (7-26-1874)
Johnson, Edmond to Elenor Ashley 8-31-1849 (9-6-1849)
Johnson, Fred to Sidney Swain 3-4-1871 (no return)
Johnson, G. D. to Margret E. Corn 12-22-1869 (12-23-1869)
Johnson, James M. to Amanda Swain 10-14-1867 (no return)
Johnson, James S. to Ivarilla D. Davis 4-30-1853
Johnson, Joseph B. to Mary E. Finley 5-10-1860
Johnson, Joseph to Rebecca Brummit 7-30-1857
Johnson, Thomas F. to Anna Corn 1-30-1868
Johnson, William to Manervga Austin 12-23-1839 (12-25-1839)
Johnston, Allen to Josephine Foreman 11-16-1857 (11-17-1857)
Johnston, Franklin to Mary E. Wiseman 3-9-1857 (3-10-1857)
Johnston, T. W. to Mattie A. Miller 1-5-1874 (no return)
Jolly, W. T. to Sarah Banks 12-13-1859
Jones, A. S. to Hannah Richardson 2-16-1865 (2-19-1865)
Jones, Abner to Mary Ann Carroll 12-23-1847 (12-28-1847)
Jones, Abram M. to Barbrey Gross 10-24-1844 (no return)
Jones, Allen B. to Sarah B. Stewart 7-15-1857
Jones, Benj. B. to Nannie E. Phillips 7-12-1858
Jones, Benjamin F. to Sarah Smith 8-1-1839
Jones, C. M. to Susan M. Horton 10-21-1859 (no return)
Jones, Charles L. to Rebecca J. Harris 9-12-1854 (9-15-1854)
Jones, Charles L. to Susan M. Horton 10-21-1858 (no return)
Jones, D. D. to C. L. Blythe 2-12-1867 (2-13-1867)
Jones, D. S. to M. S. Mitchell 12-20-1866 (12-23-1866)
Jones, F. B. to Sarah J. Wagner 8-25-1868 (no return)
Jones, G. J. to W. V. Anderson 2-1-1866 (no return)
Jones, Gray W. to Elizabeth Davidson 9-10-1846
Jones, H. T. to Nancy C. Boyd 1-16-1867 (no return)
Jones, Henry H. to Elizabeth Hammon 4-4-1854 (4-6-1854)
Jones, Henry to Martha Robertson 12-9-1865
Jones, Hugh to Nancy March 12-27-1838
Jones, James A. to Elizabeth Craten 2-8-1842
Jones, James to Mary Brown 8-28-1874 (8-29-1874)
Jones, Jessee E. to Sarah J. Thomas 10-17-1855
Jones, John C. to Emeline Wilkins 10-19-1842 (10-20-1842)
Jones, John W. to Caroline McNabb 4-10-1866
Jones, Jos.? B. to Amanda L. Thomas 12-29-1849 (12-30-1849)
Jones, L. D. to Isabella Osborn 3-6-1839 (no return)
Jones, Lorenzo D. to Eveline Mann 1-8-1852 (1-13-1852)
Jones, Ozwill to Polly Cook 12-17-1839
Jones, Richard to Mary Hasty 4-4-1860 (no return)
Jones, Robert to D. A. Mason 12-21-1868
Jones, Robt. R. to Sarah A. R. Tarpley 1-4-1858 (no return)
Jones, Robt. to D. O. (Miss) Mason 12-21-1869
Jones, Thomas W. to Cathrine E. Kenningham 10-22-1840 (no return)
Jones, Thomas to Mary Susan Francis 12-17-1846
Jones, Thos. E. to Lucind L. Starnes 7-15-1858 (7-22-1858)
Jones, Turner to Rutha Caroline Dougan 10-25-1841 (no return)
Jones, W. L. to N. H. Martin 11-21-1866 (no return)
Jones, William H. to Elizabeth M. Muse 7-10-1849
Jones, William R. to Louisa J. Horton 11-20-1843 (11-21-1843)
Jones, William to Clarrissa Berry 9-3-1841 (9-5-1841)
Jourdan, W. F. to Frazie Deason 8-20-1873
Jourdan, Wm. to Louisanah Brazelton 12-26-1870 (no return)
Keath, Wm. to Elenor Malone 4-20-1852
Keck, J. K. P. to Nancy J. Dorrell 3-1-1858 (3-2-1858)
Keck, John to Juda Lasater 5-17-1845 (5-18-1845)
Keedy, William to Nancy Powell 8-27-1845 (8-28-1845)
Keel, G. R. to Nancy Wagner 12-16-1868 (no return)
Keele, James to Sarah Cherry 10-18-1843 (no return)
Keener, Joseph to Mary M. Moton 2-15-1850
Keith, A. M. to Mary E. Brooks 8-8-1868 (no return)
Keith, Anthony N. to Ann T. Green 12-8-1850 (no return)
Keith, Daniel C. to Susan C. Bledsoe 8-26-1854 (8-27-1854)
Keith, Jack to Ellen Staples 5-4-1870 (no return)
Keith, James H. to Mollie E. Moseley 10-31-1871 (12-19-1871)
Keith, James N. to Nancy J. Larkins 2-7-1839 (2-9-1839)
Keith, John B. to Susan M. Bell 2-24-1848
Keith, John L. to Elizabeth Trigg 1-9-1847 (1-12-1847)
Keith, John to Mary Drake 2-13-1861 (2-16-1861)

Keith, Newton to Joanah England 12-28-1870 (no return)
Keith, P. B. to M. F. Keith 8-9-1869 (8-12-1869)
Keith, S. H. to Mere? Moore 9-25-1865 (9-26-1865)
Keith, Samuel H. to Nancy Johnson 11-7-1844
Keith, Samuel to Salinna Denson 1-9-1847 (1-12-1847)
Keith, Thomas A. to Violet Francis 5-7-1874 (no return)
Keith, William P. to Bernatty Holder 9-14-1843
Keith, Wm. H. to Sarah A. Horton 1-18-1872 (no return)
Keith, Wm. M. to Mollie E. Hines 11-7-1871 (no return)
Keller, John to Nancy Burt 4-8-1853 (4-12-1853)
Kelley, Charles to Elizabeth Rose 5-8-1867
Kelley, Charley to Elizabeth J. Davis 5-21-1858
Kelley, G. W. to Mary E. Gamble 9-2-1869 (with 1867)
Kelley, George to Mary Ann Stewart 2-15-1846 (no return)
Kelley, J. W. to Susan Crabtree 4-25-1839
Kelley, James S. to Nannie Gadsey 2-17-1852
Kelley, John M. to Elizabeth Brown 12-13-1866 (no return)
Kelley, John W. to Leanna Holder 8-1-1850
Kelley, Luke to Jane Noah 12-26-1857 (12-31-1857)
Kelley, Luke to Matilda J. Counts 6-18-1859
Kelley, Luke to Susan Noah 10-3-1853 (10-27-1853)
Kelley, R. J. to K. W. Acklin 6-17-1864 (6-23-1864)
Kelley, Ruben to Louisa A. Caperton 10-17-1845 (10-19-1845)
Kemp, I. to Sarah C. Smith 10-9-1867
Kennada, Sampson to Jane Pitcock 2-11-1855 (2-12-1855)
Kennedy, D. T. to Rebecca Mason 11-8-1866 (no return)
Kennerly, George T. to Levicy? Bratton 1-16-1873
Kennerly, John P. to Clarrissa Bennett 3-9-1848 (3-12-1848)
Key, Alexander G. to Ann E. Spann 8-1-1839 (no return)
Kilpatrick, Geo. F. to Ann Eliza Moseley 10-7-1849
Kilpatrick, James P. to Mary J. Badgett 4-6-1842 (4-7-1842)
Kilpatrick, John M. to Emily C. Morgan 12-27-1843 (12-28-1843)
Kilpatrick, Wm. McClain to Mary A. Riddle 9-10-1855 (no return)
Kimbro, George A. to Nannie Crick 12-6-1870 (no return)
Kimsey, John to Permintha A. Wilkins 5-5-1858 (no return)
King, Charles to Sarah E. Stewart 5-28-1872 (6-2-1872)
King, Fountain to Mary J. Sullivan 10-5-1869
King, George to Lizzie Rose 1-30-1866 (1-31-1866)
King, Isaac to Harriett Moore 12-3-1870 (12-4-1870)
King, John to Elizabeth Williams 12-4-1856 (12-5-1856)
King, R. M. to Amelia Judd 12-31-1840 (no return)
King, Samuel to Betsy Wilhite 8-8-1855 (no return)
King, William to Clary McKee 5-2-1838 (no return)
King, William to Marinda Briler 5-2-1846 (5-3-1846)
King, Wm. R. to M. E. Coker 5-19-1866 (5-25-1866)
Kiningham, A. J. to Mary A. Cowan 2-10-1870
Kiningham, A. J. to Pattie E. Porter 2-5-1872 (no return)
Kiningham, James H. to Mariah Vaughan 1-23-1852
Kiningham, John H. to Virginia E. Kiningham 12-1-1858 (12-2-1858)
Kiningham, Robt. C. to Mary G. Alexander 2-27-1855
Kiningham, W. E. to Fannie Alexander 10-24-1865 (10-25-1865)
Kiningham, W. J. to Nancy J. Mathews 3-26-1870 (3-27-1870)
Kiningham, W. M. to Jane Moore 11-7-1844
Kinney, John to Louisa Cherry 10-4-1843
Kinsey, Jno. W. M. to Bettie Panter 4-24-1874 (4-25-1874)
Kirby, S. P. to Sarah Hinton 1-3-1861
Kitchens, Daniel to Mahala Franklin 12-16-1871 (no return)
Kitchens, Daniel to Mary Ann Barbee 3-17-1851 (3-18-1851)
Kitchens, James to Martha J. Woodward 8-11-1850
Kitchens, W. B. to S. B. Spears 7-26-1869 (no return)
Kitchens, W. M. to W. C. Reynols 7-6-1871
Kitchens, William C. to Julia Ann Morgan 3-5-1846 (no return)
Kitchings, Daniel to Mary A. Bausling? 3-23-1841 (no return)
Kitchings, John to Drusia Alexander 2-25-1841
Klepper, James to Polly Jones 2-9-1838 (no return)
Knight, Andrew J. to Sarah Carroll 10-19-1854
Knight, B. F. to M. E. Holland 12-30-1865 (no return)
Knight, J. L. to R. S. Williams 10-24-1870 (no return)
Knight, James M. to Tempa McKelvey 12-22-1868
Knight, James to Amanda Jones 12-20-1848 (12-21-1848)
Knight, James to Henretta Oakley 12-11-1843 (12-14-1843)
Knight, Joseph M. to Nancy A. Hurley 2-5-1866 (no return)
Knight, Thomas to Mary E. Shelton 11-13-1874 (11-21-1874)
Knight, William D. to Sarah E. Huddleston 11-10-1846
Knott, C. C. to Nancy C. Travis 3-3-1870 (no return)

Knox, John to Mary V. Jordan 4-1-1855
Knuckles, Wm. H. to Sarah A. Linsley 12-13-1840 (12-20-1840)
Koger, Calvin to Martha Gifford 10-9-1874 (10-11-1874)
Koger, Jno. P. to Nancy P. Simpson 4-1-1871
Krotzer, H. J. to Rebecca Zerbee 10-14-1871 (10-15-1871)
Kuningham, Thos. F. to Mary E. Seargent 4-4-1861
Lackey, Allen to Nancy Fannan 2-14-1839 (no return)
Ladd, Amos to Martha Statum 8-6-1855 (8-7-1855)
Ladd, Balis to Virginia Reed 4-10-1865 (4-13-1865)
Ladd, James to Nancy Vibbert 2-15-1855
Ladd, John M. to Lucinda Jane Carroll 7-20-1841 (7-21-1841)
Ladd, Noble to Elizabeth Weaver 12-9-1850
Lakey, James to Lucinda Holder 6-12-1840 (6-15-1840)
Lambert, H. A. to Mollie Bell 12-22-1866 (no return)
Lambert, H. L. to Sarah Taylor 8-8-1840 (8-10-1840)
Lambert, John S. to Lucy Duncan 7-27-1842 (8-10-1842)
Lambert, John S. to Martha Taylor 1-20-1848
Lambert, John to Elizabeth Edwards 7-29-1846 (7-30-1846)
Lambertson, Joseph J. to Sarah Turman 1-14-1858
Landenberger, John C. to M. A. Warren 9-7-1868 (no return)
Lane, Rowland to Dosha Decherd 12-20-1844
Langan, Wm. to Ann Reed 4-16-1859
Langston, Jacob to M. M. Sandridge 7-17-1865 (7-18-1865)
Langston, James H. to M. J. McGehee 3-16-1874 (no return)
Langston, John E. to Semantha Evans 12-10-1843
Langston, Wm. H. to Paralee Kelley 12-4-1850 (12-5-1850)
Lanham, A. H. to Mary A. Garnett 12-17-1860 (12-24-1860)
Larkin, David F. to Martha A. Frame 2-6-1846
Larkin, Francis M. to Darcas Larkin 7-2-1855 (7-4-1855)
Larkin, John H. to Frances A. Stovall 8-6-1853 (8-11-1853)
Larkin, John H. to Mary Hannah 1-1-1862 (1-3-1862)
Larkin, Thos. J. to Ophelia E. Rutledge 8-20-1867 (no return)
Larkin, Wm. to Ann Gentle 7-31-1858 (no return)
Larry, John T. to Louisa C. Noah 5-29-1854
Lasater, Christopher A. to Martha N. Kennady 3-12-1856
Lasater, Green H. to Lucy Davidson 1-22-1845 (1-7-1845)
Lasater, James A. to Rebecca E. Blake 7-9-1855 (7-13-1855)
Lasater, Jefferson to Mary Grammer 2-20-1872
Lasater, John H. to Rebecca J. Brandyberry 1-14-1871
Lasater, Robert C. to Susan Davidson 12-22-1838 (no return)
Lasater, William to Mary Ann Evans 10-2-1852 (10-3-1852)
Lashbrook, L. M. to Charity Colyar 8-27-1853 (8-28-1853)
Lashbrooks, James W. to Susan Colyar 8-26-1856 (no return)
Lasiter, Hugh F. to C. E. Beard 5-14-1869 (5-16-1869)
Lasley, Thomas to Loucinda Hise 9-26-1849
Latimer, Wm. M. to Nancy E. Newman 8-20-1853 (8-25-1853)
Latta, O. C. to M. F. Collins 9-19-1874
Laughmiller, F. A. to Caroline W. Reeves 9-9-1847
Laughmiller, F. A. to Elizabeth F. Decherd 10-10-1839 (no return)
Law, William to Margret E. Parsons 5-23-1857 (no return)
Lawing, Andrew K. to Mary M. Darrell 12-21-1844
Lawrence, King to Ellen Black 2-22-1866 (no return)
Lawson, George R. to Nancy H. Warren 12-21-1855 (12-23-1855)
Lawson, Lazarus to Margret Duncan 1-2-1854 (1-3-1854)
Lawson, Levi to Georgian Sanders 2-21-1866 (2-22-1866)
Lawson, Putman to Mary A. Farmer 3-18-1854 (no return)
Layton, John H. to Eliza Jane Logan 3-9-1847 (3-11-1847)
Leach, J. W. to Nancy E. Burt 1-16-1867 (no return)
Leach, Wm. H. to Nancy Smith 10-17-1867 (no return)
League, Jurred to Amanda Birmingham 10-26-1872 (10-27-1872)
League, William T. to Nannie Hill 8-3-1871
Lee, Anderson J. to Caroline A. Renfro 2-7-1855 (2-8-1855)
Lee, Bolden P. to Mary A. Morris 10-7-1852
Lee, Edward F. to Rebecca A. Taylor 1-21-1845
Lee, James to Nancy Davis 12-25-1862
Lee, John to Maldy Ann Adkinson 3-28-1855
Lee, Stephen M. to Mary J. Jones 8-19-1856
Lee, William T. to Mary A. Jones 1-4-1850
Lee, Wm. R. to Amanda C. Monis 10-2-1851
Lee, Wm. T. to Sarah M. Jones 1-28-1858 (11-25?-1858)
Leel, F. A. to E. A. Syler 5-29-1866 (no return)
Lefeber, George H. to Eliza Jane Custer 5-12-1855 (5-13-1855)
Lefeber, George H. to Julia A. E. Stanphiel 9-3-1853 (9-4-1853)
Legg, William to Sally A. Johnson 1-27-1873 (1-29-1873)
Lenehan, Daniel to Susan Featherston 12-19-1868 (12-20-1868)

Lenehan, George to Nancy McKelvy 1-25-1872
Lenehan, Peter to Jennie Lyons 7-14-1874 (7-16-1874)
Lenehan, Thomas E. to T. E. Featherston 8-10-1872
Lesley, William C. to E. E. Hice 1-1-1848 (1-5-1848)
Lesure, L. C. to Laura Corn 10-21-1874
Leveret, James A. to C. J. Goddard 2-1-1868
Leverton, H. B. to Martha L. Stephens 6-22-1867 (7-1-1867)
Leverton, Levi to Mary A. Pearson 8-7-1865 (8-10-1865)
Lewis, Gabriel to Elizabeth Anderton 1-7-1851
Lewis, James to M. E. Williams 1-10-1874 (1-11-1874)
Lewis, M. M. W. W. to Mary C. Anderton 4-11-1855
Lewis, Steven M. to Nancy Cox 10-22-1868 (no return)
Lewis, Thomas to Sarah Cowan 10-3-1840 (10-4-1840)
Lewis, William R. to Nancy E. Carter 4-12-1849
Lexton, William C. to Elizabeth Osborn 11-2-1846 (11-5-1846)
Ligret, John B. to Rebecca A. Williams 2-2-1850 (2-6-1850)
Lilley, Jessee to Martha B. Stewart 8-13-1818 (no return)
Lillis, John to Eliza Odom 11-26-1868
Limbaugh, Joel to Sarah A Tipps 12-5-1870 (no return)
Limbaugh, John W. to Cathrine Moore 1-4-1872
Limbaugh, Michiel to Susan Tipps 10-15-1866 (no return)
Limbaugh, Peter to Judith Smith 7-17-1845 (7-18-1845)
Limbaugh, Peter to Sarah Grant 1-18-1854 (1-19-1854)
Limbaugh, Solomon to Christiana Robeson 3-19-1838 (no return)
Limbaugh, W. R. to M. J. Osborn 10-3-1868 (no return)
Limbaugh, Wark to Frances Miller 9-10-1872
Lindsley, James M. to Susan A. Taylor 8-21-1868
Lindsley, John A. to Mary Becknell 7-22-1868
Linticum, Thomas to Ellen Russell 10-7-1841
Linville, Henry to Margret Woodson 9-26-1848 (9-30-1848)
Lipscomb, Dabney D. to Julia F. Larkins 1-1-1838 (1-4-1838)
Lipscomb, J. T. to M. M. Rutledge 8-23-1869 (8-24-1869)
Lipscomb, Sherrod to Samyra Simmons 11-23-1868 (no return)
Litle, George to Mary Willis 6-13-1868 (6-14-1868)
Litle, M. W. to Ellen Noah 12-5-1865 (no return)
Litrell, Shelton to Frances Blakely 1-21-1842 (1-23-1842)
Little, A. G. to Judith Oakley 12-23-1873 (12-24-1873)
Little, A. J. to Lucy J. Phillips 1-13-1870 (no return)
Little, David A. to Sumira Wilhite 11-13-1852 (no return)
Little, John H. to Frances Lenehan 3-17-1858
Little, Richard F. to Rebecca Stewart 12-15-1853
Little, Richard to Nancy E. Kemp 11-22-1860
Lockhart, James to Adaline P. Scott 10-8-1844 (10-10-1844)
Lockhart, Thomas J. to Julian C. Vaughan 11-6-1851
Logan, James W. to Mary E. Flemming 10-31-1854 (11-2-1854)
Logan, William to Mourning Bray 8-5-1842
Long, D. S. to M. C. Barnes 3-14-1867 (3-17-1867)
Long, David S. to Alice Lenshaw 5-10-1853
Long, George W. to Martha J. Garner 9-5-1867 (9-3?-1867)
Long, Henry to Dolly Rose 11-7-1865 (11-26-1865)
Long, James to Elizabeth Garner 10-4-1866 (10-11-1866)
Long, James to Mary Jane Pack 10-31-1860
Long, Jas. to America Partin 10-25-1865 (10-29-1865)
Long, John to Sarah Gipson 1-8-1844
Long, W. C. to Emily McKelvey 7-10-1860
Long, W. J. to Miss Jernigan 3-9-1870 (no return)
Long, W. S. to Martha C. Long 12-9-1868 (no return)
Long, William to Sarah T. Farris 1-12-1848 (1-13-1848)
Looney, J. M. to M. S. Francis 10-29-1874 (no return)
Looney, James C. to Sarah Stewart 11-9-1842
Looney, John B. to Mollie Shook 12-18-1867 (12-19-1867)
Looney, W. C. to Julia A. Holder 8-10-1870 (no return)
Lovelady, Pleasant to Marthy Taylor 2-16-1850 (2-17-1850)
Lowe, Stephen to Sally Ann Williams 4-7-1838 (4-17-1838)
Luck, John to Cathrine Williamson 11-8-1838
Ludewell, Willie to Sarah E. McKinzey 7-28-1839 (no return)
Lusk, John B. to Mariel L. Roseborough 12-27-1840
Lusk, Joseph to Mary C. McCord 5-26-1847 (5-27-1847)
Lyans, Richard to Nancy D. Smith 8-18-1838 (8-23-1838)
Lyman, H. C. to Mary S. Bunn 5-1-1871 (5-7-1871)
Lyncecum, Lycurgas to Martha I. Cox 5-28-1838 (no return)
Lynch, Berry to Jane Hudley 9-21-1843 (no return)
Lynch, Calvin to Mary Kelley 7-20-1850 (7-25-1850)
Lynch, David to Lizzie Leverton 9-18-1867 (9-19-1867)
Lynch, Elijah to Elizabeth Williams 6-2-1838

Lynch, Ignashus to Franky Kelley 1-18-1850
Lynch, John D. to Elizabeth Edwards 2-22-1871 (2-24-1871)
Lynch, John D. to Nancy King 4-16-1867 (no return)
Lynch, John M. to Mary J. Holder 3-10-1874 (3-12-1874)
Lynch, John to Charity D. Prince 12-4-1872 (no return)
Lynch, John to Elizabeth Kelley 8-16-1870
Lynch, Joseph to Sarah A. Martin 1-2-1839
Lynch, Layfayette to Temperance B. Knight 2-17-1859
Lynch, Lorenza to Mary Floyd 9-15-1841
Lynch, William to Sarah J. Champion 5-29-1874 (5-31-1874)
Lynch, Wm. S. to Dicy A. Wagner 6-1-1872 (no return)
Lyons, David to Nancy Farrell 11-27-1839 (no return)
Maccay, John to Jane Hunt 5-30-1842 (6-1-1842)
Madden, M. to Louisa Sanders 9-28-1866 (9-29-1866)
Magors, William to Mary Webb 5-12-1857 (no return)
Mahaffey, Carter to Mary Jane Reed 8-16-1859 (8-18-1859)
Mahan, James to Manerva Powell 1-14-1871 (1-16-1871)
Mahathy, Hiram to Susan Berryhill 10-10-1868 (10-11-1868)
Mahu, Aron to Eliza Jane Sisk 3-31-1847 (3-4?-1847)
Mails, J. C. to Mary Brazelton 3-2-1861 (3-6-1861)
Majors, E. A. to F. A. Smith 3-21-1866 (3-22-1866)
Majors, Kindred to Mary C. Byrom 10-11-1839 (10-13-1839)
Majors, Newton to Mahala Driver 4-22-1868 (no return)
Majors, R. M. to M. L. Byrom 10-23-1867 (10-24-1867)
Majors, Smauel E. to Mary J. Chasteen 11-5-1874
Malcom, W. B. to M. E. Stanfield 3-28-1868 (no return)
Mallard, William to Jane Fortney 3-12-1858
Malone, A. K. to Margret Hill 5-21-1870 (5-22-1870)
Malone, James C. to Elizabeth Sisk 4-29-1841
Malone, Jeremiah to Elendor Dougan 6-3-1856 (no return)
Malone, Sampson M. to Corsady E. Peacock 8-2-1859
Malone, Thomas to Manerva E. Weaver 9-19-1854 (no return)
Malone, Thos. to Lucretia Green 7-31-1869
Manier, Joel J. to Elizabeth M. Poats 6-20-1846 (6-?-1846)
Mankin, James R. to Rachiel A. Robenson 2-7-1854 (no return)
Mann, Albert G. to Susan Jane Morris 10-15-1846 (10-16-1846)
Mann, George W. to Sarah Hammingtree 8-28-1860
Mann, Robert N. to Nancy J. Lipscomb 10-19-1851
Manus, M. H. to M. C. Bennett 7-20-1867 (no return)
Maples, Josiah to Elizabeth Maples 2-13-1852
Marberry, J. H. to Mary A. Allen 11-11-1867 (11-13-1867)
Marberry, Moses P. to Florida A. Martin 10-11-1858 (10-4?-1858)
March, Hayden to M. E. (Miss) Estill 2-15-1869
March, Hayden to Mary E. Finch 2-21-1839
March, John B. to Margret Miller 12-16-1856
Marlow, George M. to Mary Jane Garner 7-24-1868 (9-28-1868)
Marris, Wm. A. to Nancy J. Pruit 12-19-1851 (12-22-1851)
Marsh, John to Susan Smith 11-13-1841 (11-14-1841)
Marshall, Carroll E. to Mary Riddle 12-27-1855
Marshall, Davis to M. J. Bean 9-10-1859 (9-14-1859)
Marshall, Edward W. to Mary A. S. Brandon 12-27-1865 (12-28-1865)
Marshall, Hayden to Mary Ann Bean 11-2-1870 (11-3-1870)
Marshall, Josiah W. to Ruth Rainey (Mrs.) 2-3-1864 (2-5-1864)
Marshall, William to Musadore Curle 8-29-1849
Martin, A. H. to Nancy J. Estell 4-19-1839
Martin, Alford to Mehalia Gamble 4-16-1844 (4-17-1844)
Martin, Bradford G. to Martha Sexton 11-15-1854 (11-16-1854)
Martin, Ebenezer to Daly Smith 2-28-1842 (no return)
Martin, George R. to Fannie Faris 6-15-1870
Martin, George to Margret Yarber 7-23-1874 (7-26-1874)
Martin, Isaac N. to Sarah M. Horton 6-28-1854 (6-29-1854)
Martin, J. J. to M. J. Erwin 1-9-1867 (1-8?-1867)
Martin, J. J. to Mollie F. Williams 7-29-1868
Martin, J. W. to Susan Vace 11-24-1869 (11-25-1869)
Martin, John W. to Emiline Jeans 1-12-1858
Martin, John W. to Fidelia T. Mitchell 7-16-1851
Martin, John W. to Mary M. McNiel 12-23-1847
Martin, Samuel H. to Sarah Martin 2-16-1841 (2-21-1841)
Martin, Thomas D. to Lydia H. Miles 10-10-1838 (10-11-1838)
Martin, Thornton to E. J. Pearson 6-17-1867
Martin, W. T. to Laura Staples 7-26-1872 (7-28-1872)
Martin, William to M. E. Ragsdale 1-5-1870 (no return)
Martin, Wm. W. to Elizabeth Hines 3-2-1853 (3-3-1851?)
Mash, Wm. A. to Lucy E. Elkins 11-9-1857

Mashburn, Robert to Martha Smith 12-27-1860 (12-31-1860)
Mason, Ely to Elizabeth F. Kilpatrick 11-24-1841 (no return)
Mason, Isaac N. to Martha D. Arledge 10-3-1872
Mason, Isaac to Louiza Scott 7-2-1860
Mason, James to Frances Brown 1-27-1857
Mason, James to Margrett Garner 8-14-1865 (8-15-1865)
Mason, James to Mary Brown 10-19-1846 (10-20-1846)
Mason, James to Nancy M. Miller 1-5-1857 (1-6-1857)
Mason, John to Elizabeth Pack 8-14-1865 (8-20-1865)
Mason, John to Mary Wilson 11-24-1851 (11-27-1851)
Mason, Joseph to Lou Foster 12-2-1874 (12-3-1874)
Mason, Josiah to Darcas O. Stovall 1-9-1851
Mason, Levi to Louisa Hall 7-22-1852 (7-23-1852)
Mason, Martin to Mary S. Larkin 12-30-1870 (1-4-1871)
Mason, Martin to Sarah Bridges 12-11-1841
Mason, Posey to Manca Corbett 11-7-1865 (11-9-1865)
Mason, T. C. to M. E. Coots 3-25-1874
Mason, W. B. to Sarah A. Williams 10-13-1869
Mason, William to Cirena Dodson 7-28-1853
Mason, Wm. J. to Elizabeth Robbins 5-26-1858 (no return)
Mather, S. D. to R. H. Stamps 10-11-1865 (10-12-1865)
Mathews, Andrew to Elizabeth Holder 5-16-1843
Mathews, J. A. M. to Ella N. Jones 7-23-1874
Mathews, J. M. to M. L. Tipps 10-28-1867 (10-29-1867)
Mathews, L. S. to Elizabeth A. Stewart 2-13-1870 (2-14-1870)
Mathews, L. S. to Mary J. Stewart 9-20-1859
Mathews, Michael N. to Sarah A. Thurman 11-27-1854 (11-30-1854)
Mathews, Wm. J. to Elizabeth Rask 6-30-1860 (7-1-1860)
Mathews, Wm. J. to Mary A. Anderson 5-6-1853 (5-12-1853)
Mathews, Wm. R. to Sally A. Keith 12-19-1855 (12-20-1855)
Matlock, George G. to Susan A. Simmons 2-13-1866 (2-14-1866)
Matlock, H. H. to Sarah C. Baker 3-13-1872 (no return)
Matlock, James M., jr. to Mary Jane Dyer 5-8-1839 (5-9-1839)
Matlock, Wm. H. to Lucy E. Moore 1-30-1840
Mattenlee, Clement C. to Mary Farris 8-3-1841
Matthews, G. W. to Sophia Rebecca Noblett 11-17-1870
Matthews, John L. to Sarah Morris 6-27-1853 (no return)
Maxey, W. H. to M. E. Garner 9-5-1867
May, Alexander to Mary M. May 1-14-1856 (11-16-1856)
May, Lindsey to Cynthia Stovall 7-20-1872 (no return)
Mayes, James F. to Mary F. Roberts 8-20-1869 (no return)
Mayes, James M. to Martha Langston 2-4-1867 (2-5-1867)
Mayes, James to Nancy Foster 8-13-1870 (no return)
Mayes, Peter to Evy Peyton 10-23-1873
Mayes, William to Olley Cline 1-20-1858 (1-21-1858)
Mays, Edward to Permelia Mays 8-9-1866
Mays, Jackson L. to Prudy Ann Hill 3-5-1849
Mays, Stanford to M. H. Lucca 2-9-1860
Mays, Wm. to Mary E. Hill 11-19-1855 (no return)
McAdams, John to Fanny Jones 1-22-1865
McAfee, W. M. to Nancy Tate 9-7-1865 (no return)
McAllister, J. G. to Martha L. Malone 1-26-1872 (1-27-1872)
McAllister, Samuel to Caldonia McKissick 12-17-1867
McBee, Arnold to Iby Pelham 7-8-1867 (no return)
McBee, Jessee to Syrena McBee 9-4-1865 (9-21-1865)
McBee, Robt. to Margaret Williams 4-29-1851
McBee, Samuel to Nancy S. Wilkenson 3-12-1857
McBee, Samuel to Susan Barnes 2-14-1842
McBride, C. to Franky Caloway 9-7-1874 (no return)
McBride, George W. to Lotisha Arnold 1-25-1871 (no return)
McBride, Robt. T. to Martha Sisk 10-3-1855
McBride, T. J. to Fanny Reed 12-19-1871 (12-21-1871)
McCarter, Daniel to Pheba Spence 3-4-1844 (no return)
McClure, Francis G. to Nancy Ethridge 2-24-1858
McClure, Geo. to Mary J. Stovall 10-16-1866 (10-?-1866)
McClure, James H. to Rebecca J. Syler 5-3-1852
McClure, Jessee S. to Rhutha S. Lucas 11-28-1853
McClure, Nathaniel to Elizabeth Langston 12-18-1851
McClure, William to Martha Mayes 3-22-1858
McClure, Wm. E. to Penina E. Stovall 11-27-1865 (11-28-1865)
McClure, Wm. M. to Almira M. Roughton 12-28-1872 (no return)
McClure, Wm. M. to Mattie Vaughan 7-31-1865 (8-1-1865)
McCollum, James to P. Childers 6-14-1838
McCollum, Rufus K. to Emeline Stovall 3-11-1848 (3-16-1848)
McComb, George B. to Amanda Davis 12-19-1855 (no return)

McCord, David B. to Elizabeth H. Bell 5-17-1845 (5-20-1846?)
McCord, William P. to Hester A. Noah 3-1-1842 (no return)
McCovey, J. F. to Elizabeth Grider 2-7-1867 (2-3?-1867)
McCoy, A. J. to Sarah West 9-7-1865 (no return)
McCoy, D. H. to M. E. Jarrett 2-21-1840 (no return)
McCoy, Daniel to Dosha Deckerd 10-31-1844 (no return)
McCoy, Francis M. to Eve Welb 1-10-1856 (1-16-1856)
McCoy, James H. to Elizabeth Jane Douthet 10-14-1855
McCrary, Auston to Rebecca A. Collins 7-31-1853
McCrary, T. B. to Sarah J. Bruce 12-14-1870 (no return)
McCrary, Thos. B. to V. K. Bradford 4-27-1867 (4-28-1867)
McCroy, C. E. to Sally Vanzant 6-13-1865 (no return)
McCutcheon, Geo. S. to Cathrine H. Raggins 2-13-1843 (2-14-1843)
McCutcheon, Gordon C. to Mary Corn 8-4-1849 (8-5-1849)
McCutcheon, J. N. to C. E. Carpenter 12-18-1859 (no return)
McCutcheon, Joel G. to Emily Corn 6-17-1841 (6-20-1841)
McDanal, James to Elizabeth Wilson 6-29-1838
McDaniel, Alexander L. to Mary McKelvey 8-7-1843
McDaniel, Charles B. to Nancy L. Wakefield 1-1-1844 (1-4-1844)
McDaniel, E. R. to Unice L. Robbins 11-17-1840 (11-20-1840)
McDaniel, Edwin H. to Malissa J. Barnes 10-10-1838
McDaniel, Henry to Narcissa McKelvey 7-15-1847
McDaniel, James to Elizabeth E. Vaughan 8-8-1857 (no return)
McDaniel, Robt. to Manerva A. Baker 10-3-1872
McDaniel, Wm. to Sally Fitch 3-25-1868 (3-26-1868)
McDonald, James M. to Elizabeth Delzell 10-12-1852 (no return)
McDonald, Jesse to Mary (Mrs.) Woods 1-9-1868 (1-12-1868)
McDonald, John J. to Paralee Jackson 7-4-1859 (7-5-1859)
McElroy, Davis to Christiana E. Wakefield 4-27-1840
McElroy, J. D. to A. C. Collins 5-26-1870
McEnally, J. C. to Adaline Russell 12-8-1859
McFarlin, Robt. to Adaline Anderson 12-13-1871 (no return)
McGavock, Randal W. to Searaphina Deery 8-23-1855
McGee, Robt. H. to Idella P. Mason 11-26-1873
McGhee, William to Adaline P. Lockhart 12-28-1850 (12-30-1850)
McGlothlin, Ezekiel H. to Fannie Brown 9-17-1872 (no return)
McGowan, David to Sarah A. Thompson 3-29-1839 (no return)
McGriff, Wm. J. to Louisa Brakefield 2-24-1853
McGrue, J. H. M. to Letitia Camron 6-5-1851 (no return)
McGuire, John E. to Sarah E. Combs 4-6-1849
McHathy, John to E. Corning 10-22-1870
McIntosh, Newton C. to Nancy C. Turner 12-23-1844 (12-24-1844)
McKay, William to Elizabeth Crawford 2-1-1847
McKee, Derrell to Kiziah King 1-25-1840 (1-26-1840)
McKee, Jasper to Mariah Hill 3-14-1857 (3-15-1857)
McKelby, Thomas J. to Mollie E. Talleferro 11-13-1873
McKelvey, Captain to Elizabeth Willhite 8-16-1840
McKelvey, Elijah to Phebe A. J. Enochs 12-17-1857 (no return)
McKelvey, Jessee to Susan C. Spaun 7-15-1846 (7-16-1846)
McKelvey, John W. to Mary A. McKelvey 11-30-1842 (no return)
McKelvey, Joseph to Elizabeth Smith 11-1-1844 (11-6-1844)
McKelvey, Joseph to Rebecca Smith 7-5-1849
McKelvey, Matthew to Emeline Hill 11-6-1847 (no return)
McKelvey, Saml. to R. L. Brazier 2-5-1868 (no return)
McKelvey, Samuel to Elizabeth Embrey 7-30-1840 (no return)
McKelvey, Samuel to Lucy Ann Bass 12-8-1858 (12-9-1858)
McKelvey, WilliamB. to Martha Enochs 10-14-1857 (10-15-1857)
McKey, Jasper to Louisa King 8-26-1847
McKhenen?, John to Cyntha Thurman 1-8-1850
McKinney, James C. to Frances Holder 8-7-1854 (8-8-1854)
McKinney, R. M. to R. A. (Miss) Evans 4-25-1869 (4-24?-1869)
McKinney, Robert to Susan Holder 10-17-1847
McKinney, Russell to Elizabeth Holder 9-12-1848
McKinzey, Daniel to Julia A. Cartright 5-23-1856
McKinzie, Atwood to Sarah A. Hockersmith 2-2-1852 (2-4-1852)
McKinzie, Elijah to P. J. Hockersmith 11-15-1871
McKinzie, Elijah to Rebecca A. Branch 11-3-1857
McKinzie, John to M. J. Marshall 9-28-1866 (no return)
McKinzie, Wm. E. to J. C. Black 3-18-1868
McKnight, John H. to Sarah M. Lee 2-28-1854 (3-1-1854)
McLaughlin, E. B. to Elizabeth Majors 2-4-1839 (no return)
McLaughlin, Richard H. to Isabella C. Walker 1-16-1840
McLeroy, James W. to R. A. Scivally 9-28-1872 (no return)
McManara, J. M. to Adaline McCauly 1-31-1871
McMillion, G. W. to M. L. Crisman 12-25-1871 (12-26-1871)

McMurray, Wm. to Elizabeth A. Wadlington 5-3-1861 (5-30-1861)
McNabb, James to Sarah E. Daniel 7-28-1856
McNabb, Wm. M. to Rhoda C. Garnett 12-30-1849
McNiel, Abel to Mahala Chitwood 10-22-1840 (no return)
McNiel, E. B. to Jessee A. Kittridge 10-12-1867 (10-14-1867)
McTorrick, Thos. to Catharine Turney 3-25-1859 (no return)
Meadows, Benjamine H. to E. M. Orear 10-21-1874 (no return)
Meadows, James D. to Elizabeth Damrel 2-26-1857
Mealer, John R. to Emily J. Elliott 1-7-1858 (no return)
Megee, Jessee to Rebecca F. Wiggin 12-16-1841 (12-19-1841)
Meicher, John F. to Emma Stalder 12-23-1874 (12-24-1874)
Merrit, A. J. (Capt.) to Mary Coover 7-19-1865 (7-25-1865)
Messick, John to Willie Statum 5-5-1859 (no return)
Metcalf, George A. to Elizabeth Cunningham 8-11-1869 (no return)
Metcalf, John to Elizabeth Frame 11-19-1870 (11-20-1870)
Metcalf, Lewis to Sarah Stamper 11-6-1843 (11-9-1843)
Metcalf, William D. to Martha Morgan 12-6-1841 (12-9-1841)
Metts, L. E. to N. P. Summerford 3-2-1861 (3-3-1861)
Michiel, Ephraim to Cassy A. Pitcock 5-2-1852
Mickles, Wm. N. to Mary J. Thompson 10-8-1855 (10-10-1855)
Middleton, Charles C. to Mary Mathews 8-6-1843
Middleton, Thos. J. to Jennie Shook 8-21-1871 (no return)
Miles, Daniel to Martha Tims 2-5-1855 (2-8-1855)
Miles, G. J. to Mariah Rogers 5-2-1851 (5-3-1851)
Miles, Henry to Jane Pierce 7-1-1851 (no return)
Miles, John W. to Katy Piggeon 1-15-1873
Miles, William B. to Elizabeth McKelvey 4-7-1847 (5-27-1847)
Milham, Jefferson to Mary Armstrong 1-14-1854 (no return)
Miller, Carl to Malinda Ashley 10-7-1872 (10-8-1873?)
Miller, Edwin to Sarah A. Coleman 3-9-1853 (3-10-1853)
Miller, George G. to Elizabeth J. Oakley 3-19-1846
Miller, George G. to Mary J. Knight 8-13-1851 (no return)
Miller, George to Virginia Deaton 10-29-1842 (10-30-1842)
Miller, Gustave to Louise Colyar 3-31-1862 (4-6-1862)
Miller, Jacob to Sallie Gifford 3-9-1867
Miller, Jake to Amanda Lackray 8-15-1872
Miller, James to Sarah E. Williams 1-10-1858 (1-13-1858)
Miller, Jas. H. to Mattie Tripp 4-8-1872 (4-13-1872)
Miller, Joel to America Fraine 9-7-1863 (no return)
Miller, John H. to Ellen E. Morris 9-21-1848
Miller, John H. to Nancy E. Brazelton 12-20-1855
Miller, John J. to Mary Ann Hines 9-18-1838 (9-20-1838)
Miller, John P. to Rebecca Hendley 7-23-1839 (7-24-1839)
Miller, Joseph to Hettie (Miss) Miller 1-6-1869 (no return)
Miller, Joseph to Lucretia Mealer 2-24-1846 (2-25-1846)
Miller, Joseph to Milly Perkins 9-28-1840 (no return)
Miller, Joseph to Sarah Millikin 10-9-1872 (no return)
Miller, Josiah to Jane C. Farris 10-28-1843
Miller, Josiah to Jane Faris 6-14-1843 (6-15?-1843)
Miller, Josiah to Margrett Vinson 4-10-1848 (4-12-1848)
Miller, Lewis to Margret Pelham 8-15-1865 (8-16-1865)
Miller, Madison to Eliza A. Sisk 12-11-1856
Miller, Montgomery to Mary M. Buckner 8-22-1849 (no return)
Miller, R. B. to Sarah Pelham 3-23-1874 (3-25-1874)
Miller, Samuel M. to Joanna Hines 9-7-1872 (9-8-1872)
Miller, Thomas to Mary J. Kavanaugh 6-24-1853
Miller, Thos. G. to Susan E. Bridges 1-28-1846 (no return)
Miller, William J. to Frances A. Collins 5-1-1851
Miller, William to F. E. Prince 3-21-1868 (3-22-1868)
Miller, William to Manerva Tankesley 6-22-1867 (6-19?-1867)
Miller, Wm. G. to E. C. Brown 9-2-1868 (no return)
Miller, Wm. to Nancy J. Robinson 12-6-1853
Mills, Gilbert to Nevey Bass 6-10-1838
Mills, Joel G. to Mary Ann Moore 6-2-1849 (6-3-1849)
Mills, Nathaniel to Amanda M. Hall 4-17-1852 (no return)
Millsaps, L. W. to Mary A. Ivey 9-14-1867 (9-15-1867)
Millsaps, M. to N. C. Ivey 10-1-1866 (no return)
Millsaps, Martin V. to Hannah T. Smith 2-10-1866 (no return)
Mitchell, D. W. to Martha C. Banks 5-10-1856 (5-11-1856)
Mitchell, George W. to Marthy A. Day 12-25-1850
Mitchell, Isaac R. to Nancy M. Cobble 1-17-1857 (1-22-1857)
Mitchell, Joseph to Elizabeth Banks 11-24-1857 (no return)
Mitchell, Newton J. to Mary J. Sexton 3-24-1858
Mitchell, Solomon to Wimma Kennedy 9-9-1868
Mitchell, William M. to Fidella T. Mathews 6-11-1844
Mitchell, William to Matilda Edwards 12-24-1851 (no return)
Mitchell, Wm. P. to Lidda Banks 2-18-1856 (2-24-1856)
Mitchell, Wm. to Arrenia Smith 1-10-1856 (1-13-1856)
Modena, Thomas H. to Ann Lyons 11-16-1871 (11-18-1871)
Money, Jasper to Charlina Wilson 4-18-1868 (no return)
Money, William to E. Rice 4-7-1860 (no return)
Montgomery, Cowan to Jane Riddle 3-17-1862?
Montgomery, Daniel S. to Mary E. Wagner 2-23-1874 (2-6?-1874)
Montgomery, George W. to Mollie Turner 3-26-1874
Montgomery, John C. to Nancy Cowan 1-15-1850
Montgomery, Milton to Nancy Auston 1-19-1843
Moody, Lewis to Polly Ann Barnes 1-12-1867 (1-15-1867)
Mooney, D. H. to Lou Stringer 11-6-1869 (11-7-1869)
Moore, A. P. to M. E. Oliver 2-14-1840
Moore, F. W. to S. M. West 8-16-1871 (no return)
Moore, Freeman to Frankey A. Potts 7-27-1848
Moore, Geo. E. to M. J. Elkins 9-?-1866
Moore, H. R. to Annie E. Hunt 9-3-1860 (9-5-1860)
Moore, Henderson to Frances A. Gillespie 7-25-1848
Moore, J. L. to Calafornia Kennerly 12-21-1871
Moore, James H. to Eliza Warren 9-16-1847
Moore, James to Rebecca Jane McDonald 8-15-1855 (8-19-1855)
Moore, John W. to Lucy E. Barnes 7-11-1857 (7-14-1857)
Moore, John W. to Susan G. Miller 1-29-1844 (2-1-1844)
Moore, Machessna to Nancy Hawkins 1-8-1852 (no return)
Moore, Richard to S. K. Southerland 8-29-1872 (9-1-1872)
Moore, S. J. to Nancy Vanzant 12-20-1871 (1-2-1872)
Moore, W. A. to Mary E. Elkin 1-31-1860 (no return)
Mooris, Ed, jr. to Mollie E. Davidson 6-2-1871 (7-3-1871)
Morgan, George to Louisa Metcalf 2-21-1844 (2-22-1844)
Morgan, James D. to P. P. Thomas 11-28-1853 (12-1-1853)
Morgan, M. C. to Nancy J. Edwards 2-19-1855 (no return)
Morris, Alfred P. to Margret B. Knight 1-8-1856
Morris, Benj. F. to Polly Ann Morris 9-27-1871
Morris, Benjamin to Catharine Gilliam 1-14-1845
Morris, C. T. to Elizabeth E. Wilkerson 11-29-1865 (12-3-1865)
Morris, C. to M. J. Yates 9-19-1859 (9-20-1859)
Morris, Edward to Lucinda Gifford 12-15-1849
Morris, Henry B. to Nancy A. Allen 1-18-1856 (1-24-1856)
Morris, James to Frances W. Sutton 10-4-1853
Morris, John F. to Mahala Warren 5-9-1845 (5-13-1845)
Morris, John H. to Mary E. Farris 3-16-1848
Morris, John to Jemima Hill 5-2-1842 (no return)
Morris, Larkin to Angeline Helton 8-1-1874 (no return)
Morris, Larkin to Dinah Logan 7-5-1849
Morris, Larkin to Nancy A. Morris 2-27-1842
Morris, Robert to Elizabeth Sells 9-1-1869 (no return)
Morris, Rolin to Sarah A. Morris 3-25-1874
Morris, Rowlin to Sarah Bane 11-10-1868
Morris, Saml. to Lydia A. Little 10-31-1865
Morris, W. C. to Mary Jane Finney 5-21-1857 (no return)
Morris, William to Lizzie Hill 1-26-1870 (2-1-1870)
Morris, William to Piety A. E. Swann 9-14-1842 (no return)
Morris, William to Rilda Smith 12-29-1870
Moseley, Hartwell to Mary A. Holder 11-30-1855
Moseley, John R. to Mary A. Hunt 2-5-1858 (no return)
Moseley, John R. to Nancy Y. Farris 5-10-1847 (5-13-1847)
Moseley, P. S. to F. M. Patrick 11-5-1867 (11-6-1867)
Mosely, Thomas F. to A. V. H. Simmons 12-10-1859
Moses, Joseph to Mary A. Runnels 4-29-1857 (no return)
Moss, Eli to Indiana C. M. Sharp 8-20-1853
Mullen, John G. to Oma Carter 8-26-1845 (8-27-1845)
Mullins, Andrew to Louisa Carter 9-28-1842 (9-30-1842)
Mullins, Joel to Nancy M. Cobb 3-8-1855
Mullins, Thomas R. to Izzibiah Carter 8-22-1846 (8-26-1846)
Murphy, Robt. J. to Frances Escridge 12-17-1839
Murrell, Thomas C. to Louisa Simmons 5-13-1856
Murrell, W. E. to Eliza Gregory 11-7-1866 (no return)
Murrell, Z. R. to A. Rengar 2-11-1868 (2-13-1868)
Murrell, Zachariah to Adaline Anderson 8-14-1849
Muse, Joab B. to Sophia W. Shasteen 9-12-1856
Muse, Joshua to Ledy Short 1-19-1843
Muse, Joshua to Mary Ann Holcom 6-22-1856
Muse, Kindred P. to Sarah E. Sims 8-23-1855
Muse, Thos. E. to Edeva Johnson 1-3-1867 (no return)

Musgrove, Solomon to Mary Isbell 9-21-1865
Myers, Bishly A. to Clementine Francis 3-26-1840 (no return)
Myers, Thomas S. to Lucinda Gamble 7-15-1850 (7-16-1850)
Myres, J. M. to Mary F. Garner 4-20-1871 (4-20-1872?)
Myres, Thomas J. to Rachiel Loyd 3-26-1850
Myrick, A. S. to Mary Martin 4-8-1839
Nail, H. to Cynthia S. Boren 12-21-1867 (12-22-1867)
Nance, James R. to Arbella Erwin 4-19-1854 (4-20-1854)
Nassamer, Joseph to Hellen Robinson 12-22-1860
Neal, Henderson to Nancy M. Robertson 12-26-1872
Neal, J. F. to R. M. Tipps 1-5-1874
Neal, J. M. to Nancy M. Neal 4-9-1859 (4-10-1859)
Neal, James H. to Sarah F. Daniel 2-11-1846
Neal, John A. to Hannah A. Brazelton 11-16-1852 (11-17-1852)
Neal, John W. to Louisa J. Williams 1-3-1853 (1-6-1853)
Neal, Wm. H. to Mary Sanders 3-31-1859 (4-1-1859)
Neal, Wm. H. to Nancy C. Sanders 2-13-1850 (2-14-1850)
Nelson, George H. to Jennette N. Wilson 2-28-1850
Nelson, Henry to Mary Nelson 6-11-1851
Nelson, James A. to Mary A. E. Cobb 2-21-1871 (2-23-1871)
Nelson, James M. to Nancy P. Rogers 3-9-1853 (3-10-1853)
Nelson, Jno. B. to Margret Clark 2-8-1854 (2-9-1854)
Nelson, John to Margret Rogers 6-29-1845 (no return)
Nelson, Jonas A. to Jennie Perry 6-1-1874
Nelson, Leroy to Lusa Jane Baley 3-9-1850 (3-12-1850)
Nelson, P. A. to Lucy Haynes 2-5-1866 (2-11-1866)
Nemmo, A. V. to Frances C. Drake 8-13-1856
Nevels, G. to Elizabeth Helton 1-20-1859
Nevil, Carrel to Sarah Seargent 12-27-1866 (no return)
Nevill, H. to Dorah Corn 11-26-1866 (no return)
Nevill, W. P. to N. P. Reagin 8-28-1866 (no return)
Nevills, A. to E. J. Anderson 10-17-1859 (10-20-1859)
Nevils, George W. to Sarah Cross 7-9-1857
Newberry, Alexander N. to Lucinda Cowan 11-9-1848
Newberry, J. P. to Maggie Williams 10-15-1874 (no return)
Newberry, James C. to Angeline Baxter 7-30-1850
Newberry, Robert C. to Elizabeth A. McCollister 8-24-1843
Newberry, Saml. H. to Jennie L. Knight 1-11-1872
Newel, William to Mary F. Rich 9-23-1871 (9-24-1871)
Newman, Andrew to Elizabeth Kimbro 1-14-1854 (1-16-1854)
Newman, George to Cathrine Barnett 8-28-1856
Newman, J. M. to Adelia M. Burt 1-17-1874 (1-18-1874)
Newman, Joseph to Mary P. T. Ragsdale 11-10-1842
Newman, Robert to Mary Parks 8-6-1866 (no return)
Newman, Tazwell W. to Sarah C. Buchanan 3-11-1851
Newman, Thomas A. to Manerva D. Keith 2-13-1851
Newman, Wm. G. to Julia F. Logan 8-18-1853
Newman, John N. to Margaret A. Latamore 7-13-1854
Nichols, Charles B. to Barthena Baxter 12-29-1855 (12-30-1855)
Nichols, James B. to Sarah E. Hiltohn 3-8-1849 (no return)
Nichols, James S. to Samantha J. Stewart 12-27-1856
Nichols, James to Ann S. Huddleston 11-29-1849
Nichols, Wilson to Sarah McBee 5-22-1845 (5-28-1845)
Nicks, H. K. P. to R. A. Muse 12-22-1866 (no return)
Nimmo, James P. to A. E. Hughes 12-16-1852 (6-26-1853)
Nippers, Pleas to Mary Mahaffey 9-?-1870 (9-8-1870)
Nixon, Benjamin to Rebecca E. Lasater 8-1-1874 (8-13-1874)
Nixon, F. M. to Artemecia Perryman 9-24-1870 (9-28-1870)
Noah, John to Telitha Hendrix 5-30-1839
Noah, Peter J. to Ann E. Bowling 5-23-1857 (5-24-1857)
Noah, Thos. J. to E. E. Hatchett 1-19-1860 (no return)
Noah, Wm. H. to Sarah A. Moseley 9-8-1868
Noblett, Joshua to Elizabeth Branch 9-6-1871 (9-7-1871)
Noe, Abram to Susan Brittian 8-14-1850 (8-15-1850)
Noe, James W. to Mary L. Wakefield 1-17-1859 (no return)
Norman, Joseph to Rebecca Sewell 10-16-1855
Norwood, Andrew J. to Caroline Guthrie 4-24-1841
Norwood, Henry to Amanda Cowen 9-4-1868 (9-6-1868)
Norwood, Samuel to Pegg Perry 10-6-1873
Nowlin, Sherrod G. to Ruthy Methvin 8-12-1841
Nuckles, Barbe to Mary E. Embry 8-12-1852
Nuckles, Wm. to Mary Witt 3-21-1872 (3-24-1872)
Oakley, Asa D. to July L. Gillespie 10-29-1842 (10-30-1842)
Oakley, Asa D. to Mary L. Kennerly 1-16-1854 (1-17-1854)
Oakley, Francis m. to Harriett Suddarth 11-25-1851

Oakley, James A. to Mary A. Oakley 3-26-1846
Oakley, James S. to Martha E. Syler 1-27-1857
Oakley, John W. to E. C. Mosel 1-6-1847 (1-7-1847)
Oakley, R. F. to M. F. Lyons 5-4-1868 (no return)
Oakley, Richard F. to Frances Oakley 9-16-1856 (no return)
Oakley, Samuel R. to Mary J. Hill 1-9-1847 (1-10-1847)
Oakley, Thomas G. to Emeline Janes 2-20-1850
Oakley, Thomas J. to Marah? E. Roseborough 1-17-1859 (1-18-1859)
Oakley, Thomas P. to Martha Jane Jones 12-22-1846 (12-24-1846)
Oakley, William L. to Musadora C. Gillaspie 11-12-1846
Odam, Steven to Charlott Catchings 7-7-1859 (7-8-1859)
Odear, B. to Dinty Rose 6-19-1869 (6-17?-1869)
Odonnel, Constantine O. to Deliah Suiter 3-2-1851
Officer, Robt. W. to Lota Venable 12-20-1871 (12-25-1871)
Oldwell, I. A. to Mary C. Turner 12-17-1867
Oliver, Armstead R. to Delitha Partin 6-1-1857
Oliver, Charles C. to Issabell Hill 7-28-1853 (7-29-1853)
Oliver, William to Margrett Mathews 1-18-1849
Oppell, Charles to Ida C. Tuttle 10-11-1870 (no return)
Orear, E. M. to Telithia Hedgepeth 9-12-1872
Orear, William to Elizabeth Swords 7-7-1853 (7-8-1853)
Orear, Wm. J. to Elizabeth Covey 1-31-1852 (no return)
Osborn, Isaac to Sarah Downum 2-5-1849 (2-8-1849)
Osborn, Isham to Mary Allen 10-25-1855
Osborn, Isham to Matilda Downum 9-7-1853
Osborn, Levi P. to Elizabeth McDaniel 1-22-1845
Osborn, Nathaniel to Nancy Sexton 1-15-1849 (1-17-1849)
Osborn, Wm. to Jane Ladd 12-26-1870 (no return)
Osborn, Wm. to Martha Majors 1-24-1854 (1-25-1854)
Osborne, J. F. to Sarah J. Black 7-31-1858 (8-1-1858)
Osborne, John to Caroline Baker 5-29-1839 (6-6-1839)
Osbourn, B. A. to Sarah E. Weaver 2-5-1855
Overby, Henderson to Harriette E. Gorden 9-15-1868 (9-16-1868)
Owens, M. L. to Nancy Farris 6-17-1868
Pack, Jefferson to Margret Pelham 9-8-1866 (no return)
Pack, John M. to N. C. (Miss) Thomison 12-12-1868 (12-13-1868)
Pack, Joseph to Serena Pelham 5-7-1854
Pack, Nathaniel to Cathrine Deckerd 1-5-1843 (1-12-1843)
Pack, Thomas to Nancy Singleton 8-10-1843
Pack, Thomas to Sallie Singleton 11-19-1858 (11-21-1858)
Pack, Thos. to Nancy Singleton 8-14-1865 (8-15-1865)
Pack, William to Jane Kelley 8-14-1865 (8-16-1865)
Pack, William to Margrett Stewart 2-9-1843
Pack, Wm. to Denty Rose 5-20-1851
Pack, Wm. to Mary A. Stevens 8-7-1865 (8-10-1865)
Paine, John to Pattie Linch 7-27-1848
Panther, William to Nancy J. Miller 5-22-1865 (no return)
Parham, J. W. to Symanth Chasteen 12-16-1873 (12-17-1873)
Parham, Louis B. to Agnes B. Crisman 6-15-1870
Parker, Michiel to Martha Sample 1-26-1867 (no return)
Parks, Ambors to Nancy M. Smith 5-3-1851 (5-4-1851)
Parks, Benj. F. to Mary E. Burt 3-31-1851 (4-6-1851)
Parks, Elijah to Louisa Collins 5-5-1848 (5-6-1848)
Parks, George J. to Synthia Davis 7-20-1848 (7-21-1848)
Parks, H. L. to Sallie Hunt 5-23-1867
Parks, Isaac to Elizabeth Rogers 9-6-1848 (9-8-1848)
Parks, J. M. to E. Z. Brazier 8-24-1859
Parks, James S. to Martha Roleman 8-3-1849 (no return)
Parks, James to Rachiel Chavors 9-30-1854 (10-1-1854)
Parks, John W. to Maggie Cotton 9-20-1866 (no return)
Parks, John to Elizabeth Shavers 4-12-1855 (4-22-1855)
Parks, John to Martha Hester 1-13-1855 (no return)
Parks, John to Susan G. Enochs 2-22-1854 (2-23-1854)
Parks, Joseph C. to Amanda M. Pitcock 9-28-1852
Parks, Perry H. to Luvinia Featherston 7-6-1857 (7-7-1857)
Parks, Thomas to Nancy Chambers 12-26-1840 (no return)
Parks, Wm. A. to Louisa Syler 12-19-1855 (no return)
Parks, Wm. A. to Rebecca Roleman 2-14-1849 (2-15-1849)
Parks, Wm. B. to Adeline Wiseman 12-22-1852 (12-23-1852)
Parks, Wm. S. to Elizabeth McQueen 8-3-1846 (8-5-1846)
Partin, Danl. W. to Louisa Carroll 1-2-1850 (1-3-1850)
Partin, Henry to Elizabeth A. Finch 7-6-1853 (no return)
Partin, John W. to M. J. Tipps 9-1-1859 (no return)
Partin, John to Mary A. Morris 12-28-1853 (12-29-1853)
Partin, Marion to Mary Jane Hill 7-27-1847

Partin, Samuel to Elizabeth Shaw 8-28-1851
Partin, W. S. to Elizabeth Sanders 3-25-1868 (3-26-1868)
Partin, Wm. to Martha Gross 10-7-1868 (10-8-1868)
Parton, Nathaniel to Mary Royalty 7-14-1838 (7-15-1838)
Pasley, Thomas to Susannah Davis 8-18-1838 (8-30-1838)
Patterson, David to Feba Hargess 2-24-1851
Patterson, W. W. to Sarah A. Foster 10-9-1865 (10-10-1865)
Pattie, Thornton S. to Mildred V. Acklin 9-26-1846
Patton, W. T. to H. C. Vanzant 7-5-1866 (7-12-1866)
Patty, H. C. to Evalena Embrey 10-3-1866 (10-4-1866)
Paul, William to Mahala Sentor 11-10-1848
Payne, A. to D. Fergerson 6-8-1867 (6-9-1867)
Payne, B. to B. A. Lynch 10-31-1859 (11-3-1859)
Payne, Calvin C. to Sarah M. Williams 2-28-1853 (3-3-1853)
Payne, David to Nancy Rose 1-28-1867 (no return)
Payne, J. N. to Annie E. J. Brown 8-25-1874 (no return)
Payne, J. S. to Priscilla Crisman 12-24-1870 (no return)
Payne, James to Hetty Crabtree 9-22-1851
Payne, James to Priscilla Crisman 12-26-1870 (no return)
Payne, Jefferson to Elizabeth Hendley 1-1-1859 (no return)
Payne, John R. to Niagra Ann Thomas 2-25-1874 (2-27-1874)
Payne, John to Matilda Lynch 10-6-1857 (10-27-1857)
Payne, Joseph S. to Margrett Daniel 3-12-1869 (3-17-1869)
Payne, Robt. to Nancy Mahan 9-18-1858 (9-19-1858)
Payne, S. P. to Sarah Hill 8-26-1868
Payne, William to Sallie A. Vanzant 3-17-1870 (?-?-1870)
Payne, Wm. to Jerusha Patton 8-1-1865 (8-5-1865)
Pearson, J. R. to Sarah Jerrell 12-8-1862 (12-9-1862)
Pearson, James K. to Nancy M. Darwin 9-18-1873
Pearson, James to B. A. Hawkins 9-20-1868
Pearson, Joseph to Mary A. Fowler 11-28-1864 (12-1-1864)
Pearson, Richard B. to Sarah A. Dougan 12-11-1857 (no return)
Pearson, Robert to Louisa Jackson 4-5-1852
Pearson, Robt. to Rachael Davis 9-21-1858 (9-23-1858)
Pearson, Samuel to Eliza C. Whitson 7-8-1838 (7-12-1838)
Pearson, Solomon to Martha Bennette 9-3-1873
Pearson, Thos. to Elizabeth Pellum 8-7-1865 (8-8-1865)
Pearson, William M. to Frances Shores 10-11-1847 (10-13-1847)
Pelham, James to Mary C. Leverton 3-28-1874 (3-30-1874)
Pellann, Mark to Elizabeth Steel 9-29-1860 (9-31-1860)
Pellham, William to E. (Miss) Huffman 6-5-1869 (6-13-1869)
Pellum, Nathan to Franky A. Barnes 1-30-1866 (2-4-1866)
Pellum, Shadrick to Margrett Prince 2-14-1842 (2-20-1842)
Pennington, James N. to Sarah J. Simms 7-8-1867 (7-10-1867)
Pennington, John to Sarah McLyea 8-13-1839 (no return)
Pennington, W. G. to Luticia A. Pennington 11-26-1868
Perkins, Henry to Tennessee Furgerson 8-4-1873
Perkins, Jesse to Elizabeth Caperton 4-11-1843
Perkins, Jessee C. to Nancy M. Miller 9-27-1853
Perkins, Joseph J. to Lucinda Edwards 1-8-1846
Perry, Commadore to Angeline Dial 4-18-1874
Perry, David to Cyntha Hill 3-11-1874 (3-12-1874)
Perry, George to Sarah J. Finney 3-22-1871 (no return)
Perry, Harrison to Elizabeth Kennerly 5-27-1858 (no return)
Perry, Jeremiah to Mary A. Garner 2-28-1842
Perry, John A. to Mary Allen 7-26-1868
Perry, John to Nancy Sanders 12-3-1868
Perry, John to Ryna Gipson 9-20-1851 (9-21-1851)
Perry, Mathew N. to Zerilda E. Vaughn 10-4-1849
Perry, Patrick L. to Musadora C. Hendricks 10-4-1852 (10-5-1852)
Perry, Solomon to Elizabeth Hill 6-5-1845
Perry, Thomas to Eliza Williams 2-16-1855 (2-18-1855)
Perry, Thos. to Sarah Coker 9-1-1865
Perry, William to Lethia Allen 12-29-1842 (1-1-1843)
Perry, William to Mary Gibson 9-15-1842 (no return) [*]
Perryman, A. L. to Laura G. Long 1-9-1867 (1-10-1867)
Person, Wm. to E. Boggs 10-18-1859
Petty, William W. to Sarah Ann Porter 11-12-1844
Petty, Wm. T. to Mary E. Black 8-31-1850
Phelps, John to Eliza Hill 7-31-1851
Phillips, E. K. to Anna Mitchell 2-3-1874 (2-5-1874)
Phillips, James A. to Frances M. Hill 10-4-1838
Phillips, Jessee A. to Areyminty D. Cobb 8-26-1845 (8-27-1845)
Phillips, John M. to Louisa Gray 3-15-1845 (3-16-1845)
Phillips, John T. to Lucy A. E. Darnaby 10-8-1850

Phillips, William H. to Elizabeth Saxton 1-12-1846 (1-13-1846)
Pickeny, Julius to Mary Yarborough 7-15-1871 (7-16-1871)
Pickett, George W. to Sarah Ann Pulliun 12-10-1846
Pike, Josiah to Angeror A. Williams 3-4-1843 (3-5-1843)
Pinkerton, Samuel S. to Emma C. Jackson 7-26-1855 (7-30-1855)
Pitcock, Jacob to Sarah A. Donaldson 3-25-1858 (no return)
Pitcock, James to Tranquilla Williams 10-11-1842 (10-13-1842)
Pitcock, Stephen M. to Euphany Kilpatrick 10-10-1850
Pitman, Jas. to Susan Wilson 1-15-1866 (no return)
Pitman, Moses to Polly King 6-12-1844
Pitts, Henry H. to Susan F. Burks 11-20-1866 (no return)
Pless, John to Jemima Corn 12-19-1868
Plummer, Frank E. to M. F. Hopkins 2-26-1872 (no return)
Pockrous, Greenberry to Paralee Brady 8-17-1855
Poe, A. J. to Ida A. Muse 8-9-1859 (8-10-1859)
Poe, Abram F. to Elizabeth Shasteen 1-6-1851
Poe, D. K. to S. M. J. Parks 12-11-1869 (12-16-1869)
Poe, Ezra H. to Sarah Hill 8-23-1851 (no return)
Poe, John to Frances Poe 7-18-1840 (7-20-1840)
Poe, Thomas B. to Winney A. Hutton 3-15-1853? (3-15-1854)
Poe, Thos. L. to Susan J. Ray 12-27-1871 (1-2-1872)
Poe, Wm. M. to Nancy J. Johnson 12-14-1853
Poens, John to Mary Darrell 11-28-1871 (11-29-1871)
Pollock, John to Nancy Weaver 1-22-1847 (1-24-1847)
Pollock, Samuel to Lucinda Cook 12-30-1846
Porter, J. A. to Lou Hines 8-14-1871 (no return)
Porter, Jas. M. to Ann March 8-30-1871
Posey, B. B. to Rachael Goff 12-19-1855 (12-25-1855)
Posey, Bartly to Sarah Looney 7-23-1853
Posey, H. K. to S. A. Wood 3-2-1868 (no return)
Posey, Hiram K. to Ann Mitchell 7-23-1853
Posey, John to Sarah Mize 2-3-1871 (no return)
Posey, O. M. to Elizabeth Dodson 11-18-1853 (11-21-1853)
Posey, Olive M. to Angeline Malone 12-25-1847
Posey, Oliver M. to Martha Berryhill 1-20-1848 (7-4-1848)
Powell, George B. to Musadora E. Jones 5-4-1843
Powell, J. C. to Laura Pope 9-22-1874 (8?-27-1874)
Powell, John to Nancy Ellis 2-1-1845 (2-2-1845)
Powell, R. R. to Mollie (Miss) McGee 6-3-1869 (no return)
Powell, William M. to Elizabeth Ellis 9-5-1846 (9-6-1846)
Power, Jos. W. to Josia Smith 1-15-1867 (no return)
Power, Nathaniel T. to Elizabeth A. Acklin 12-18-1844
Powers, A. J. to Sarah A. Miller 10-25-1871 (no return)
Powers, George W. to Martha Montgomery 11-19-1841
Powers, Henderson to Mary A. Coulson 1-7-1868 (1-8-1868)
Powers, Mathew to Mary Gore 11-14-1865 (11-16-1865)
Pratt, Jeremiah to Elizabeth M. Compton 1-5-1850 (1-6-1850)
Pratt, Jeremiah to L. M. Cooper 6-15-1860 (6-17-1860)
Pream, Andrew J. to Sarah G. Morris 12-31-1855
Preitt, Uriah to Hannah Franklin 2-28-1856
Price, Albert to Margret A. Young 6-23-1853
Price, Richard F. to Rebecca Williams 1-3-1856 (no return)
Price, Robt. to M. M. Driver 6-10-1868 (6-14-1868)
Prince, Hardy to Lucinda Williams 9-6-1844
Prince, John to Elizabeth Pack 6-6-1851
Prince, Jonathan J. to Mary Hammer 9-24-1847 (9-26-1847)
Prince, Milford to Mary Foster 11-26-1853 (11-27-1853)
Prince, Nathan to Sarah Garner 10-13-1853
Prince, Newton to Delila Ford 8-22-1834
Prince, Silas to Candis Ashley 7-22-1871 (no return)
Prince, William to Ellen McBee 6-13-1868 (no return)
Prince, William to Jane Holt 10-30-1851
Prince, William to Lucinda Lynch 3-24-1841
Prince, Wm. to Louisa Garner 10-13-1853
Protter, Henry to Margret Stringer 3-19-1872
Pryor, James J. to Nannie Brazelton 4-26-1870 (4-29-1870)
Pryor, Wm. J. to Jennie Estill 9-11-1867
Pulliam, E. to R. E. (Miss) Tipps 5-8-1869 (5-9-1869)
Pulliam, J. E. to R. E. (Miss) Tipps 5-8-1869 (no return)
Pulliam, John to Pitor Ann Pickett 7-30-1846
Pulliam, Nicholass J. to Mariah Hise 12-24-1842 (12-25-1842)
Purdom, Wm. H. to Sarah C. Gossage 12-31-1868
Pursley, Thomas E. to Sarah E. Cagle 6-21-1871 (6-28-1871)
Puryor, William to Mary E. Pitt 10-3-1838 (10-4-1838)
Putman, Fleming to M. L. Kitchens 5-27-1870 (?-?-1870)

Putman, John to Nancy S. Vaughn 12-24-1859 (12-29-1859)
Pyland, James M. to Cinda Weaver 11-20-1866 (no return)
Pyland, James to Sally Lastor 10-2-1838 (10-4-1838)
Pylant, J. M. to Nancy Latimore 12-26-1866
Pylant, Kimberly to Emily Carpenter 11-25-1843 (11-26-1843)
Pylant, Stephen to Martha E. Lasater 6-3-1841
Pylant, William H. to Nelly Cook 12-4-1844
Pylant, William T. to Lizzie Mangrum 2-18-1871
Pylant, Wm. H. to Elizabeth A. Carpenter 12-25-1849
Qualls, C. R. to Adaline Bland 7-20-1871
Qualls, R. A. to Samantha Davis 1-20-1870
Qualls, Wm. to Mary E. Hazup 10-13-1869
Quinn, Hugh M. to Margret M. Coker 10-17-1866 (10-28-1866)
Radford, Robt. to Vickey Gipson 8-19-1857 (no return)
Ragin, James R. to Nancy Goodloe 3-24-1847 (3-25-1847)
Ragsdale, William N. to Justine Hodges 10-5-1839 (10-6-1839)
Ragsdale, William N. to Martha R. Purvers 8-24-1841 (9-7-1841)
Raines, Benza to Lucy Rutledge 7-11-1859 (7-12-1859)
Rallston, W. C. to Cyntha Gillaspie 1-17-1871 (no return)
Ramsey, Harrison to Lucinda Jones 2-28-1845 (3-5-1845)
Ramsey, Samuel to Lucy A. Harris 8-14-1855 (8-15-1855)
Randle, S. A. to Nancy Chitwood 12-10-1866
Randol, W. R. C. to L. C. Fagg 12-9-1872 (12-10-1872)
Randolph, Willie B. to Ruth Ann (Miss) Blanton 7-19-1847 (7-22-1847)
Raney, Thos. B. to M. E. Poe 12-31-1859 (11-22-1859?)
Rash, Saml. E. to Mary A. Allison 7-24-1853
Rather, Samuel B. to Sallie P. Wilson 6-29-1874 (6-30-1874)
Rawlins, E. M. to Douzella Reagin 8-1-1870 (8-4-1870)
Rawlins, John A. T. to Jane E. Martin 10-4-1844 (10-9-1844)
Ray, A. C. to M. C. Holt 2-18-1868 (2-19-1868)
Ray, Alfred to Christiana E. Hice 10-1-1851
Ray, Benj. J. to Nancy A. Byrom 2-4-1850 (no return)
Ray, G. G. T. to Martha E. Shasteen 11-9-1874 (11-10-1874)
Ray, G. M. to Jennie W. Estill 11-20-1873 (no return)
Ray, Hezekiah to Phebe J. Rauney? 9-29-1856 (no return)
Ray, Richard to Susan A. Kinney 2-4-1854 (2-5-1854)
Ray, Samuel P. to Lucy T. Parks 10-14-1852
Ray, Wm. C. to Christa E. Smith 1-7-1850 (1-9-1850)
Reader, John to Mary A. Guinn 5-9-1850 (5-12-1850)
Reagin, C. G. to N. B. Corn 12-9-1859 (12-11-1859)
Reagin, J. A. to Miss J. A. Oglesby 5-19-1869 (5-20-1869)
Reagin, John A. to Mahala Tate 10-29-1853 (11-1-1853)
Reagin, John C. to Adaline Tipps 1-30-1867 (4-23-1867)
Reagin, M. P. to Jane W. Goodloe 9-13-1849
Reagin, Thos. J. to Nancy Anderson 12-29-1859
Reed, Benjamin to Sarah A. Miller 4-21-1853
Reed, Charles A. to Mary J. Brandon 1-29-1874
Reed, Franklin to Mahala Haley 8-27-1839
Reed, Isaac to Elizabeth Brannan 6-28-1856 (no return)
Reed, Isaac to Rebecca Long 10-28-1841 (11-2-1841)
Reed, Josiah to Malinda Guarant 8-9-1842 (8-14-1842)
Reed, Levi to Elizabeth Tarbor 2-11-1854 (2-12-1854)
Reed, Robert T. to Mattie J. Keith 4-20-1874 (no return)
Reed, Samuel to Dorcas Cherry 11-12-1866 (11-22-1866)
Reed, Shipman to Elizabeth Taylor 7-12-1869 (7-13-1870?)
Reed, Shipman to Letty Campbell 9-16-1851 (9-18-1851)
Reed, W. G. to Frances E. Freeman 12-11-1872 (12-12-1872)
Reed, William F. to Nancy J. Williams 1-20-1873 (1-23-1873)
Reedy, Thos. L. to F. J. Thompson 8-7-1865 (8-10-1865)
Reeves, Prudence to John F. Robertson 11-28-1855 (11-19-1855)
Reeves, Robt. W. to Kate Anderson 12-24-1874
Renegar, Calvin to Elizabeth M. Franklin 11-1-1865 (11-3-1865)
Renegar, W. H. to Jane Hallowell 8-2-1858 (no return)
Renfro, F. C. to Ella Carter 12-16-1870 (no return)
Renfro, Jas. to Eliza Grammer 1-10-1872 (1-11-1872)
Renfro, John A. to M. C. Cole 11-24-1868 (no return)
Revis, A. W. to L. T. Cole 11-3-1869 (no return)
Revis, Andrew W. to Elizabeth N. Cobb 8-12-1847
Revis, J. A. to Ann Eliza Smith 11-19-1866 (no return)
Revis, Jonathan J. to Sarah A. Cates 1-18-1852 (1-20-1852)
Reynolds, D. S. to F. S. Nuckles 8-?-1865 (no return)
Reynolds, Dosier T. to Aseneth A. Little 3-17-1858 (3-18-1858)
Reynolds, E. F. to Sarah McKerns 5-17-1867
Reynolds, J. C. to Malinda Pollock 10-4-1858 (10-16-1858)
Reynolds, P. D. to Haley George 2-14-1859 (no return)
Reynolds, W. M. to Victoria Fanning 9-26-1858
Reynolds, William M. to Patsy Duncan 12-12-1839 (12-19-1839)
Reynolds, Wm. M. to S. R. E. Pollock 9-14-1859 (9-15-1859)
Rhodes, James M. to Margrett Chavers 7-29-1874 (7-30-1874)
Rhodes, John B. to L. Hynds 12-24-1860
Rice, D. C. to M. J. Crabtree 9-14-1860 (9-23-1860)
Rice, Isiah to Betty Miller 7-3-1869 (7-4-1869)
Rice, James P. to Sarah Reed 9-21-1853
Rice, Noah to Polly Mason 9-2-1839 (no return)
Rich, A. J. to Sarah E. Evans 10-6-1852 (10-7-1852)
Rich, Joseph M. to Mary E. Adams 9-10-1873 (9-11-1873)
Rich, M. H. to M. J. Robinson 2-25-1862 (2-26-1862)
Rich, Martial H. to Frances E. Ford 10-24-1844
Rich, Thomas J. to Eliza E. Cartright 3-24-1857
Rich, Williamson to Zilpha C. McClure 8-27-1855 (no return)
Richardson, Amos to Sarah Ann Gilliam 5-10-1856 (5-11-1856)
Richardson, Bernard to Martha Wade 12-11-1845 (no return)
Richardson, Calvin to Margaret Richardson 5-19-1853
Richardson, J. T. to Sophia Covey 11-29-1870 (12-1-1870)
Richardson, Reubin to Margret Gipson 1-25-1850
Richardson, W. T. to Sarah Hicks 7-25-1867 (7-29-1867)
Richardson, William C. to Harriett Reed 10-16-1844
Richardson, William R. to Martha Gipson 12-25-1860
Richison, Ruben to Dida Nabors 1-23-1841 (no return)
Ricketts, John to Nancy E. Hill 11-17-1856
Riddle, Jerry to Sarah Mason 1-24-1843 (1-26-1843)
Riddle, Linton to Sarah Boyce 10-5-1848
Riddle, Tyree to E. A. Goodloe 11-15-1871 (no return)
Riddle, Tyree to Hannah E. Lawson 8-17-1859
Riggins, John J. to Malinda Hammontree 5-5-1842 (5-15-1842)
Rile, William to Elizabeth Cole 9-28-1848
Riley, P. J. to Sophia Anderson 8-1-1868 (8-2-1868)
Riley, Patrick J. to Lucy Anderson 5-9-1860
Riley, Wm. to Pateena Sexton 7-29-1848 (7-30-1848)
Rippy, Levi F. to Jane N. Knight 7-24-1855 (7-26-1855)
Rivers, Thomas to Mary A. Trigg 11-12-1843 (11-13-1843)
Roach, James P. to Susanah Hall 8-31-1854
Roach, Wm. C. to Amanda M. Hall 9-6-1858
Robbins, Eligah D. to Mary E. B. Moore 6-1-1843
Robbins, Milo to Margret A. Almond 4-12-1856 (4-13-1856)
Robenson, S. M. to A. P. Robenson 8-12-1865 (no return)
Roberson, James N. to Hannah L. Hill 12-24-1874
Roberson, James to Nancy A. Brinsfield 3-18-1854 (3-21-1854)
Roberson, Michael to Elizabeth Seargent 6-26-1854
Roberson, William to Mary McKinzey 8-5-1844
Roberts, Benj. to E. J. Tucker 4-14-1841
Roberts, Hansford H. to Mary E. Lynch 3-7-1851
Roberts, James to Nancy C. Warren 10-19-1866 (no return)
Roberts, John to Mary Christian 6-6-1838 (6-3?-1838)
Roberts, Phillip to Lucy Ann Barnes 9-7-1848 (9-8-1848)
Robertson, Allen F. to Elizabeth J. Staples 12-14-1847 (12-16-1847)
Robertson, Jack to Mariah Brown 1-29-1873
Robertson, James to Martha Robertson 7-1-1858 (no return)
Robertson, John F. to Prudence A. Reeves 11-28-1855 (11-29-1855)
Robeson, Neapolean to Caroline Ludewell 2-7-1838 (no return)
Robinson, F. M. to Julia A. Gattis 1-15-1866 (1-17-1866)
Robinson, James to Eliza Hutchins 2-18-1840
Robinson, John M. to Martha Yarborough 9-12-1866 (no return)
Robinson, Newton M. to Nancy E. Gattis 1-22-1861 (1-23-1861)
Robinson, Virgil to M. Garner 12-16-1867
Roddy, A. J. to Elizabeth Statum 12-24-1870 (no return)
Rodgers, James M. to Nancy M. Awalt 1-6-1848 (1-7-1848)
Rodgers, Joseph to Julia Parks 1-7-1850
Rogers, C. B. to Mary Brewer 2-21-1841 (no return)
Rogers, George F. to Mary Awalt 2-3-1853
Rogers, Isaac to Mary Jetton 5-30-1872 (5-31-1872)
Rogers, James to Margret Nelson 6-9-1859
Rogers, Jessee to Harriett Thompson 8-3-1865 (12-11-1864?)
Rogers, Jessee to Sarah Holland 6-13-1859
Rogers, Jessee to Susan Sutton 1-15-1839
Rogers, John B. to Nancy Stewart 7-30-1850
Rogers, John W. to Sarah E. Nelson 8-6-1857
Rogers, Joseph to Nancy Nelson 9-10-1858
Rogers, Patrick to Julia Welch 7-16-1853 (7-18-1853)

Rogers, S. C. to Mary J. Burt 5-9-1848 (5-10-1848)
Rogers, S. P. to Bettie Wagner 10-13-1870
Rogers, Thos. S. to Nancy J. Graves 10-15-1855 (no return)
Rogers, Thos. S. to Nancy Myors 9-6-1856 (9-10-1856)
Rogers, W. J. to E. A. Taft 12-13-1865 (12-18-1865)
Rogers, Wade M. to Mattie A. McClure 7-29-1873 (no return)
Rogers, William P. to Sarah Gofer 11-26-1860
Rogers, William to Margrett Perkins 4-14-1871
Rogers, William to Pelina Jane West 4-11-1874 (4-12-1874)
Roleman, Spencer to Delila Barbee 8-6-1849 (8-7-1849)
Rollins, Joseph to Elizabeth Carroll 11-14-1840 (no return)
Rollman, Spencer to Mary A. Brennan 3-8-1855
Rolman, Henry to Luraney Weaver 7-23-1846
Rolman, J. S. to N. N. M. Hice 2-6-1860 (no return)
Romius, Thomas M. to C. P. M. E. A. Guanant 8-14-1849
Rose, Alexander to Judith Banks 12-18-1847 (12-19-1847)
Rose, Henry to Jane Clenny 5-19-1865
Rose, Hugh L. to Martha L. Garner 11-3-1855 (11-4-1855)
Rose, James to Mary E. Guinn 3-3-1870 (3-6-1870)
Rose, Martin V. to Dolly Garner 8-2-1856
Rose, Randolph, jr. to Cathrine J. Hale 9-11-1851 (9-16-1851)
Rose, Seborn to Viny Kezzort 12-22-1865 (12-24-1865)
Rose, Solomon to Lucinda Lynch 11-4-1869 (11-8-1869)
Rose, Stephen to Sarah Pearson 6-1-1843
Rose, Thomas to Margret Pellum 8-29-1865 (8-30-1865)
Rose, Waman L. to Nancy Davis 6-14-1849
Rose, Wm. M. to Elizabeth Long 5-21-1861 (5-22-1861)
Roseborough, S. R. to Martha C. Colyar 1-7-1857 (no return)
Roseborough, Samuel to Mary Bratton 11-28-1844
Roseborough, William H. to Cacy Simmons 11-12-1844
Rossin, James N. to Cynthia Morris 1-2-1849
Roton, Jon to Simonie? Templeton 2-12-1866 (no return)
Rousser, Wm. M. to M. E. Anderson 1-15-1866 (no return)
Rowlett, Columbus to Lucinda Jane Byrom 3-10-1855
Rowlett, Thomas W. to Millie R. Bicknell 10-4-1872 (10-24-1872)
Royalty, John O. to Mary Hill 1-2-1841? (1-2-1842)
Royalty, Joseph to Nancy Mitchell 1-2-1845
Royton, Thos. to Marila Simpson 1-23-1860 (no return)
Rucker, Thos. G. to Susan E. Smith 5-11-1865 (no return)
Runnells, Jonathan M. to Syntha Sanders 8-10-1839
Runnels, Barney M. to Betsy Crocket 9-13-1838
Runnels, Jessee G. to Nancy Ann Sanders 8-11-1856 (8-12-1856)
Russell, B. S. to Mary C. Cleek 5-3-1867 (5-5-1867)
Russell, J. N. to Emily Renegar 9-15-1870 (no return)
Russell, John to Jane Denson 11-1-1843 (11-2-1843)
Russell, Rufus S. to Semirah Campbell 1-24-1843 (1-26-1843)
Russell, Samuel to Amanda M. Taylor 2-26-1848 (3-2-1848)
Russell, William to Amanda Hill 10-18-1843
Russell, William to Mary A. Taylor 8-26-1848
Russey, Alford W. to Elvira J. Williams 1-15-1854
Russey, B. F. to Emma Maxwell 7-1-1867
Russey, C. B. to Willie K. Turner 12-2-1874 (12-3-1874)
Russey, J. W. to Frances V. Brooks 6-3-1866 (7-1-1866)
Russey, James M. to Mary B. Burt 11-15-1848 (no return)
Russey, M. B. to M. E. Temple 7-18-1868 (7-19-1868)
Russey, Wm. M. to Virginia L. McNabb 7-28-1847 (7-29-1847)
Rutledge, Admiral N. to Rosannah Counts 12-5-1851 (12-10-1851)
Sanders, Benjamin to Anna Holly 5-4-1846 (5-27-1846)
Sanders, Elijah to N. J. Paden 4-7-1860 (4-8-1860)
Sanders, Felix G. to Eliza Oliver 11-17-1842 (11-?-1842)
Sanders, Felix H. to Emily Grammor 9-3-1853 (9-4-1853)
Sanders, Geo. W. to M. P. Smith 11-19-1866 (no return)
Sanders, H. F. to B. J. Grammer 3-25-1870 (3-27-1870)
Sanders, Harpeth to Louisa Hise 1-3-1861
Sanders, Henry to Patsey Phillips 1-2-1844 (1-15-1844)
Sanders, John F. to Elizabeth Henkle 9-28-1870 (9-29-1870)
Sanders, John T. to Fannie L. Martin 11-18-1865 (11-19-1865)
Sanders, Ruben Z. to Nancy A. Williams 12-31-1871 (no return)
Sanders, Stephen C. to Eliza J. Lee 3-1-1849
Sanders, Thomas to Elizabeth Dorsett 3-2-1853 (3-3-1853)
Sanders, Thomas to Mary A. McDaniel 1-7-1841
Sanders, W. M. to Jane L. Daniel 2-10-1859 (no return)
Sanders, Wesley to Harriett Qualls 12-6-1853
Sanders, William to Julia Greenlee 1-14-1839 (no return)
Sandford, James to Martha Usleton 9-27-1838

Sandridge, F. M. to R. E. Cummings 10-25-1866 (10-26-1866)
Sandridge, Nimrod to Elizabeth Smith 8-26-1858 (8-29-1858)
Sandridge, Pendleton F. to Frances A. Oliver 7-26-1842 (8-2-1842)
Sandridge, Wm. P. to Sarah Qualls 12-27-1853 (12-29-1853)
Sansom, J. J. to Jane Maynus 1-9-1868 (1-10-1868)
Sansom, Jas. to Martha Hill 10-25-1865 (10-29-1865)
Sansom, Martin to N. C. Pollock 12-31-1867
Sartin, L. R. to Jennie Hawkins 11-5-1873 (11-6-1873)
Saunders, Ivey to Susan Rutledge 2-2-1852 (no return)
Saunders, J. B. to Elizabeth Morris 8-23-1859 (no return)
Saunders, James to Mary L. Morris 10-25-1859 (10-26-1859)
Schmidt, Phillip to Mary Jane Basdon 1-16-1855 (1-19-1855)
Schrom, John G. to Mary A. Souder 8-26-1869
Scivally, G. R. to Leah J. Matlock 3-1-1866 (3-2-1866)
Scivally, John J. to Amelia Ann Owins 1-25-1849 (2-2-1849)
Scivally, ___ to Martha Bean 1-5-1870 (no return)
Scivily, J. V. to Caroline Tribble 12-21-1868 (12-23-1868)
Scott, E. M. to Lucy Norris 8-11-1870 (no return)
Scrivener, Ruben to Nancy W. Bell 3-8-1847 (3-11-1847)
Seargeant, John B. to Jennie Prince 10-21-1874 (no return)
Seargent, Campbell to Elizabeth A. Jackson 12-11-1856
Seargent, George M. to Malinda McBee 9-14-1874 (9-13?-1874)
Seargent, James to Serena Cowan 10-28-1868 (10-29-1868)
Seaton, B. C. to R. J. Gilbert 12-16-1871 (12-17-1871)
Seaton, Wm. to Julia Seatyon 1-21-1868 (no return)
Seay, George to Mary Grabarr 7-15-1873 (12-16-1873)
Seivally, Jasper N. to Vinece J. Vanzant 7-17-1856
Seivilly, Martin to Nancy McJohns 3-4-1853 (3-10-1853)
Sells, A. J. to Nancy Stephens 9-24-1866 (no return)
Sells, Benj. to Mary A. Stewart 8-9-1838
Sells, J. P. to L. C. Sells 8-26-1869 (no return)
Sells, James H. to Lizzie Summers 1-5-1873? (6-11-1874)
Sells, John to Elizabeth McCrary 8-30-1846
Sells, John to Sarah Walker 2-3-1842
Sells, P. G. to Elizabeth Holder 9-5-1866 (no return)
Sells, Solomon to Lucy Taylor 12-26-1839
Setliff, James I. to Arabella W. Johnson 1-25-1872
Sewell, Abram to Roda A. Burnam 8-18-1842
Sewell, Henry to Permelia Baxter 2-27-1847 (2-28-1847)
Sewell, Simpson to Mary M. Riggins 9-8-1849 (9-9-1849)
Sexton, James to Nancy Riddicks 7-19-1856 (7-20-1856)
Shapard, H. F. to Cordelia Gattis 1-14-1868 (1-15-1868)
Sharber, Samuel to Caroline (Miss) Bucher 11-24-1869 (11-25-1869)
Sharp, Geo. W. to Martha Daniel 12-1-1866 (no return)
Sharp, George W. to Sarah E. Finch 12-18-1844 (12-19-1844)
Sharp, James W. to Amelia Ann Sharp 6-11-1857
Sharp, Jesse to Margrett L. Wallace 3-30-1844
Sharp, R. E. to Jane Berryhill 8-31-1872
Sharp, Richard to Indiana C. M. Spain 5-16-1839
Sharp, Wm. W. to Susan Finch 4-9-1851 (4-10-1851)
Shasteen, Benj. to Frances P. Rogers 1-4-1859
Shasteen, E. B. to Elizabeth Magors 10-25-1860
Shasteen, Ezekiel F. to Terrissa Rogers 9-15-1857
Shasteen, James E. to Caroline Cook 7-17-1856
Shasteen, Saml. J. to Mary Weaver 12-20-1853
Shasteen, Thomas to Martha Looney 7-27-1843
Shasteen, Thomas to Sarah Brunage 1-15-1848 (1-17-1848)
Shasteen, Wm. to Mary A. E. Smith 11-20-1856
Shasteen, Wm. to Polina E. Byrom 9-23-1856
Shaw, B. W. to M. F. Davis 12-30-1859 (no return)
Shaw, Samuel to Lucinda Burrow 8-8-1846
Shearl, Lewis H. to Jane Wiley 11-17-1860 (11-18-1860)
Shed, James M. to Margret Sims 12-2-1839 (12-3-1839)
Shelton, Ambros to Cathrine H. Parks 9-8-1851
Shelton, Geo. W. to Elizabeth Winkler 8-16-1846 (8-17-1846)
Shelton, H. A. to Lucy Phillips 11-25-1867 (11-26-1867)
Shelton, James to Elizabeth Wood 8-11-1865 (8-25-1865)
Shelton, William to Sarah Weaver 2-11-1851
Shepard, R. H. to L. J. Williams 3-5-1861 (3-11-1861)
Shepard, Richard to Mary Pearson 12-20-1864 (12-21-1864)
Sherdon, William to Mary Hoosier 9-12-1849 (9-13-1849)
Sherrell, John to Eliza Long 11-14-1846 (no return)
Sherrell, Samuel T. to Mary E. Banks 11-28-1872
Sherrill, Henry to Ardena Farrow 9-14-1855 (no return)
Shivers, Charley to Rutha A. Trevis? 4-18-1866 (4-19-1866)

Shook, George A. to Sarah A. C. Newman 3-21-1850
Shook, James K. to Eliza H. Green 10-10-1844
Shook, W. G. to A. F. Baird 11-15-1858 (11-16-1858)
Shores, Hilliard R. to Frances Pearson 4-28-1852 (4-29-1852)
Short, General to Lizzie Linsy 11-1-1869 (11-4-1869)
Short, Rubin to Julia A. Austin 12-1-1866 (no return)
Short, Thomas to Rebbeca D. Sims 7-25-1843
Shoup, Francis A. to Esther A. Elliott 6-26-1871
Shropshire, James to Nancy Ray 9-29-1843
Shropshire, William to Mary McCoy 5-24-1851 (5-27-1851)
Shulls, Jessee to Charlott Burks 9-22-1841 (10-9-1841)
Shutters, Wm. M. to Dosia D. Kellogg 8-27-1870 (no return)
Side, Samuel W. to Laura E. Hines 3-24-1869 (no return)
Sikes, Thomas to Mary King 2-10-1843
Sills, Daniel to Eliza Jane Parks 2-14-1849
Sills, Henry L. to Issabella Sparks 9-26-1852
Simeon, Solomon to Sarah Ann Byrum 3-18-1848 (3-23-1848)
Simmons, George W. to Susan A. Nelson 8-27-1853 (8-28-1853)
Simmons, George to Mary E. Tickel 11-28-1871
Simmons, J. J. to Sarah C. Curtis 1-17-1869 (1-?-1869)
Simmons, James A. to Nancy J. Shutters 3-20-1871 (no return)
Simmons, James to Margaret Calaway 4-26-1851
Simmons, John to Annie L. Pennington 12-18-1872
Simmons, Martin to Mary Ann Pack 9-25-1872 (9-26-1872)
Simmons, Peter to Jane A. Hurt 9-22-1854
Simmons, William to Susan Stokes 9-29-1853 (10-4-1853)
Simpson, A. J. to Terressa Rogers 4-6-1846 (4-9-1846)
Simpson, Bird M. to Julia C. Andrews 1-4-1857 (1-5-1857)
Simpson, Green B. to Mary Houston 12-24-1850
Simpson, Henry H. to Mildred V. Cowan 11-6-1848 (11-12-1848)
Simpson, John to Nancy Griffin 1-28-1867
Simpson, Joseph to Martha Burt 2-13-1849
Simpson, L. N. to Lucinda C. Smith 9-18-1855
Simpson, Nelson to Elizabeth Adkins 9-2-1839
Simpson, Rice to Sarah A. Muse 12-17-1856 (12-18-1856)
Simpson, Stephen to Nancy King 5-1-1865 (no return)
Simpson, Washington P. to Mary C. Travis 9-9-1858 (9-10-1858)
Simpson, William to Ann S. Houston 11-5-1851
Sims, A. M. to Evaline Winkler 11-28-1841 (12-2-1841)
Sims, Elisha H. to Sally Ann Herriford 10-24-1838 (no return)
Sims, Jonathan to Sarah Jane Smith 2-19-1867 (2-23-1867)
Sims, L. S. to Martha A. Handley 11-13-1866 (11-14-1866)
Sims, Nathan to M. A. Oliver 2-15-1844
Sims, Nathan to Susan Gray 2-10-1845 (2-15-1845)
Sims, Richard F. to Cornelia E. Reeves 1-28-1853
Sims, S. D. to Julia S. Embrey 4-11-1859 (4-12-1859)
Sims, William to Susan P. Grills 10-1-1840
Singer, John W. to Mary J. Darwin 12-28-1864 (1-1-1865)
Singleton, Daniel to Rena Pellam 11-23-1865 (11-28-1865)
Singleton, J. H. to Mary Adair 2-4-1860 (no return)
Singleton, Robert to Mary J. Payne 2-10-1870 (no return)
Sisco, Flemming J. to Mary E. Hill 10-30-1858 (not executed)
Sisk, Abner to Elizabeth Sparks 4-8-1850
Sisk, D. J. to Lafebe Foster 5-28-1862 (5-30-1862)
Sisk, D. J. to M. D. Denso 1-4-1860 (1-5-1860)
Sisk, Daniel to Martha J. Denson 11-9-1849
Sisk, Elijah to Nancy Suthard 11-23-1843
Sisk, George to Margrett Shasteen 5-16-1846 (5-17-1846)
Sisk, George to Martha Denson 10-12-1854
Sisk, James J. to Mary Trigg 7-22-1873 (no return)
Sisk, John to Lydia Burks 2-12-1850 (2-21-1850)
Sisk, Jos. P. to Hester A. Noah 10-4-1858
Skidmore, James T. to Margret E. Sells 10-25-1855 (10-26-1855)
Skidmore, Wm. to A. E. C. Farmer 7-12-1860 (7-9-1860?)
Skyrme, Edward J. to Mary E. Russey 6-6-1855 (6-7-1855)
Slatter, John Thos. to Hesther Ann Sims 12-15-1846
Sloan, R. F. to Annie Stewart 8-12-1869 (no return)
Sloman, B. S. to M. E. Johnson 9-20-1865 (9-21-1865)
Smart, E. F. to M. M. Slot ?-26-1870 (with Sept.)
Smith, Abram to Cathrine Hall 9-11-1851
Smith, Alex to Elizabeth Weaver 12-15-1858 (12-16-1858)
Smith, Alex to Susan Cone 3-24-1874 (6-9-1874)
Smith, Andrew to Barbary E. Gross 8-14-1872 (no return)
Smith, Benj. F. to Martha E. Darnaby 1-23-1855
Smith, Bennett B. to Caroline Downum 5-11-1844 (5-12-1844)

Smith, Chaney to Lucinda Riddle 1-6-1857 (1-7-1857)
Smith, Christian to Tempy Embrey 3-10-1846
Smith, David D. to Martha Davidson 7-26-1838 (8-7-1838)
Smith, David to Lucy McDaniel 5-10-1847 (5-11-1847)
Smith, Dennis to Margret V. Ellis 8-15-1868 (8-16-1868)
Smith, Edward to Angeline Barnes 11-21-1870
Smith, F. M. to Terrissa Gist 3-3-1854
Smith, Felix E. to Mary S. Mann 10-18-1856 (10-23-1856)
Smith, G. M. to F. A. Fagg 12-25-1867 (12-26-1867)
Smith, G. W. to Mary F. Speck 12-23-1867 (12-20-1867)
Smith, G. W. to Sallie Carter 11-24-1870
Smith, George H. to M. E. McClure 10-18-1874 (11-9-1874)
Smith, Hardy H. to Susan A. Young 10-25-1841 (10-17?-1841)
Smith, Henry L. to Nancy Ann Williams 11-26-1872
Smith, Ira J. to Elizabeth Atkins 12-23-1847
Smith, J. A. to Luticia Barton 12-31-1868 (no return)
Smith, J. A. to N. C. Cobb 10-2-1867
Smith, J. B. to Mary J. Cobble 1-5-1861 (1-6-1861)
Smith, J. N. to F. M. Cobble 10-17-1867
Smith, J. P. to L. E. Carter 11-1-1869
Smith, James A. to Josephine Hasty 6-8-1865
Smith, James C. to Mary Smith 3-16-1871 (no return)
Smith, James R. to Robecca J. McClure 10-4-1858
Smith, James W. to Marinda E. Fox 3-9-1853 (no return)
Smith, James to Mary Ann Hill 2-20-1872 (2-21-1872)
Smith, John B. to Cordelia Burt 11-15-1854
Smith, John B. to Elizabeth Byrom 6-5-1845
Smith, John C. to Sarah J. Kennedy 1-10-1858
Smith, John D. to Martha Stiles 1-6-1857 (1-11-1857)
Smith, John W. to Emelia McKelvey 7-20-1846 (8-5-1846)
Smith, John W. to Mary Simpson 12-31-1838 (1-1-1839)
Smith, John W. to Nancy L. Little 6-4-1853 (6-5-1853)
Smith, John to Easter Ann Pickett 4-23-1840 (no return)
Smith, John to Mary A. Tipps 6-23-1851 (no return)
Smith, John to Sarah M. McCord 3-3-1845 (no return)
Smith, Joseph M. to Elizabeth A. Starnes 8-4-1860 (8-9-1860)
Smith, Josephus to Elizabeth Cavern 1-30-1846 (2-1-1846)
Smith, Joshua jr. to Margret Wakefield 9-4-1839 (no return)
Smith, Joshua to J. L. Sides 10-16-1869 (no return)
Smith, Larkin to Eliza Barnes 7-5-1859
Smith, Lorenza D. to Sarah E. Anderson 2-19-1872 (no return)
Smith, M. C. to M. W. Brown 8-20-1873 (no return)
Smith, Marion to Eliza J. Sides 9-29-1870
Smith, N. M. to Sally Dyer 9-2-1865 (9-3-1865)
Smith, Napoleon B. to Karon C. Lipscomb 3-30-1850 (3-31-1850)
Smith, R. C. to Mourning W. Miller 6-4-1839
Smith, Robt. S. to Sarah Farris 8-10-1865 (8-13-1865)
Smith, Robt. to Jane Jones 6-17-1847
Smith, Robt. to Mahala Sargent 5-30-1851 (6-1-1851)
Smith, Robt. to Nancy Norman 1-15-1848
Smith, Samuel C. to Sarah A. Syler 11-18-1852
Smith, Solomon W. to Temperance K. Bibb 11-16-1846 (11-17-1846)
Smith, T. B. to Allie M. Carter 1-1-1872 (1-3-1872)
Smith, T. J. to S. J. Collins 7-20-1867 (no return)
Smith, Thos. F. to L. C. Davis 8-10-1870 (8-11-1870)
Smith, Tobias D. to Sarah A. Fleming 8-15-1853 (8-18-1853)
Smith, W. B. to F. D. Pollock 7-19-1869 (7-20-1869)
Smith, W. W. to Mary J. Connway 3-25-1848 (3-28-1848)
Smith, Wallis E. to Sarah A. Butler 4-26-1871 (4-27-1871)
Smith, William H. to Georgiana M. Hopkins 5-18-1871
Smith, William to Delila Yates 12-18-1838
Smith, William to Esther Baggett 1-28-1850 (1-30-1850)
Smith, Wm. C. to Permenta J. Carr 12-6-1857 (12-13-1857)
Smith, Wm. to Jane Weddington 6-5-1856 (no return)
Smith, Wm. to Nancy A. Rogers 2-18-1865 (2-19-1865)
Smith, Zachriah to Nancy Warren 1-2-1872 (1-3-1872)
Smith, Zack to M. J. Stamps 10-5-1859 (no return)
Sneed, John M. to Susan Morris 4-30-1844 (5-1-1844)
Sneed, Thomas P. to Frances M. Talifarro 8-14-1842
Snoddy, John to Eliza Wedington 9-24-1857 (9-25-1857)
Snodgrass, F. A. to Malinda J. Shelton 9-7-1871
Sore?, John to Louisa Kirkindall 3-15-1850 (3-18-1850)
Sors, George W. to Cynthia A. Webb 12-26-1849
South, Henry W. to Sarah E. Seaton 9-24-1856 (9-25-1856)
South, Isaac T. to Hester A. Roughton 10-17-1874 (10-18-1874)

South, M. V. to Nancy E. Dixon 9-2-1871 (no return)
South, William T. to Mary C. Gilbert 12-14-1872 (12-19-1872)
Southerland, A. J. to Melvina (Miss) Tankesley 12-3-1869
Sparks, Joseph to Sarah Sandidge 12-7-1843 (12-19-1843)
Sparks, Lawson to Charity Sparks 7-29-1845
Sparks, William to Elizabeth Hannah Sells 9-30-1870
Spears, A. M. to M. E. Kitchens 5-7-1866 (5-10-1866)
Spears, J. P. to M. J. Lewis 12-15-1871 (12-17-1871)
Speck, George to Halley Awalt 2-5-1839
Speck, Henderson to Hannah Davis 2-23-1853
Speck, Milton to Amanda Thompson 2-28-1871
Speck, Rufus to Barsheba Syler 3-7-1869
Speck, William to Matilda Brimage 11-11-1847
Spence, John A. to Nancy Carr 1-14-1849
Spence, Richard D. to Martha Jane Stewart 5-3-1844
Spencer, James F. to Susan Foster 7-10-1865 (7-12-1865)
Spencer, James M. to Emily Gregory 3-21-1859 (3-22-1859)
Spencer, James M. to Emily Gregory 3-21-1859 (3-27-1859)
Spencer, Morgan to Sofa Franklin 9-10-1845 (9-11-1845)
Spencer, T. E. to N. L. Wiseman 10-2-1865 (10-5-1865)
Spilter, John R. to Sarah A. Custer 10-7-1851
Spindle, Wm. R. A. to Siotha Franklin 4-1-1844 (4-4-1844)
Spray, J. K. to Mary Cunningham 2-17-1866
Stafford, Jesse F. to Sarah E. Osborn 10-25-1865 (10-26-1865)
Stafford, Wm. to Fanny Kelley 12-31-1868
Stalcups, Samuel to Eliza Hinkle 12-1-1857 (12-2-1857)
Stallcup, Elias to Caroline Finley 2-22-1868 (2-23-1868)
Stamper, Dewit C. to Juliet F. McCutcheon 12-18-1856
Stamper, George W. to Mary M. Moore 3-10-1846
Stamper, Robt. to F. E. Hamilton 8-27-1870 (8-29-1870)
Stamps, Daniel B. to Elizabeth Ann Oldham 8-19-1844 (8-22-1844)
Stamps, Nathan D. to Winney Embrey 9-21-1838 (9-27-1838)
Stands, W. J. to Ellen Best 12-10-1873
Staples, Cary to Susan Keith 9-11-1843
Staples, David to Minerva Branch 3-2-1848
Staples, John to Elizabeh Larkin 7-15-1851 (7-16-1851)
Staples, William C. to Josephine Miller 10-5-1842 (10-6-1842)
Starkey, James to Mary Ertes 11-15-1852
Starnes, B. C. to Mary E. Powers 10-25-1871 (no return)
Starnes, Benjamin C. to Temperance J. Knight 1-13-1849 (no return)
Starnes, Joseph L. to Margrett Bible 1-22-1840 (1-24-1840)
Starnes, William P. to Amanda J. Knight 6-20-1838 (6-21-1838)
Statham, Jessee D. to Eveline Hightower 1-3-1841
Statum, Dean to Mary Downum 10-23-1851 (10-24-1851)
Statum, James to Sarah A. Stevenson 4-30-1856 (5-1-1856)
Statum, M. D. to M. J. Davis 8-29-1872
Statum, S. H. to Mary Mitchell 7-22-1856 (7-27-1856)
Statum, Tate to Elizabeth J. Hiles 3-5-1858 (3-7-1858)
Statum, William D. to Lucy Claxton 9-7-1843
Statum, William to Lucy Bradberry 5-9-1846 (5-11-1846)
Statum, William to Mary Tipps 3-30-1854
Statum, Wm. to Elizabeth F. Barnett 6-13-1859
Steel, B. R. to Emily Connell 2-20-1855 (2-22-1855)
Steel, George D. to Mary A. Hill 2-10-1866 (2-11-1866)
Steel, George to Nancy Steel 1-27-1866 (no return)
Steel, James to Malissa Ashley 1-21-1871 (1-22-1871)
Steel, John to Jane Matlock 4-2-1854
Steel, Robert to Nancy Holliway 3-31-1866 (4-4-1866)
Stephens, Andrew to Margrett Garner 1-8-1843
Stephens, Arther N. to Catherine Hice 4-7-1851 (4-9-1851)
Stephens, Dennis to Caroline Turley 7-4-1856 (7-8-1856)
Stephens, Enoch to Mary Sikes 4-18-1848
Stephens, George to Martha Pratt 11-28-1874
Stephens, Isaac to Ritta Sisk 8-6-1847 (8-?-1847)
Stephens, J. C. to Mary J. Huston 11-5-1874 (no return)
Stephens, J. N. T. to Louisa Southerland 12-10-1866 (no return)
Stephens, Jacob to Jane Coker 12-8-1856
Stephens, John F. to Nancy Newberry 10-18-1838
Stephens, M. N. to A. (Miss) Knight 12-24-1868
Stephens, Robt. to Darcas Davis 7-20-1866 (no return)
Stephens, Ruben P. to Susan H. Stamps 2-5-1849
Stephens, Samuel to Elizabeth Teters 9-26-1855 (9-27-1855)
Stephens, Taylor to Martha Bennett 3-18-1870 (?-?-1870)
Stephens, Thos. to Martha J. West 9-21-1865 (9-26-1865)
Stephens, William to Sarah Gambol 7-27-1871 (7-30-1871)

Stevens, W. R. to M. C. Finley 8-7-1869 (no return)
Stevenson, J. P. to M. A. Teasdel 4-15-1869 (4-23-1869)
Stewart, A. C. to Bettie Smith 7-19-1871
Stewart, Anthony D. to Rebecca Holland 10-1-1846
Stewart, Anthony G. to Mary E. Bowers 8-26-1872 (8-27-1872)
Stewart, Bazil to Eliza E. Troop 10-14-1853 (no return)
Stewart, Bledsoe to Lydia Gonce 2-19-1846
Stewart, Bledsoe to Parina Jackson 5-19-1852 (5-23-1852)
Stewart, Charles H. to Arena Simpson 9-10-1867 (9-13-1867)
Stewart, Enoch to Nancy Holder 10-2-1847 (10-3-1847)
Stewart, F. M. to Martha E. Carter 8-17-1872 (no return)
Stewart, F. M. to S. A. (Miss) Simpson 12-29-1868
Stewart, H. P. to Mary C. Harris 11-26-1867
Stewart, Hamilton to Charity Stewart 11-28-1853 (11-29-1853)
Stewart, I. N. to E. Long 2-17-1868
Stewart, Isaac G. to Mary J. Skidmore 3-5-1857
Stewart, J. M. to Elizabeth Brazelton 11-16-1870 (no return)
Stewart, John to Elizabeth Dechard 5-9-1852
Stewart, John to Jennie (Miss) Price 1-20-1874 (1-28-1874)
Stewart, Joseph to Sally Kelley 6-1-1841
Stewart, William C. to Sarah A. Dotson 3-21-1872 (3-25-1872)
Stewart, William to Mary Newman 8-13-1853 (8-14-1853)
Stewart, William to Nancy Elliott 6-7-1841
Stewart, William to Sarah Reasoner 2-17-1851
Stewart, William to Zella Crabtree 4-25-1850
Stewart, Willis to Martha J. Mathews 6-11-1854
Stewman, Geo. W. to Rutha A. Tipps 7-14-1869 (no return)
Stewman, John H. to Mary J. Jarnagan 8-11-1865 (no return)
Stewman, R. A. to M. M. Dixson 6-16-1859 (no return)
Stewman, W. C. to Cyntha E. King 9-5-1870 (9-21-1870)
Stewman, William to Paralee Smith 1-31-1857
Stewman?, William to Elizabeth Tucker 8-17-1849
Stokes, Jonathan R. to Charlotte Nelson 7-14-1856
Stone, Allen to Sarah Howard 2-16-1856 (no return)
Stone, Samuel to Any Ladd 2-4-1848 (no return)
Stone, Samuel to Nancy Jane Price 11-28-1866 (no return)
Stone, William to Matilda Hollin 7-12-1841 (no return)
Stovall, Benj. R. to Mary Stiles 6-30-1854 (7-2-1854)
Stovall, George W. to Mary E. Syler 7-4-1855 (7-5-1855)
Stovall, John R. to Sarah A. McCollum 2-9-1850 (2-14-1850)
Stovall, Joseph to Martha A. Lucas 7-9-1850 (7-?-1850)
Stovall, Thomas J. to Saphrona E. Johnson 8-4-1873 (no return)
Stovall, Warren to Mary Jane Mays 4-19-1849
Stranco, George R. to Ann E. Huddleston 1-5-1869
Street, Anthony to Frances H. Gillespie 10-17-1843
Streeter, John to Susn Bent 6-11-1840
Stringer, James to Mary B. Darrell 7-1-1871 (7-9-1871)
Stroud, Preston B. to Mary Jane Stamper 7-27-1847 (7-28-1847)
Stuart, Anthony to Cathrine Young 2-2-1871 (no return)
Stubblefield, John to Harriet Wilkinson 1-15-1849 (1-16-1849)
Stubblefield, William R. to Jane Nelson 12-17-1844
Stubblefield, Wm. A. to Angeline Sells 7-6-1872
Stubblefield, Wm. J. to Salina C. Nelson 7-7-1846
Sturdevant, J. M. to Elizabeth W. Robinson 6-10-1855
Styles, Wm. C. to Mary C. Tipps 12-29-1865 (12-31-1865)
Sublett, John F. to Dicey A. Temple 1-7-1843 (1-8-1843)
Sublett, John G. to Laura E. Jones 9-3-1873 (no return)
Sublett, Thomas A. to Frances L. Stephens 8-25-1856
Sublett, W. B. to Elizabeth Carter 8-24-1848
Sublett, W. B. to Mary A. Blackwood 1-1-1867 (no return)
Sullidin, Thomas to Mary Walsh 7-26-1853
Sullivan, John to Elizabeth Seargent 10-23-1854 (10-25-1854)
Sullivan, Patrick to Catharine Fitzgibbons 10-30-1854 (10-31-1854)
Sullivan, Patrick to Cathrine Taylor 10-23-1854 (10-24-1854)
Summerford, John to Nicy P. Kenerly 1-25-1853
Summers, J. C. to Martha J. Sells 8-29-1865 (8-30-1865)
Summers, Thomas to Sally Wells 1-26-1846
Surratt, John to Julia A. Cox 9-7-1865 (no return)
Suter, John to Lucinda Bryant 11-21-1852
Sutherland, Joshua to Mary Rusell 1-19-1842 (no return)
Sutherland, Wm. to H. Pratt 10-17-1859 (no return)
Sutterin, Anderson to Sarah Barnes? 11-3-1849
Sutton, John to Angeline Garner 8-7-1865 (8-10-1865)
Swan, G. W. to Eliza Swan 9-24-1859 (no return)
Swann, E. D. to Margrett Wilhoite 9-20-1870

Swann, Edward D. to Matilda Covey 4-25-1854 (no return)
Swann, Edwin D. to Martha McKeel 9-6-1849 (9-7-1849)
Swann, Jacob to Sarah Garrett 7-4-1853
Swann, John A. to Katharine Barnes 12-27-1840
Swann, Mathew to Feraby E. Howard 7-5-1854 (no return)
Swann, Samuel to Jemima Hunt 1-14-1853
Swann, William to Martha Jane Seargent 6-4-1844
Swann, Wm. B. to Sarah Taylor 11-29-1850
Swearengame, Ferney to Nancy J. Bradford 8-23-1866
Swearingame, Ferney to Matilda Perry 3-14-1850 (3-17-1850)
Swearingin, Timothy to Mary Nevills 7-21-1866 (no return)
Swords, George to Elizabeth Williason 10-6-1846
Syler, Alex P. to Milly Grant 2-1-1871 (2-2-1871)
Syler, Isaac P. to Sarah E. Neal 1-7-1874
Syler, J. F. to Ruth Mann 1-16-1867
Syler, J. W. to Sue V. Mann 10-10-1867 (10-13-1867)
Syler, John W. to Judith E. Mann 5-3-1849 (no return)
Syler, Robt. to Ann Pearson 11-17-1853
Taft, Amos to Judith E. Taft 3-30-1857 (4-1-1857)
Taft, James A. to E. A. Rigeway 11-20-1860 (11-21-1860)
Taft, Wm. M. to Mary J. Coldwell 11-22-1852
Talleferro, Edwin J. to Sarah J. Warren 1-30-1851
Tally, M. W. to Mary E. Karnes 1-18-1872
Tally, Mathew to Angelina M. Hendrix 12-18-1842
Tankersley, C. M. to Melvina McClure 11-23-1868 (11-21?-1868)
Tankersley, William R. to Mary (Miss) Prewett 4-2-1874 (4-5-1874)
Tankersley, Wm. J. to Nancy Anderson 8-14-1853
Tankesley, C. D. to Elizabeth Gifford 8-13-1869 (no return)
Tankesley, Riley to nna Sugg 5-1-1871
Tankesley, W. M. to Ellen Terrell 2-9-1866
Tankesley, Willis to K. E. Bradford 8-7-1867 (8-8-1867)
Tankesley, Wm. M. to M. S. Eggleston 3-31-1868 (no return)
Tapscott, C. F. to A. M. Sanders 11-30-1870 (no return)
Tarman, Benjamin to Martha J. Nipins 11-2-1858 (11-6-1858)
Tarpley, A. N. to Sarah A. Gilbert 8-29-1866 (no return)
Tarpley, James M. to Mary E. Hubbard 2-2-1858 (2-4-1858)
Tarply, James to Mary E. R. Hubbard 2-2-1858 (no return)
Tarrant, Reuben to Jane C. B. Hatchett 1-29-1859 (1-30-1859)
Tarwater, George to Caroline Groom 12-6-1846 (12-7-1846)
Tarwater, Noah to Harriet Elizebeth Nippers 7-15-1867 (7-16-1867)
Tarwaters, Noah to Julia Ann Cole 7-6-1857 (no return)
Tate, A. D. to R. P. Wade 9-28-1868
Tate, Robert to Martha . Gossage 3-7-1867
Tate, Samuel M. to Cathrine Anderson 9-9-1843 (9-10-1843)
Tate, Washington to Eliza McNiel 12-20-1848 (no return)
Tatum, Webster to Lou E. Gray 9-3-1873 (9-4-1873)
Taylor, Andrew J. to Sarah T. Roberson 8-18-1874 (8-20-1874)
Taylor, Benjamin to Sarah P. Lee 7-13-1842 (no return)
Taylor, Daniel H. to Mary Oliver 11-12-1842 (11-13-1842)
Taylor, Elijah T. to Celia Brown 8-30-1852 (9-2-1852)
Taylor, Elijah to Mary E. Corn 5-28-1868
Taylor, G. D. to Bettie Garner 12-22-1865 (1-12-1866)
Taylor, George M. to Drusetta Jackson 10-5-1852
Taylor, George W. to Caroline Baker 2-17-1858 (no return)
Taylor, George to Peggy Walker 9-12-1841
Taylor, Henry B. to Sarah Kennedy 1-16-1854 (1-18-1854)
Taylor, James to Anna Wells 11-22-1845
Taylor, James to Mary Strambler 12-2-1845 (no return)
Taylor, Jeremiah to Sarah Majors 1-4-1856
Taylor, John H. to M. E. Hurley 12-7-1868
Taylor, John H. to Unice McDaniel 12-20-1852
Taylor, John to Susan Nelson 7-7-1853
Taylor, Joseph C. to Julia A. Wagner 10-4-1853
Taylor, Joseph to Elizabeth A. Matlock 7-27-1839
Taylor, Joseph to Martha J. Moonham 6-1-1854
Taylor, Miles to Margret Nugent 8-17-1838 (8-19-1838)
Taylor, Samuel M. to Sarah Suiter 3-10-1850
Taylor, Shadrick to Martha E. Skidmore 12-13-1866
Taylor, Thomas R. to Nancy Martin 2-3-1840 (no return)
Taylor, W. N. to Lucy Wakefield 7-24-1854 (7-27-1854)
Taylor, WM. E. to Malinda J. Turney 7-24-1855
Taylor, William P. to Martha E. Phillips 2-6-1850 (2-13-1850)
Teasdale, Robinson to Martha A. Estill 12-13-1842 (12-14-1842)
Temple, Charles B. to Martha J. Malone 12-21-1872 (12-26-1872)
Temple, Solomon A. to Winey J. Duncan 8-15-1855

Templeton, Columbus to Amanda Taylor 3-23-1854
Templeton, Jasper to Lucy F. Johnson 12-11-1857
Terril, Thomas to Jane Pack 11-28-1873 (11-30-1873)
Terrill, D. C. to Ellen Finney 10-19-1856
Teters, G. W. to Rachel Wagner 8-1-1859 (8-11-1859)
Teters, Isham to Mariah E. Tripp 12-18-1852 (12-23-1852)
Thacker, Richard B. to Nancy Green 2-12-1841 (2-21-1841)
Thomas, A. to E. Price 10-8-1867 (10-10-1867)
Thomas, Hugh to Elizabeth M. Porter 12-30-1852 (1-3-1853)
Thomas, J. A. to M. E. Jones 9-5-1870 (no return)
Thomas, James M. to Febe P. Parks 1-30-1849
Thomas, James to Martha Francis 12-3-1846 (12-5-1846)
Thomas, John J. to Dora C. Bates 10-24-1872
Thomas, John R. to Caroline Holder 10-18-1873 (no return)
Thomas, W. C. to Mary Short 12-30-1865 (no return)
Thomas, William H. to Martha Brown 8-23-1873
Thomas, Wm. to Jennie Westmoreland 6-14-1866 (no return)
Thomas?, Silas to Elenor A. Rose 4-21-1850
Thomason, Gileroy to Malinda Cannon 10-26-1874 (no return)
Thompson, A. to H. Jetton 1-9-1860
Thompson, Adam to Hannah Mircer 3-12-1853 (3-13-1853)
Thompson, Daniel to Martha J. Parks 3-7-1844
Thompson, Ezekiel G. to Mary A. Jones 3-11-1857 (3-12-1857)
Thompson, G. W. to Allice Clark 7-1-1872 (7-7-1872)
Thompson, G. W. to Charlotta Hart 11-9-1858 (11-11-1858)
Thompson, George to Frances Frazier 1-28-1870 (1-29-1870)
Thompson, Nevills A. to Frances J. Counts 10-3-1855 (no return)
Thompson, Newton to Sarah Tate 5-2-1854 (5-5-1854)
Thompson, W. L. to Helena Garnett 4-27-1871 (no return)
Thompson, William G. to Mary Ann Cope 4-22-1848 (4-26-1848)
Thompson, William L. to Sallie A. Power 3-11-1873 (3-12-1873)
Thornsberry, Benj. L. to Nancy C. Ferrill 12-20-1854
Thurman, John to Elizabeth Matthews 9-25-1850 (9-26-1850)
Thurston, John J. to Anna Hardey 5-8-1856
Tims, A. M.? to Jane Winkler 11-21-1855 (no return)
Tinsley, Henry Clay to Arrena Banks 1-16-1867 (no return)
Tinsley, William R. to Malisa Chilton 8-4-1847 (8-5-1847)
Tipps, D. B. to L. E. Hilton 5-16-1871 (5-18-1871)
Tipps, D. to M. Higginbotham 1-25-1870 (no return)
Tipps, George S. to Mary Eliza Noak 12-23-1851 (12-30-1851)
Tipps, George W. to Pheba Emaline Webb 8-20-1860 (8-23-1860)
Tipps, J. C. to Mary Brown 12-20-1859 (no return)
Tipps, J. F. to J. Lynbough 12-28-1859 (no return)
Tipps, J. F. to M. J. Tipps 11-20-1866 (no return)
Tipps, Jacob to Jane Brown 9-23-1868 (9-24-1868)
Tipps, James C. to Mary D. Stovall 8-30-1858 (9-2-1858)
Tipps, John to Mary A. Parks 11-13-1854 (11-16-1854)
Tipps, Joseph W. to Martha E. Green 10-17-1870 (10-18-1870)
Tipps, Joshua F. to Polly Weaver 10-29-1846
Tipps, Leander to Matilda Cobble 7-23-1858 (7-25-1858)
Tipps, Peter to Louisa C. Moore 8-15-1840 (8-20-1840)
Tipps, Thomas J. to Susan F. Higginbotham 1-7-1858 (1-10-1858)
Tipps, W. C. to Nancy J. Bean 10-21-1867 (10-24-1867)
Tipps, William J. to Permelia A. Higgenbotham 12-8-1860 (12-10-1860)
Tipton, Sherman to Sarah S. Hatchett 10-13-1851
Tomlinson, Lorenzo S. to Alley Mays 2-10-1866 (2-12-1866)
Tomlinson, W. H. to Delila E. Jones 12-6-1871 (12-12-1871)
Townsend, Parks S. to Sarah S. Coover 11-16-1854
Travis, A. J. to M. E. Vanzant 11-8-1866
Travis, Alfred H. to Euphria S. Turner 8-18-1845
Travis, James E. to Martha Stovall 11-23-1840
Travis, James P. to N. P. (Miss) Coldwell 2-9-1869 (2-11-1869)
Tribble, John J. to Sue McDaniel 2-4-1867 (2-?-1867)
Trigg, Alanson to Olive E. Arnett 5-18-1853 (5-18-1854)
Trigg, H. A. to Nancy C. Syler 10-4-1866 (no return)
Trigg, Levi to Ann Stovall 1-1-1866 (no return)
Trigg, Marshal W. to Ann Miller 10-4-1842 (10-6-1842)
Tripp, Alexander to Sarah Campbell 8-27-1874 (8-30-1874)
Tripp, E. F. to Angeline Powels 9-2-1865 (9-5-1865)
Trolenger, C. D. to Issabella Hammons 4-14-1859
Troxler, J. C. to Margret A. H. Parks 12-5-1866 (no return)
Troy, Patrick to Sarah Kale 2-2-1854 (2-3-1854)
Trussel, W. M. to Elizabeth Simpson 11-2-1844 (no return)
Trussell, Matthew to Nancy Wells 6-12-1846

Tucker, David A. to Mollie T. (Miss) Golden 4-23-1873 (no return)
Tucker, G. to Mary Honey 2-10-1868 (2-11-1868)
Tucker, Robt. W. to Jane Bridges 12-25-1849
Tucker, T. L. to Margret McKinzie 8-25-1859
Tucker, Wiley to Lee A. Armstrong 12-29-1870 (no return)
Tulley, H. F. to Emma Sitze 10-30-1873
Tulley, John A. to Margreet A. Meeks 7-29-1840
Tune, D. M. to Elizabeth Kennerly 5-2-1859
Turley, Alfred to Sarah Sisk 1-8-1842 (1-9-1842)
Turman, Benjamin B. to Eliza Bledsoe 8-28-1845
Turner, Charles L. to Mary Jane Spindle 1-10-1842 (1-12-1842)
Turner, F. M. to Mag E. (Miss) Miller 11-19-1867 (no return)
Turner, Francis to Adaline Embrey 2-6-1845
Turner, Henry S. to Elizabeth Kavanaugh 1-8-1852
Turner, J. M. to Malissa Baggett 2-25-1852
Turner, John B. to Mary Matthews 1-12-1843 (1-13-1843)
Turner, Jones L. to M. E. Oakley 2-22-1872 (no return)
Turner, Peter to Cassandra W. Garner 5-10-1851 (6-10-1851)
Turner, Plesant G. to Ruth H. Woods 2-3-1845 (2-4-1845)
Turner, R. J. to Mary E. Oliver 12-9-1857 (12-10-1857)
Turner, Wm. E. to Cornelia J. Ledbetter 7-1-1873 (7-2-1873)
Turner, Wm. T. to Mary E. Arnett 4-10-1850 (no return)
Turney, H. L. to Lizzie A. Estill 10-29-1859 (10-30-1859)
Turney, J. W. to Allice Manuel 9-11-1869 (9-5?-1869)
Turney, John M. to Paulina McCoy 6-27-1853 (not executed)
Turney, John to Julia Gifford 1-15-1855
Turney, Michael to Elizabeth Farris 12-27-1843 (12-28-1843)
Turney, Miller F. to Annis Crisman 1-31-1856
Underwood, John A. to Martha Jane King 2-6-1841
Usley, Thos. to Nancy J. Miller 1-3-1858 (1-4-1858)
Vandiver, George W. to E. J. Davis 8-11-1866 (8-10?-1866)
Vandozier, Allen to Mary Morris 10-11-1843 (10-12-1843)
Vann, Jessee to Arrina Powell 7-8-1851
Vanoleck, Abram to Emma Jones 8-27-1856 (no return)
Vanzant, Isaac to Lucy J. Blanton 11-26-1860 (11-27-1860)
Vanzant, Isaac to M. J. McElroy 2-8-1860 (2-9-1860)
Vanzant, Jacob H. to Jennie Williams 10-10-1867 (no return)
Vanzant, Joel to A. E. Matlock 9-15-1868 (no return)
Vanzant, Joel to Sally Limbaugh 12-22-1838 (no return)
Vanzant, Leonidas to Sarah E. Williams 3-18-1846
Vaughan, J. P. to Sarah A. Lumpkins 2-14-1867
Vaughan, Joseph to Martha Richardson 6-24-1868
Vaughan, Wm. to Sarah J. McGrew 10-5-1854
Vaughn, David to Martha A. Southerland 3-7-1850 (3-10-1850)
Vaughn, H. R. to B. A. Majors 12-24-1866 (no return)
Vaughn, James S. to Mary C. Wiggs 12-22-1858 (no return)
Vaughn, John F. to J. F. Laughmiller 5-10-1866
Vaughn, Robt. to Percie Stewart 12-26-1860
Vaughn, S. S. P. to H. R. Knight 6-16-1868 (6-17-1868)
Vaughn, S. S. to Tennessee Anderson 12-4-1866 (no return)
Vaughn, Wm. to Martha Enghram 5-7-1868 (no return)
Vaun, Will Edw. to Jane E. Curle 6-9-1841 (no return)
Vaun, William to Mary Jane Powell 9-3-1855 (9-4-1855)
Vernier, Victor to Louisa Sands 1-15-1868 (1-21-1868)
Vernor, Benjamin to Nancy Russell 9-2-1839 (9-3-1839)
Vibbart, James H. to Sarah Ladd 9-7-1854
Victory, William to Margret Gist 3-5-1855
Vincent, Benjamin to Nannie Money 6-17-1870
Vincent, William R. to Margrett E. Coleman 3-3-1847 (3-4-1847)
Vinson, Benj. J. to Zeppy Nelson 12-12-1866 (12-?-1866)
Vinson, Jessee to Nancy L. Downum 12-3-1850
Wade, Benj. F. to Sarah A. Miller 5-19-1845
Wade, F. B. to R. A. (Miss) Wood 8-31-1867
Wade, F. B. to Sally Vaughn 7-24-1865
Wade, Farley B. to Lotty Gage 8-6-1848
Wade, John to Jennie Holiday 12-13-1869 (no return)
Wade, John to Jennie Holliday 12-13-1870
Wade, R. P. to Nancy Magby 10-11-1865 (10-12-1865)
Waggoner, James M. to Josephine Janson 3-18-1871 (3-19-1871)
Waggoner, James M. to Mary A. Higginbotha 9-29-1857 (10-11-1857)
Waggoner, W. S. to S. Brown 11-15-1869
Wagner, Andrew J. to Frances E. Knight 7-25-1844 (7-28-1844)
Wagner, E. A.? to E. A. Knight 12-9-1841
Wagner, Edmond R. to Attillia May 1-18-1844
Wagner, Geo. W. to Mary E. May 4-10-1845

Wagner, George W. to Elizabeth Newberry 3-12-1852
Wagner, George W. to Martha Partin 11-6-1873 (11-11?-1873)
Wagner, George to Elizabeth Walls 2-23-1847
Wagner, James to Mary Hudson 12-22-1842
Wagner, John to Huldah Brannan 2-19-1841 (no return)
Wagner, Joseph T. to Nancy J. Higginbotham 1-7-1856 (1-13-1856)
Wagner, Robinson to Elizabeth Riddle 5-9-1839 (no return)
Wagner, Solomon to Adaline Bennett 8-9-1869 (no return)
Wagner, Solomon to Margret McKelvey 11-30-1865
Wagner, Wm. to Mary Dickerson 7-14-1852 (7-15-1852)
Wagner, Wm. to Mary Singleton 6-21-1840 (6-28-1840)
Wagner?, John to Lucinda Ellis 11-11-1851
Wagnewr?, John to Lucinda Ellis 11-11-1851
Wagoner, A. J. to Nancy Riddle 10-22-1860
Waitt, Geo. W. to Jane H. Scott 12-24-1845 (12-20?-1845)
Wakefield, James H. to Rosanah M. Bean 1-22-1853 (1-27-1853)
Wakefield, William T. to Mary L. Hatchett 12-21-1857 (12-23-1857)
Waldman, Peter to Virginia A. Purvis 9-13-1848
Walker, B. G. to Gilley (Miss) Holder 9-7-1868 (9-9-1868)
Walker, F. B. to Nancy Crownover 9-15-1866 (no return)
Walker, Geo. to Betsy Wagner 2-18-1840 (no return)
Walker, Hemphey M. to Nancy C. Johnson 1-31-1848 (2-9-1848)
Walker, J. A. to Nancy E. Weaver 12-23-1867 (12-24-1867)
Walker, James to Caroline McKelvy 7-26-1856 (no return)
Walker, James to M. (Miss) Lynch 2-26-1842
Walker, Richard F. to Sarah J. Cobb 1-7-1850 (1-9-1850)
Walker, Wallace E. to Martha Ann Williamson 12-3-1846
Wallace, Henry to Peggy Hill 11-11-1839 (no return)
Wallace, Hiram to Ann Brown 3-30-1839 (no return)
Wallace, John to S. E. (Miss) Hopkins 1-19-1869 (1-20-1869)
Wallace, Wm. to Lucy Bohanan 10-26-1866 (no return)
Wallraven, V. E. to Sarah A. L. Oyler 5-20-1871 (5-21-1871)
Walls, D. B. to M. M. Coker 8-6-1872 (8-8-1872)
Walls, Daniel to Sally Kersey 9-7-1839 (no return)
Walls, Francis to Eliza J. Clark 5-11-1870
Walls, Henry M. to Martha Berryhill 7-22-1852 (7-23-1852)
Walls, James W. to Elizabeth Ann Hays 5-23-1849
Walls, Josiah T. to Mary A. Ellis 10-19-1854
Walls, R. to Margret Hill 11-2-1867
Walls, Richard to Mary Anderson 6-13-1850
Walls, Wm. M. to Amelia Anderson 5-23-1850
Walraven, Orange to Julia Ann Malone 8-20-1856 (no return)
Walton, James to Cathrine Head 8-11-1859
Wamack, Isham R. to Lydia A. Tarbor 6-19-1852 (6-20-1852)
Wanger, Fredrick to Mary Sumbruen 11-6-1871 (11-8-1871)
Ward, Wm. C. to Martha A. Brannan 3-15-1856 (3-16-1856)
Warner, George W. to Fannie W. Estill 12-20-1865
Warren, Charles B. to Mary Justin 3-28-1872 (no return)
Warren, Geo. W. to Susan Sublett 1-1-1849 (1-2-1849)
Warren, George W. to Jane Taylor 3-7-1846 (3-15-1846)
Warren, Isaac R. to Sarah D. Stamps 3-31-1851 (no return)
Warren, James H. to E. H. McClain 7-3-1867 (no return)
Warren, John to Clementine Brooks 6-21-1860
Warren, Preston to Mary Janes 9-5-1838 (9-6-1838)
Washam, William to Dolly Claxton 9-8-1857
Watkins, Absalom to Mary J. Biddle 10-17-1854 (10-18-1854)
Watkins, George to Oliver Cline 2-6-1855 (no return)
Watson, Addison to Elizabeth Mays 3-23-1872
Watson, Henry to Allice Mathews 8-27-1872 (8-29-1872)
Watson, Henry to Allice Matthews 8-2-1872 (no return)
Watson, Mathew W. to Rebecca Smith 11-27-1838 (no return)
Watson, Shelton to Mary Shaers? 2-15-1841 (no return)
Watt, Robt. L. to Mary Harris Phelin 2-3-1872 (2-6-1872)
Watterson, W. D. to Livia Brazelton 12-4-1867
Watts, Joseph B. to Mary E. Swain 5-21-1858 (no return)
Weatherford, Alexr. to Lucinda R. Clark 12-10-1854 (12-17-1854)
Weatherford, Wm. H. to Amanda Newman 1-31-1856
Weaver, D. W. to N. T. Byrom 8-10-1869 (no return)
Weaver, Elias to Susan Ann Morris? 9-10-1846 (no return)
Weaver, Henry to Patsy Morgan 5-?-1839
Weaver, John R. to Mary C. Byrum 10-24-1855
Weaver, John to Marrissa Blaget 11-24-1865 (no return)
Weaver, John to Mary Ann Cole 2-19-1846
Weaver, Patton to Mary McKnight 8-23-1859 (no return)
Weaver, Peter to Jane Syrrat 2-26-1845 (no return)

Weaver, Samuel to Mary C. Collins 9-10-1847 (9-12-1847)
Weaver, Samuel to Nancy Hill 10-17-1838 (10-20-1838)
Weaver, W. H. to Lucy Weaver 12-8-1860 (12-11-1860)
Weaver, W. N. to Angeline Tripp 11-26-1873 (11-27-1873)
Weaver, William to Julia Ann Lawson 12-20-1870 (no return)
Weaver, William to Manerva Dyer 2-19-1850
Weaver, Wm. to Nancy Jane Mickles 7-7-1855
Webb, James to Nancy S. McCoy 1-10-1845 (no return)
Webb, Jas. F. to H. E. Jones 1-25-1871
Webb, T. J. to N. E. Keith 11-21-1866
Webb, Wm. W. to Lucy A. Roleman 8-9-1855
Webb, Z. W. to S. E. Runnells 1-1-1866 (1-3-1866)
Wedington, L. G. to M. G. Parks 12-9-1869 (no return)
Wedington, Wm. E. to Mary M. Young 9-27-1860
Weeks, Samuel to Levina Chasteen 11-20-1843 (11-21-1843)
Weeks, Samuel to Patsey Noah 4-4-1842 (no return)
Welch, Abram to America Heith 4-10-1858 (4-11-1858)
Welch, John E. to Mary Weaver 12-3-1851
Wells, B. to Mary Kitchens 8-29-1868
Wells, Daniel to Barbary Perry 2-2-1853
Wells, David to Milly Catchings 12-14-1851
Wells, J. H. to M. L. (Miss) Clark 4-5-1869 (no return)
Wells, James to Jane Stephens 8-5-1871 (8-16-1871)
Wells, James to Zilpha M. Simpson 7-3-1846 (7-5-1846)
Wells, Jas. to Margret E. West 12-21-1871 (12-23-1871)
Wells, John to Mandy Furgerson 8-18-1873
Wells, M. C. to N. E. Payne 9-5-1859 (9-6-1859)
Wells, Mc? to Josephine West 7-31-1865 (8-2-1865)
Wells, Thos. S. to Nancy J. Trussel 6-7-1847 (6-12-1847)
Wensell, Peter to Marena Pylant 2-14-1870 (no return)
West, Euveh? M. to Manery J. Norwood 7-19-1846
West, George M. to Mary Sells 7-6-1871 (7-9-1871)
West, H. B. to M. J. Patton 9-22-1859
West, Jno. R. to Martha J. Crabtree 1-3-1859 (2-17-1859)
West, John to Lucy A. McLeod 11-27-1854 (11-30-1854)
West, John to ____ Crabtree 1-31-1859 (no return)
West, Sim to Mollie H. Patrick 2-16-1870 (2-17-1870)
Wetherford, Wm. to Margret McCord 7-15-1846 (not executed)
Whaley, Edward to Mary A. Couch 10-28-1848 (11-2-1848)
Whaley, George E. to Julitty Parks 1-2-1847 (1-3-1847)
Wheeler, Ambrose to Patsey Singleton 4-27-1838
Whitby, Green B. to Priscilla Williams 2-5-1855 (3-15-1855)
White, George W. to Mary A. Hutchins 11-16-1847
White, James N.? to Sallie Ann Handly 3-1-1853 (no return)
White, Mark H. to Nannie L. Ransom 11-20-1873
White, Thomas to Ruth Campbell 12-1-1856
Whitesides, Frank D. to Lillie B. (Miss) Slatter 4-22-1874
Whitesides, J. J. to Mollie E. Farris 12-18-1871 (no return)
Whitesides, Thomas C. to Margret Robinson 5-24-1838
Whitlock, James M. to Mary E. Smith 1-4-1858 (1-7-1858)
Whitson, Stephen to Martha Pylant 9-28-1870 (no return)
Whitworth, William M. to Louisa C. Black 2-3-1854 (2-5-1854)
Wicker, William to Polly E. Alexander 6-25-1874 (7-28-1874)
Wier, James to Mary Baker 1-30-1846 (2-1-1846)
Wiggs, Alexander R. to Mary Mariah Hawkins 9-3-1846
Wilcox, Dora to Sarah Stephens 4-12-1872
Wilder, John to Malinda Partin 3-12-1852
Wildman, William to Jane Warren 9-7-1854
Wileman, Levi R. to Mary A. Colyar 1-12-1853 (1-14-18530
Wiley, E. P. to Martha A. Anderson 9-25-1856 (no return)
Wiley, J. K. P. to M. J. Churchman 12-1-1868 (no return)
Wiley, Jno. to Sarah E. Garner 12-16-1868 (no return)
Wilhelms, Thomas to Margret E. Dillon 8-15-1854 (8-16-1854)
Wilhite, Welburn to Elizabeth J. Litle 9-10-1846
Wilhoit, Pearce to Sarah Henshaw 12-30-1867
Wilhoite, Pearce to Mary Mason 5-13-1852
Wilkerson, George W. to Mary J. Stubblefield 1-31-1874 (2-5-1874)
Wilkerson, George to Martha Hollis 8-11-1866 (no return)
Wilkerson, John B. to Malinda Jackson 10-2-1851
Wilkerson, John to Nancy Sells 3-13-1872 (3-14-1872)
Wilkerson, Lewis to Elizabeth Kelley 4-2-1840
Wilkerson, Miles to Elizabeth H. Fitzpatrick 1-26-1859 (no return)
Wilkerson, William C. to Nancy Champion 7-18-1842 (7-21-1842)
Wilkerson, William to Unieca A. Green 3-26-1852 (3-27-1852)
Wilkins, C. A. to Sarah C. Jones 10-18-1845

Wilkinson, Abner to C. A. Oliver 8-11-1841 (no return)
Wilkinson, B. B. to Elizabeth A. Hutchins 7-18-1843 (7-25-1843)
Wilkinson, John to Sarah Henson 11-22-1846
Wilkinson, Thomas P. to Sally Stubblefield 2-28-1849
Wilkinson, W. L. to Nancy Stubblefield 8-4-1841 (8-6-1841)
Willard, Lafayette to Emeline Davis 1-24-1855
Willcoxen, A. A. to Sarah A. Stephens 12-10-1867 (no return)
Willetts, H. D. to Kate (Miss) Davis 10-10-1868
Willhoite, John to Mahala Nixon 10-18-1866 (no return)
Willhoite, Wilbourn to Sarah Damron 10-3-1865
Williams, A. F. to M. A. Holder 8-30-1866
Williams, A. to Ann Stewart 10-15-1868 (no return)
Williams, Absalom to Susanah Holland 9-29-1842
Williams, Arrington C. to Mariah W. Hill 9-30-1856 (no return)
Williams, C. C. to M. R. Faucett 7-4-1874 (7-5-1874)
Williams, C. C. to Mary E. Bennett 1-29-1868 (1-30-1868)
Williams, Claborn N. to Martha A. Hatchett 2-2-1854 (2-7-1854)
Williams, Crawford H. to Frances Brittian 1-3-1853 (1-6-1853)
Williams, Daniel M. to Emeline Robinson 12-10-1850
Williams, Daniel M. to Mary Jane Busby 3-27-1858 (3-28-1858)
Williams, Francis M. to Cordelia Thurman 11-29-1849
Williams, Fredrick to Elizabeth Farris 12-21-1869
Williams, G. W. to M. A. Whitlock 3-26-1868 (3-28-1868)
Williams, H. S. to Emily Mathews 2-15-1844
Williams, Hardin to Jane Yates 6-6-1842
Williams, Hardin to Sarah Smith 2-25-1845 (2-26-1845)
Williams, Henderson to Lucy Jane Moseley 11-29-1849
Williams, Henry to Sarah P. Clifton 1-3-1858
Williams, J. T. W. to Louisa Horton 11-30-1874 (12-4-1874)
Williams, J. W. to Mary F. McNabb 1-5-1841 (no return)
Williams, James H. to Prudence Francis 8-29-1848
Williams, James R. to Laura Moore 12-24-1873 (12-25-1873)
Williams, James R. to Martha J. Bradford 9-9-1850 (9-12-1850)
Williams, James to Matilda Edwards 3-18-1854 (3-19-1854)
Williams, John H. to Mary Myers 9-13-1850 (9-15-1850)
Williams, John L. B. to Peggy J. Stewart 8-6-1856 (8-7-1856)
Williams, John W. to Elizabeth Ethridge 8-19-1857 (no return)
Williams, John W. to Elizabeth Ethridge 8-19-1859 (no return)
Williams, John to E. K. Corn 1-1-1872 (1-4-1872)
Williams, John to Elizabeth Barnes 12-25-1843
Williams, John to Phebe Lasan 6-15-1838 (8-8-1838)
Williams, Leroy P. to Martha Hill 3-9-1843
Williams, Leut to Violet McIlherron 12-31-1840 (no return)
Williams, Marian W. to Jane E. Green 9-22-1849 (9-23-1849)
Williams, Matthew to Eliza A. Carter 1-4-1849
Williams, Peter A. to Mary McKinzie 10-4-1839
Williams, Peter to Jane Seargent 6-28-1866 (no return)
Williams, S. C. M. to M. E. Holland 9-19-1867
Williams, Sherrod to Elizabeth McCutcheon 12-21-1850 (12-22-1850)
Williams, T. J. to Elizabeth Hill 1-2-1861 (1-3-1861)
Williams, W. W. to Susan Counts 12-8-1866 (no return)
Williams, William E. to Mary Miller no date (with May 1848)
Williams, William H. to Lucy R. Caperton 12-29-1845 (12-30-1845)
Williams, William I. to Elizabeth A. Stubblefield 6-1-1838
    (no return)
Williams, William to Sarah Rose 8-4-1870 (no return)
Williamson, Alford to Nancy Pitcock 9-23-1843 (no return)
Williamson, Beverly M. to Eleanor Dougan 7-31-1838 (no return)
Williamson, James to Cathrine J. Darrell 12-23-1843 (no return)
Williamson, James to Martha Jane Thomas 6-6-1849
Williamson, William to Nancy Buckhart 5-15-1847 (no return)
Williford, C. N. to Sarah Day 12-30-1840 (no return)
Williford, John S. to Margrett Cook 12-7-1839 (no return)
Willis, A. J. to Eliza Wagner 11-28-1870 (no return)
Willis, John A. to Sarah McDaniel 9-3-1847 (no return)
Willis, Larkin to Cyrina C. Anderson 9-4-1848 (9-24-1848)
Willis, Michael to Martha Anderson 9-20-1856
Willis, Peter to Amanda Arnett 11-25-1851
Willis, Wm. H. to Susan Vanzant 11-25-1851
Wilmarding, Wm. E. to Mary A. Gregg 6-27-1872 (no return)
Wilson, G. B. to Mary Ann Bean 8-25-1859 (8-26-1859)
Wilson, J. C. to M. Bennett 12-19-1867
Wilson, Jas. to Sarah Bennett 3-10-1869 (3-11-1869)
Wilson, John to Nancy J. Dotson 9-15-1860 (9-16-1860)
Wilson, Samuel to Amanda Dotson 3-13-1871 (no return)

Wilson, William to Malissa Nelson 6-13-1857 (6-14-1857)
Windows, Richard to Lucinda Davis 11-10-1865 (no return)
Winford, G. R. to N. P. Anderson 12-10-1867 (12-11-1867)
Winford, John to Mary Ann Price 10-27-1845
Winford, Robert to M. J. Vann 5-12-1869
Winford, W. F. to Eliza E. Taylor 1-21-1859 (1-27-1859)
Winford, Wm. W. to Mary F. Anderson 11-20-1858 (11-23-1858)
Winfro, John A. to Sarah A. Wade 7-13-1866
Wingait, J. A. to Susan Rate 3-27-1872 (3-28-1872)
Winkler, Alfred E. to Elizabeth Conn 8-4-1853
Winkler, Ephram to Mary Benson 11-24-1856 (11-25-1856)
Winkler, Marion to Sarah Webb 1-30-1854
Winn, George W. to C. C. Wileman 2-15-1844 (2-21-1844)
Winters, Joseph to Lurinda Pearson 3-13-1872 (3-14-1872)
Winton, Joseph to Lucinda Pearson 3-13-1872 (3-14-1872)
Winton, Wm. to Elizabeth Fults 1-20-1873
Wiseman, Andrew J. to Martha C. Smith 6-6-1842 (no return)
Wiseman, Charles M. to Eliza J. Wakefield 10-5-1850 (no return)
Wiseman, J. C. to Sophia Hickman 3-29-1841 (no return)
Wiseman, J. E. to S. E. Webb 9-23-1870
Wiseman, J. M. to E. W. Bowling 1-16-1871 (1-19-1871)
Wiseman, James P. to M. M. (Miss) Bowlin 2-27-1869 (2-28-1869)
Wiseman, John J. to Susan A. Bean 10-3-1874 (10-4-1874)
Wiseman, John to Susan Linebaugh 9-15-1856
Wiseman, Martin V. to Mary A. Wakefield 9-1-1856 (9-9-1856)
Wiseman, R. C. to Mary E. Smith 1-18-1859 (no return)
Wiseman, W. M. to N. C. Taylor 9-5-1859 (
Wiseman, Wilson D. to Nancy M. Hammontree 1-24-1850 (1-27-1850)
Witcher, Wm. to Mary Jane Crismond 9-9-1869
Womack, A. L. J. to Elizabeth Corn 1-5-1843
Womack, C. W. to N. McDuffie 8-6-1859 (8-7-1859)
Womack, E. C. to Emaline Slator 7-26-1858
Womack, James W. to Fannie E. Pylant 9-11-1873 (9-12-1873)
Wood, Baldwin H. to Mary E. Anderson 5-9-1853 (5-?-1853)
Wood, Bazil to Mary McDaniel 10-12-1851
Wood, Charles to Betsy Smith 4-16-1839
Wood, James E. to Canzada Ayres 6-3-1853 (6-5-1853)
Wood, John B. to M. E. (Mrs.) Marshall 8-9-1870 (8-11-1870)
Wood, Joseph M. to Susan E. Blanton 8-18-1853
Wood, Perry to Marilla J. Mitchell 3-28-1872
Wood, Peter to Laura Kendry 10-9-1872
Wood, Pleasant B. to Nancy P. Sneede 12-5-1842 (12-15-1842)
Wood, William M. to Nancy L. Osborn 3-18-1873 (3-20-1873)
Wood, Wm. W. to Mary A. Corn 10-4-1855
Woodall, Joel A. to Sarah Douglass 1-26-1839 (no return)
Woodall, W. A. to Margret Brison 10-20-1866 (10-21-1866)
Woodard, A. C. to Nancy Branch 3-25-1870 (no return)
Woodard, A. J. to Rebecca Raney 9-9-1871
Woodard, Wm. to Julia Rodgers 10-17-1868
Woods, Charles F. to Sumira A. Mann 2-27-1851
Woods, Garland M. to Nancy M. Bostick 12-23-1865 (12-24-1865)
Woods, J. H. to Mary Holder 11-18-1856
Woods, J. K. to Mary J. Bass 11-22-1870 (11-24-1870)
Woods, James M. to Eliza Miller 5-19-1859
Woods, James M. to Miggie Birchenaugh 6-17-1871 (6-19-1871)
Woods, James to Annie Earp 11-23-1842
Woods, Thomas H. to Althuna Russell 1-20-1858 (1-21-1858)
Woods, W. J. to J. L. Lipscomb 12-23-1868 (no return)
Woods, W. M. to Mary J. Arnett 6-17-1851
Woodson, Martin to Margret Wells 6-4-1844 (6-11-1844)
Woodward, W. B. to Elizabeth Lockhart 12-21-1870 (12-22-1870)
Worn, John to Margret Orear 9-12-1859
Worsham, Isaac P. to Susan C. Alexander 4-18-1842 (4-?-1842)
Wright, Hannible to Susan Hockersmith 11-18-1856 (12-21-1856)
Wright, J. F. to S. J. Todd 1-4-1870 (no return)
Wright, James F. to Mary J. Gentle 10-22-1866 (no return)
Wright, Newton M. to Emma E. Ford 1-25-1871
Wright, R. S. to M. A. Buchanan 2-26-1868
Wright, Virgil C. to Mary A. Hill 4-1-1857
Wright, William M. to Musadora M. Bean 1-12-1848 (1-14-1848)
Yates, Andrew to Jane Gifford 6-6-1856
Yates, William to Martha Byrom 1-5-1839 (1-6-1839)
Young, A. C. to Mary Allen 5-28-1858
Young, Abram to M. C. Hughes 10-28-1869 (no return)
Young, David to Ala Jenkins 2-8-1849
Young, Elizabeth A. to David A. Franklin 11-8-1849 (11-9-1849)
Young, Isaac to Mary S. Holder 9-25-1867 (no return)
Young, J. D. to Nancy J. Payne 5-17-1871 (no return)
Young, Jacob A. to Elizabeth S. Jones 4-10-1872
Young, James H. to Cyrena Lucas 3-16-1843
Young, James H. to Mary Eskridge 3-8-1852 (3-11-1852)
Young, John W. to Susan M. Wedington 3-4-1873
Young, John to Clamensia Francis 8-26-1848 (8-27-1848)
Young, Mordent to Louisa Waisen? 5-18-1839
Young, T. W. to M. A. Arnold 7-22-1859 (7-24-1859)
Young, Willis Wilson to Eliza Ball 12-26-1840 (12-29-1840)
Young, Wilson to Sarah A. Crabtree 2-11-1874 (no return)
Young, Wm. D. to Martha J. Wiseman 1-4-1858

Ables, Rachiel to B. B. Brandon 5-27-1861 (5-28-1861)
Acklin, Elizabeth A. to Nathaniel T. Power 12-18-1844
Acklin, Julia D. to Pleasant Hill 1-17-1850
Acklin, K. W. to R. J. Kelley 6-17-1864 (6-23-1864)
Acklin, Mildred C. to Thomas J. Jackson 3-29-1853
Acklin, Mildred V. to Thornton S. Pattie 9-26-1846
Adair, Mary B. to John Ellis 7-4-1838
Adair, Mary to J. H. Singleton 2-4-1860 (no return)
Adam, Ann to David Hise 9-19-1860 (9-23-1860)
Adams, Martha A. to John Bennett 10-6-1853 (10-7-1853)
Adams, Mary E. to Joseph M. Rich 9-10-1873 (9-11-1873)
Adams, Rebecca A. to J. W. Cullins 4-6-1867 (4-9-1867)
Adams, Sarah B. to Willis S. Brakefield 1-14-1852
Adcock, Louisa J. to Wm. L. Haislep 5-8-1858 (no return)
Adcock, M. J. to Joseph Green 2-6-1860 (2-8-1860)
Adcock, N. A. to Robert Green 7-6-1859 (7-7-1859)
Adkerson, Emeline to John B. Howard 10-12-1869 (no return)
Adkins, Elizabeth to Nelson Simpson 9-2-1839
Adkinson, Maldy Ann to John Lee 3-28-1855
Aldman, Charity A. to Jas. H. Chafin 11-12-1858 (no return)
Aldman, Charity Ann to John H. Chafin 11-12-1858 (11-14-1858)
Alexander, Anna to William B. Crisman 7-31-1860
Alexander, Drusia to John Kitchings 2-25-1841
Alexander, Fannie to W. E. Kiningham 10-24-1865 (10-25-1865)
Alexander, Letha Jane to Edward S. Bowman 4-7-1841 (no return)
Alexander, Mary G. to Robt. C. Kiningham 2-27-1855
Alexander, Polly E. to William Wicker 6-25-1874 (7-28-1874)
Alexander, Susan C. to Isaac P. Worsham 4-18-1842 (4-?-1842)
Allen, Armentha to Wm. J. Bledsoe 12-21-1849 (12-22-1849)
Allen, Lethia to William Perry 12-29-1842 (1-1-1843)
Allen, Martha Ann to Solomon Bowers 12-17-1846 (12-18-1846)
Allen, Martha to John W. Alman 1-11-1855
Allen, Mary A. to J. H. Marberry 11-11-1867 (11-13-1867)
Allen, Mary to A. C. Young 5-28-1858
Allen, Mary to Isham Osborn 10-25-1855
Allen, Mary to John A. Perry 7-26-1868
Allen, Nancy A. to Henry B. Morris 1-18-1856 (1-24-1856)
Allen, Nancy to John Blakemore 7-12-1860
Allison, M. J. to A. Foster 2-15-1864 (2-16-1864)
Allison, Mary A. to Saml. E. Rash 7-24-1853
Almond, Margret A. to Milo Robbins 4-12-1856 (4-13-1856)
Alspaugh, Cyntha T. to Robt. S. Donaldson 3-14-1871 (3-10?-1871)
Alspaugh, H. E. to Thos. Foster 2-10-1868 (2-11-1868)
Anderson, Adaline to Robt. McFarlin 12-13-1871 (no return)
Anderson, Adaline to Zachariah Murrell 8-14-1849
Anderson, Amelia to Wm. M. Walls 5-23-1850
Anderson, America to John Berry 6-7-1839 (8-4-1839)
Anderson, Cathrine to Samuel M. Tate 9-9-1843 (9-10-1843)
Anderson, Cyrina C. to Larkin Willis 9-4-1848 (9-24-1848)
Anderson, E. J. to A. Nevills 10-17-1859 (10-20-1859)
Anderson, Elizabeth to John M. Holder 9-21-1847 (9-27-1847)
Anderson, Kate to Robt. W. Reeves 12-24-1874
Anderson, Lucy to Patrick J. Riley 5-9-1860
Anderson, M. C. to Thomas Combs 11-8-1869 (no return)
Anderson, M. E. to Wm. M. Rousser 1-15-1866 (no return)
Anderson, M. J. to A. S. Bledsoe 6-6-1867
Anderson, Martha A. to E. P. Wiley 9-25-1856 (no return)
Anderson, Martha to A. H. Johnson 7-20-1852
Anderson, Martha to Joseph C. Cook 9-10-1838
Anderson, Martha to Michael Willis 5-20-1856
Anderson, Mary A. to Wm. J. Mathews 5-6-1853 (5-12-1853)
Anderson, Mary E. to Baldwin H. Wood 5-9-1853 (5-?-1853)
Anderson, Mary F. to Wm. W. Winford 11-20-1858 (11-23-1858)
Anderson, Mary to Richard Walls 6-13-1850
Anderson, N. P. to G. R. Winford 12-10-1867 (12-11-1867)
Anderson, Nancy Ann to W. A. Breeden 11-4-1860 (11-8-1860)
Anderson, Nancy to Thos. J. Reagin 12-29-1859
Anderson, Nancy to Wm. J. Tankersley 8-14-1853
Anderson, Sarah E. to Lorenza D. Smith 2-19-1872 (no return)
Anderson, Sarah to Lemuel W. Gonce 10-15-1848
Anderson, Sophia to P. J. Riley 8-1-1868 (8-2-1868)
Anderson, T. W. to Muer Grevany 10-7-1859 (10-9-1859)
Anderson, Tennessee to S. S. Vaughn 12-4-1866 (no return)
Anderson, W. V. to G. J. Jones 2-1-1866 (no return)
Anderton, Elizabeth to Gabriel Lewis 1-7-1851

Anderton, Elizabeth to John Buchanan 1-4-1841 (1-5-1841)
Anderton, Mary C. to M. M. W. W. Lewis 4-11-1855
Andrews, Julia C. to Bird M. Simpson 1-4-1857 (1-5-1857)
Arledge, Julia A. to Jesse S. Counts 12-20-1854 (12-21-1854)
Arledge, Martha D. to Isaac N. Mason 10-3-1872
Arledge, Mary G. to Sylvester Days 4-2-1867
Armstrong, Lee A. to Wiley Tucker 12-29-1870 (no return)
Armstrong, Martha to J. E. Armstrong 9-4-1868 (no return)
Armstrong, Mary to Jefferson Milham 1-14-1854 (no return)
Armstrong, S. E. to B. D. Gipson 7-13-1872 (7-14-1872)
Arnett, Amanda to Peter Willis 11-25-1851
Arnett, Mary E. to Wm. T. Turner 4-10-1850 (no return)
Arnett, Mary J. to W. M. Woods 6-17-1851
Arnett, Olive E. to Alanson Trigg 5-18-1853 (5-18-1854)
Arnold, Lotisha to George W. McBride 1-25-1871 (no return)
Arnold, M. A. to T. W. Young 7-22-1859 (7-24-1859)
Arnold, Mary C. to R. W. Jackson 5-17-1873 (5-18-1873)
Arnold, Mary to George W. Cobb 1-12-1849
Arnold, Rebecca Ann to James M. Bean 6-7-1857
Arnold, Sarah Jane to Obediah Bradford 7-11-1873 (7-13-1873)
Ashley, Candis to Silas Prince 7-22-1871 (no return)
Ashley, Elenor to Edmond Johnson 8-31-1849 (9-6-1849)
Ashley, Eliza J. to William R. Davis 10-31-1874 (11-2-1874)
Ashley, Elizabeth to Silas Donaldson 12-19-1849 (1-9-1850)
Ashley, Eunice to Young A. Ivey 9-26-1846 (9-27-1846)
Ashley, Lucinda A. to Henderson Dotson 10-16-1865 (10-17-1865)
Ashley, Malinda to Carl Miller 10-7-1872 (10-8-1873?)
Ashley, Malissa to James Steel 1-21-1871 (1-22-1871)
Ashley, Nancy to John Davis 8-23-1855 (no return)
Askins, Mary to D. A. Conner 2-4-1840
Atchley, Sarah A. to Wm. P. Baxter 10-11-1851
Atkins, Elizabeth to Ira J. Smith 12-23-1847
Atkins, Elizabeth to John Fry 6-30-1866 (7-4-1866)
Auden, Mary J. to Lewis D. Hall 8-19-1871 (no return)
Austin, Jane to Jasper S. Hamilton 5-24-1855 (5-30-1855)
Austin, Julia A. to Rubin Short 12-1-1866 (no return)
Austin, Manervga to William Johnson 12-23-1839 (12-25-1839)
Auston, Nancy to Milton Montgomery 1-19-1843
Awalt, Cathrine to John Compton 10-3-1849 (10-4-1849)
Awalt, Evey L. to K. H. Berford 10-28-1843 (11-7-1843)
Awalt, Halley to George Speck 2-5-1839
Awalt, Mary to George F. Rogers 2-3-1853
Awalt, Nancy M. to James M. Rodgers 1-6-1848 (1-7-1848)
Awalt, Rose Ann to David Baker 3-2-1854
Ayres, Canzada to James E. Wood 6-3-1853 (6-5-1853)
Backwell, Lizzie to Wm. T. Allen 4-11-1866 (no return)
Badgett, Mary J. to James P. Kilpatrick 4-6-1842 (4-7-1842)
Baggett, Esther to William Smith 1-28-1850 (1-30-1850)
Baggett, Issabella m. to John Bevil 1-9-1854
Baggett, Julia Ann to Richard S. Downum 7-16-1846
Baggett, Malissa to J. M. Turner 2-25-1852
Baggett, Mary Jane to George W. Anderson 1-6-1866 (no return)
Baggett, S. A. to J. B. Hardy 12-18-1869
Baines, Nancy to Moses jr. Hill 8-26-1847
Baird, A. F. to W. G. Shook 11-15-1858 (11-16-1858)
Baites, Harriett to Ruben Dixon 1-17-1838
Baker, A. C. (Miss) to John W. Armstrong 1-19-1869 (1-21-1869)
Baker, Caroline to George W. Taylor 2-17-1858 (no return)
Baker, Caroline to John Osborne 5-29-1859 (6-6-1859)
Baker, E. A. to J. W. Fly 9-28-1866 (no return)
Baker, Elia J. to Thomas M. H. Hunger 2-14-1870 (no return)
Baker, Elizabeth to James Hilton 9-9-1852
Baker, Ellea J. to Thos. H. M. Hunter 2-14-1870
Baker, Eunice E. to Elijah H. Hall 3-24-1874 (3-25-1874)
Baker, Levina to R. C. Andrews 2-12-1842
Baker, Malinda to Thomas S. Houston 10-12-1841
Baker, Manerva A. to Robt. McDaniel 10-3-1872
Baker, Mary L. to Sion S. Brazier 11-22-1841
Baker, Mary to Allen Greenlee 9-14-1852 (9-15-1852)
Baker, Mary to James Wier 1-30-1846 (2-1-1846)
Baker, Rosauna M. to Samuel P. Cole 9-1-1841 (no return)
Baker, Sarah C. to H. H. Matlock 3-13-1872 (no return)
Baley, Lusa Jane to Leroy Nelson 3-9-1850 (3-12-1850)
Ball, Eliza to Willis Wilson Young 12-26-1840 (12-29-1840)
Ballard, Harriett to Orange Goff 1-1-1872 (1-3-1872)

Ballard, Susan (Miss) to Robt. Gambol 5-2-1874 (5-3-1874)
Bane, Sarah to Rowlin Morris 11-10-1868
Banels?, Lucinda to Moses Hill 3-18-1854
Banks, Arrena to Henry Clay Tinsley 1-16-1867 (no return)
Banks, Elizabeth to Joseph Mitchell 11-24-1857 (no return)
Banks, Elizabeth to William Blackwood 12-26-1849 (12-27-1849)
Banks, Glathy to Andrew Edwards 11-24-1857 (no return)
Banks, Judith to Alexander Rose 12-18-1847 (12-19-1847)
Banks, Lidda to Wm. P. Mitchell 2-18-1856 (2-24-1856)
Banks, Mahulda to Kirby W. Goolsby 9-9-1842 (9-14-1842)
Banks, Martha C. to D. W. Mitchell 5-10-1856 (5-11-1856)
Banks, Mary A. to William Gilliam 1-25-1858 (1-28-1858)
Banks, Mary E. to Samuel T. Sherrell 11-28-1872
Banks, Miss Joicy to J. J. Banks 1-7-1869
Banks, Nancy C. to John F. L. Banks 12-2-1850
Banks, Sarah to W. T. Jolly 12-13-1859
Banks, Sarah to William A. Edwards 8-2-1855
Barbee, Delila to Spencer Roleman 8-6-1849 (8-7-1849)
Barbee, Mary Ann to Daniel Kitchens 3-17-1851 (3-18-1851)
Bardy, Emma J. to R. E. Fagg 11-28-1870 (11-30-1870)
Barnes, Angeline to Edward Smith 11-21-1870
Barnes, E. (Miss) to A. C. Cleaveland 7-8-1867
Barnes, Eliza to Larkin Smith 7-5-1859
Barnes, Elizabeth H. to Newborn W. Gwinn 4-6-1842
Barnes, Elizabeth to John Williams 12-25-1843
Barnes, Frankey to Samuel Hays 6-2-1849 (6-3-1849)
Barnes, Franky A. to Nathan Pellum 1-30-1866 (2-4-1866)
Barnes, Jane to M. C. Greer 1-31-1855
Barnes, Katharine to John A. Swann 12-27-1840
Barnes, Louisa to Ansel Clepton 1-3-1859 (no return)
Barnes, Lucy Ann to Phillip Roberts 9-7-1848 (9-8-1848)
Barnes, Lucy B. to Daniel Guin 10-2-1853
Barnes, Lucy E. to John W. Moore 7-11-1857 (7-14-1857)
Barnes, M. C. to D. S. Long 3-14-1867 (3-17-1867)
Barnes, M. E. (Miss) to J. W. Anderson 5-19-1869 (5-20-1869)
Barnes, M. J. to Riley Gwinn 11-20-1865 (11-21-1865)
Barnes, Mahala to Meredith Catchings 12-9-1853 (12-11-1853)
Barnes, Malinda to Joshua Hill 2-5-1849
Barnes, Malissa J. to Edwin H. McDaniel 10-10-1838
Barnes, Margrett to George W. Farris 3-18-1842 (3-20-1842)
Barnes, Mary to Grifen Garner 5-1-1852
Barnes, Niny to Jon O. Carrol 3-9-1849
Barnes, Polly Ann to Lewis Moody 1-12-1867 (1-15-1867)
Barnes, Rachiel to Jourdan Banks 12-31-1838
Barnes, Susan to Samuel McBee 2-14-1842
Barnes?, Sarah to Anderson Sutterin 11-3-1849
Barnett, Cathrine to George Newman 8-28-1856
Barnett, Elizabeth F. to Wm. Statum 6-13-1859
Bartlett, Aura A. to Thomas P. Gannaway 10-22-1851
Bartlett, Mary to Thomas Daniel 2-4-1851 (2-6-1851)
Barton, Luticia to J. A. Smith 12-31-1868 (no return)
Basdon, Mary Jane to Phillip Schmidt 1-16-1855 (1-19-1855)
Bass, Lucy Ann to Samuel McKelvey 12-8-1858 (12-9-1858)
Bass, Mary J. to J. K. Woods 11-22-1870 (11-24-1870)
Bass, Mary J. to John Berry 6-5-1852
Bass, Mary S. to Wilson Buckner 5-23-1872
Bass, Nevey to Gilbert Mills 6-10-1838
Bates, Caroline to William Holder 7-25-1840 (7-26-1840)
Bates, Dora C. to John J. Thomas 10-24-1872
Bausling?, Mary A. to Daniel Kitchings 3-23-1841 (no return)
Baxter, Angeline to James C. Newberry 7-30-1850
Baxter, Barthena to Charles B. Nichols 12-29-1855 (12-30-1855)
Baxter, Nancy to Ross B. Berry 2-15-1855
Baxter, Permelia to Henry Sewell 2-27-1847 (2-28-1847)
Bean, Eliza (Miss) to Alex Allen 3-2-1869 (no return)
Bean, Elizabeth to John L. Brandon 10-19-1874 (no return)
Bean, M. J. to Davis Marshall 9-10-1859 (9-14-1859)
Bean, Margret to Jackson Hill 8-22-1857
Bean, Martha to _____ Scivally 1-5-1870 (no return)
Bean, Mary Ann to G. B. Wilson 8-25-1859 (8-26-1859)
Bean, Mary Ann to Hayden Marshall 11-2-1870 (11-3-1870)
Bean, Musadora M. to William M. Wright 1-12-1848 (1-14-1848)
Bean, Nancy J. to W. C. Tipps 10-21-1867 (10-24-1867)
Bean, Rosanah M. to James H. Wakefield 1-22-1853 (1-27-1853)
Bean, Susan A. to John J. Wiseman 10-3-1874 (10-4-1874)

Bean, Susan M. to Wm. C. Awalt 9-20-1854 (9-21-1854)
Beard, C. E. to Hugh F. Lasiter 5-14-1869 (5-16-1869)
Beck, Elmyra A. to Wm. Bomer 11-7-1855
Beckley, Polly H. to William R. Furman 3-6-1843 (3-12-1843)
Becknell, Mary to John A. Lindsley 7-22-1868
Beckum, Nancy to Abel G. Baggett 1-19-1847
Bell, Elizabeth H. to David B. McCord 5-17-1845 (5-20-1846?)
Bell, Mary M. to Joh Counts 1-11-1847 (1-12-1847)
Bell, Mollie to H. A. Lambert 12-22-1866 (no return)
Bell, Nancy W. to Ruben Scrivener 3-8-1847 (3-11-1847)
Bell, Sarah E. to James Gann 7-19-1872
Bell, Susan M. to John B. Keith 2-24-1848
Bennet, M. A. to W. C. Heathcoat 10-13-1869 (no return)
Bennett, Adaline to Solomon Wagner 8-9-1869 (no return)
Bennett, Annie to Wm. R. Green 3-16-1870
Bennett, Clarrissa to John P. Kennerly 3-9-1848 (3-12-1848)
Bennett, M. C. to M. H. Manus 7-20-1867 (no return)
Bennett, M. E. to A. R. Elkins 7-25-1866 (no return)
Bennett, M. M. to B. R. Bostick 9-16-1866 (9-18-1866)
Bennett, M. to J. C. Wilson 12-19-1867
Bennett, Martha to Taylor Stephens 3-18-1870 (?-?-1870)
Bennett, Mary E. to C. C. Williams 1-29-1868 (1-30-1868)
Bennett, Nancy A. to Alexander Henley 1-21-1868 (1-23-1868)
Bennett, Sarah to Jackson Dial 12-13-1853
Bennett, Sarah to Jas. Wilson 3-10-1869 (3-11-1869)
Bennett, Sarah to Joseph M. Bratton 1-5-1849
Bennette, Martha to Solomon Pearson 9-3-1873
Benson, Mary to Ephram Winkler 11-24-1856 (11-25-1856)
Bent, Susn to John Streeter 6-11-1840
Berry, Clarrissa to William Jones 9-3-1841 (9-5-1841)
Berry, Hannah to William Crownover 3-19-1845
Berry, Susanah to George Crabtree 7-8-1841
Berryhill, Jane to R. E. Sharp 8-31-1872
Berryhill, Martha to Henry M. Walls 7-22-1852 (7-23-1852)
Berryhill, Martha to Oliver M. Posey 1-20-1848 (7-4-1848)
Berryhill, Susan to Hiram Mahathy 10-10-1868 (10-11-1868)
Besley, N? J. to W. P. Darwin 2-18-1868 (no return)
Best, Ellen to W. J. Stands 12-10-1873
Bibb, Temperance K. to Solomon W. Smith 11-16-1846
 (11-17-1846)
Bible, Margrett to Joseph L. Starnes 1-22-1840 (1-24-1840)
Bice, Nancy to Thomas Hutchinson 7-30-1855 (8-1-1855)
Bickley, Mary J. to William L. Collins 12-3-1860 (12-11-1860)
Bickley, Sarah M. to James W. Gillespie 5-7-1856
Bicknell, Lucy C. to William T. Gilbert 10-24-1872 (10-27-1872)
Bicknell, Millie R. to Thomas W. Rowlett 10-4-1872 (10-24-1872)
Biddle, Mary J. to Absalom Watkins 10-17-1854 (10-18-1854)
Binkley, Ida to G. M. Inglass 7-29-1869 (8-?-1869)
Binkley, Susan to Hugh Gillmour 3-24-1873 (3-27-1873)
Birchenaugh, Miggie to James M. Woods 6-17-1871 (6-19-1871)
Birmingham, Amanda to Jurred League 10-26-1872 (10-27-1872)
Bishop, Mary Jane to Samuel Gifford 6-14-1858
Black, Ellen to King Lawrence 2-22-1866 (no return)
Black, J. C. to Wm. E. McKinzie 3-18-1868
Black, Louisa C. to William M. Whitworth 2-3-1854 (2-5-1854)
Black, Mary C. to John P. Hefner 10-12-1850 (10-13-1850)
Black, Mary E. to Wm. T. Petty 8-31-1850
Black, Sarah J. to J. F. Osborne 7-31-1858 (8-1-1858)
Black, Susanah L. to W. A. Harris 8-8-1865 (9-8-1865)
Blackwood, Eliza Jane to Richard N. Farris 1-22-1844 (1-23-1844)
Blackwood, Margret F. to Johnsy Blackwood 4-29-1839
Blackwood, Mary A. to W. B. Sublett 1-1-1867 (no return)
Blades, S. E. to J. A. Jackson 11-16-1864
Blaget, Marrissa to John Weaver 11-24-1865 (no return)
Blake, F. E. to J. J. Hammontree 3-13-1868 (3-16-1868)
Blake, Jane E. to Milton L. Byrom 7-8-1856 (7-9-1856)
Blake, Rebecca E. to James A. Lasater 7-9-1855 (7-13-1855)
Blakely, Frances to Shelton Litrell 1-21-1842 (1-23-1842)
Blakely, Martha to William Bryant 4-1-1838 (4-6-1838)
Bland, Adaline to C. R. Qualls 7-20-1871
Blanton, Lucy J. to Isaac Vanzant 11-26-1860 (11-27-1860)
Blanton, Ruth Ann (Miss) to Willie B. Randolph 7-19-1847
 (7-22-1847)
Blanton, Susan E. to Joseph M. Wood 8-18-1853
Bledsoe, Ann to John G. Brazelton 1-10-1839

Bledsoe, Eliza to Benjamin B. Turman 8-28-1845
Bledsoe, Linda to Bayless Jett 7-18-1859 (7-19-1859)
Bledsoe, Mary F. to William M. Cowan 3-11-1857
Bledsoe, Suffronia H. to Francis D. Huddleston 12-14-1843
Bledsoe, Susan C. to Daniel C. Keith 8-26-1854 (8-27-1854)
Blivins, M. A. to P. P. Jackson 8-3-1869 (no return)
Blythe, C. L. to D. D. Jones 2-12-1867 (2-13-1867)
Blythe, Jane to Thomas Damron 6-12-1855 (6-13-1855)
Bobo, Roda H. to H. G. W. Grant 10-22-1840 (no return)
Boggs, E. to Wm. Person 10-18-1859
Boggs, Elizabeth J. to William Cummings 8-19-1852 (8-25-1852)
Bohanan, Lucy to Wm. Wallace 10-26-1866 (no return)
Boman, Margrett to S. B. Austen 3-3-1867
Borem, N. A. H. to Joseph M. Bratton 1-18-1845 (1-22-1845)
Boren, Cynthia S. to H. Nail 12-21-1867 (12-22-1867)
Boren, Mahala A. to S. J. Boggs 10-30-1867
Boren, Malissa E. to John F. Harmoning 9-23-1872 (no return)
Borum, Maria to John M. Bennett 2-15-1844
Borum, Sarah E. to Nathan N. Garnett 4-19-1856 (4-20-1856)
Bostick, Mary to Presley R. Buckner 11-4-1856 (11-6-1856)
Bostick, Nancy M. to Garland M. Woods 12-23-1865 (12-24-1865)
Boswell, M. E. to G. W. Dorsey 9-18-1872 (no return)
Bouldwin, Josephine to Hardeman Harman 5-31-1853 (no return)
Bowens, Mary to Marion Brown 2-20-1854 (2-25-1854)
Bowers, M. C. to J. C. Fletcher 9-16-1867 (no return)
Bowers, Mary E. to Anthony G. Stewart 8-26-1872 (8-27-1872)
Bowers, R. J. to J. F. Ingalls 3-3-1868
Bowlin, M. M. (Miss) to James P. Wiseman 2-27-1869 (2-28-1869)
Bowling, Ann E. to Peter J. Noah 5-23-1857 (5-24-1857)
Bowling, E. W. to J. M. Wiseman 1-16-1871 (1-19-1871)
Bowling, Martha J. to Simeon W. Horton 7-20-1843
Bowling, Nancy to Jacob M. Bean 5-11-1840
Boyce, Sarah to Linton Riddle 10-5-1848
Boyd, Elizabeth to William Finney 3-21-1861
Boyd, Mary to Bird Grills 11-8-1838
Boyd, Nancy C. to H. T. Jones 1-16-1867 (no return)
Bradberry, Lucy to William Statum 5-9-1846 (5-11-1846)
Bradberry, Mary J. to A. C. Baggett 9-14-1852 (9-15-1852)
Bradford, C. M. to A. W. Bradford 8-31-1859 (no return)
Bradford, Celia m. to A. W. Bradford 8-31-1859 (no return)
Bradford, K. E. to Willis Tankesley 8-7-1867 (8-8-1867)
Bradford, Martha J. to James R. Williams 9-9-1850 (9-12-1850)
Bradford, Mary R. to Dawson B. Elliott 12-23-1849
Bradford, Mary to Jessee Guinn 8-13-1870 (8-14-1870)
Bradford, Nancy J. to Ferney Swearengame 8-23-1866
Bradford, Rebecca H. to Elias Ashley 4-7-1848
Bradford, Sarah to Thos. Clark 9-25-1847 (9-26-1847)
Bradford, Sophia to Jourdan Ashley 7-19-1841 (7-23-1841)
Bradford, V. K. to Thos. B. McCrary 4-27-1867 (4-28-1867)
Bradley, Nancy to L. B. Ethridge 10-14-1874 (10-15-1875?)
Brady, Paralee to Greenberry Pockrous 8-17-1855
Brakefield, Cathrine A. to P. B. Hawkins 12-13-1855
Brakefield, Louisa to Wm. J. McGriff 2-24-1853
Brakefield, Mary K. to S. W. Buckner 3-10-1874
Brakefield, Sarah to Jack Hawkins 11-15-1873 (11-16-1873)
Branch, Elizabeth to Benjamin Hutton 1-15-1859 (no return)
Branch, Elizabeth to Joshua Noblett 9-6-1871 (9-7-1871)
Branch, Louisa to John Cobble 12-1-1860 (12-2-1860)
Branch, M. L. to D. P. Baker 12-6-1865 (12-7-1865)
Branch, Mary Jane to Jacob Burris 6-24-1839
Branch, Minerva to David Staples 3-2-1848
Branch, Nancy to A. C. Woodard 3-25-1870 (no return)
Branch, Rebecca A. to Elijah McKinzie 11-3-1857
Brandon, Mary A. S. to Edward W. Marshall 12-27-1865 (12-28-1865)
Brandon, Mary J. to Charles A. Reed 1-29-1874
Brandyberry, Rebecca J. to John H. Lasater 1-14-1871
Brannan, Elizabeth to Isaac Reed 6-28-1856 (no return)
Brannan, Huldah to John Wagner 2-19-1841 (no return)
Brannan, Martha A. to Wm. C. Ward 3-15-1856 (3-16-1856)
Brannon, Lucinda to William C. Boice 7-26-1838
Brannon, M. (Miss) to M. Busby 12-15-1868 (12-18-1868)
Brasford, Elizabeth to Alford Burt 7-4-1840 (7-5-1840)
Bratton, Julia D. M. M. to Z. R. Dotson 12-28-1854 (12-10?-1854)
Bratton, Levicy? to George T. Kennerly 1-16-1873

Bratton, Mary to Samuel Roseborough 11-28-1844
Bratton, Nancy E. to Jacob M. Anderson 9-11-1855
Bray, Mourning to William Logan 8-5-1842
Brazelton, A. E. to J. M. B. Carlton 3-23-1869
Brazelton, Elizabeth to J. M. Stewart 11-16-1870 (no return)
Brazelton, Hannah A. to John A. Neal 11-16-1852 (11-17-1852)
Brazelton, Jane E. to William W. Estill 1-5-1852
Brazelton, Livia to W. D. Watterson 12-4-1867
Brazelton, Louisanah to Wm. Jourdan 12-26-1870 (no return)
Brazelton, Mary H. to Ross B. Cowan 12-8-1840 (no return)
Brazelton, Mary to J. C. Mails 3-2-1861 (3-6-1861)
Brazelton, Matilda E. to James T. Green 11-29-1871 (11-30-1871)
Brazelton, Nancy E. to John H. Miller 12-20-1855
Brazelton, Nannie to James J. Pryor 4-26-1870 (4-29-1870)
Brazelton, Sinna J. to Samuel M. Hawkins 12-20-1855
Brazier, E. Z. to J. M. Parks 8-24-1859
Brazier, Martha to Abel Greenlee 2-24-1853 (3-3-1853)
Brazier, Mary J. to W. G. Brazelton 12-9-1868 (no return)
Brazier, R. L. to Saml. McKelvey 2-5-1868 (no return)
Breeden, Sarah P. to James G. Collins 10-3-1840 (10-4-1840)
Brennan, Mary A. to Spencer Rollman 3-8-1855
Brewer, Mary to C. B. Rogers 2-21-1841 (no return)
Brewer, Nancy to George Barnes 11-22-1869 (no return)
Brewer, Rebecca to J. L. Brewer 2-11-1870 (no return)
Bridges, Jane to Robt. W. Tucker 12-25-1849
Bridges, Sarah to Martin Mason 12-11-1841
Bridges, Susan E. to Thos. G. Miller 1-28-1846 (no return)
Briler, Marinda to William King 5-2-1846 (5-3-1846)
Brimage, Matilda to William Speck 11-11-1847
Brimage, Mickey to John Awalt 7-18-1846 (7-19-1846)
Brinkley, Emeline to James Guinn 5-31-1853
Brinsfield, Nancy A. to James Roberson 3-18-1854 (3-21-1854)
Brison, Margret to W. A. Woodall 10-20-1866 (10-21-1866)
Brittian, Frances to Crawford H. Williams 1-3-1853 (1-6-1853)
Brittian, Susan to Abram Noe 8-14-1850 (8-15-1850)
Brooks, Clementine to John Warren 6-21-1860
Brooks, Frances V. to J. W. Russey 6-3-1866 (7-1-1866)
Brooks, Mary E. to A. M. Keith 8-8-1868 (no return)
Brouglimans?, Rebecca J. to Andrew S. Holder 10-16-1856 (no return)
Brown, Amanda M. to C. M. Crabtree 5-22-1866 (no return)
Brown, Ann to Hiram Wallace 3-30-1839 (no return)
Brown, Annie E. J. to J. N. Payne 8-25-1874 (no return)
Brown, Callie to D. K. Becknell 9-4-1865 (9-5-1865)
Brown, Celia to Elijah T. Taylor 8-30-1852 (9-2-1852)
Brown, E. C. to Wm. G. Miller 9-2-1868 (no return)
Brown, Elizabeth to John M. Kelley 12-13-1866 (no return)
Brown, Fannie to Ezekiel H. McGlothlin 9-17-1872 (no return)
Brown, Frances to James Mason 1-27-1857
Brown, Gracy E. to James H. Holt 11-19-1873 (11-20-1873)
Brown, Jane to Jacob Tipps 9-23-1868 (9-24-1868)
Brown, Louisa E. to A. B. Darrell 4-11-1844
Brown, M. J. to James W. Brazier 11-3-1868
Brown, M. W. to M. C. Smith 8-20-1873 (no return)
Brown, Mariah to Jack Robertson 1-29-1873
Brown, Martha to Alexander Farnsworth 1-22-1869
Brown, Martha to William H. Thomas 8-23-1873
Brown, Mary A. to William D. Holder 8-25-1873
Brown, Mary E. to Joseph Hammer 10-26-1847
Brown, Mary E. to Richard C. Farris 1-30-1854 (1-31-1854)
Brown, Mary to J. C. Tipps 12-20-1859 (no return)
Brown, Mary to James Jones 8-28-1874 (8-29-1874)
Brown, Mary to James Mason 10-19-1846 (10-20-1846)
Brown, N. A. M. to N. L. Davis 11-21-1865 (11-22-1865)
Brown, N. J. to James R. Beaver 9-11-1871
Brown, Nancy A. to James Alley 5-4-1838 (5-6-1838)
Brown, Nancy to Moses Bradley 4-2-1853 (4-4-1853)
Brown, S. to W. S. Waggoner 11-15-1869
Brown, Susan F. to A. E. Edmonson 12-8-1868
Brown, Susan to Joshua F. Awalt 10-4-1858 (no return)
Browning, Lucinda to Minor Carroll 9-26-1838
Bruce, Mary F. to L. P. Elliott 3-21-1867
Bruce, Sarah A. to J. R. Anderson 12-14-1870 (no return)
Bruce, Sarah J. to T. B. McCrary 12-14-1870 (no return)
Brummit, Rebecca to Joseph Johnson 7-30-1857

Brunage, Sarah to Thomas Shasteen 1-15-1848 (1-17-1848)
Bryant, Lucinda to John Suter 11-21-1852
Bryant, Manerva (Miss) to Thomas Bennette 1-14-1874 (1-15-1874)
Bryant, Margrett to William Hill 2-6-1839 (no return)
Bryant, Susan to Pinkney Allen 12-18-1873 (12-19-1873)
Buchanan, Amanda to Dr. William S. Green 5-10-1838
Buchanan, C. M. E. J. to S. J. Ivey 6-8-1857 (6-9-1857)
Buchanan, Catharine to Hugh Francis 4-12-1838
Buchanan, M. A. to R. S. Wright 2-26-1868
Buchanan, Mary E. to William W. Brazelton 11-18-1847
Buchanan, Nancy Jane to James M. Anderson 10-20-1846
Buchanan, Sarah C. to Tazwell W. Newman 3-11-1851
Bucher, Caroline (Miss) to Samuel Sharber 11-24-1869 (11-25-1869)
Buckhart, Nancy to William Williamson 5-15-1847 (no return)
Buckner, M. A. to Samuel Gilliam 1-2-1869 (1-7-1869)
Buckner, M. E. to J. M. Holland 2-9-1871
Buckner, Malinda E. to Henry G. Hamption 7-3-1858 (7-6-1858)
Buckner, Mariah E. to Squire J. Hawkins 12-17-1851 (12-18-1851)
Buckner, Mary J. F. to J. J. Baker 12-11-1871 (12-4-1871)
Buckner, Mary M. to Montgomery Miller 8-22-1849 (no return)
Buckner, S. A. to Benj. Bostick 1-15-1870 (1-16-1870)
Buckner, Sallie to James M. Elkins 12-18-1865 (12-19-1865)
Buckner, Sallie to Jos. M. Holland 2-21-1860 (no return)
Bunn, Mary S. to H. C. Lyman 5-1-1871 (5-7-1871)
Burgess, Jemima to Henry M. Ballard 5-5-1838 (5-6-1838)
Burkes, Charlott to Richard Burkes 9-27-1838 (no return)
Burks, Charlott to Jessee Shulls 9-22-1841 (10-9-1841)
Burks, Lydia to John Sisk 2-12-1850 (2-21-1850)
Burks, Sarah to Nathan Henshaw 1-2-1855
Burks, Susan F. to Henry H. Pitts 11-20-1866 (no return)
Burnam, Roda A. to Abram Sewell 8-18-1842
Burnett, Louisa A. to Henry Creciate 2-24-1872 (2-28-1872)
Burrough, Elizabeth to John W. Brown 12-25-1849 (no return)
Burrow, Lucinda to Samuel Shaw 8-8-1846
Burt, Adelia M. to J. M. Newman 1-17-1874 (1-18-1874)
Burt, Cordelia to John B. Smith 11-15-1854
Burt, Frances L. to John S. Davis 3-31-1842
Burt, Malinda to John Dougherty 8-18-1852 (8-19-1852)
Burt, Martha to Joseph Simpson 2-13-1849
Burt, Mary B. to James M. Russey 11-15-1848 (no return)
Burt, Mary E. to Benj. F. Parks 3-31-1851 (4-6-1851)
Burt, Mary J. to S. C. Rogers 5-9-1848 (5-10-1848)
Burt, Nancy E. to J. W. Leach 1-16-1867 (no return)
Burt, Nancy to John Keller 4-8-1853 (4-12-1853)
Busby, Mary Jane to Daniel M. Williams 3-27-1858 (3-28-1858)
Bush, S. F. to L. C. Bowen 12-18-1871
Butler, Sarah A. to Wallis E. Smith 4-26-1871 (4-27-1871)
Byrom, Elizabeth to John B. Smith 6-5-1845
Byrom, Lucinda Jane to Columbus Rowlett 3-10-1855
Byrom, Lucinda to Dennis Holder 12-21-1853 (12-22-1853)
Byrom, M. L. to R. M. Majors 10-23-1867 (10-24-1867)
Byrom, Martha to William Yates 1-5-1839 (1-6-1839)
Byrom, Mary C. to Kindred Majors 10-11-1839 (10-13-1839)
Byrom, N. C. to Wm. M. Hasty 8-2-1865 (8-3-1865)
Byrom, N. T. to D. W. Weaver 8-10-1869 (no return)
Byrom, Nancy A. to Benj. J. Ray 2-4-1850 (no return)
Byrom, Nancy C. to James C. Evans 11-13-1855 (11-15-1855)
Byrom, Nancy C. to Wm. H. Byrom 6-4-1852
Byrom, Polina E. to Wm. Shasteen 9-23-1856
Byrum, Mary C. to John R. Weaver 10-24-1855
Byrum, Sarah Ann to Solomon Simeon 3-18-1848 (3-23-1848)
Cagle, Sarah E. to Thomas E. Pursley 6-26-1871 (6-28-1871)
Calaway, Margaret to James Simmons 4-26-1851
Call, Rebecca to James Bledsoe 9-12-1851
Callahan, Mary to Wilson Cunningham 2-25-1871 (no return)
Callaway, Julia to M. A. Anderson 12-31-1843 (no return)
Calloway, Susan Eveline to Newton Couch 8-30-1866 (8-31-1866)
Caloway, Franky to C. McBride 9-7-1874 (no return)
Camp, Permelia to Joseph Cowling 1-13-1841 (1-?-1841)
Campbell, Ann to Coleman Arledge 11-3-1851 (11-4-1851)
Campbell, Letty to Shipman Reed 9-16-1851 (9-18-1851)
Campbell, Margarett E. to Nathan H. Dickey 4-27-1853 (4-28-1853)
Campbell, Mary A. to Alfred Collins 9-9-1842 (9-12-1842)
Campbell, Polly Ann to Marion Campbell 6-15-1858 (no return)
Campbell, R. A. to Wm. E. Dewitt 5-10-1860
Campbell, Ruth to Thomas White 12-1-1856
Campbell, Sarah to Alexander Tripp 8-27-1874 (8-30-1874)
Campbell, Semirah to Rufus S. Russell 1-24-1843 (1-26-1843)
Camron, Letitia to J. H. M. McGrue 6-5-1851 (no return)
Canady, H. A. to Michael Howard 8-4-1858 (no return)
Cannon, Malinda to Gileroy Thomason 10-26-1874 (no return)
Cantrell, Mary A. to Thomas J. Howard 6-24-1851
Caperton, Elizabeth to Jesse Perkins 4-11-1843
Caperton, Louisa A. to Ruben Kelley 10-17-1845 (10-19-1845)
Caperton, Lucy R. to William H. Williams 12-29-1845 (12-30-1845)
Caraway, Louisa Adaline to Elbert W. Custer 10-19-1841 (10-25-1841)
Cardon, E. J. (Mrs.) to G. G. Gilbert 1-22-1869 (no return)
Caroll, Margret to James Faris 10-3-1838 (no return)
Carpenter, C. E. to J. N. McCutcheon 12-18-1859 (no return)
Carpenter, Elizabeth A. to Wm. H. Pylant 12-25-1849
Carpenter, Emily to Kimberly Pylant 11-25-1843 (11-26-1843)
Carr, Betsey to Jessee Beaver 11-1-1838
Carr, Nancy to John A. Spence 1-14-1849
Carr, Permenta J. to Wm. C. Smith 12-6-1857 (12-13-1857)
Carr, Rachiel to James Goff 7-17-1851
Carroll, Elizabeth to Joseph Rollins 11-14-1840 (no return)
Carroll, Hannah to Mathew Courtney 3-19-1858 (3-20-1858)
Carroll, Louisa to Danl. W. Partin 1-2-1850 (1-3-1850)
Carroll, Lucinda Jane to John M. Ladd 7-20-1841 (7-21-1841)
Carroll, Mary Ann to Abner Jones 12-23-1847 (12-28-1847)
Carroll, Nancy to Robt. Chilton 9-20-1844 (9-22-1844)
Carroll, Sarah to Andrew J. Knight 10-19-1854
Carson, Mary to William B. Harris 7-23-1844
Carter, Allie M. to T. B. Smith 1-1-1872 (1-3-1872)
Carter, Eliza A. to Matthew Williams 1-4-1849
Carter, Elizabeth to W. B. Sublett 8-24-1848
Carter, Ella to F. C. Renfro 12-16-1870 (no return)
Carter, Izzibiah to Thomas R. Mullins 8-22-1846 (8-26-1846)
Carter, L. E. to J. P. Smith 11-1-1869
Carter, Louisa to Andrew Mullins 9-28-1842 (9-30-1842)
Carter, Martha E. to F. M. Stewart 8-17-1872 (no return)
Carter, Mollie K. to Alford Eaton 7-31-1867 (8-1-1867)
Carter, N. A. (Mrs.) to R. S. Corn 2-14-1871
Carter, Nancy E. to William R. Lewis 4-12-1849
Carter, Oma to John G. Mullen 8-26-1845 (8-27-1845)
Carter, Sallie to G. W. Smith 11-24-1870
Cartright, Eliza E. to Thomas J. Rich 3-24-1857
Cartright, Julia A. to Daniel McKinzey 5-23-1856
Cashin, Roselinda to Vincent B. Ferrell 5-8-1843 (no return)
Casteel, Lucretia to J. H. Burt 1-24-1866 (1-25-1866)
Catchings, Charlott to Steven Odam 7-7-1859 (7-8-1859)
Catchings, Milly to David Wells 12-14-1851
Catchings, Sarah to Larkin B. Garner 9-26-1841
Cates, Sarah A. to Jonathan J. Revis 1-18-1852 (1-20-1852)
Cauffe, Velia A. to T. J. Eals 2-10-1861 (2-11-1861)
Cavern, Elizabeth to Josephus Smith 1-30-1846 (2-1-1846)
Cavin, M. J. to Oliver Davis 4-29-1860 (no return)
Cavin, Malinda to Wiley Edwards 12-1-1857 (no return)
Cemray, Eliza to W. J. Gordon 2-3-1874 (2-4-1874)
Chambers, Nancy to Thomas Parks 12-26-1840 (no return)
Chambers, Sarah M. to John J. Hudgins 8-9-1859 (8-11-1859)
Champion, Nancy to William C. Wilkerson 7-18-1842 (7-21-1842)
Champion, Polly to Daniel Champion 11-21-1845
Champion, Sarah J. to William Lynch 5-29-1874 (5-31-1874)
Chapman, Mary Ann to William B. Brannan 5-29-1846
Chartan, Zay to Robt. H. Bryant 8-27-1874 (no return)
Chasteen, Levina to Samuel Weeks 11-20-1843 (11-21-1843)
Chasteen, Mary J. to Smauel E. Majors 11-5-1874
Chasteen, Sarah to John F. Graves 10-23-1858 (10-29-1858)
Chasteen, Symanth to J. W. Parham 12-16-1873 (12-17-1873)
Chavers, Malinda to James A. Davis 2-10-1858
Chavers, Margrett to James M. Rhodes 7-29-1874 (7-30-1874)
Chavors, Mary to James A. Deaton 9-30-1851 (10-2-1851)
Chavors, Rachiel to James Parks 9-30-1854 (10-1-1854)
Cheny, Mary A. to William Estill 2-13-1867 (no return)
Cherry, C. to Williamson Brannon 2-26-1840 (no return)
Cherry, Dorcas to Samuel Reed 11-12-1866 (11-22-1866)
Cherry, Louisa to John Kinney 10-4-1843
Cherry, Mary E. to David A. Hendley 12-5-1874 (12-6-1874)
Cherry, Matilda to James F. Griffin 4-14-1859 (no return)

Cherry, Sarah to James Keele 10-18-1843 (no return)
Childers, P. to James McCollum 6-14-1838
Chilton, Malisa to William R. Tinsley 8-4-1847 (8-5-1847)
Chilton, Mary J. to Wm. P. Gardner 11-7-1850
Chinch, Elizabeth to Ellick Clark 8-25-1846 (no return)
Chitwood, Mahala to Abel McNiel 10-22-1840 (no return)
Chitwood, Nancy to S. A. Randle 12-10-1866
Christian, Mary to John Roberts 6-6-1838 (6-3?-1838)
Christy, Nancy to John Franks 4-25-1846 (4-26-1846)
Church, Lucinda E. to James Collins 5-28-1852 (5-30-1852)
Church, Mary to Geo. P. Heath 2-16-1839 (2-17-1839)
Church, Mary to George P. Heath 1-17-1839
Churchman, M. J. to J. K. P. Wiley 12-1-1868 (no return)
Clanton, Mary to Wm. Buchanan 4-23-1858 (no return)
Clark, Allice to G. W. Thompson 7-1-1872 (7-7-1872)
Clark, Eliza J. to Francis Walls 5-11-1870
Clark, Lucinda R. to Alexr. Weatherford 12-10-1854 (12-17-1854)
Clark, M. L. (Miss) to J. H. Wells 4-5-1869 (no return)
Clark, Margret to Jno. B. Nelson 2-8-1854 (2-9-1854)
Clark, Martha L. to John Boswell 12-30-1874 (no return)
Clark, Martha to William Burks 12-5-1860 (12-9-1860)
Clark, Nancy J. to J. R. Bradford 8-24-1860 (8-26-1860)
Clark, Sarah to C. C. Curl 3-18-1873 (6-29-1873)
Claxton, Dolly to William Washam 9-8-1857
Claxton, Lucy to William D. Statum 9-7-1843
Claxton, Mary to Wesley Clanton 4-18-1858 (no return)
Cleek, Mary C. to B. S. Russell 5-3-1867 (5-5-1867)
Clements, Florinda to James H. Estill 2-12-1851 (2-13-1851)
Clements, Mary Bula to James F. Jenkins 12-6-1869 (12-7-1869)
Clenny, Jane to Henry Rose 5-19-1865
Clifton, Mary Ann to Franklin T. Gipson 6-4-1858 (no return)
Clifton, Sarah P. to Henry Williams 1-3-1858
Clifton, Sarah to James A. Edwards 9-5-1866 (9-31?-1866)
Cline, Oliver to George Watkins 2-6-1855 (no return)
Cline, Olley to William Mayes 1-20-1858 (1-21-1858)
Cluck, Cynthia J. to John Busby 5-22-1849
Cobb, Areyminty D. to Jessee A. Phillips 8-26-1845 (8-27-1845)
Cobb, Elizabeth N. to Andrew W. Revis 8-12-1847
Cobb, M. E. to M. M. Cates 9-25-1865 (no return)
Cobb, Mary A. E. to James A. Nelson 2-21-1871 (2-23-1871)
Cobb, N. C. to J. A. Smith 10-2-1867
Cobb, Nancy M. to Joel Mullins 3-8-1855
Cobb, Sarah J. to Richard F. Walker 1-7-1850 (1-9-1850)
Cobble, C. A. to Rederick P. Brown 11-16-1870 (10-12-1870?)
Cobble, Elizabeth to David Honey 10-13-1870
Cobble, F. M. to J. N. Smith 10-17-1867
Cobble, Mary J. to J. B. Smith 1-5-1861 (1-6-1861)
Cobble, Matilda to Leander Tipps 7-23-1858 (7-25-1858)
Cobble, Nancy M. to Isaac R. Mitchell 1-17-1857 (1-22-1857)
Coffrey, Mary to John Cameron 11-27-1854 (11-30-1854)
Coggins, M. (Mrs.) to John Clemons 3-18-1871 (3-19-1871)
Coker, Elizabeth to John Gilliam 9-18-1845
Coker, Elmster? to William Hays 6-9-1857
Coker, Jane to Jacob Stephens 12-8-1856
Coker, M. E. to Wm. R. King 5-19-1866 (5-25-1866)
Coker, M. M. to D. B. Walls 8-6-1872 (8-8-1872)
Coker, Margret M. to Hugh M. Quinn 10-17-1866 (10-28-1866)
Coker, Mary C. to Jessee D. Gipson 2-6-1866
Coker, Sarah to Thos. Perry 9-1-1865
Coldwell, Mary J. to Wm. M. Taft 11-22-1852
Coldwell, N. P. (Miss) to James P. Travis 2-9-1869 (2-11-1869)
Cole, Elizabeth to William Rile 9-28-1848
Cole, Fannie to P. M. Greene 6-2-1869 (6-24-1869)
Cole, Julia Ann to Noah Tarwaters 7-6-1857 (no return)
Cole, L. T. to A. W. Revis 11-3-1869 (no return)
Cole, M. C. to John A. Renfro 11-24-1868 (no return)
Cole, M. J. to P. M. Green 6-?-1869 (no return)
Cole, Mary A. to John H. Bridgeway 4-9-1842 (no return)
Cole, Mary Ann to John Weaver 2-19-1846
Cole, Mollie M. to W. G. Crane 9-22-1871
Cole, Nancy C. to James M. Daulton 11-14-1843 (11-16-1843)
Cole, Rachel to A. W. Barbee 5-17-1849 (5-18-1849)
Coleman, Margrett E. to William R. Vincent 3-3-1847 (3-4-1847)
Coleman, Sarah A. to Edwin Miller 3-9-1853 (3-10-1853)
Collins, A. C. to J. D. McElroy 5-26-1870

Collins, Emeline to James R. Banks 11-4-1856
Collins, Frances A. to William J. Miller 5-1-1851
Collins, Louisa to Elijah Parks 5-5-1848 (5-6-1848)
Collins, M. F. to O. C. Latta 9-19-1874
Collins, Mary C. to Samuel Weaver 9-10-1847 (9-12-1847)
Collins, Rebecca A. to Auston McCrary 7-31-1853
Collins, S. J. to George Garner 9-5-1867 (9-13-1868?)
Collins, S. J. to T. J. Smith 7-20-1867 (no return)
Colyar, Cathrine to Adam L. Hyder 1-4-1848 (1-6-1848)
Colyar, Charity to L. M. Lashbrook 8-27-1853 (8-28-1853)
Colyar, Elizabeth to John Curtis 1-21-1842 (1-23-1842)
Colyar, Louise to Gustave Miller 3-31-1862 (4-6-1862)
Colyar, Martha C. to S. R. Roseborough 1-7-1857 (no return)
Colyar, Mary A. to Levi R. Wileman 1-12-1853 (1-14-18530
Colyar, Nancy to Robt. Elkin 1-1-1857
Colyar, Permelia to Brazilla F. Harris 2-17-1855 (2-18-1855)
Colyar, Sarah to William Houston 12-24-1860
Colyar, Susan to James W. Lashbrooks 8-26-1856
Combs, Sarah E. to John E. McGuire 4-6-1849
Comings, Elizabeth to John Coker 5-9-1849
Compton, Elizabeth M. to Jeremiah Pratt 1-5-1850 (1-6-1850)
Conaway, Eliza to Andrew Dotson 3-24-1873 (no return)
Cone, Susan to Alex Smith 3-24-1874 (6-9-1874)
Conn, Elizabeth to Alfred E. Winkler 8-4-1853
Conn, Sarah A. to Robert A. Berryhill 8-2-1852
Connell, Emily to B. R. Steel 2-20-1855 (2-22-1855)
Connway, Mary J. to W. W. Smith 3-25-1848 (3-28-1848)
Cook, Caroline to James E. Shasteen 7-17-1856
Cook, Josephene to David Buttrick 4-25-1865 (no return)
Cook, Lucinda to Samuel Pollock 12-30-1846
Cook, M. J. to J. W. Holt 12-17-1873 (12-18-1873)
Cook, Margrett to John S. Williford 12-7-1839 (no return)
Cook, Mary to Daniel B. Armstrong 10-15-1846
Cook, Nancy A. to Nathaniel J. Brown 1-7-1850 (1-9-1850)
Cook, Nelly to William H. Pylant 12-4-1844
Cook, Pelina to Hoden Hill 8-30-1845 (8-31-1845)
Cook, Polly to Ozwill Jones 12-17-1839
Cooley, Mary to James Isbell 6-28-1871
Cooper, L. M. to Jeremiah Pratt 6-15-1860 (6-17-1860)
Cooper, Mary A. to Enoch D. Fox 10-16-1853 (10-17-1853)
Coots, M. E. to T. C. Mason 3-25-1874
Coots, Sarah to Duke Johnson 7-25-1874 (7-26-1874)
Coover, Mary to A. J. (Capt.) Merrit 7-19-1865 (7-25-1865)
Coover, Sarah S. to Parks S. Townsend 11-16-1854
Cope, Mary Ann to William G. Thompson 4-22-1848 (4-26-1848)
Corbett, Manca to Posey Mason 11-7-1865 (11-9-1865)
Corn, Anna to Thomas F. Johnson 1-30-1868
Corn, Dorah to H. Nevill 11-26-1866 (no return)
Corn, E. K. to John Williams 1-1-1872 (1-4-1872)
Corn, Elizabeth to A. L. J. Womack 1-5-1843
Corn, Elizabeth to John Hail 9-9-1851
Corn, Ellen to George Crewgar 4-16-1866 (4-?-1866)
Corn, Emily to Joel G. McCutcheon 6-17-1841 (6-20-1841)
Corn, Jemima to John Pless 12-19-1868
Corn, Laura to L. C. Lesure 10-21-1874
Corn, M. E. to G. W. Duncan 10-7-1869 (no return)
Corn, Malissa to Richard S. Corn 3-28-1842 (3-31-1842)
Corn, Margret F. to G. D. Johnson 12-22-1869 (12-23-1869)
Corn, Mary A. to M. Corn 2-26-1870 (no return)
Corn, Mary A. to Wm. W. Wood 10-4-1855
Corn, Mary E. to Elijah Taylor 5-28-1868
Corn, Mary to Gordon C. McCutcheon 8-4-1849 (8-5-1849)
Corn, N. B. to C. G. Reagin 12-9-1859 (12-11-1859)
Corn, Sarah to John A. Corn 12-27-1845
Corn, T. K. to Boulin Clark 10-14-1879 (10-15-1868?)
Corning, E. to John McHathy 10-22-1870
Cosents, Elizabeth to Jacob J. Bridges 12-1-1857 (no return)
Cotton, Maggie to John W. Parks 9-20-1866 (no return)
Couburn, Sarah E. to Martin Dukes 10-6-1873 (10-8-1873)
Couch, E. to Alexander Davis 11-25-1859 (no return)
Couch, Mary A. to Edward Whaley 10-28-1848 (11-2-1848)
Coulson, Mary A. to Henderson Powers 1-7-1868 (1-8-1868)
Coulson, Sarah A. to T. C. Cunningham 12-31-1873 (1-1-1874)
Counts, Emeline to Joseph Campbell 11-2-1848
Counts, Frances J. to Nevills A. Thompson 10-3-1855 (no return)

Counts, M. J. to Samuel Hamer 8-9-1869 (no return)
Counts, Matilda J. to Luke Kelley 6-18-1859
Counts, Rosannah to Admiral N. Rutledge 12-5-1851 (12-10-1851)
Counts, Sophia to Robt. Holiday 9-3-1873
Counts, Susan to W. W. Williams 12-8-1866 (no return)
Covey, Elizabeth to Wm. J. Orear 1-31-1852 (no return)
Covey, Esther to Samuel Hinkle 8-24-1850 (9-7-1850)
Covey, Matilda to Edward D. Swann 4-25-1854 (no return)
Covey, Sophia to J. T. Richardson 11-29-1870 (12-1-1870)
Cowan, Elizabeth A. to John Fuqua 11-5-1857 (no return)
Cowan, Lucinda to Alexander N. Newberry 11-9-1848
Cowan, Mary A. to A. J. Kiningham 2-10-1870
Cowan, Mildred V. to Henry H. Simpson 11-6-1848 (11-12-1848)
Cowan, Nancy to John C. Montgomery 1-15-1850
Cowan, Sarah L. to A. R. David 4-5-1847 (4-6-1847)
Cowan, Sarah to Thomas Lewis 10-3-1840 (10-4-1840)
Cowan, Serena to James Seargent 10-28-1868 (10-29-1868)
Cowen, Amanda to Henry Norwood 9-4-1868 (9-6-1868)
Cox, Julia A. to John Surratt 9-7-1865 (no return)
Cox, Malinda J. to David Addington 6-1-1842 (6-2-1842)
Cox, Martha I. to Lycurgas Lyncecum 5-28-1838 (no return)
Cox, Nancy to Steven M. Lewis 10-22-1868 (no return)
Crabtree, Caroline to E. H. Colton 12-23-1868 (12-24-1868)
Crabtree, Hetty to James Payne 9-22-1851
Crabtree, M. J. to D. C. Rice 9-14-1860 (9-23-1860)
Crabtree, M. J. to J. W. Adcock 12-14-1867 (no return)
Crabtree, Martha J. to Jno. R. West 1-3-1859 (2-17-1859)
Crabtree, Sarah A. to Wilson Young 2-11-1874 (no return)
Crabtree, Susan to J. W. Kelley 4-25-1839
Crabtree, Zella to William Stewart 4-25-1850
Crabtree, ____ to John West 1-31-1859 (no return)
Craig, Sarah to Ephriam Bradford 12-4-1860
Craten, Elizabeth to James A. Jones 2-8-1842
Crawford, Elizabeth to William McKay 2-1-1847
Crawford, M. J. to T. C. Farris 12-20-1871
Crawford, Sarah E. to William Bishop 10-10-1871
Crenshaw, Mattie to James P. Holman 8-16-1870 (9-16-1870)
Crick, Matilda H. to John A. Byrum 12-3-1855 (12-5-1855)
Crick, Nannie to George A. Kimbro 12-6-1870 (no return)
Crisman, Agnes B. to Louis B. Parham 6-15-1870
Crisman, Annis to Miller F. Turney 1-31-1856
Crisman, M. L. to G. W. McMillion 12-25-1871 (12-26-1871)
Crisman, Priscilla to J. S. Payne 12-24-1870 (no return)
Crisman, Priscilla to James Payne 12-26-1870 (no return)
Crismond, Mary Jane to Wm. Witcher 9-9-1869
Crocket, Betsy to Barney M. Runnels 9-13-1838
Cross, Sarah to George W. Nevils 7-9-1857
Crowden, Eliza to William Adcock 1-30-1850 (1-31-1850)
Crowder, Mary to Lancen Hunt 8-7-1841
Crowders, Lucinda to David Hunt 6-26-1851
Crownover, Jane to John Clark 9-26-1874 (9-27-1874)
Crownover, Martha to John Dotson 12-17-1856 (12-18-1856)
Crownover, Melvina to William Edwards 9-3-1850
Crownover, Nancy to F. B. Walker 9-15-1866 (no return)
Crutchfield, Nancy to Wm. Graham 12-2-1865 (12-4-1865)
Crutchfield, Ruthy C. to William M. Hall 11-29-1873 (11-9?-1873)
Cumins, Jane to William Coker 4-4-1843 (4-5-1843)
Cummings, R. E. to F. M. Sandridge 10-25-1866 (10-26-1866)
Cunningham, Elizabeth to George A. Metcalf 8-11-1869 (no return)
Cunningham, Mary to J. K. Spray 2-17-1866
Cunningham, Sarah to Hezekiah Faris 4-25-1843 (4-26-1843)
Curle, Jane E. to Will Edw. Vaun 6-9-1841 (no return)
Curle, Martha A. to Hiram Brown 12-15-1842
Curle, Mary J. to Nathan M. Ivey 12-6-1857 (no return)
Curle, Musadore to William Marshall 8-29-1849
Curle, T. J. to J. W. Byrom 4-11-1865 (4-13-1865)
Curtis, Sarah C. to J. J. Simmons 1-17-1869 (1-?-1869)
Custer, Ann to J. W. Hardee 12-22-1866 (no return)
Custer, Eliza Jane to George H. Lefeber 5-12-1855 (5-13-1855)
Custer, Elizabeth to Orin Hill 10-27-1840
Custer, Sarah A. to John R. Spilter 10-7-1851
Custer, Sarah F. to G. S. Farris 3-8-1865
Dampon, Mrtha to Lewis Donaldson 1-26-1865 (1-2?-1865)
Damrel, Elizabeth to James D. Meadows 2-26-1857
Damron, Catherine to William Damron 5-10-1855

Damron, Ellan to L. B. Ethridge 4-18-1872 (no return)
Damron, Mary E. to H. M. Gault 8-14-1871 (no return)
Damron, Sarah L. to A. J. Fullmore 3-14-1853 (3-24-1853)
Damron, Sarah to Wilbourn Willhoite 10-3-1865
Daniel, Jane L. to W. M. Sanders 2-10-1859 (no return)
Daniel, Margrett to Joseph S. Payne 3-12-1869 (3-17-1869)
Daniel, Martha to Geo. W. Sharp 12-1-1866 (no return)
Daniel, Sarah E. to James McNabb 7-28-1856
Daniel, Sarah F. to James H. Neal 2-11-1846
Darnaby, Lucy A. E. to John T. Phillips 10-8-1850
Darnaby, Martha E. to Benj. F. Smith 1-23-1855
Darnaby, Nancy to William Davis 1-27-1841 (1-28-1841)
Darnell, Elizabeth to John O. Boggs 1-8-1855
Darnell, Mary Jane to Benjamin D. Gipson 12-20-1845 (12-30-1845)
Darrel, Naoma A. to Thomas A. Clark 4-20-1858
Darrell, Cathrine J. to James Williamson 12-23-1843 (no return)
Darrell, Julia A. to John K. Embrey 1-24-1843 (no return)
Darrell, Mary B. to James Stringer 7-1-1871 (7-9-1871)
Darrell, Mary B. to Robt. P. Hester 7-7-1853 (7-8-1853)
Darrell, Mary M. to Andrew K. Lawing 12-21-1844
Darrell, Mary to John Poens 11-28-1871 (11-29-1871)
Darrell, Nancy to Henry Hall 1-13-1848
Darrell, Naoma A. to Thomas A. Clark 4-20-1858 (no return)
Darrow, Susanah E. to James P. Cobb 8-29-1856
Darwin, Easther to Abram Dalley 2-14-1873
Darwin, Elizabeth to Daniel Hannah 12-18-1869
Darwin, Elizabeth to George M. Hockersmith 12-30-1847
Darwin, M. E. to John H. Bass 10-21-1867 (10-24-1867)
Darwin, Mary J. to John W. Singer 12-28-1864 (1-1-1865)
Darwin, Nancy M. to James K. Pearson 9-18-1873
Davidson, Elizabeth to Gray W. Jones 9-10-1846
Davidson, Lucy to Green H. Lasater 1-22-1845 (1-7-1845)
Davidson, Martha to David D. Smith 7-26-1838 (8-7-1838)
Davidson, Mollie E. to Ed, jr. Mooris 6-2-1871 (7-3-1871)
Davidson, Nancy to Grant T. Hamilton 12-9-1841
Davidson, Susan to Robert C. Lasater 12-22-1838 (no return)
Davis, Amanda to George B. McComb 12-19-1855 (no return)
Davis, Amanda to Patrick Gallaugher 4-30-1858 (no return)
Davis, Darcas to Robt. Stephens 7-20-1866 (no return)
Davis, E. J. to George W. Vandiver 8-11-1866 (8-10?-1866)
Davis, Elizabeth J. to Charley Kelley 5-21-1858
Davis, Emeline to Lafayette Willard 1-24-1855
Davis, Hannah to Henderson Speck 2-23-1853
Davis, Ivarilla D. to James S. Johnson 4-30-1853
Davis, Kate (Miss) to H. D. Willetts 10-10-1868
Davis, L. C. to Thos. F. Smith 8-10-1870 (8-11-1870)
Davis, Lucinda to Richard Windows 11-10-1865 (no return)
Davis, M. F. to B. W. Shaw 12-30-1859 (no return)
Davis, M. J. to M. D. Statum 8-29-1872
Davis, Nancy to James Lee 12-25-1862
Davis, Nancy to Waman L. Rose 6-14-1849
Davis, Rachael to Robt. Pearson 9-21-1858 (9-23-1858)
Davis, Rebecca to George Brewer 12-28-1859 (2-29-1860)
Davis, Sallie to J. L. Arnold 10-6-1874 (no return)
Davis, Samantha to R. A. Qualls 1-20-1870
Davis, Susannah to Thomas Pasley 8-18-1838 (8-30-1838)
Davis, Synthia to George J. Parks 7-20-1848 (7-21-1848)
Day, Marthy A. to George W. Mitchell 12-25-1850
Day, Sarah to C. N. Williford 12-30-1840 (no return)
Dean, Mary A. to J. A. Byrom 10-12-1869
Deason, Frazie to W. F. Jourdan 8-20-1873
Deaton, Mary Ann to Wm. M. Evans 2-14-1849
Deaton, Virginia to George Miller 10-29-1842 (10-30-1842)
Dechard, Amelia to Jessee C. Foreman 2-21-1857 (2-25-1857)
Dechard, Elizabeth to John Stewart 5-9-1852
Decherd, C. C. to John Coburn 11-23-1866 (no return)
Decherd, Dosha to James Bennett 12-8-1852
Decherd, Dosha to Rowland Lane 12-20-1844
Decherd, Elizabeth F. to F. A. Laughmiller 10-10-1839 (no return)
Decherd, Louisa F. to Efford Friend 9-11-1854 (9-12-1854)
Decherd, Sophia to Samuel Black 6-28-1853
Deckerd, Cathrine to Nathaniel Pack 1-5-1843 (1-12-1843)
Deckerd, Dosha to Daniel McCoy 10-31-1844 (no return)
Deerin, Mary to Jacob Holt 4-19-1866 (no return)
Deery, Searaphina to Randal W. McGavock 8-23-1855

Delzell, Elizabeth to James M. McDonald 10-12-1852 (no return)
Delzell, Lucy A. to W. M. Griffin 9-2-1859 (9-4-1859)
Delzell, Mary to Joe Berryhill 12-17-1874 (12-19-1874)
Denso, M. D. to D. J. Sisk 1-4-1860 (1-5-1860)
Denson, Catherine to Henry Crawford 2-25-1860 (2-29-1860)
Denson, Elizabeth to Samuel Frazier 1-21-1846 (1-22-1846)
Denson, Frances L. to Patton M. Black 11-1-1848 (11-2-1848)
Denson, Harriett to John W. Burks 9-21-1858 (9-22-1858)
Denson, Jane to John Russell 11-1-1843 (11-2-1843)
Denson, Martha J. to Daniel Sisk 11-9-1849
Denson, Martha to George Sisk 10-12-1854
Denson, Mary to Wm. P. Burk 2-19-1857
Denson, Salinna to Samuel Keith 1-9-1847 (1-12-1847)
Denton, Anna to Lindsay Jackson 8-24-1843
Devenport, Luvina to Samuel Duckworth 5-15-189 (no return)
Dial, Angeline to Commadore Perry 4-18-1874
Dial, Angeline to George Hill 5-10-1871
Dial, Dicy to David Anderson 8-1-1867 (8-4-1867)
Dial, Hannah to Wiseman Adcock 4-8-1844
Dial, Ibby to L. G. Bennett 7-27-1847 (7-30-1847)
Dickenson, Adaline to Andrew B. Anderson 4-17-1841 (4-18-1841)
Dickerson, Mary to Wm. Wagner 7-14-1852 (7-15-1852)
Dickson, C. S. to Geo. W. Hefner 1-10-1866 (1-11-1866)
Dillon, Margret E. to Thomas Wilhelms 8-15-1854 (8-16-1854)
Dixon, Nancy E. to M. V. South 9-2-1871 (no return)
Dixson, M. M. to R. A. Stewman 6-16-1859 (no return)
Dobson, Martha H. to Edward B. Farris 11-12-1850 (11-13-1850)
Dodson, Cirena to William Mason 7-28-1853
Dodson, Elizabeth to O. M. Posey 11-18-1853 (11-21-1853)
Donaldson, Narcissa A. to Wm. Cluck 8-7-1858 (8-10-1858)
Donaldson, Sarah A. to Jacob Pitcock 3-25-1858 (no return)
Dorrell, Briggett to Timothy Dougan 10-21-1854 (10-24-1854)
Dorrell, Nancy J. to J. K. P. Keck 3-1-1858 (3-2-1858)
Dorsett, Elizabeth to Thomas Sanders 3-2-1853 (3-3-1853)
Dossey, Susan to James W. Franklin 4-19-1848 (4-21-1848)
Dotson, Amanda to Samuel Wilson 3-13-1871 (no return)
Dotson, Eliza to A. M. Gross 7-22-1867
Dotson, Lucy to Wm. T. Harrison 10-17-1872
Dotson, Mary E. to Rufus Dotson 11-28-1871 (12-17-1871)
Dotson, Nancy J. to John Wilson 9-15-1860 (9-16-1860)
Dotson, Sarah A. to William C. Stewart 3-21-1872 (3-25-1872)
Dougan, Eleanor to Beverly M. Williamson 7-31-1838 (no return)
Dougan, Elendor to Jeremiah Malone 6-3-1856 (no return)
Dougan, Rutha Caroline to Turner Jones 10-25-1841 (no return)
Dougan, Sarah A. to Richard B. Pearson 12-11-1857 (no return)
Douglass, Sarah to Joel A. Woodall 1-26-1839 (no return)
Douthet, Elizabeth Jane to James H. McCoy 10-14-1855
Downum, Caroline to Bennett B. Smith 5-11-1844 (5-12-1844)
Downum, Mary to Dean Statum 10-23-1851 (10-24-1851)
Downum, Matilda to Isham Osborn 9-7-1853
Downum, Nancy L. to Jessee Vinson 12-3-1850
Downum, Sarah to Isaac Osborn 2-5-1849 (2-8-1849)
Drake, Frances C. to A. V. Nemmo 8-13-1856
Drake, Mary to John Keith 2-13-1861 (2-16-1861)
Drake, Musadora to Henry Harig 9-30-1853
Dravit, Sarah Jane to Francis A. Bartles 8-17-1865
Driver, Cynthia to Lewis Hill 9-14-1838 (9-24-1838)
Driver, M. M. to Robt. Price 6-10-1868 (6-14-1868)
Driver, Mahala to Newton Majors 4-22-1868 (no return)
Duboice, Mary to Thomas Hill 7-24-1838
Duboise, S. E. to Redmon Cruse 10-14-1869 (no return)
Duddue, M. A. to C. C. Garner 2-4-1874 (2-5-1871?)
Dumpley, Margrett to William Devim 2-26-1851
Dunbar, Rebecca to Peter Brown 1-1-1840
Duncan, Dicy to Andrew J. Duncan 12-23-1839
Duncan, Elizabeth to Thomas Anderson 5-6-1852 (5-7-1852)
Duncan, L. J. (Miss) to J. B. Boyce 1-12-1869 (no return)
Duncan, Lucy to John S. Lambert 7-27-1842 (8-10-1842)
Duncan, Margret to Lazarus Lawson 1-2-1854 (1-3-1854)
Duncan, Martisha to E. H. Ikard 1-1-1851 (1-2-1851)
Duncan, Mary to George W. Gipson 11-7-1872 (11-9-1872)
Duncan, Mary to James Burks 12-23-1871
Duncan, Mattie J. to C. F. Blair 12-19-1866 (12-20-1866)
Duncan, Patsy to William M. Reynolds 12-12-1839 (12-19-1839)
Duncan, Sarah to Joel Chitwood 1-21-1843 (1-22-1843)

Duncan, T. T. to J. B. Corn 12-22-1868 (12-23-1868)
Duncan, Terrissa K. to Payton S. Corn 9-12-1850
Duncan, Winey J. to Solomon A. Temple 8-15-1855
Durham, Frances to William C. Edwards 9-17-1846
Durham, Mary to G. L. Baker 11-26-1874 (11-27-1874)
Dyal, Martha to Nelson Finney 1-15-189 (1-17-1839)
Dyer, Manerva to William Weaver 2-19-1850
Dyer, Mary Jane to James M., jr. Matlock 5-8-1839 (5-9-1839)
Dyer, Sally to N. M. Smith 9-2-1865 (9-3-1865)
Earp, Annie to James Woods 11-23-1842
Easley, Pamey to Willim C. Hally 10-5-1838 (10-11-1838)
Edwards, Elizabeth to John D. Lynch 2-22-1871 (2-24-1871)
Edwards, Elizabeth to John Lambert 7-29-1846 (7-30-1846)
Edwards, Lucinda to Joseph J. Perkins 1-8-1846
Edwards, Matilda to James Williams 3-18-1854 (3-19-1854)
Edwards, Matilda to William Mitchell 12-24-1851 (no return)
Edwards, Nancy J. to M. C. Morgan 2-19-1855 (no return)
Eggleston, M. S. to Wm. M. Tankesley 3-31-1868 (no return)
Eggleston, Mary E. to Charles F. Burt 10-13-1856 (10-14-1856)
Egleston, Bessie to R. M. Dubose 12-16-1873 (12-18-1873)
Elkin, Mary E. to W. A. Moore 1-31-1860 (no return)
Elkins, Lucy E. to Wm. A. Mash 11-9-1857
Elkins, M. J. to Geo. E. Moore 9-?-1866
Elliott, Ellen to J. P. Francis 8-3-1868 (no return)
Elliott, Emily J. to John R. Mealer 1-7-1858 (no return)
Elliott, Esther A. to Francis A. Shoup 6-26-1871
Elliott, Judy A. m. to John Jackson 8-18-1866 (no return)
Elliott, Nancy to William Stewart 6-7-1841
Ellis, Elizabeth to William M. Powell 9-5-1846 (9-6-1846)
Ellis, Lucinda to John Wagner? 11-11-1851
Ellis, Lucinda to John Wagnewr? 11-11-1851
Ellis, Margret V. to Dennis Smith 8-15-1868 (8-16-1868)
Ellis, Mary A. to Josiah T. Walls 10-19-1854
Ellis, Nancy to John Powell 2-1-1845 (2-2-1845)
Ellitt, Judy Ann Mexico to John Jackson 8-18-1866 (no return)
Elmore, Marinda J. to Edward E. S. Howard 11-4-1851 (no return)
Elps, Ulis to E. G. Duckworth 9-23-1867 (9-26-1867)
Embrey, Adaline to Francis Turner 2-6-1845
Embrey, Eliza W. to Jessee B. Corn 9-2-1858
Embrey, Elizabeth to Samuel McKelvey 7-30-1840 (no return)
Embrey, Evalena to H. C. Patty 10-3-1866 (10-4-1866)
Embrey, Julia S. to S. D. Sims 4-11-1859 (4-12-1859)
Embrey, Lucy to James B. Garner 4-8-1841
Embrey, M. F. to John P. Hinton 11-15-1865
Embrey, Mary to Thomas Howard 4-24-1845
Embrey, Tempy to Christian Smith 3-10-1846
Embrey, Winney to Nathan D. Stamps 9-21-1838 (9-27-1838)
Embry, Mary E. to Barbe Nuckles 8-12-1852
Enghram, Martha to Wm. Vaughn 5-7-1868 (no return)
England, Frances C. to Andrew Jackson Brazelton 10-22-1839
England, Joanah to Newton Keith 12-28-1870 (no return)
England, Martha A. to Peter T. Hurt 4-23-1850
Englet, N. E. to John G. Hannah 6-21-1870 (no return)
Enochs, Laura V. to Samuel P. Bowling 5-10-1873 (5-14-1873)
Enochs, Martha to WilliamB. McKelvey 10-14-1857 (10-15-1857)
Enochs, Phebe A. J. to Elijah McKelvey 12-17-1857 (no return)
Enochs, Rebecca to William Higden 8-21?-1849 (8-24-1849?)
Enochs, Susan G. to John Parks 2-22-1854 (2-23-1854)
Epps, Elvira to Mathew J. S. Brown 9-14-1854
Ertes, Mary to James Starkey 11-15-1852
Erwin, Arbella to James R. Nance 4-19-1854 (4-20-1854)
Erwin, M. J. to J. J. Martin 1-9-1867 (1-8?-1867)
Escridge, Frances to Robt. J. Murphy 12-17-1839
Eskridge, Elizabeth L. to Coleman Franklin 11-11-1845
Eskridge, Mary to James H. Young 3-8-1852 (3-11-1852)
Eskridge, Rebecca J. to Samuel M. Farmer 11-14-1843 (11-21-1843)
Estell, Nancy J. to A. H. Martin 4-19-1839
Estill, Agnes E. to Arther S. Colyar 12-9-1847
Estill, Ann W. to Harrison T. Carr 1-15-1856
Estill, Elizabeth to Charles P. Cochran 5-24-1855
Estill, Elizabeth to Joseph M. Burrough 12-8-1840 (no return)
Estill, Fannie W. to George W. Warner 12-20-1865
Estill, Jane E. to Elmore R. Horton 1-25-1856
Estill, Jemima C. to John H. Decherd 8-5-1851
Estill, Jennie W. to G. M. Ray 11-20-1873 (no return)

Estill, Jennie to Wm. J. Pryor 9-11-1867
Estill, Lelia T. to Merrier W. Garner 1-6-1848
Estill, Lizzie A. to H. L. Turney 10-29-1859 (10-30-1859)
Estill, M. E. (Miss) to Hayden March 2-15-1869
Estill, Martha A. to Robinson Teasdale 12-13-1842 (12-14-1842)
Estill, Mary L. to Joseph W. Carter 11-18-1847
Etherly, Elizabeth A. to James S. Gillaspie 8-14-1858 (8-15-1858)
Etherly, Missouri C. to R. S. Donaldson 12-10-1856 (12-11-1856)
Ethridge, Elizabeth to John W. Williams 8-19-1857 (no return)
Ethridge, Elizabeth to John W. Williams 8-19-1859 (no return)
Ethridge, Nancy to Francis G. McClure 2-24-1858
Evans, Mary Ann to William Lasater 10-2-1852 (10-3-1852)
Evans, R. A. (Miss) to R. M. McKinney 4-25-1869 (4-24?-1869)
Evans, Sarah E. to A. J. Rich 10-6-1852 (10-7-1852)
Evans, Semantha to John E. Langston 12-10-1843
Ewing, M. E. to William Holbert 4-19-1860 (no return)
Fagg, F. A. to G. M. Smith 12-25-1867 (12-26-1867)
Fagg, L. C. to W. R. C. Randol 12-9-1872 (12-10-1872)
Fannan, Nancy to Allen Lackey 2-14-1839 (no return)
Fanning, Elizabeth to James A. Hudgins 9-7-1865 (10-8-1865)
Fanning, Victoria to W. M. Reynolds 9-26-1858
Faris, Ann F. to William Brazelton 1-8-1851 (no return)
Faris, Elender to Richard Jackson 5-25-1849
Faris, Eliza Jane to H. L. Farris 2-15-1866
Faris, Fannie to George R. Martin 6-15-1870
Faris, Jane to Josiah Miller 6-14-1843 (6-15?-1843)
Faris, Lottie Ann to Walter Braly 4-3-1851 (4-4-1851)
Faris, Lucy J. to James S. Faris 12-20-1854 (12-21-1854)
Faris, Manervia to William jr. Brazelton 9-23-1846 (no return)
Faris, Margret E. to Solomon S. Groves 8-17-1872 (no return)
Faris, Martha M. to Luke Hale 12-24-1851
Faris, Mary Louisa to Armstead Campbell 9-14-1846 (9-16-1846)
Farmer, A. E. C. to Wm. Skidmore 7-12-1860 (7-9-1860?)
Farmer, Mary A. to Putman Lawson 3-18-1854 (no return)
Farmer, Mary H. to Thomas O. Garvin 3-2-1848
Farmer, Sarah to John L. Bishop 6-6-1855
Farmer, Sarena to D. H. Haverse? 3-28-1846
Farrell, Nancy to David Lyons 11-27-1839 (no return)
Farris, Amanda A. to G. I. Dishroom 6-5-1867
Farris, Amandy E. to John C. Holder 3-12-1846
Farris, Ann C. to Francis M. Green 1-30-1871 (no return)
Farris, Ann to Wm. D. Faris 3-30-1843
Farris, Edetha (Mrs.) to J. D. Eslick 10-11-1870 (no return)
Farris, Elizabeth to Fredrick Williams 12-21-1869
Farris, Elizabeth to Michael Turney 12-27-1843 (12-28-1843)
Farris, Elvira A. to John Dolby 12-23-1852 (12-26-1852)
Farris, Eveline to Thomas D. Farris 2-18-1841 (no return)
Farris, Fannie to Ephram Bryant 9-18-1873 (9-15?-1873)
Farris, Glathia T. to John Jeans 1-24-1871 (1-23?-1871)
Farris, Jane C. to Josiah Miller 10-28-1843
Farris, Jane to Michael Hufman 11-20-1849
Farris, Jennie T. to S. M. Jackson 12-14-1870 (no return)
Farris, Lucinda to Sidney Downum 12-23-1858
Farris, Mary Ann to W. H. Davis 12-2-1874 (12-3-1874)
Farris, Mary E. to Henry B. Flemming 11-14-1870
Farris, Mary E. to John H. Morris 3-16-1848
Farris, Mary J. to C. C. Holder 7-17-1858 (7-18-1858)
Farris, Mary V. to Hugh Blackwood 12-26-1850
Farris, Mary to Clement C. Mattenlee 8-3-1841
Farris, Matilda E. to Phinnis W. Center 8-12-1874 (8-18-1874)
Farris, Mollie E. to J. J. Whitesides 12-18-1871 (no return)
Farris, Nancy Y. to John R. Moseley 5-10-1847 (5-13-1847)
Farris, Nancy to M. L. Owens 6-17-1868
Farris, S. C. to Wm. M. Cowan 2-14-1870 (no return)
Farris, Sarah E. to Thomas Cunningham 1-31-1861
Farris, Sarah T. to William Long 4-12-1848 (4-13-1848)
Farris, Sarah to Robt. S. Smith 8-10-1865 (8-13-1865)
Farrow, Ardena to Henry Sherrill 9-14-1855 (no return)
Faucett, M. R. to C. C. Williams 7-4-1874 (7-5-1874)
Featherston, Luvinia to Perry H. Parks 7-6-1857 (7-7-1857)
Featherston, Susan to Daniel Lenehan 12-19-1868 (12-20-1868)
Featherston, T. E. to Thomas E. Lenehan 8-10-1872
Fergeson, D. to A. Payne 6-8-1867 (6-9-1867)
Fergeson, Martha to Wiley Gambel 2-7-1856
Fergeson, Sarah to Joseph M. Arnold 10-7-1855

Ferrell, Elender to Thomas D. W. Anderson 4-21-1858 (no return)
Ferrill, Nancy C. to Benj. L. Thornsberry 12-20-1854
Finch, Elizabeth A. to Henry Partin 7-6-1853 (no return)
Finch, Elizabeth M. to Samuel Hayter 9-26-1846
Finch, Frances E. to W. T. Denson 9-14-1867 (9-15-1867)
Finch, Martha Ann to Samuel Hinkle 10-5-1870
Finch, Mary E. to Hayden March 2-21-1839
Finch, Nancy K. to Rich Hill 1-4-1855
Finch, Rebecca to Alford H. Johnson 12-18-1845
Finch, Sarah E. to George W. Sharp 12-18-1844 (12-19-1844)
Finch, Susan to Wm. W. Sharp 4-9-1851 (4-10-1851)
Finley, Caroline to Elias Stallcup 2-22-1868 (2-23-1868)
Finley, M. C. to W. R. Stevens 8-7-1869 (no return)
Finley, Mary E. to Joseph B. Johnson 5-10-1860
Finney, Eleanor to Ruben Greenlee 12-24-1845
Finney, Elizabeth to Simon W. Bennett 1-18-1854
Finney, Ellen to D. C. Terrill 10-19-1856
Finney, Ellen to Wm. Bishop 3-27-1868 (3-29-1868)
Finney, Margret to Alfred H. Anderson 11-5-1855 (11-11-1855)
Finney, Mary Jane to W. C. Morris 5-21-1857 (no return)
Finney, Polly to James Dial 7-3-1844 (7-5-1844)
Finney, Sarah J. to George Perry 3-22-1871 (no return)
Fisher, Carrie to Hugo Hopfold 7-15-1873 (7-28-1873)
Fitch, Caroline to A. J. Gossage 12-16-1843 (12-17-1843)
Fitch, Mary J. to Asa Jarnagan 8-8-1866 (no return)
Fitch, Sally to William Gossage 2-12-1838 (2-15-1838)
Fitch, Sally to Wm. McDaniel 3-25-1868 (3-26-1868)
Fitzgerald, Mary to Huston Hill 8-?-1854 (8-1-1854)
Fitzgibbons, Catharine to Patrick Sullivan 10-30-1854 (10-31-1854)
Fitzpatrick, Elizabeth H. to Miles Wilkerson 1-26-1859 (no return)
Fleming, Sarah A. to Tobias D. Smith 8-15-1853 (8-18-1853)
Flemming, Mary E. to James W. Logan 10-31-1854 (11-2-1854)
Fletcher, E. P. to Wm. H. Acklin 12-6-1847 (12-7-1847)
Fletcher, Mary A. to Henry Dennis 9-13-1852 (9-19-1852)
Floyd, Christiana to Joshua Holder 12-21-1847
Floyd, Mary to Lorenza Lynch 9-15-1841
Ford, Delila to Newton Prince 8-22-1854
Ford, Emma E. to Newton M. Wright 1-25-1871
Ford, Frances E. to Martial H. Rich 10-24-1844
Ford, Hannah to Henry Dabs 3-4-1844 (3-6-1844)
Ford, Kesiah to Jeremiah Holt 5-6-1859 (5-8-1859)
Ford, Mary Ann to Jerry Holder 1-30-1846 (2-1-1846)
Foreman, Josephine to Allen Johnston 11-16-1857 (11-17-1857)
Foreman, Mary to Enoch Holt 12-7-1842 (12-8-1842)
Forshee, Caledonia to James H. Collins 12-17-1871 (no return)
Fortney, Jane to William Mallard 3-12-1858
Foster, Ann to Thos. Foster 9-24-1870
Foster, Eliza to Welbourn L. Farmer 10-19-1844 (10-20-1844)
Foster, Elizabeth to R. H. Chasteen 12-20-1859 (12-23-1859)
Foster, Lafebe to D. J. Sisk 5-28-1862 (5-30-1862)
Foster, Lou to Joseph Mason 12-2-1874 (12-3-1874)
Foster, Mary to Milford Prince 11-26-1853 (11-27-1853)
Foster, Nancy to James Mayes 8-13-1870 (no return)
Foster, Sarah A. to W. W. Patterson 10-9-1865 (10-10-1865)
Foster, Susan to James F. Spencer 7-10-1865 (7-12-1865)
Fowler, Mary A. to Joseph Pearson 11-28-1864 (12-1-1864)
Fowler, Susan E. to A. M. Cox 12-21-1865
Fox, Marinda E. to James W. Smith 3-9-1853 (no return)
Fraine, America to Joel Miller 9-7-1863 (no return)
Frame, Cynthia to John Baker 3-11-1844 (3-14-1844)
Frame, Elizabeth to John Metcalf 11-19-1870 (11-20-1870)
Frame, Martha to David F. Larkin 2-6-1846
Frame, Martha L. to W. R. Baggett 10-13-1859
Frame, Mary A. to Ruben W. Bales 2-16-1843
Frame, Phebias M. to Henry Hill 1-1-1841 (1-3-1841)
Frame, Rachael L. to Thomas Hutcherson 9-17-1857 (no return)
Francis, Clamensia to John Young 8-26-1848 (8-27-1848)
Francis, Clementine to Bishly A. Myers 3-26-1840 (no return)
Francis, Julia A. to Samuel Bowers 7-22-1851
Francis, Leaunah to Dyer Holder 2-15?-1838 (2-20-1838)
Francis, M. S. to J. M. Looney 10-29-1874 (no return)
Francis, Martha Jane to John Gross 11-26-1846 (11-30-1846)
Francis, Martha to James Thomas 12-3-1846 (12-5-1846)
Francis, Mary E. to Joseph Carter 4-24-1851
Francis, Mary Susan to Thomas Jones 12-17-1846

Francis, Mary to Noel Greer 11-7-1838 (11-8-1838)
Francis, Prudence to James H. Williams 8-29-1848
Francis, Violet to Thomas A. Keith 5-7-1874 (no return)
Franklin, David A. to Elizabeth A. Young 11-8-1849 (11-9-1849)
Franklin, Elizabeth M. to Calvin Renegar 11-1-1865 (11-3-1865)
Franklin, Elizabeth to Henry Cowan 9-28-1839 (9-29-1839)
Franklin, Hannah to Uriah Preitt 2-28-1856
Franklin, Lucinda to Alford Burt 12-22-1848
Franklin, Mahala to Daniel Kitchens 12-16-1871 (no return)
Franklin, Manerva to John Easterwood 4-11-1870
Franklin, Martha to William L. Frame 1-31-1844 (2-1-1844)
Franklin, Musadora to Isaac Estill 4-13-1853
Franklin, Nancy C. to Elisha Guinn 12-28-1846
Franklin, Rhoda P. to William W. Decher 12-23-1846 (12-24-1846)
Franklin, Siotha to Wm. R. A. Spindle 4-1-1844 (4-4-1844)
Franklin, Sofa to Morgan Spencer 9-10-1845 (9-11-1845)
Franks, Sarah E. to Lewis H. Hall 8-31-1865 (9-2-1865)
Frazier, Frances to George Thompson 1-28-1870 (1-29-1870)
Freeman, Frances E. to W. G. Reed 12-11-1872 (12-12-1872)
Freeman?, Mary E. to Andrew Duboise 3-27-1845 (no return)
Frost, Lyda to Elijah Alexander 8-18-1859 (8-19-1859)
Fults, Elizabeth to Wm. Winton 1-20-1873
Furgerson, Jane to Wm. Hoosier 8-4-1865 (8-7-1865)
Furgerson, Mandy to John Wells 8-18-1873
Furgerson, Tennessee to Henry Perkins 8-4-1873
Gadsey, Nannie to James S. Kelley 2-17-1852
Gage, Lotty to Farley B. Wade 8-6-1848
Gainer, Harriett to Bailey Hill 7-14-1857 (7-16-1857)
Gainer, Nancy Jane to Peter Barnes 7-2-1849
Gamble, Elizabeth to Jessee Briant 5-6-1851
Gamble, Elizabeth to William J. Farris 5-4-1841
Gamble, Lucinda to Thomas S. Myers 7-15-1850 (7-16-1850)
Gamble, Mary E. to G. W. Kelley 9-2-1869 (with 1867)
Gamble, Mehalia to Alford Martin 4-16-1844 (4-17-1844)
Gamble, Milley to Wiley Edwards 10-27-1843
Gambol, Mary M. to John W. Fitzpatrick 10-23-1867 (no return)
Gambol, Sarah to William Stephens 7-27-1871 (7-30-1871)
Garner, Angeline to John Sutton 8-7-1865 (8-10-1865)
Garner, Bettie to G. D. Taylor 12-22-1865 (1-12-1866)
Garner, C. A. to Geo. W. Farris 5-1-1845
Garner, Cassandra W. to Peter Turner 5-10-1851 (6-10-1851)
Garner, Cathrine H. to Francis T. Estill 2-12-1846
Garner, Dolly to Martin V. Rose 8-2-1856
Garner, Elizabeth to J. L. Brown 5-26-1860 (5-27-1860)
Garner, Elizabeth to James Craig 2-20-1843 (2-23-1843)
Garner, Elizabeth to James Long 10-4-1866 (10-11-1866)
Garner, Louisa to Wm. Prince 10-13-1853
Garner, M. E. to W. H. Maxey 9-5-1867
Garner, M. to Virgil Robinson 12-16-1867
Garner, Margret to James Hendly 12-25-1866
Garner, Margrett to Allen Gipson 1-3-1855
Garner, Margrett to Andrew Stephens 1-8-1843
Garner, Margrett to James Mason 8-14-1865 (8-15-1865)
Garner, Martha J. to George W. Long 9-5-1867 (9-3?-1867)
Garner, Martha L. to Hugh L. Rose 11-3-1855 (11-4-1855)
Garner, Mary A. to Jeremiah Perry 2-28-1842
Garner, Mary F. to J. M. Myres 4-20-1871 (4-20-1872?)
Garner, Mary Jane to George M. Marlow 7-24-1868 (9-28-1868)
Garner, Mary S. to James H. Davis 7-12-1842 (no return)
Garner, Mary S. to John Garner 6-26-1873 (6-27-1873)
Garner, Mary to A. Clifton 6-29-1859
Garner, Rachiel to John Berry 8-23-1858
Garner, Rebecca to Wilson C. Jackson 8-3-1854
Garner, Samira to H. G. W. Grant 9-15-1844
Garner, Sarah E. to Jno. Wiley 12-16-1868 (no return)
Garner, Sarah to James H. Collins 10-13-1873 (10-16-1873)
Garner, Sarah to Nathan Prince 10-13-1853
Garnett, Helena to W. L. Thompson 4-27-1871 (no return)
Garnett, Martha J. to John F. Cody 4-10-1865
Garnett, Mary A. to A. H. Lanham 12-17-1860 (12-24-1860)
Garnett, Rhoda C. to Wm. M. McNabb 12-30-1849
Garrett, Elizabeth C. to William H. Gilliam 5-23-1844 (5-25-1844)
Garrett, M. J. to J. R. Boyd 11-30-1847 (no return)
Garrett, Mary A. to James Gilliam 5-4-1842

Garrett, Mary to Ross B. Cowan 3-12-1857
Garrett, Sarah to Jacob Swann 7-4-1853
Gattis, Cordelia to H. F. Shapard 1-14-1868 (1-15-1868)
Gattis, Julia A. to F. M. Robinson 1-15-1866 (1-17-1866)
Gattis, Nancy E. to Newton M. Robinson 1-22-1861 (1-23-1861)
Gentle, Ann to Wm. Larkin 7-31-1858 (no return)
Gentle, Mary J. to James F. Wright 10-22-1866 (no return)
George, Haley to P. D. Reynolds 2-14-1859 (no return)
George, Marinda E. to N. F. Anderson 9-14-1865 (no return)
George, Susan to Sampson Gifford 1-12-1870 (no return)
Gibson, Martha to W. G. Gibson 1-11-1865 (1-12-1865)
Gibson, Mary to William Perry 9-15-1842 (no return)[*]
Gifford, Elizabeth to C. D. Tankesley 8-13-1869 (no return)
Gifford, Emeline to Thos. Davis 2-21-1867 (no return)
Gifford, Jane to Andrew Yates 6-6-1856
Gifford, Julia to John Turney 1-15-1855
Gifford, Lucinda to Edward Morris 12-15-1849
Gifford, Martha to Arther Bradford 5-1-1853
Gifford, Martha to Calvin Koger 10-9-1874 (10-11-1874)
Gifford, Nancy to John M. Crabtree 12-25-1856
Gifford, Sallie to Jacob Miller 3-9-1867
Gilbert, Mary C. to William T. South 12-14-1872 (12-19-1872)
Gilbert, Mollie to Stephen Becknell 12-5-1873 (no return)
Gilbert, R. J. to B. C. Seaton 12-16-1871 (12-17-1871)
Gilbert, Rebecca to James R. Graham 4-4-1853 (4-18-1853)
Gilbert, Sarah A. to A. N. Tarpley 8-29-1866 (no return)
Gillaspie, Cyntha to W. C. Raliston 1-17-1871 (no return)
Gillaspie, Lucinda to Jos. Clark 10-6-1859
Gillaspie, Lurana A. to Tipton L. Gillaspie 9-28-1854
Gillaspie, Musadora C. to William L. Oakley 11-12-1846
Gillespie, Cynthia to John Englent 10-3-1871 (no return)
Gillespie, Frances A. to Henderson Moore 7-25-1848
Gillespie, Frances H. to Anthony Street 10-17-1843
Gillespie, July L. to Asa D. Oakley 10-29-1842 (10-30-1842)
Gillespie, Paulina A. to James H. Gillespie 1-9-1856 (1-10-1856)
Gilliam, Ann to Isaac Gibson 9-20-1843 (9-21-1843)
Gilliam, Catharine to Benjamin Morris 1-14-1845
Gilliam, Eliza to John H. Ashley 9-1-1843 (no return)
Gilliam, Nancy to John Gipson 9-24-1849 (9-25-1849)
Gilliam, Nancy to William Brown 6-23-1842
Gilliam, Sarah A. to A. M. Garrett 9-16-1840 (9-20-1840)
Gilliam, Sarah Ann to Amos Richardson 5-10-1856 (5-11-1856)
Gilliam, Sarah E. to James C. Jackson 8-18-1874 (8-28-1874)
Gipson, A. E. to W. D. Collins 5-25-1874 (3?-31-1874)
Gipson, Angeline to P. H. Helton 6-2-1847 (6-4-1847)
Gipson, Delitha to R. J. Gillespie 4-20-1872 (4-22-1872)
Gipson, Elizabeth to Jessee R. Hill 12-29-1849 (12-30-1849)
Gipson, Magret to John Banks 2-9-1846
Gipson, Mahala to Henry A. Driver 1-23-1845 (1-26-1845)
Gipson, Margaret to Obediah Bean 3-24-1853
Gipson, Margret to Reubin Richardson 1-25-1850
Gipson, Martha J. to John J. Hendley 5-6-1872 (5-8-1872)
Gipson, Martha to William R. Richardson 12-25-1860
Gipson, Mary to Washington Austin 12-20-1845
Gipson, Nancy J. to Wm. Dossett 7-6-1854 (7-9-1854)
Gipson, Nancy to John Garner 8-1-1848 (8-2-1848)
Gipson, Phebia to John Hill 4-18-1850 (4-21-1850)
Gipson, Ryna to John Perry 9-20-1851 (9-21-1851)
Gipson, Sallie A. to James Harrison 12-23-1867 (no return)
Gipson, Sarah Ann to Francis M. Hill 12-18-1860 (12-14?-1860)
Gipson, Sarah to John Hill 3-22-1848
Gipson, Sarah to John Long 1-8-1844
Gipson, Susan to George W. Garner 12-29-1851
Gipson, Vickey to Robt. Radford 8-19-1857 (no return)
Gipsoni, Milly to Melmuth Coker 1-1-1841
Gist, Margret to William Victory 3-5-1855
Gist, Terrissa to F. M. Smith 3-3-1854
Glaze, Julia Ann to William Dotson 9-18-1847 (9-19-1847)
Glover, Milly J. to Isaac H. Hall 5-23-1857 (5-24-1857)
Gocher, T. E. to J. M. Ikard 6-11-1866 (no return)
Goddard, C. J. to James A. Leveret 2-1-1868
Gofer, Sarah to William P. Rogers 11-26-1860
Goff, Frances to George Brewer 10-24-1865 (10-25-1865)
Goff, Rachael to B. B. Posey 12-19-1855 (12-25-1855)
Golden, Mollie T. (Miss) to David A. Tucker 4-23-1873 (no return)

Goldin, Margaret to John A. Combs 12-12-1843 (no return)
Gonce, Lydia to Bledsoe Stewart 2-19-1846
Goodloe, E. A. to Tyree Riddle 11-15-1871 (no return)
Goodloe, Jane W. to M. P. Reagin 9-13-1849
Goodloe, Nancy to James R. Ragin 3-24-1847 (3-25-1847)
Goodman, Susan to David Gipson 11-13-1852 (no return)
Gorden, Harriette E. to Henderson Overby 9-15-1868 (9-16-1868)
Gore, Elizabeth to Hayden Hunt 11-27-1849 (no return)
Gore, Ginnatha to James Hampton 1-2-1845
Gore, Louisa to Thomas Gore 9-29-1851
Gore, Mary to Mathew Powers 11-14-1865 (11-16-1865)
Gore, Nancy to Thomas H. Fares 1-5-1842 (no return)
Gossage, Martha . to Robert Tate 3-7-1867
Gossage, Mary A. to John Hester 4-1-1854 (no return)
Gossage, Sally to H. A. Bingham 2-26-1840
Gossage, Sarah C. to Wm. H. Purdom 12-31-1868
Gover, Elizabeth to Benjamin Elliott 12-18-1846
Grabarr, Mary to George Seay 7-15-1873 (12-16-1873)
Graham, Elizabeth A. to Benj. W. Corn 3-19-1849 (3-20-1849)
Graham, Sarah E. to Joel Blackwell 1-24-1843
Grammer, B. J. to H. F. Sanders 3-25-1870 (3-27-1870)
Grammer, Eliza to Jas. Renfro 1-10-1872 (1-11-1872)
Grammer, Mary to Jefferson Lasater 2-20-1872
Grammor, Emily to Felix H. Sanders 9-3-1853 (9-4-1853)
Grant, E. C. to Robert Dean 12-23-1866 (no return)
Grant, Lucinda to Nathan Davis 3-31-1855 (4-1-1855)
Grant, Milly to Alex P. Syler 2-1-1871 (2-2-1871)
Grant, Sarah to Peter Limbaugh 1-18-1854 (1-19-1854)
Graves, Florence M. to G. E. Folwell 8-1-1865 (8-2-1865)
Graves, Mary J. to George W. Gan 9-7-1867 (9-8-1867)
Graves, Nancy J. to Thos. S. Rogers 10-15-1855 (no return)
Graves, Sarah to M. A. Bradberry 6-10-1866 (no return)
Graves, Sophia to Chas. W. Chasteen 9-27-1855
Gray, Lou E. to Webster Tatum 9-3-1873 (9-4-1873)
Gray, Louisa to John M. Phillips 3-15-1845 (3-16-1845)
Gray, Mary E. to W. T. Dardis 2-23-1842 (no return)
Gray, Rachiel to Hiram J. Carter 9-28-1872 (10-1-1872)
Gray, Rachiel to Jacob Goodman 9-21-1849
Gray, Susan to Nathan Sims 2-10-1845 (2-15-1845)
Graybill, Susan to James Cole 11-14-1871 (11-16-1871)
Green, Ann A. to James C. Bowdon 12-24-1847
Green, Ann T. to Anthony N. Keith 12-8-1850 (no return)
Green, Eliza H. to James K. Shook 10-10-1844
Green, Jane E. to Marian W. Williams 9-22-1849 (9-23-1849)
Green, Lucretia to Thos. Malone 7-31-1869
Green, Malinda to James Anderson 12-31-1868 (no return)
Green, Martha E. to Joseph W. Tipps 10-17-1870 (10-18-1870)
Green, Martha to Tillman Arledge 10-29-1842 (10-30-1842)
Green, Mary F. to Jonathan Elbords 9-13-1844
Green, Mary to William G. Jenkins 3-7-1840 (no return)
Green, Nancy W. to Robt. J. Green 11-17-1840 (11-19-1840)
Green, Nancy to Richard B. Thacker 2-12-1841 (2-21-1841)
Green, S. S. to J. M. Colton 2-14-1870 (no return)
Green, Sarah Ann to Daniel Ashbrook 11-26-1849
Green, Susan (Mrs.) to John Crawford 9-15-1869 (no return)
Green, Unieca A. to William Wilkerson 3-26-1852 (3-27-1852)
Greenlee, Julia to William Sanders 1-14-1839 (no return)
Greenlee, Louisa to Thornton Goolsby 6-18-1844
Greenlee, Nancy to Josiah Hill 2-8-1849
Greer, Sarah J. to James T. Fitzpatrick 10-11-1865 (10-12-1865)
Gregg, Mary A. to Wm. E. Wilmarding 6-27-1872 (no return)
Gregory, Eliza to W. E. Murrell 11-7-1866 (no return)
Gregory, Emily to James M. Spencer 3-21-1859 (3-22-1859)
Gregory, Emily to James M. Spencer 3-21-1859 (3-27-1859)
Gregory, Jemima to James W. Davis 9-3-1855 (9-?-1855)
Grider, Elizabeth to J. F. McCovey 2-7-1867 (2-3?-1867)
Griffin, Frances to Chesley B. Bostic 12-13-1842 (12-10?-1842)
Griffin, Nancy to John Simpson 1-28-1867
Grills, Susan P. to William Sims 10-1-1840
Grizzard, Laura to George W. Hale 1-26-1852 (1-29-1852)
Groom, Caroline to George Tarwater 12-6-1846 (12-7-1846)
Gross, Barbary E. to Andrew Smith 8-14-1872 (no return)
Gross, Barbrey to Abram M. Jones 10-24-1844 (no return)
Gross, Martha to Wm. Partin 10-7-1868 (10-8-1868)
Gross, Mary to John B. Francis 6-30-1842

Gross, Rosanna to Stephen M. Francis 4-8-1841 (no return)
Guanant, C. P. M. E. A. to Thomas M. Romius 8-14-1849
Guarant, Malinda to Josiah Reed 8-9-1842 (8-14-1842)
Guess, Elizabeth to Abram Baggett 10-26-1844 (10-27-1844)
Guin, Susan to Anthony Bradfort 7-15-1850
Guinn, Manerva to Anderson Hill 3-25-1841
Guinn, Margret to Jordan Alexander 4-10-1854
Guinn, Mary A. to John Reader 5-9-1850 (5-12-1850)
Guinn, Mary E. to James Rose 3-3-1870 (3-6-1870)
Guinn, Ury to Davy Hill 3-13-1844 (3-16-1844)
Gunn, Nancy to William Capshaw 1-8-1840
Guthery, Sarah to William Decker 12-24-1850 (12-25-1850)
Guthree, Hannah to John Dyal 3-24-1841 (no return)
Guthrie, Caroline to Andrew J. Norwood 4-24-1841
Hacher, Nannie V. to W. P. Allen 11-23-1872 (10?-10-1873)
Haislep, Nancy J. m. to Joseph G. Burt 8-22-1857 (no return)
Hale, Cathrine J. to Randolph, jr. Rose 9-11-1851 (9-16-1851)
Hale, Margrett A. to Anthony Hunt 5-6-1874 (no return)
Haley, Mahala to Franklin Reed 8-27-1839
Hall, A. E. (Miss) to A. T. Crawford 3-20-1869 (3-21-1869)
Hall, Amanda M. to Nathaniel Mills 4-17-1852 (no return)
Hall, Amanda M. to Wm. C. Roach 9-6-1858
Hall, Cathrine to Abram Smith 9-11-1851
Hall, Hulda to Wm. R. Ellis 11-6-1871 (no return)
Hall, Louisa to Levi Mason 7-22-1852 (7-23-1852)
Hall, Martha J. to John A. Ellis 12-4-1871 (no return)
Hall, Susanah to James P. Roach 8-31-1854
Hallowell, Jane to W. H. Renegar 8-2-1858 (no return)
Hamilton, F. E. to Robt. Stamper 8-27-1870 (8-29-1870)
Hammer, Mary to Jonathan J. Prince 9-24-1847 (9-26-1847)
Hammer, Matilda to John M. Bass 12-19-1867 (no return)
Hammingtree, Sarah to George W. Mann 8-28-1860
Hammon, Elizabeth to Henry H. Jones 4-4-1854 (4-6-1854)
Hammonds, Cathrine to James H. Anderson 5-31-1869 (no return)
Hammons, Elizabeth to W. D. Bethel 5-19-1859
Hammons, Issabella to C. D. Trolenger 4-14-1859
Hammontree, Malinda to John J. Riggins 5-5-1842 (5-15-1842)
Hammontree, Nancy M. to Wilson D. Wiseman 1-24-1850 (1-27-1850)
Handley, Martha A. to L. S. Sims 11-13-1866 (11-14-1866)
Handly, Sallie Ann to James N.? White 3-1-1853 (no return)
Haney, Aurenia to Alford Harny 11-15-1856 (11-16-1856)
Haning, Sophia to David A. Heytt 12-12-1855 (no return)
Hanks, Mary to John Buchanan 12-1-1857
Hanley, Nancy J. M. to Jos. G. Burt 8-23-1858
Hannah, Jane to George Gillaspie 3-7-1852 (3-8-1852)
Hannah, Lizzie to James Bledsoe 3-16-1865
Hannah, M. J. to J. H. Foster 2-29-1868 (3-1-1868)
Hannah, Mary to John H. Larkin 1-1-1862 (1-3-1862)
Hannah, S. A. to N. M. Horton 11-15-1858 (11-16-1858)
Hannah, Sallie A. to Newton Horton 11-15-1859 (no return)
Hannah, Sallie A. to Newton M. Horton 11-15-1858 (no return)
Haralson, Vic to Perry Harrison 9-5-1867
Harden, Polly Ann to John Hardin 12-25-1850 (no return)
Hardey, Anna to John J. Thurston 5-8-1856
Hardy, Leah to D. G. Branch 2-3-1866 (no return)
Hardyman, Elizabeth to J. R. Higginbotham 3-19-1869 (3-23-1869)
Hargess, Feba to David Patterson 2-24-1851
Harington, Mariah to Jessee Bradford 5-6-1858 (no return)
Harris, A. M. to Wm. Boatman 9-26-1865 (10-3-1865)
Harris, C. E. to William M. Holland 11-1-1870 (no return)
Harris, Lucy A. to Samuel Ramsey 8-14-1855 (8-15-1855)
Harris, Mary C. to H. P. Stewart 11-26-1867
Harris, Rebecca J. to Charles L. Jones 9-12-1854 (9-15-1854)
Harrison, Nancy F. to James B. Baggett 10-1-1849 (no return)
Hart, Charlotta to G. W. Thompson 11-9-1858 (11-11-1858)
Hart, Missouria to John H. Duncan 12-22-1866 (12-23-1866)
Hasket, Sarah A. to John Gour 7-7-1842
Haskin, Martha to D. S. Gross 11-22-1870 (11-23-1870)
Hasty, Josephine to James A. Smith 6-8-1865
Hasty, Mary to James M. C. Davenport 12-7-1844 (12-8-1844)
Hasty, Mary to Richard Jones 4-4-1860 (no return)
Hasty, Sarah to J. K. Cobb 2-9-1842 (2-10-1842)
Hatchett, E. E. to Thos. J. Noah 1-19-1860 (no return)
Hatchett, Elizabeth to Wm. R. Arnett 1-3-1853 (1-4-1853)
Hatchett, Jane C. B. to Reuben Tarrant 1-29-1859 (1-30-1859)

Hatchett, Martha A. to Claborn N. Williams 2-2-1854 (2-7-1854)
Hatchett, Mary L. to William T. Wakefield 12-21-1857 (12-23-1857)
Hatchett, Olivia to John O. Bridges 9-19-1867
Hatchett, Sarah S. to Sherman Tipton 10-13-1851
Hatchett, Susan to Felix Green 1-11-1858 (no return)
Hatchett, Susan to John T. Green 12-20-1846 (12-24-1846)
Hatton, Elizabeth A. to Nathan, jr. Green 1-18-1844
Hawkins, B. A. to James Pearson 9-20-1868
Hawkins, Jennie to L. R. Sartin 11-5-1873 (11-6-1873)
Hawkins, Mary Mariah to Alexander R. Wiggs 9-3-1846
Hawkins, Nancy to Machessna Moore 1-8-1852 (no return)
Haws, Elizabeth to John R. Clay 7-17-1848
Haynes, Lucy to P. A. Nelson 2-5-1866 (2-11-1866)
Hays, Caroline to Jonas Barnes 5-18-1849 (5-20-1849)
Hays, Eliza to Benjamin Byrom 10-18-1847 (10-19-1847)
Hays, Elizabeth Ann to James W. Walls 5-23-1849
Hays, Ellen to John Hill 11-7-1865 (11-24-1865)
Hays, Mary to Daniel M. Bates 2-13-1849
Hazup, Mary E. to Wm. Qualls 10-13-1869
Head, Cathrine to James Walton 8-11-1859
Heaston, Mary Ann to Archibald M. Breeden 9-2-1845 (9-?-1845)
Heathcoat, Martha A. to William Adams 12-13-1852 (12-14-1852)
Hedgepeth, Telithia to E. M. Orear 9-12-1872
Hefner, Sarah C. to Peter Harden 3-4-1859
Heith, America to Abram Welch 4-10-1858 (4-11-1858)
Helton, Angeline to Larkin Morris 8-1-1874 (no return)
Helton, Elizabeth to G. Nevels 1-20-1859
Helton, Sarah E. to Andron Chasteen 11-29-1858 (11-30-1858)
Henderson, Julia to Joseph Carter 9-20-1853
Henderson, Susan F. to William M. Bradford 2-16-1848
Hendley, Amanda to James Coarton 11-7-1865 (11-24-1865)
Hendley, Amanda to Wm. Filpot 9-9-1869 (no return)
Hendley, D. to James A. Hilton 12-7-1874 (12-8-1874)
Hendley, Elizabeth to Jefferson Payne 1-1-1859 (no return)
Hendley, Mary to Z. J. Ellison 5-2-1844
Hendley, Nancy A. to William T. Garner 7-6-1874
Hendley, Rebecca to John P. Miller 7-23-1839 (7-24-1839)
Hendley, Virginia to Mathew B. Davidson 3-2-1867 (3-4-1867)
Hendly, S. A. to H. Barnett 8-2-1867
Hendricks, Caroline to Eli Chambers 8-11-1856 (8-14-1856)
Hendricks, Matilda to W. S. S. Haynes 8-15-1867 (9-15-1867)
Hendricks, Musadora C. to Patrick L. Perry 10-4-1852 (10-5-1852)
Hendricks, Nancy E. to Isham Epps 12-24-1849 (12-25-1849)
Hendricks, Susan to William P. Black 1-7-1868 (no return)
Hendrix, Angelina M. to Mathew Tally 12-18-1842
Hendrix, Telitha to John Noah 5-30-1839
Heniford, Tenner E. to J. R. Bratton 11-29-1870 (12-1-1870)
Henkle, Elizabeth to John F. Sanders 9-28-1870 (9-29-1870)
Henley, Martha to F. B. Faris 7-11-1838 (7-?-1838)
Henley, Tennessee to Allen Hill 4-20-1872
Hensey?, Sarah to James Crafford 3-26-1854
Henshaw, Eliza to Henry Crawford 10-29-1839
Henshaw, Sarah to Pearce Wilhoit 12-30-1867
Henson, Lotta to James Holder 5-8-1874 (5-17-1874)
Henson, Sarah to John Wilkinson 11-22-1846
Herriford, Rachael to Thomas S. Camp 3-7-1838 (no return)
Herriford, Sally Ann to Elisha H. Sims 10-24-1838 (no return)
Herring, Jennie to A. H. Horton 8-17-1869 (no return)
Herrington, Susan to J. M. Coots 6-2-1874 (6-3-1874)
Hessey, Mary E. to Thos. J. Gossage 3-10-1868
Hester, Martha to John Parks 1-13-1855 (no return)
Hice, Catherine to Arther N. Stephens 4-7-1851 (4-9-1851)
Hice, Christiana E. to Alfred Ray 10-1-1851
Hice, E. E. to William C. Lesley 1-1-1848 (1-5-1848)
Hice, N. N. M. to J. S. Rolman 2-6-1860 (no return)
Hice, Sophia C. to Henderson Church 8-9-1854
Hickman, Elizabeth C. to William C. Eggleston 10-28-1857 (10-29-1857)
Hickman, Sophia to J. C. Wiseman 3-29-1841 (no return)
Hicks, Sarah to W. T. Richardson 7-25-1867 (7-29-1867)
Higgenbotham, Permelia A. to William J. Tipps 12-8-1860 (12-10-1860)
Higginbotha, Mary A. to James M. Waggoner 9-29-1857 (10-11-1857)
Higginbotham, M. to D. Tipps 1-25-1870 (no return)
Higginbotham, Mary A. to John J. Fletcher 11-21-1854 (not executed)
Higginbotham, Nancy J. to Joseph T. Wagner 1-7-1856 (1-13-1856)
Higginbotham, Susan F. to Thomas J. Tipps 1-7-1858 (1-10-1858)
Highamer, Sarah (Mrs.) to A. B. Cummings 1-29-1861 (11?-29-1861)
Hightower, Eveline to Jessee D. Statham 1-3-1841
Hiles, Elizabeth J. to Tate Statum 3-5-1858 (3-7-1858)
Hill, Amanda to William Russell 10-18-1843
Hill, Amelia A. to Thos. H. Finch 2-8-1854
Hill, Cyntha to David Perry 3-11-1874 (3-12-1874)
Hill, Cyntha to Lemuel Guinn 4-27-1870 (no return)
Hill, Eliza to John Phelps 7-31-1851
Hill, Elizabeth to Andrew Gipson 3-2-1849 (3-4-1849)
Hill, Elizabeth to Hosea Bohana 2-21-1866 (no return)
Hill, Elizabeth to Jessee Ethridge 8-24-1853 (8-25-1853)
Hill, Elizabeth to Solomon Perry 6-5-1845
Hill, Elizabeth to T. J. Williams 1-2-1861 (1-3-1861)
Hill, Emeline to Matthew McKelvey 11-6-1847 (no return)
Hill, Emily to Hasten Dial 6-29-1850
Hill, Frances M. to James A. Phillips 10-4-1838
Hill, Hannah L. to James N. Roberson 12-24-1874
Hill, Issabell to Charles C. Oliver 7-28-1853 (7-29-1853)
Hill, Jane to Wm. Brewer 8-20-1867 (8-22-1867)
Hill, Jemima to John Morris 5-2-1842 (no return)
Hill, Lizzie to William Morris 1-26-1870 (2-1-1870)
Hill, Malinda to Joseph Barnes 2-3-1849 (2-4-1849)
Hill, Malinda to Joshua Franklin 11-23-1846 (11-24-1846)
Hill, Margret to A. K. Malone 5-21-1870 (5-22-1870)
Hill, Margret to R. Walls 11-2-1867
Hill, Mariah W. to Arrington C. Williams 9-30-1856 (no return)
Hill, Mariah to Jasper McKee 3-14-1857 (3-15-1857)
Hill, Martha to Burrell Campbell 11-9-1838 (no return)
Hill, Martha to Jas. Sansom 10-25-1865 (10-29-1865)
Hill, Martha to Leroy P. Williams 3-9-1843
Hill, Mary A. to George D. Steel 2-10-1866 (2-11-1866)
Hill, Mary A. to Virgil C. Wright 4-1-1857
Hill, Mary Ann to James Smith 2-20-1872 (2-21-1872)
Hill, Mary E. to Flemming J. Sisco 10-30-1858 (not executed)
Hill, Mary E. to Wm. Mays 11-19-1855 (no return)
Hill, Mary J. to John L. Gipson 1-15-1853
Hill, Mary J. to Samuel R. Oakley 1-9-1847 (1-10-1847)
Hill, Mary Jane to Marion Partin 7-27-1847
Hill, Mary to Huston Hill 7-26-1854
Hill, Mary to John Fitzgerald 8-4-1851
Hill, Mary to John O. Royalty 1-2-1841? (1-2-1842)
Hill, Nancy E. to John Ricketts 11-17-1856
Hill, Nancy to Samuel Weaver 10-17-1838 (10-20-1838)
Hill, Nannie to William T. League 8-3-1871
Hill, Peggy to Henry Wallace 11-11-1839 (no return)
Hill, Prudy Ann to Jackson L. Mays 3-5-1849
Hill, Rosana to W. R. Hockersmith 12-14-1867
Hill, S. E. to H. P. Hughes 4-20-1870
Hill, Sallie A. to M. Davis 2-26-1870 (no return)
Hill, Sallie to Wm. Bishop 9-30-1867
Hill, Sarah to Ezra H. Poe 8-23-1851 (no return)
Hill, Sarah to Hiram Anderson 5-13-1850
Hill, Sarah to Jas. Doty 7-5-1871
Hill, Sarah to S. P. Payne 8-26-1868
Hill, Sarah to Samuel Barnet? 8-20-1856
Hill, Sarah to Samuel Bramet? (no dates)
Hill, Susan to James Brinkley 11-6-1872 (no return)
Hill, Telitha to Rolin Hill 4-30-1873
Hiltohn, Sarah E. to James B. Nichols 3-8-1849 (no return)
Hilton, L. E. to D. B. Tipps 5-16-1871 (5-18-1871)
Hines, Elizabeth to Wm. W. Martin 3-2-1853 (3-3-1851?)
Hines, Joanna to Samuel M. Miller 9-7-1872 (9-8-1872)
Hines, Laura E. to Samuel W. Side 3-24-1869 (no return)
Hines, Lou to J. A. Porter 8-14-1871 (no return)
Hines, M. L. to W. S. Embrey 12-10-1870 (no return)
Hines, Mary Ann to John J. Miller 9-18-1838 (9-20-1838)
Hines, Mollie E. to Wm. M. Keith 11-7-1871 (no return)
Hines, Sarah L. to John S. Farris 11-29-1839
Hinkle, Eliza to Samuel Stalcups 12-1-1857 (12-2-1857)
Hinton, Sarah to S. P. Kirby 1-3-1861
Hise, Anna V. to George W. L. Heath 1-25-1851 (1-26-1851)
Hise, Loucinda to Thomas Lasley 9-26-1849
Hise, Louisa to Harpeth Sanders 1-3-1861

Hise, Lucy E. to Esquire Hockersmith 1-20-1866 (1-21-1866)
Hise, Mariah to Nicholass J. Pulliam 12-24-1842 (12-25-1842)
Hise, Sarah S. E. to George W. Brown 1-17-1866
Hockersmith, P. J. to Elijah McKinzie 11-15-1871
Hockersmith, Sarah A. to Atwood McKinzie 2-2-1852 (2-4-1852)
Hockersmith, Sarah to J. L. Hise 11-14-1868 (11-15-1868)
Hockersmith, Susan to Hannible Wright 11-18-1856 (12-21-1856)
Hodge, Sarah to Isaac Cook 7-11-1871 (no return)
Hodges, Justine to William N. Ragsdale 10-5-1839 (10-6-1839)
Holcom, Mary Ann to Joshua Muse 6-22-1856
Holcomb, Eliza to A. L. Crabtree 11-26-1866 (12-12-1866)
Holden, Sarah to D. M. Baytes 3-18-1841 (no return)
Holder, America M. to George W. Crabtree 12-27-1873 (1-1-1873?)
Holder, Bernatty to William P. Keith 9-14-1843
Holder, Caroline to John R. Thomas 10-18-1873 (no return)
Holder, Elizabeth to Andrew Mathews 5-16-1843
Holder, Elizabeth to John Holder 9-2-1852
Holder, Elizabeth to P. G. Sells 9-5-1866 (no return)
Holder, Elizabeth to Russell McKinney 9-12-1848 (no return)
Holder, Emeline to E. B. Byrom 11-23-1868
Holder, Frances to James C. McKinney 8-7-1854 (8-8-1854)
Holder, Gilley (Miss) to B. G. Walker 9-7-1868 (9-9-1868)
Holder, Huldah to William Elliott 11-7-1844 (11-17-1844)
Holder, Julia A. to W. C. Looney 8-10-1870 (no return)
Holder, Leanna to John W. Kelley 8-1-1850
Holder, Lucinda to Jacob Holt 9-26-1838 (9-27-1838)
Holder, Lucinda to James Lakey 6-12-1840 (6-15-1840)
Holder, Lucy to Isaac Jernegan 8-19-1852
Holder, Lucy to Joseph Grier 10-5-1854
Holder, M. A. to A. F. Williams 8-30-1866
Holder, M. J. to E. F. Dickson 9-9-1868 (9-10-1868)
Holder, Mahulda to William Holder 8-24-1843
Holder, Martha to James A. Hoges 3-19-1853 (3-24-1853)
Holder, Mary A. to Hartwell Moseley 11-30-1855
Holder, Mary J. to John M. Lynch 3-10-1874 (3-12-1874)
Holder, Mary S. to Isaac Young 9-25-1867 (no return)
Holder, Mary to J. H. Woods 11-18-1856
Holder, Nancy to Enoch Stewart 10-2-1847 (10-3-1847)
Holder, Sarah to B. W. Harrison 8-20-1859 (8-21-1859)
Holder, Sarah to Elijah Jearnegan 12-30-1852
Holder, Sarah to Stanford Anthony 9-12-1843
Holder, Susan to Robert McKinney 10-17-1847
Holiday, Jennie to John Wade 12-13-1869 (no return)
Holiway, L. J. to John Barnes 10-4-1872 (10-25-1872)
Holland, M. E. to B. F. Knight 12-30-1865 (no return)
Holland, M. E. to S. C. M. Williams 9-19-1867
Holland, Mary to Green Brazelton 3-16-1843 (3-17-1843)
Holland, Rebecca to Anthony D. Stewart 10-1-1846
Holland, Sarah to Jessee Rogers 6-13-1859
Holland, Susanah to Absalom Williams 9-29-1842
Holland, Temmie to S. C. Hoge 11-19-1872 (no return)
Holliday, Jennie to John Wade 12-13-1870
Hollin, Matilda to William Stone 7-12-1841 (no return)
Hollis, Martha to George Wilkerson 8-11-1866 (no return)
Holliway, Nancy to Robert Steel 3-31-1866 (4-4-1866)
Holly, Anna to Benjamin Sanders 5-4-1846 (5-27-1846)
Holt, E. E. to Jones A. Hudgins 11-7-1867
Holt, Jane to William Prince 10-30-1851
Holt, Lucinda to J. H. Holder 9-14-1871 (no return)
Holt, M. C. to A. C. Ray 2-18-1868 (2-19-1868)
Holt, Mary C. to James Ivey 5-30-1843 (5-31-1843)
Holt, Mary C. to Solomon L. Daniel 11-19-1873 (11-20-1875)
Holt, S. E. to W. F. Holder 10-13-1869 (no return)
Holt, T. C. to John Gipson 7-29-1869
Holt, T. C. to W. R. Daniel 9-23-1869
Home, Maggie to William H. Barnes 8-21-1872 (no return)
Honey, Mary to G. Tucker 2-10-1868 (2-11-1868)
Hooper, Elizabeth to John Gunter 7-7-1869 (no return)
Hooser, Harriett to Berry Barnes 12-15-1839
Hoosier, Mary to William Sherdon 9-12-1849 (9-13-1849)
Hope, Laura to Richard S. Ayers 9-5-1874 (9-6-1874)
Hopkins, Emily to Geo. W. Day 7-9-1842 (7-10-1842)
Hopkins, Georgiana M. to William H. Smith 5-18-1871
Hopkins, M. F. to Frank E. Plummer 2-26-1872 (no return)
Hopkins, Rebecca to Benjamin Cherry 3-2-1846

Hopkins, S. B. to John L. Daniel 3-4-1843 (no return)
Hopkins, S. E. (Miss) to John Wallace 1-19-1869 (1-20-1869)
Hopper, Kiziah to Minor Anderson 9-14-1839 (9-15-1839)
Horton, Louisa J. to William R. Jones 11-20-1843 (11-21-1843)
Horton, Louisa to J. T. W. Williams 11-30-1874 (12-4-1874)
Horton, Mary A. to Elisha Bobo 11-21-1842 (11-29-1842)
Horton, Sarah A. to Wm. H. Keith 1-18-1872 (no return)
Horton, Sarah M. to Isaac N. Martin 6-28-1854 (6-29-1854)
Horton, Sarah W. to Silas M. Green 1-10-1848
Horton, Susan M. to C. M. Jones 10-21-1859 (no return)
Horton, Susan M. to Charles L. Jones 10-21-1858 (no return)
Horton, Susan M. to James M. Crutcher 11-8-1848 (11-9-1848)
Hosier, Elizabeth to David Grooms 2-10-1854
Houston, Ann S. to William Simpson 11-5-1851
Houston, Marinda to Wm. M. Evans 11-10-1852
Houston, Mary to Green B. Simpson 12-24-1850
Howard, Feraby E. to Mathew Swann 7-5-1854 (no return)
Howard, Matt to Robt. Holland 12-27-1866 (no return)
Howard, Sarah to Allen Stone 2-16-1856 (no return)
Howe, Cyntha A. to Benj. J. Ingram 9-27-1844 (9-30-1844)
Howell, Nancy to J. H. Hessey 12-24-1870 (no return)
Howk, M. E. to E. J. Howard 11-25-1858
Hubbard, Mary E. R. to James Tarply 2-2-1858 (no return)
Hubbard, Mary E. to James M. Tarpley 2-2-1858 (2-4-1858)
Huddleston, Ann E. to George R. Stranco 1-5-1869
Huddleston, Ann S. to James Nichols 11-29-1849
Huddleston, Sarah E. to William D. Knight 11-10-1846
Hudgins, Mary A. to Joseph A. Ford 12-15-1858
Hudley, Jane to Berry Lynch 9-21-1843 (no return)
Hudson, Elizabeth to Joseph S. Hopper 11-9-1842 (11-10-1842)
Hudson, Mary to James Wagner 12-22-1842
Huffman, E. (Miss) to William Pellham 6-5-1869 (6-13-1869)
Huggins, Gustia J. to J. W. Duckworth 12-5-1870 (12-7-1870)
Hugh, Sarah E. to Benj. F. Crabtree 5-4-1866 (no return)
Hughes, A. E. to James P. Nimmo 12-16-1852 (6-26-1853)
Hughes, M. C. to Abram Young 10-28-1869 (no return)
Hughs, A. S. to Wm. C. Harrison 9-24-1866 (no return)
Human, Cynthia to William Abanathy 8-17-1872 (8-18-1872)
Hunt, Annie E. to H. R. Moore 9-3-1860 (9-5-1860)
Hunt, Ede to William Corn 8-3-1840 (8-6-1840)
Hunt, Jane to John Maccay 5-30-1842 (6-1-1842)
Hunt, Jemima to Samuel Swann 1-14-1853
Hunt, M. O. to Ulysees Bates 8-10-1868 (8-11-1868)
Hunt, Mary A. to John R. Moseley 2-5-1858 (no return)
Hunt, Sallie to H. L. Parks 5-23-1867
Hurley, M. E. to John H. Taylor 12-7-1868
Hurley, Nancy A. to Joseph M. Knight 2-5-1866 (no return)
Hurst, Agness B. to Archibald D. Cadzon 1-9-1873
Hurt, Jane A. to Peter Simmons 9-22-1854
Hurt, Sarah to John Frost 1-17-1851 (1-19-1851)
Huston, Mary J. to J. C. Stephens 11-5-1874 (no return)
Hutcherson, Elizabeth to Isaac B. Bennett 3-27-1852 (3-28-1852)
Hutchins, Eliza to James Robinson 2-18-1840
Hutchins, Elizabeth A. to B. B. Wilkinson 7-18-1843 (7-25-1843)
Hutchins, Mary A. to George W. White 11-16-1847
Hutchins, Roena R. to Seth W. Houghton 11-2-1848 (no return)
Hutchins, Virginia P. to Levi Q. Ayers 12-29-1851 (12-30-1851)
Hutchinson, Nancy to John Diggom 4-28-1853
Hutton, Margrett E. to Bennett C. Barney 5-28-1856
Hutton, Winney A. to Thomas B. Poe 3-15-1853? (3-15-1854)
Hyder, Mollie to S. J. Green 7-29-1870 (no return)
Hynds, L. to John B. Rhodes 12-24-1860
Ikard, Martha to S. Douglas 12-30-1870 (no return)
Ingram, Mary Jane to Adam Hancock 12-13-1849
Ingram, Sarah to William Cornelius 1-12-1846 (no return)
Isbel, Hannah to William Bowman 8-8-1839 (9-15-1839)
Isbell, Jane to Flemming Culver 11-30-1866
Isbell, Mary to Solomon Musgrove 9-21-1865
Ivey, Anna J. to W. A. Branch 6-1-1872 (no return)
Ivey, Mary A. to L. W. Millsaps 9-14-1867 (9-15-1867)
Ivey, N. C. to M. Millsaps 10-1-1866 (no return)
Ivey, Sarah E. to Jesse Daniel 7-19-1858 (7-21-1858)
Ivey, Sarah Jane to James W. Helton 9-15-1869 (9-16-1869)
Ivey, Telitha to Jerry Dean 7-20-1868 (no return)
Jackson, Adaline to William Champion 10-23-1848 (10-24-1848)

Jackson, Drusetta to George M. Taylor 10-5-1852
Jackson, Elizabeth A. to Campbell Seargent 12-11-1856
Jackson, Emma C. to Samuel S. Pinkerton 7-26-1855 (7-30-1855)
Jackson, Hetty to Andrew Garner 12-17-1872 (12-26-1872)
Jackson, Louisa to Robert Pearson 4-5-1852
Jackson, Malinda to John B. Wilkerson 10-2-1851
Jackson, Paralee to John J. McDonald 7-4-1859 (7-5-1859)
Jackson, Parina to Bledsoe Stewart 5-19-1852 (5-23-1852)
Jackson, Phoebe A. to John E. Bobo 11-27-1855
Jackson, Rebecca to Champion Guinn 10-16-1841 (no return)
Jackson, Susan to James Holder 10-19-1866 (no return)
Janes, Editha to John W. Farris 9-21-1859
Janes, Emeline to Thomas G. Oakley 2-20-1850
Janes, Margret to H. F. Byrom 11-1-1870 (no return)
Janes, Mary to Preston Warren 9-5-1838 (9-6-1838)
Janson, Josephine to James M. Waggoner 3-18-1871 (3-19-1871)
Jarnagan, Mary J. to John H. Stewman 8-11-1865 (no return)
Jarrett, M. E. to D. H. McCoy 2-21-1840 (no return)
Jeans, Emiline to John W. Martin 1-12-1858
Jenkins, Ala to David Young 2-8-1849
Jenkins, Jane to Benjamin Hill 5-14-1853
Jenkins, Lucretia to Franklin Hill 8-30-1849
Jenkins, Margrett to Patrick Ferrell 8-20-1849
Jernegan, Martha to William Guthrie 1-24-1868 (no return)
Jernigan, Miss to W. J. Long 3-9-1870 (no return)
Jerrell, Sarah to J. R. Pearson 12-8-1862 (12-9-1862)
Jestin, Ellen H. to Wm. C. Cox 12-8-1853
Jett, Sarah to Stephen Allen 2-14-1851 (no return)
Jetton, H. to A. Thompson 1-9-1860
Jetton, Mary to Isaac Rogers 5-30-1872 (5-31-1872)
Jetton, Mary to J. C. Bryant 6-15-1871
Jinkins, Susan A. to Wm. W. Carter 4-8-1857 (4-9-1857)[*]
Johnson, Arabella W. to James I. Setliff 1-25-1872
Johnson, C. to E. R. Bean 11-24-1869 (no return)
Johnson, Edeva to Thos. E. Muse 1-3-1867 (no return)
Johnson, Lucy F. to Jasper Templeton 12-11-1857
Johnson, M. E. to B. S. Sloman 9-20-1865 (9-21-1865)
Johnson, Martha E. to John H. Birdsong 10-16-1848
Johnson, Nancy C. to Hemphey M. Walker 1-31-1848 (2-9-1848)
Johnson, Nancy J. to Wm. M. Poe 12-14-1853
Johnson, Nancy to Samuel H. Keith 11-7-1844
Johnson, Rebecca to John A. Brensfield 5-28-1859
Johnson, Sally A. to William Legg 1-27-1873 (1-29-1873)
Johnson, Saphrona E. to Thomas J. Stovall 8-4-1873 (no return)
Johnston, Josephene R. to Brice P. Gray 11-17-1870
Johnston, Miss Mattie to G. E. Banks 1-10-1870 (12?-10-1870)
Joiner, Charity to Jacob Hammers 10-15-1858 (10-17-1858)
Jolly, Malinda to Robt. Cavin 2-22-1854 (2-23-1854)
Jolly, Sharlotta T. to Joel Deshields 1-11-1851
Jones, Amanda to James Knight 12-20-1848 (12-21-1848)
Jones, America to Pinkney Adams 12-20-1860
Jones, Caroline to Isaac Dial 9-3-1846
Jones, Caroline to William A. Francis 9-15-1846
Jones, Cordelia to Joseph Darnell 8-31-1867 (9-1-1867)
Jones, Cyrena to John A. L. Brown 11-28-1846 (11-30-1846)
Jones, Delila E. to W. H. Tomlinson 12-6-1871 (12-12-1871)
Jones, Eliza to Thos. A. Easlick 11-15-1859
Jones, Eliza to Thos. A. Easlick 11-15-1859 (no return)
Jones, Elizabeth S. to Jacob A. Young 4-10-1872
Jones, Elizabeth to H. L. Byrom 11-10-1869
Jones, Elizabeth to John A. Dollins 1-11-1847 (no return)
Jones, Ella N. to J. A. M. Mathews 7-23-1874
Jones, Emeline to John Horton 12-22-1870 (no return)
Jones, Emma to Abram Vanoleck 8-27-1856 (no return)
Jones, Fanny to John McAdams 1-22-1865
Jones, H. E. to Jas. F. Webb 1-25-1871
Jones, Jane to Robt. Smith 6-17-1847
Jones, Laura E. to John G. Sublett 9-3-1873 (no return)
Jones, Lucinda to Harrison Ramsey 2-28-1845 (3-5-1845)
Jones, M. A. W. to J. W. Gray 2-12-1872 (2-13-1872)
Jones, M. E. to J. A. Thomas 9-5-1870 (no return)
Jones, M. M. to E. F. Campbell 9-23-1871 (no return)
Jones, Martha Jane to Thomas P. Oakley 12-22-1846 (12-24-1846)
Jones, Mary A. to Ezekiel G. Thompson 3-11-1857 (3-12-1857)
Jones, Mary A. to William H. Gilbert 1-15-1842 (1-17-1842)

Jones, Mary A. to William T. Lee 1-4-1850
Jones, Mary Ann to John Brown 10-27-1838
Jones, Mary J. to Jackson H. Cobble 5-7-1851 (5-8-1851)
Jones, Mary J. to Stephen M. Lee 8-19-1856
Jones, Mary M. to Thomas L. Chilton 10-19-1857 (10-20-1857)
Jones, Musadora E. to George B. Powell 5-4-1843
Jones, N. E. to W. F. Easterly 6-3-1871 (6-7-1871)
Jones, Nancy to Samuel P. Hilton 1-17-1843 (no return)
Jones, Polly to James Klepper 2-9-1838 (no return)
Jones, Rhoda A. to Thomas Cox 9-21-1854
Jones, S. M. to J. W. Gray 2-24-1868 (2-25-1868)
Jones, Sarah C. to C. A. Wilkins 10-18-1845
Jones, Sarah J. to Z. Fagg 3-21-1871 (3-23-1871)
Jones, Sarah M. to Wm. T. Lee 1-28-1858 (11-25?-1858)
Jones, Semira to John Gross 11-9-1842 (11-10-1842)
Jones, Susan to David Dyal 4-27-1839 (4-28-1839)
Jones, Synthia to James R. Byrom 8-9-1842 (8-11-1842)
Jones, T. H. (Miss) to Robert Harris 1-19-1870 (no return)
Jones, Tempy to Thomas Foster 1-17-1839
Jordan, A. C. to Edwin B. Byrom 1-9-1861 (1-10-1861)
Jordan, Mary V. to John Knox 4-1-1855
Judd, Amelia to R. M. King 12-31-1840 (no return)
Justin, Mary S. to D. L. Buckner 10-28-1873 (no return)
Justin, Mary to Charles B. Warren 3-28-1872 (no return)
Kale, Sarah to Patrick Troy 2-2-1854 (2-3-1854)
Karnes, Mary E. to M. W. Tally 1-18-1872
Kavanaugh, Elizabeth to Henry S. Turner 1-8-1852
Kavanaugh, Mary J. to Thomas Miller 6-24-1853
Keal, Permelia to William Gunn 12-11-1844 (no return)
Keath, Sarah M. to P. W. Brewer 2-1-1858 (2-5-1858)
Keaton, Clarisa to H. R. Bennett 9-20-1838 (9-?-1838)
Keel, M. E. to G. H. Gunn 11-29-1870 (12-1-1870)
Keel, Sarah to Henry R. Gilliam 6-2-1853
Keelin, Frances to Daniel Conley 4-2-1855 (4-9-1855)
Keith, Lucy S. to M. P. Hines 11-20-1866 (11-21-1866)
Keith, M. F. to P. B. Keith 8-9-1869 (8-12-1869)
Keith, Manerva D. to Thomas A. Newman 2-13-1851
Keith, Mary A. to A. L. Hyder 9-21-1840 (9-22-1840)
Keith, Mary A. to B. F. Harris 2-20-1871 (2-21-1871)
Keith, Mattie J. to Robert T. Reed 4-20-1874 (no return)
Keith, N. E. to T. J. Webb 11-21-1866
Keith, Nancy to Wm. S. Buchanan 8-1-1850
Keith, S. E. to Henry T. Garner 8-10-1872 (8-15-1872)
Keith, Sally A. to Wm. R. Mathews 12-19-1855 (12-20-1855)
Keith, Susan to Cary Staples 9-11-1843
Keith, Susan to Giles W. Bass 10-12-1839 (no return)
Kelley, Angeline to William Garner 10-21-1857
Kelley, Elizabeth to John Lynch 8-16-1870
Kelley, Elizabeth to Lewis Wilkerson 4-2-1840
Kelley, Fanny to Wm. Stafford 12-31-1868
Kelley, Franky to Ignashus Lynch 1-18-1850
Kelley, Jane to William Pack 8-14-1865 (8-16-1865)
Kelley, Josie B. to N. S. Cowan 9-25-1867
Kelley, M. J. (Miss) to John Garner 4-24-1866 (no return)
Kelley, Mary to Calvin Lynch 7-20-1850 (7-25-1850)
Kelley, Paralee to Wm. H. Langston 12-4-1850 (12-5-1850)
Kelley, Sally to Joseph Stewart 6-1-1841
Kellogg, Dosia D. to Wm. M. Shutters 8-27-1870 (no return)
Kemp, Lucinda to Wiley Jetton 10-25-1852 (no return)
Kemp, Nancy E. to Richard Little 11-22-1860
Kendry, Laura to Peter Wood 10-9-1872
Kenerly, Nicy P. to John Summerford 1-25-1853
Kennady, Martha N. to Christopher A. Lasater 3-12-1856
Kennedy, M. E. to Joseph V. Cagle 1-21-1871 (no return)
Kennedy, Nancy to John W. Howard 10-30-1859 (no return)
Kennedy, S. J. to Wm. Jacks 1-31-1870 (2-3-1870)
Kennedy, Sarah to John C. Smith 1-10-1858
Kennedy, Sarah to Henry B. Taylor 1-16-1854 (1-18-1854)
Kennedy, Wimma to Solomon Mitchell 9-9-1868
Kennerly, Calafornia to J. L. Moore 12-21-1871
Kennerly, Elizabeth to D. M. Tune 5-2-1859
Kennerly, Elizabeth to Harrison Perry 5-27-1858 (no return)
Kennerly, Leatha J. to William jr. Durham 1-4-1851 (1-5-1851)
Kennerly, Litha J. to Clement Featherston 1-20-1858 (no return)
Kennerly, Mary L. to Asa D. Oakley 1-16-1854 (1-17-1854)

Kennerly, Nancy to Powell Darwin 1-14-1839 (no return)
Kennerly, Nannie to Wm. Harris 7-25-1866 (no return)
Kennerly, S. to John Harris 12-17-1874 (12-20-1874)
Kenningham, Cathrine E. to Thomas W. Jones 10-22-1840 (no return)
Kersey, Sally to Daniel Walls 9-7-1839 (no return)
Kezzort, Viny to Seborn Rose 12-22-1865 (12-24-1865)
Kilpatrick, Elizabeth F. to Ely Mason 11-24-1841 (no return)
Kilpatrick, Euphany to Stephen M. Pitcock 10-10-1850
Kilpatrick, N. S. to W. M. Donaldson 4-22-1859 (4-24-1859)
Kimbro, Elizabeth to Andrew Newman 1-14-1854 (1-16-1854)
King, Barbary A. to William George 2-22-1842 (3-3-1842)
King, Cyntha E. to W. C. Stewman 9-5-1870 (9-21-1870)
King, Deliley to Dennis Barnes 12-22-1841
King, Kiziah to Derrell McKee 1-25-1840 (1-26-1840)
King, Louisa to Jasper McKey 8-26-1847
King, Martha Jane to John A. Underwood 2-6-1841
King, Mary to Thomas Sikes 2-10-1843
King, Nancy to John D. Lynch 4-16-1867 (no return)
King, Nancy to Stephen Simpson 5-1-1865 (no return)
King, Polly to Moses Pitman 6-12-1844
Kiningham, Mary A. to J. H. Bowers 5-30-1866 (5-?-1866)
Kiningham, Virginia E. to John H. Kiningham 12-1-1858 (12-2-1858)
Kinney, Susan A. to Richard Ray 2-4-1854 (2-5-1854)
Kirby, Mary to John B. Elliott 12-5-1856
Kirby, S. T. to Jordan Hays 7-12-1865
Kirkendol, Hester A. R. to Wm. Brazelton 6-4-1868 (6-29-1868)
Kirkendol, Mary A. to Wm. Hicks 3-23-1872 (3-24-1872)
Kirkindall, Louisa to John Sore? 3-15-1850 (3-18-1850)
Kitchens, Eliza E. to Thos. M. Davis 12-17-1853
Kitchens, M. E. to A. M. Spears 5-7-1866 (5-10-1866)
Kitchens, M. L. to Fleming Putman 5-27-1870 (?-?-1870)
Kitchens, Malissa to Bailey Hill 1-29-1845 (1-30-1845)
Kitchens, Malissa to Wm. Crownover 1-13-1872
Kitchens, Manerva J. to Robt. Davis 8-6-1849 (8-9-1849)
Kitchens, Mary V. to William C. Davis 9-22-1857
Kitchens, Mary to B. Wells 8-29-1868
Kittridge, Jessee A. to E. B. McNiel 10-12-1867 (10-14-1867)
Knight, A. (Miss) to M. N. Stephens 12-24-1868
Knight, A. J. to A. G. Headden 8-21-1865
Knight, Amanda J. to William P. Starnes 6-20-1838 (6-21-1838)
Knight, Charlotte T. to James M. Bratton 8-29-1860 (8-30-1860)
Knight, E. A. to E. A.? Wagner 12-9-1841
Knight, Frances E. to Andrew J. Wagner 7-25-1844 (7-28-1844)
Knight, H. R. to S. S. P. Vaughn 6-16-1868 (6-17-1868)
Knight, Jane N. to Levi F. Rippy 7-24-1855 (7-26-1855)
Knight, Jennie L. to Saml. H. Newberry 1-11-1872
Knight, Margret B. to Alfred P. Morris 1-8-1856
Knight, Margrett S. to Levi P. Carroll 10-18-1873 (10-19-1873)
Knight, Martha E. to J. T. Hamilton 10-15-1867 (no return)
Knight, Mary Ann to Wm. J. Blackwood 1-17-1852 (no return)
Knight, Mary J. to George G. Miller 8-13-1851 (no return)
Knight, Mary M. to Robt. Darwin 4-22-1847
Knight, S. C. to R. G. Conn 7-30-1868 (no return)
Knight, Sarah A. to Melton Bolin 5-1-1865 (no return)
Knight, Sarah to Edward A. Jackson 7-7-1853
Knight, Sophia to John Coldwell 2-12-1868 (2-13-1868)
Knight, Temperance B. to Layfayette Lynch 2-17-1859
Knight, Temperance J. to Benjamin C. Starnes 1-13-1849 (no return)
Knight, Winford to Wm. H. Corn 7-25-1859 (7-28-1859)
Knuckles, Mourning to Ralph Arnold 7-27-1847 (8-3-1847)
Knuckles, Sarah to William Bishop 1-22-1846
Koger, Charlotta to Benjamin Clark 11-7-1868 (11-12-1868)
Lackray, Amanda to Jake Miller 8-15-1872
Ladd, Any to Samuel Stone 2-4-1848 (no return)
Ladd, Jane to Wm. Osborn 12-26-1870 (no return)
Ladd, Lucinda to James W. Arnold 6-17-1872
Ladd, Sarah to James H. Vibbart 9-7-1854
Lakey, Harriett to James Davison 1-7-1841
Lakey, Mariah to Lewis Holder 5-19-1841
Lamb, Nancy M. to James M. Clay 6-9-1843
Lambert, Anna to John S. Acree 4-6-1867 (4-7-1867)
Langston, Elizabeth to Nathaniel McClure 12-18-1851
Langston, Martha to James M. Mayes 2-4-1867 (2-5-1867)
Langston, Mary J. to Benj. Bragg 1-16-1858 (1-17-1858)

Lanham, Sophia to Newton J. Gattis 8-27-1873
Large, Harriett E. to A. S. Cooper 4-29-1861
Larkin, Darcas to Francis M. Larkin 7-2-1855 (7-4-1855)
Larkin, Elizabeh to John Staples 7-15-1851 (7-16-1851)
Larkin, Jane E. to James L. Hatchett 3-21-1859 (no return)
Larkin, Mary S. to Martin Mason 12-30-1870 (1-4-1871)
Larkins, Julia F. to Dabney D. Lipscomb 1-1-1838 (1-4-1838)
Larkins, Nancy J. to James N. Keith 2-7-1839 (2-9-1839)
Lasan, Phebe to John Williams 6-15-1838 (8-8-1838)
Lasater, Euphrasha E. to John L. Edwards 10-3-1850
Lasater, Fidella J. to Hubbard H. Huggins 10-14-1858 (10-4?-1858)
Lasater, Juda to John Keck 5-17-1845 (5-18-1845)
Lasater, Martha E. to Stephen Pylant 6-3-1841
Lasater, Mary to Thomas J. Hill 12-20-1855 (12-23-1855)
Lasater, Rebecca E. to Benjamin Nixon 8-1-1874 (8-13-1874)
Lasater, Sarah A. to David Banks 1-23-1852 (1-25-1852)
Lasater, Susan to George Fontain 11-24-1865 (no return)
Lasater, Virginia C. to Thomas F. Dollins 10-18-1848
Lastor, Sally to James Pyland 10-2-1838 (10-4-1838)
Latamore, Margaret A. to John N. Newnan 7-13-1854
Latimore, Nancy to J. M. Pylant 12-26-1866
Laughinhouse, D. D. to John A. Douglass 12-13-1854
Laughmiller, J. F. to John F. Vaughn 5-10-1866
Laughmiller, Mary A. to George S. Dickens 12-10-1873 (12-11-1873)
Lawson, Hannah E. to Tyree Riddle 8-17-1859
Lawson, Julia Ann to William Weaver 12-20-1870 (no return)
Lawson, Rebecca to J. H. Allen 2-13-1866 (2-15-1866)
Ledbetter, Cornelia J. to Wm. E. Turner 7-1-1873 (7-2-1873)
Lee, Eliza J. to Stephen C. Sanders 3-1-1849
Lee, Frances M. to Hugh L. Erwin 2-21-1854 (2-26-1854)
Lee, Heneretta D. to John W. Frame 3-22-1854
Lee, Martha Elen to George W. Allen 7-15-1847 (7-16-1847)
Lee, Mary A. to Geo. W. Brannan 2-11-1856 (2-15-1856)
Lee, Polly Ann to Elijah Bice 8-16-1847 (8-17-1847)
Lee, Sarah M. to John H. McKnight 2-28-1854 (3-1-1854)
Lee, Sarah P. to Benjamin Taylor 7-13-1842 (no return)
Lefeber, Mary (Miss) to Thomas Arledge 12-9-1869
Lenehan, Frances to John H. Little 3-17-1858
Lenshaw, Alice to David S. Long 5-10-1853
Lenton, Mary E. to James Barnett 3-6-1865 (3-7-1865)
Leonard, Margret E. to John O. Dotson 10-24-1867
Leounard, Fannie to John A. Cox 2-15-1867
Lestor, Salina to Richard Faris 2-14-1855 (2-15-1855)
Leverton, Lizzie to David Lynch 9-18-1867 (9-19-1867)
Leverton, Mary C. to James Pelham 3-28-1874 (3-30-1874)
Lewis, Elizabeth to John W. Byrom 6-13-1868 (6-14-1868)
Lewis, Elizabeth to William Cowan 10-4-1842 (10-2?-1842)
Lewis, M. J. to J. P. Spears 12-15-1871 (12-17-1871)
Lewis, Sarah Jane to Robert Brown 8-29-1846 (8-30-1846)
Lewis, Sevil to Charles Crisman 10-20-1853 (10-21-1853)
Liles, Eliza A. to John W. Casteel 9-12-1853 (9-13-1853)
Liles, Frances to James Dent 7-14-1844
Limbaugh, Elizabeth to Morgan T. Hefner 5-10-1854
Limbaugh, M. C. to M. C. Hall 2-24-1874 (2-26-1874)
Limbaugh, Melvina to Richmond A. Groves 12-28-1849 (12-30-1849)
Limbaugh, Sally to Joel Vanzant 12-22-1838 (no return)
Linch, Pattie to John Paine 7-27-1848
Lindsey, Eliza to A. B. Floyd 3-20-1872 (3-21-1872)
Linebaugh, Charlotte to John F. Church 9-15-1859 (9-18-1859)
Linebaugh, Susan to John Wiseman 9-15-1856
Linsley, Sarah A. to Wm. H. Knuckles 12-13-1840 (12-20-1840)
Linsy, Lizzie to General Short 11-1-1869 (11-4-1869)
Lipscomb, Ellen to James I. Gardner 5-6-1871 (5-7-1871)
Lipscomb, J. L. to W. J. Woods 12-23-1868 (no return)
Lipscomb, Karon C. to Napoleon B. Smith 3-30-1850 (3-31-1850)
Lipscomb, Nancy J. to Robert N. Mann 10-19-1851
Lipscomb, Tehpenis? to Clinton A. Heurst? 7-16-1838 (7-17-1838)
Litle, Elizabeth J. to Welburn Wilhite 9-10-1846
Little, Aseneth A. to Dosier T. Reynolds 3-17-1858 (3-18-1858)
Little, Lydia A. to Saml. Morris 10-31-1865
Little, Missouri to H. Allred 1-15-1867 (1-16-1867)
Little, Nancy L. to John W. Smith 6-4-1853 (6-5-1853)
Little, Rebecca C. to Thomas Campbell 12-12-1849 (12-13-1849)
Little, Sarah F. to T. D. W. Anderson 10-7-1866
Lockhart, Adaline P. to William McGhee 12-28-1850 (12-30-1850)

Lockhart, Elizabeth to W. B. Woodward 12-21-1870 (12-22-1870)
Logan, Angie to Thaddeus Foster 7-4-1865 (7-5-1865)
Logan, Dinah to Larkin Morris 7-5-1849
Logan, Eliza Jane to John H. Layton 3-9-1847 (3-11-1847)
Logan, Irena to Wm. F. Elliott 10-17-1844
Logan, Julia F. to Wm. G. Newman 8-18-1853
Loney, Margrett to Levi Isbell 3-28-1844 (no return)
Long, Cathrine to Jackson Garner 1-8-1843
Long, Cathrine to Jessee Allen 8-29-1842 (8-31-1842)
Long, E. to I. N. Stewart 2-17-1868
Long, Eliza to John Sherrell 11-14-1846 (no return)
Long, Elizabeth to Wm. M. Rose 5-21-1861 (5-22-1861)
Long, Laura G. to A. L. Perryman 1-9-1867 (1-10-1867)
Long, Malinda to Green Hill 3-10-1848 (3-12-1848)
Long, Malinda to James Golliday 4-10-1867
Long, Martha C. to W. S. Long 12-9-1868 (no return)
Long, Rebecca to Isaac Reed 10-28-1841 (11-2-1841)
Long, Sarah to Jordan Banks 8-24-1843
Long, Susan J. to Michael Cannady 10-3-1866 (no return)
Long, Vicca to Amos Gipson 4-8-1853
Looney, Eliza J. to Solomon Holder 1-9-1841
Looney, Martha to Thomas Shasteen 7-27-1843
Looney, Sarah to Bartly Posey 7-23-1853
Lovell, Jennie to J. W. Gouce 4-22-1870 (no return)
Lovell, Jennie to Jno. W. Gouce 4-22-1870 (5-1-1870)
Loyd, Rachiel to Thomas J. Myres 3-26-1850
Lucas, Amy to James Burkes 12-26-1839
Lucas, Cyrena to James H. Young 3-16-1843
Lucas, Martha A. to Joseph Stovall 7-9-1850 (7-?-1850)
Lucas, Martha to John Burkes 6-28-1839
Lucas, Mary C. to Thomas M. Burk 10-15-1847
Lucas, Nancy C. to Rufus C. Foster 2-11-1856 (no return)
Lucas, Rhutha S. to Jessee S. McClure 11-28-1853
Lucca, M. H. to Stanford Mays 2-9-1860
Luchan?, Mary A. to Stephen Carter 2-26-1849
Ludewell, Caroline to Neapolean Robeson 2-7-1838 (no return)
Ludewell, Nancy to William Carroll 6-25-1838 (no return)
Lumpkins, Sarah A. to J. P. Vaughan 2-14-1867
Lynbough, J. to J. F. Tipps 12-28-1859 (no return)
Lynch, B. A. to B. Payne 10-31-1859 (11-3-1859)
Lynch, Elizabeth C. to Giles A. Bennett 1-4-1846 (1-14-1846)
Lynch, Elzira to William I. Decherd 8-20-1848
Lynch, Franky A. to Meredith Garner 5-21-1867 (no return)
Lynch, Hattie to W. C. Gipson 1-8-1866 (1-9-1866)
Lynch, Lucinda to Solomon Rose 11-4-1869 (11-8-1869)
Lynch, Lucinda to William Prince 3-24-1841
Lynch, Lucy D. to Francis M. Jackson 9-15-1853
Lynch, M. (Miss) to James Walker 2-26-1842
Lynch, Margrett to Erasmus G. Brewer 7-15-1846
Lynch, Mary E. to Hansford H. Roberts 3-7-1851
Lynch, Matilda to John Payne 10-6-1857 (10-27-1857)
Lynch, Nancy to Amos Garner 9-5-1846 (9-6-1846)
Lynch, Sally Ann to Taylor Garner 4-4-1872
Lynch, Sopherias M. to Caleb C. Call 9-1-1841 (9-3-1841)
Lynch, Vina to Joe Buckner 12-12-1868 (no return)
Lyon, E. F. to W. W. Brittain 12-13-1871
Lyons, Ann to Thomas H. Modena 11-16-1871 (11-18-1871)
Lyons, Jennie to Peter Lonehan 7-14-1874 (7-16-1874)
Lyons, M. F. to R. F. Oakley 5-4-1868 (no return)
Magbee, Mary J. to Lemuel Furgarson 3-25-1867 (3-31-1867)
Magby, Nancy to R. P. Wade 10-11-1865 (10-12-1865)
Magors, Elizabeth to E. B. Shasteen 10-25-1860
Mahafee, Sarah to Lewis Berryhill 2-27-1863 (3-1-1863)
Mahaffey, Mary to Pleas Nippers 9-?-1870 (9-8-1870)
Mahan, Nancy to Robt. Payne 9-18-1858 (9-19-1858)
Mahathy, Margrett to Wm. Champion 8-21-1869 (8-29-1869)
Mahon, Elvira to Luke Gray 8-1-1850
Mains?, Martha E. to Benjamin Fraure 9-7-1848
Maise, Jane to David J. Hill 12-25-1856 (12-26-1856)
Majors, B. A. to H. R. Vaughn 12-24-1866 (no return)
Majors, E. to G. W. Holder 9-3-1868
Majors, Elizabeth to E. B. McLaughlin 2-4-1839 (no return)
Majors, Juda to Josias Gunn 12-20-1838 (1-1-1839)
Majors, Martha to Wm. Osborn 1-24-1854 (1-25-1854)
Majors, Missouri C. to Moses A. Baggett 11-27-1848 (11-29-1848)

Majors, Sarah to Jeremiah Taylor 1-4-1856
Malcom, Fanny to Samuel A. Hannah 6-2-1866 (no return)
Mallard, Jane to C. C. Hill 8-15-1856 (8-17-1856)
Malone, Angeline to Olive M. Posey 12-25-1847
Malone, Elenor to Wm. Keath 4-20-1852
Malone, Julia Ann to Orange Walraven 8-20-1856 (no return)
Malone, Margret J. to Edward Fogortey 7-3-1858 (7-5-1858)
Malone, Martha J. to Charles B. Temple 12-21-1872 (12-26-1872)
Malone, Martha L. to J. G. McAllister 1-26-1872 (1-27-1872)
Malone, Mary E. to Nathaniel T. Francis 9-3-1849
Malone, Sarah E. to John Furgeson 8-17-1865
Malone, Sarah to Jeptha Holsonback 6-8-1852 (6-9-1852)
Mangrum, Lizzie to William T. Pylant 2-18-1871
Mangrum, S. C. to J. M. Gillmore 6-21-1869 (6-10?-1869)
Mann, Emma E. to Jos. B. Bogle 1-22-1874
Mann, Eveline to Lorenzo D. Jones 1-8-1852 (1-13-1852)
Mann, Judith E. to John W. Syler 5-3-1849 (no return)
Mann, Mary S. to Felix E. Smith 10-18-1856 (10-23-1856)
Mann, Ruth to J. F. Syler 1-16-1867
Mann, Sue V. to J. W. Syler 10-10-1867 (10-13-1867)
Mann, Sumira A. to Charles F. Woods 2-27-1851
Manuel, Allice to J. W. Turney 9-11-1869 (9-5?-1869)
Maples, Elizabeth to Josiah Maples 2-13-1852
Marberry, V. C. to C. W. Blackwell 4-30-1867
March, Ann to Jas. M. Porter 8-30-1871
March, Harriet to Amanzey B. Gordon 9-10-1838 (9-11-1838)
March, Nancy to Hugh Jones 12-27-1838
Marks, Bettie (Miss) to Robert C. Handley 1-26-1869
Marks, Kate to William H. Davis 1-14-1873 (1-15-1873)
Marks, Mag (Miss) to J. B. Fitzpatrick 11-20-1867
Markum, Marinda to John Guthry 8-6-1853
Marlow, Caraline to William Garner 3-23-1858 (3-25-1858)
Marshall, Eliza E. to Ezekael M. Bean 8-19-1854 (8-22-1854)
Marshall, M. E. (Mrs.) to John B. Wood 8-9-1870 (8-11-1870)
Marshall, M. J. to John McKinzie 9-28-1866 (no return)
Marshall, Manerva F. to P. R. Helton 1-6-1872 (1-7-1872)
Marshall, Martha A. to Robt. C. Hines 5-4-1865
Marshall, Sarah L. to Thomas Hise 7-28-1856 (8-3-1856)
Martin, Arie E. to Jas. H. P. Byrom 12-28-1871
Martin, E. A. to Wm. L. Cherry 9-18-1873
Martin, Fannie L. to John T. Sanders 11-18-1865 (11-19-1865)
Martin, Florida A. to Moses P. Marberry 10-11-1858 (10-4?-1858)
Martin, Frances L. to John Chitwood 12-8-1838 (12-25-1838)
Martin, Hulda to Douglass Hendrix 10-?-1839 (no return)
Martin, Jane E. to John A. T. Rawlins 10-4-1844 (10-9-1844)
Martin, Mary to A. S. Myrick 4-8-1839
Martin, N. H. to W. L. Jones 11-21-1866 (no return)
Martin, Nancy to Thomas R. Taylor 2-3-1840 (no return)
Martin, Rachiel to Samuel Bridges 8-11-1842
Martin, Sarah A. to Joseph Lynch 1-2-1839
Martin, Sarah to Samuel H. Martin 2-16-1841 (2-21-1841)
Mash, Delila to Hiram Glass 7-25-1853 (7-26-1853)
Mason, D. A. to Robert Jones 12-21-1868
Mason, D. O. (Miss) to Robt. Jones 12-21-1869
Mason, Ellen to Tillman Arledge 7-10-1855
Mason, Idella P. to Robt. H. McGee 11-26-1873
Mason, Louisa J. to Newton Dodson 9-23-1850 (9-25-1850)
Mason, Mary M. to John T. Hatchet 1-21-1861 (1-22-1861)
Mason, Mary to Pearce Wilhoite 5-13-1852
Mason, Maud H. to Wm. B. Gossage 12-10-1873
Mason, Polly to Noah Rice 9-2-1839 (no return)
Mason, Rebecca to D. T. Kennedy 11-8-1866 (no return)
Mason, Sarah to Jerry Riddle 1-24-1843 (1-26-1843)
Mason, Sarah to Warren H. Clark 12-25-1872 (12-26-1872)
Mathews, Allice to Henry Watson 8-27-1872 (8-29-1872)
Mathews, Emily to H. S. Williams 2-15-1844
Mathews, Fidella T. to William M. Mitchell 6-11-1844
Mathews, Jane to Thos. W. Chastain 12-10-1857 (12-13-1857)
Mathews, M. F. to W. L. Handley 11-15-1865
Mathews, Margrett to William Oliver 1-18-1849
Mathews, Martha E. E. to William W. Grady 1-8-1840
Mathews, Martha J. to Willis Stewart 6-11-1854
Mathews, Mary to Charles C. Middleton 8-6-1843
Mathews, Nancy J. to W. J. Kiningham 3-26-1870 (3-27-1870)
Mathews, Sarah A. to Samuel B. Gover 8-16-1853

Mathews, Sarah to Wm. L. Handley 9-12-1853 (9-13-1853)
Matlock, A. E. to Joel Vanzant 9-15-1868 (no return)
Matlock, Elizabeth A. to Joseph Taylor 7-27-1839
Matlock, Jane to John Steel 4-2-1854
Matlock, Leah J. to G. R. Scivally 3-1-1866 (3-2-1866)
Mattenbee, Mary to Joseph Howell 2-1-1858 (no return)
Mattenlee, Isabel to W. T. Brakefield 12-2-1859 (no return)
Matthews, Allice to Henry Watson 8-2-1872 (no return)
Matthews, Elizabeth to John Thurman 9-25-1850 (9-26-1850)
Matthews, Mary to George W. Carroll 7-8-1843 (7-9-1843)
Matthews, Mary to John B. Turner 1-12-1843 (1-13-1843)
Mattie, Joanna to John Embrick 9-18-1871 (9-21-1871)
Maxwell, Emma to B. F. Russey 7-1-1867
May, Attillia to Edmond R. Wagner 1-18-1844
May, Elizabeth to Layton W. Campbell 1-30-1856
May, Mary E. to Geo. W. Wagner 4-10-1845
May, Mary M. to Alexander May 1-14-1856 (11-16-1856)
Mayes, Martha to William McClure 3-22-1858
Mayes, Susan to Hardy H. Ethridge 3-2-1857 (3-3-1857)
Maynus, Jane to J. J. Sansom 1-9-1868 (1-10-1868)
Mays, Alley to Lorenzo S. Tomlinson 2-10-1866 (2-12-1866)
Mays, Elizabeth to Addison Watson 3-23-1872
Mays, Mary Jane to Warren Stovall 4-19-1849
Mays, Permelia to Edward Mays 8-9-1866
Mayse, Mary A. to Louis Houston 7-16-1872 (7-18-1872)
McBee, Deboriah to Charles P. Crownover 8-16-1846
McBee, Ellen to William Prince 6-13-1868 (no return)
McBee, Malinda to George M. Seargent 9-14-1874 (9-13?-1874)
McBee, Sarah to Wilson Nichols 5-22-1845 (5-28-1845)
McBee, Syrena to Jessee McBee 9-4-1865 (9-21-1865)
McBride, S. E. to F. M. Forbes 12-3-1870 (12-4-1870)
McCall, Anna to Jessee Adams 10-2-1843
McCarty, Mary to Volentine Fulcher 2-8-1838
McCarver, Nancy to James Corin 3-29-1856 (3-30-1856)
McCarver, Vina to Moses Hill 2-20-1841 (2-21-1841)
McCauly, Adaline to J. M. McManara 1-31-1871
McClain, E. H. to James H. Warren 7-3-1867 (no return)
McClure, Elizabeth to James L. Edwards 12-31-1840 (no return)
McClure, L. J. to W. H. Dixon 10-25-1854
McClure, M. E. to George H. Smith 10-18-1874 (11-9-1874)
McClure, Martha to James Ethridge 8-29-1864 (8-11-1864)
McClure, Mattie A. to Wade M. Rogers 7-29-1873 (no return)
McClure, Melvina to C. M. Tankersley 11-23-1868 (11-21?-1868)
McClure, Nancy to Danl. Boren 7-10-1872 (7-11-1872)
McClure, Polly to Alexander M. Crawford 8-7-1841
McClure, Rebecca J. to James R. Smith 10-4-1858
McClure, Zilpha C. to Williamson Rich 8-27-1855 (no return)
McCollister, Elizabeth A. to Robert C. Newberry 8-24-1843
McCollum, Amanda M. to Thomas J. Darwin 9-18-1850 (9-19-1850)
McCollum, Sarah A. to John R. Stovall 2-9-1850 (2-14-1850)
McCord, E. R. to G. H. Bridges 1-1-1859 (no return)
McCord, Elizabeth to Manville H. Bridges 1-1-1859 (no return)
McCord, Margret to Wm. Wetherford 7-15-1846 (not executed)
McCord, Martha to John Gross 1-16-1861
McCord, Mary C. to Joseph Lusk 5-26-1847 (5-27-1847)
McCord, Sarah M. to John Smith 3-3-1845 (no return)
McCord, Sarah to Samuel A. Harris 10-24-1843 (11-7-1843)
McCord, Susanah J. to John C. Bell 6-21-1845 (5-20-1846)
McCoy, Martha J. to August P. Darrell 4-19-1854
McCoy, Mary to William Shropshire 5-24-1851 (5-27-1851)
McCoy, Nancy S. to James Webb 1-10-1845 (no return)
McCoy, Paulina to John M. Turney 6-27-1853 (not executed)
McCrary, Elizabeth to John Sells 8-30-1846
McCullock, Josephene to Wm. Farris 9-26-1873
McCutcheon, Elizabeth to Sherrod Williams 12-21-1850 (12-22-1850)
McCutcheon, Juliet F. to Dewit C. Stamper 12-18-1856
McDaniel, Elizabeth to Levi P. Osborn 1-22-1845
McDaniel, Lucy to David Smith 5-10-1847 (5-11-1847)
McDaniel, Mary A. to Thomas Sanders 1-7-1841
McDaniel, Mary to Bazil Wood 10-12-1851
McDaniel, Mary to Calvin D. Diel 1-10-1849
McDaniel, Sarah Ann to Thomas D. W. George 4-18-1850
McDaniel, Sarah to John A. Willis 9-3-1847 (no return)
McDaniel, Sue to John J. Tribble 2-4-1867 (2-?-1867)
McDaniel, Unice to John H. Taylor 12-20-1852

McDavid, Mary to John D. Gray 4-11-1848 (4-12-1848)
McDonald, Rebecca Jane to James Moore 8-15-1855 (8-19-1855)
McDuffie, N. to C. W. Womack 8-6-1859 (8-7-1859)
McElroy, C. E. to Isaac H. Hall 10-25-1859 (10-26-1859)
McElroy, M. J. to Isaac Vanzant 2-8-1860 (2-9-1860)
McElvoy, Sallie E. to Geo. S. Byrom 2-23-1870 (2-24-1870)
McGee, Martha A. to Dean A. Fletcher 12-26-1854 (12-27-1854)
McGee, Mollie (Miss) to R. R. Powell 6-3-1869 (no return)
McGehee, M. J. to James H. Langston 3-16-1874 (no return)
McGowan, Nancy to Daniel Gore 8-2-1844
McGrew, Sarah J. to Wm. Vaughan 10-5-1854
McIlheran, Margret to W. R. Francis 2-12-1840 (no return)
McIlherron, Violet to Leut Williams 12-31-1840 (no return)
McJohns, Nancy to Martin Seivilly 3-4-1853 (3-10-1853)
McKee, Clary to William King 5-2-1838 (no return)
McKee, Eliza to John Ethridge 3-19-1840
McKeel, Martha to Edwin D. Swann 9-6-1849 (9-7-1849)
McKelby, W. F. to J. R. Champion 3-25-1869 (no return)
McKelvey, Elizabeth to William B. Miles 4-7-1847 (5-27-1847)
McKelvey, Emelia to John W. Smith 7-20-1846 (8-5-1846)
McKelvey, Emily to W. C. Long 7-10-1860
McKelvey, Frances to Francis M. Bennett 11-24-1857 (11-26-1857)
McKelvey, Issabella to Alexr. Duncan 12-11-1865 (12-14-1865)
McKelvey, Margret to Solomon Wagner 11-30-1865
McKelvey, Mary A. to John W. McKelvey 11-30-1842 (no return)
McKelvey, Mary E. to J. J. Combs 10-28-1873
McKelvey, Mary to Alexander L. McDaniel 8-7-1843
McKelvey, Nancy to William Delzell 12-8-1852 (12-7?-1852)
McKelvey, Narcissa to Henry McDaniel 7-15-1847
McKelvey, Tempa to James M. Knight 12-22-1868
McKelvy, Caroline to James Walker 7-26-1866 (no return)
McKelvy, Nancy to George Lenehan 1-25-1872
McKerns, Sarah to E. F. Reynolds 5-17-1867
McKinzey, Mary to William Roberson 8-5-1844
McKinzey, Sarah E. to Willie Ludewell 7-28-1839 (no return)
McKinzie, Margret to T. L. Tucker 8-25-1859
McKinzie, Mary to Peter A. Williams 10-4-1839
McKissick, Caldonia to Samuel McAllister 12-17-1867
McKnight, Mary to Patton Weaver 8-23-1859 (no return)
McKnight, Nancy to Allen Hill 8-24-1867
McLeod, Lucy A. to John West 11-27-1854 (11-30-1854)
McLyea, Sarah to John Pennington 8-13-1839 (no return)
McNabb, Caroline to John W. Jones 4-10-1866
McNabb, Mary F. to J. W. Williams 1-5-1841 (no return)
McNabb, Mary L. to Julias M. Habeck 2-5-1856
McNabb, Virginia L. to Wm. M. Russey 7-28-1847 (7-29-1847)
McNiel, Adaline to Richard S. Corn 10-29-1846 (10-?-1846)
McNiel, Eliza to Washington Tate 12-20-1848 (no return)
McNiel, Mary M. to John W. Martin 12-23-1847
McPherson, Lizzie to William Bickerson 3-1-1872
McQueen, Elizabeth to Wm. S. Parks 8-3-1846 (8-5-1846)
McWhirter, Amanda to H. L. Greenlee 10-8-1867 (no return)
Mealer, Lucretia to Joseph Miller 2-24-1846 (2-25-1846)
Mederis, Sarah C. to Thomas Fitzgibbons 6-8-1872
Meeks, Margreet A. to John A. Tulley 7-29-1840
Meredith, Elizabeth to B. H. Emerson 11-10-1840
Meredith, Nancy to Wiley S. Embrey 12-1-1857 (no return)
Metcalf, Elizabeth C. to John W. Damron 4-24-1855
Metcalf, Louisa to George Morgan 2-21-1844 (2-22-1844)
Metcalf, Mary E. to Warner E. Driskell 11-13-1852 (11-14-1852)
Metcalf, S. L. to A. W. Collins 2-26-1868
Methvin, Ruthy to Sherrod G. Nowlin 8-12-1841
Mickles, Nancy Jane to Wm. Weaver 7-7-1855
Middleton, Nancy to John Jacoway 11-24-1844
Miler, Cathrine to Baley Coleman 7-14-1851
Miles, Elizabeth to W. M. Hays 12-24-1867
Miles, Lydia H. to Thomas D. Martin 10-10-1838 (10-11-1838)
Miles, Mary J. to David Armstrong 9-25-1854 (no return)
Miles, Mary Jane to Wm. Brinsfield 12-4-1856 (12-10-1856)
Miller, Ann to Marshal W. Trigg 10-4-1842 (10-6-1842)
Miller, Betty to Isiah Rice 7-3-1869 (7-4-1869)
Miller, Eliza to Charley Hodge 12-28-1870 (no return)
Miller, Eliza to James M. Woods 5-19-1859
Miller, Frances to Wark Limbaugh 9-10-1872
Miller, Georgia A. to James I. Hamelton 1-9-1873

Miller, Hettie (Miss) to Joseph Miller 1-6-1869 (no return)
Miller, Isbel to Thomas Bradford 9-21-1843 (9-24-1843)
Miller, Josephine to William C. Staples 10-5-1842 (10-6-1842)
Miller, Laura L. to E. D. Anderson 1-13-1872 (no return)
Miller, Lizzie to Milton Anderson 5-28-1866 (5-29-1866)
Miller, Mag E. (Miss) to F. M. Turner 11-19-1867 (no return)
Miller, Margret to John B. March 12-16-1856
Miller, Mary Ann to Fedrick G. Farris 3-26-1845 (3-23?-1845)
Miller, Mary J. to Z. N. Carroll 9-7-1865
Miller, Mary to William E. Williams no date (with May 1848)
Miller, Mattie A. to T. W. Johnston 1-5-1874 (no return)
Miller, Mourning W. to R. C. Smith 6-4-1839
Miller, Nancy A. to Obidiah Bean 8-22-1857
Miller, Nancy J. to Thos. Usley 1-3-1858 (1-4-1858)
Miller, Nancy J. to William Panther 5-22-1865 (no return)
Miller, Nancy M. to James Mason 1-5-1857 (1-6-1857)
Miller, Nancy M. to Jessee C. Perkins 9-27-1853
Miller, Rebecca to Goodman Burrow 3-18-1854 (3-19-1854)
Miller, Sarah A. to A. J. Powers 10-25-1871 (no return)
Miller, Sarah A. to Benj. F. Wade 5-19-1845
Miller, Sarah A. to Benjamin Reed 4-21-1853
Miller, Sarah J. to James A. England 11-30-1843
Miller, Sarah to Obadiah Burks 12-16-1874 (12-20-1874)
Miller, Susan G. to John W. Moore 1-29-1844 (2-1-1844)
Millikin, Sarah to Joseph Miller 10-9-1872 (no return)
Mills, Nicey to John Henson 11-13-1865
Minnix, Rhoda A. to Eli Frazier 10-26-1840 (no return)
Mircer, Hannah to Adam Thompson 3-12-1853 (3-13-1853)
Mitchell, Ann to Hiram K. Posey 7-23-1853
Mitchell, Anna to E. K. Phillips 2-3-1874 (2-5-1874)
Mitchell, Caroline to William R. Banks? 12-12-1845 (12-14-1845)
Mitchell, Fidelia T. to John W. Martin 7-16-1851
Mitchell, Louisa J. to James A. Banks 10-14-1854 (10-15-1854)
Mitchell, M. S. to D. S. Jones 12-20-1866 (12-23-1866)
Mitchell, Marilla J. to Perry Wood 3-28-1872
Mitchell, Martha A. to Isaac Hutton 8-18-1856 (8-19-1856)
Mitchell, Mary Jane to James B. Hutton 8-9-1856 (8-12-1856)
Mitchell, Mary to S. H. Statum 7-22-1856 (7-27-1856)
Mitchell, Nancy to Joseph Royalty 1-2-1845
Mitchell, Orpha M. to W. T. Garner 1-12-1870 (12?-13-1870)
Mitchell, Sarah A. to W. R. James 11-20-1872
Mize, Sarah to John Posey 2-3-1871 (no return)
Modena, Martha A. to Alexr. W. Hale 7-21-1851 (7-22-1851)
Modena, Virginia E. to M. D. Embrey 5-2-1860 (5-3-1860)
Moffitt, Ann Eliza to Thomas Finch 12-16-1846 (12-17-1846)
Money, Malinda to Solomon Dotson 2-26-1843
Money, Nannie to Benjamin Vincent 6-17-1873
Monis, Amanda C. to Wm. R. Lee 10-2-1851
Montgomery, Jane to William L. Gist 10-19-1848
Montgomery, Laura to William Crownover 1-22-1874 (1-25-1874)
Montgomery, M. F. to A. J. Hines 12-14-1872 (no return)
Montgomery, Martha to George W. Powers 11-19-1841
Montgomery, Mary J. to Joseph Crownover 9-11-1867
Moody, Ann to Jessee Barnes 1-17-1867
Moody, Mary Jane to Bird Barnes 9-26-1866 (9-21?-1866)
Mooney, Mary Jane to John Grider 6-28-1866 (7-1-1866)
Mooney, Virginia S. to Jos. H. Cunningham 9-4-1851 (not executed)
Moonham, Martha J. to Joseph Taylor 6-1-1854
Moore, Cathrine to John W. Limbaugh 1-4-1872
Moore, Charlotta to Lewis Anderson 12-15-1840 (12-17-1840)
Moore, Eliza to William Holland 12-17-1856
Moore, Harriett to Isaac King 12-3-1870 (12-4-1870)
Moore, Jane to W. M. Kiningham 11-7-1844
Moore, Laura to James R. Williams 12-24-1873 (12-25-1873)
Moore, Louisa C. to Peter Tipps 8-15-1840 (8-20-1840)
Moore, Lucy E. to Wm. H. Matlock 1-30-1840
Moore, Malinda E. to Champion C. Cleveland 12-10-1857
Moore, Maria L. to Henry N. Hise 1-13-1838 (1-14-1838)
Moore, Mary Ann to Joel G. Mills 6-2-1849 (6-3-1849)
Moore, Mary E. B. to Eligah D. Robbins 6-1-1843
Moore, Mary E. to Samuel H. Cowan 3-5-1840 (no return)
Moore, Mary J. to Hugh Holland 10-20-1857 (no return)
Moore, Mary J. to Hugh Holland 10-20-1859 (no return)
Moore, Mary Lee to Henry Coolen 6-12-1865 (6-13-1865)
Moore, Mary M. to George W. Stamper 3-10-1846
Moore, Mattie to J. D. Arnett 1-1-1872 (1-3-1872)
Moore, Mere? to S. H. Keith 9-25-1865 (9-26-1865)
Moore, Nancy J. to Joseph N. Chapman 1-5-1852 (no return)
Moore, Rachiel J. to Joshua P. Cole 10-12-1841
Moore, Sarah to Robert Hines 8-3-1848 (no return)
Moore, Virginia A. to James Campbell 9-16-1848
Morgan, Emeline to Seth H. Hall 7-19-1854 (7-23-1854)
Morgan, Emily C. to John M. Kilpatrick 12-27-1843 (12-28-1843)
Morgan, Julia Ann to William C. Kitchens 3-5-1846 (no return)
Morgan, Margret H. to Moses J. Hardin 3-16-1847 (3-17-1847)
Morgan, Martha to William D. Metcalf 12-6-1841 (12-9-1841)
Morgan, Mary Ann to Russell B. Bridges 10-22-1856 (no return)
Morgan, Patsy to Henry Weaver 5-?-1839
Morgan, Rebecca P. to Jacob P. Awalt 1-2-1839 (no return)
Morill, Mary to Hardin Hill 10-9-1839 (no return)
Moris, Fanny E. to Asbury M. Byrom 11-25-1874
Morris, Bethenay to Wilson H. Clark 3-22-1849
Morris, Cynthia L. to Josiah C. Brown 8-30-1855
Morris, Cynthia to James N. Rossin 1-2-1849
Morris, D. A. to James Bagley 6-17-1867 (no return)
Morris, Elizabeth to J. B. Saunders 8-23-1859 (no return)
Morris, Elizabeth to J. S. Douglass 4-11-1866 (no return)
Morris, Ellen E. to John H. Miller 9-21-1848
Morris, Ellen to W. T. Finney 11-3-1866 (no return)
Morris, Hannah to William Farris 6-29-1874
Morris, Mariah to Henry Clark 10-25-1855
Morris, Mary A. to Bolden P. Lee 10-7-1852
Morris, Mary A. to John Partin 12-28-1853 (12-29-1853)
Morris, Mary Jane to Albert G. Green 10-29-1842 (11-3-1842)
Morris, Mary L. to James Saunders 10-25-1859 (10-26-1859)
Morris, Mary to Allen Vandozier 10-11-1843 (10-12-1843)
Morris, Nancy A. to J. B. Hudgins 12-23-1858
Morris, Nancy A. to Larkin Morris 2-27-1842
Morris, Nancy C. to A. W. Cobble 12-27-1865 (12-28-1865)
Morris, Polly Ann to Benj. F. Morris 9-27-1871
Morris, R. C. to C. C. Cook 2-9-1856 (2-10-1856)
Morris, Rabella to Isaac Bynum 7-28-1856 (7-29-1856)
Morris, Rebecca E. to J. H. Holt 3-18-1862 (3-20-1862)
Morris, Sarah A. to Rolin Morris 3-25-1874
Morris, Sarah G. to Andrew J. Pream 12-31-1855
Morris, Sarah to David W. Bynum 6-26-1844 (6-27-1844)
Morris, Sarah to John L. Matthews 6-27-1853 (no return)
Morris, Susan Jane to Albert G. Mann 10-15-1846 (10-16-1846)
Morris, Susan to John M. Sneed 4-30-1844 (5-1-1844)
Morris?, Susan Ann to Elias Weaver 9-10-1846 (no return)
Morrow, N. J. to John Hoosier 8-4-1865 (8-10-1865)
Mosel, E. C. to John W. Oakley 1-6-1847 (1-7-1847)
Moseley, Ann Eliza to Geo. F. Kilpatrick 10-7-1849
Moseley, Annie to J. W. Carter 11-2-1869 (11-4-1869)
Moseley, F. E. to A. P. Blackwell 3-13-1872 (no return)
Moseley, Lucy J. to Charles L. Blanton 5-30-1850 (no return)
Moseley, Lucy Jane to Henderson Williams 11-29-1849
Moseley, Mollie E. to James H. Keith 10-31-1871 (12-19-1871)
Moseley, Sarah A. to Wm. H. Noah 9-8-1868
Moseley, Sarah M. to Charles A. Coleman 12-27-1852 (12-28-1852)
Moton, Mary M. to Joseph Keener 2-15-1850
Mullikin, Jennie to S. W. Houghton 12-6-1858 (12-7-1858)
Mullin, Frances to Moses Cleavland 8-23-1858 (8-22?-1858)
Murphy, Celester to Samuel D. Eddie 1-24-1868
Murrell, Sarah W. to Zachariah G. Hurley 11-29-1848
Muse, Elizabeth M. to William H. Jones 7-10-1849
Muse, Ida A. to A. J. Poe 8-9-1859 (8-10-1859)
Muse, M. C. to J. H. Holt 10-27-1856 (10-29-1856)
Muse, Maria to West S. Childers 1-12-1839 (1-17-1839)
Muse, Mary A. to George W. Hill 12-18-1844 (12-19-1844)
Muse, Mary Ann to Thomas Green 5-11-1849 (5-13-1849)
Muse, Nancy C. to George W. Corn 8-22-1850
Muse, Omega C. to John H. Ivey 12-27-1852 (12-30-1852)
Muse, R. A. to H. K. P. Nicks 12-22-1866 (no return)
Muse, Rebecca B. to H. T. Hudgins 8-30-1866 (no return)
Muse, Rebecca to Wilson Holder 1-14-1842 (1-16-1842)
Muse, Rebecca to Wm. R. Green 4-21-1849 (no return)
Muse, Sarah A. to Rice Simpson 12-17-1856 (12-18-1856)
Muse, Sarah to William Hill 6-6-1850
Myers, Mary to John H. Williams 9-13-1850 (9-15-1850)

Myors, Nancy to Thos. S. Rogers 9-6-1856 (9-10-1856)
Myrick, Eliza J. to Wm. J. Collins 10-13-1856 (10-14-1856)
Nabors, Dida to Ruben Richison 1-23-1841 (no return)
Nally, Emma to W. F. Holder 8-29-1867 (no return)
Nance, M. A. to S. Best 4-17-1866 (4-18-1866)
Nash, America J. to Rush Claxton 6-5-1858 (no return)
Nash, Martha A. to Eliott C. Davis 7-26-1855
Neal, Eliza J. to William Church 6-13-1867
Neal, Josephine to J. W. Irby 10-9-1858
Neal, Mary M. to Henderson Church 11-28-1859
Neal, Mary to Joseph Damron 10-29-1870 (11-1-1870)
Neal, N. E. to Wm. E. Bishop 1-12-1871 (1-11?-1871)
Neal, Nancy M. to J. M. Neal 4-9-1859 (4-10-1859)
Neal, Narcissa to Richard Hall 2-18-1839 (no return)
Neal, Sarah E. to Isaac P. Syler 1-7-1874
Nelson, Charlotte to John Collins 3-2-1849
Nelson, Charlotte to Jonathan R. Stokes 7-14-1856
Nelson, Elizabeth J. to Wm. W. Cannon 3-4-1852 (3-5-1852)
Nelson, Elizabeth to George B. Damrel 1-19-1859
Nelson, Jane to William R. Stubblefield 12-17-1844
Nelson, Malissa to William Wilson 6-13-1857 (6-14-1857)
Nelson, Margret to James Rogers 6-9-1859
Nelson, Mary to Henry Nelson 6-11-1851
Nelson, Nancy to Joseph Rogers 9-10-1858
Nelson, Salina C. to Wm. J. Stubblefield 7-7-1846
Nelson, Sarah E. to John W. Rogers 8-6-1857
Nelson, Susan A. to George W. Simmons 8-27-1853 (8-28-1853)
Nelson, Susan to John Taylor 7-7-1853
Nelson, Zeppy to Benj. J. Vinson 12-12-1866 (12-?-1866)
Neville, Elizabeth to B. F. Anderson 8-21-1867 (8-22-1867)
Nevills, Mary to Timothy Swearingin 7-21-1866 (no return)
Newberry, Elizabeth to George W. Wagner 3-12-1852
Newberry, Nancy to John F. Stephens 10-18-1838
Newberry, Susan to Alford E. Cowan 10-12-1853 (10-13-1853)
Newman, Amanda to Wm. H. Weatherford 1-31-1856
Newman, Malinda J. to George W. Barnes 8-31-1855 (9-3-1855)
Newman, Mary A. to John T. Drake 1-10-1854 (no return)
Newman, Mary to Lewis Furney 1-7-1860 (1-8-1860)
Newman, Mary to William Stewart 8-13-1853 (8-14-1853)
Newman, Nancy E. to Wm. M. Latimer 8-20-1853 (8-25-1853)
Newman, Sarah A. C. to George A. Shook 3-21-1850
Nichols, E. A. to H. Gauff 11-30-1867 (no return)
Nichols, Martha Jane to James C. Brannon 8-8-1846 (8-14-1846)
Nichols, Mary to E. Boothman 3-10-1868 (no return)
Nichols, Nancy to William Foster 8-15-1855 (no return)
Nichols, Sallie A. (Miss) to A. L. Haggard 11-13-1867
Nichols, Sarah J. to John Goulden 11-18-1852
Night, Betsy to Daniel Conaway 3-2-1845
Nipins, Martha J. to Benjamin Tarman 11-2-1858 (11-6-1858)
Nippers, Harriet Elizabeth to Noah Tarwater 7-15-1867 (7-16-1867)
Nippers, Tennessee to Thos. Culver 6-28-1871
Nixon, Elizabeth to P. L. Hudgins 9-19-1866 (no return)
Nixon, Lurany R. to John W. Banks 12-23-1874
Nixon, Mahala to John Willhoite 10-18-1866 (no return)
Noah, Ellen to M. W. Litle 12-5-1865 (no return)
Noah, Hester A. to Jos. P. Sisk 10-4-1858
Noah, Hester A. to William P. McCord 3-1-1842 (no return)
Noah, Jane to Luke Kelley 12-26-1857 (12-31-1857)
Noah, Louisa C. to John T. Larry 5-29-1854
Noah, Margret to F. M. Horton 4-?-1859
Noah, Margrett to Abram Brazelton 12-22-1857 (12-23-1857)
Noah, Mary J. to James M. Glover 6-13-1857 (6-14-1857)
Noah, Mary to A. Campbell 12-28-1840
Noah, Patsey to Samuel Weeks 4-4-1842 (no return)
Noah, Susan to Luke Kelley 10-3-1853 (10-27-1853)
Noak, Mary Eliza to George S. Tipps 12-23-1851 (12-30-1851)
Noblett, Sophia Rebecca to G. W. Matthews 11-17-1870
Noe, Ary to Cornelius Holder 12-17-1847 (12-19-1847)
Noe, Mary to Archibald Campbell 7-26-1840
Norman, Elizabeth to Morgan Garner 4-26-1838 (no return)
Norman, Nancy to Robt. Smith 1-15-1848
Norman, Sarah to Hiram Guess 10-20-1842
Norris, L. H. to Ruben Farris 11-2-1869 (11-3-1869)
Norris, Lucy to E. M. Scott 8-11-1870 (no return)
Norwood, Manery J. to Euveh? M. West 7-19-1846

Nuckles, F. S. to D. S. Reynolds 8-?-1865 (no return)
Nuckles, Hannah to Jasper L. Horton 10-6-1856 (10-7-1856)
Nuckles, Mary A. to Oliver H. Bridges 1-4-1840
Nuckles, Suffey to Richard Chilton 4-2-1867 (4-3-1867)
Nugent, Emiley E. to Benj. Cheny 4-27-1854
Nugent, Margret to Miles Taylor 8-17-1838 (8-19-1838)
Nugent, Martha to George W. Dossett 6-28-1858 (no return)
Oakley, Anna E. to James H. Crawley 5-14-1867
Oakley, Eliza A. to James M. Darwin 7-15-1852 (7-16-1852)
Oakley, Elizabeth J. to George G. Miller 3-19-1846
Oakley, Frances to Richard F. Oakley 9-16-1856 (no return)
Oakley, Henretta to James Knight 12-11-1843 (12-14-1843)
Oakley, Judith to A. G. Little 12-23-1873 (12-24-1873)
Oakley, Judith to Nathan Gillaspie 10-24-1859
Oakley, M. E. to Jno. Hampton 1-13-1868 (no return)
Oakley, M. E. to Jones L. Turner 2-22-1872 (no return)
Oakley, Mary A. to James A. Oakley 3-26-1846
Oakley, Musadore to Samuel Hill 1-14-1857
Odear, M. C. to J. B. Elliott 12-2-1871 (12-3-1871)
Odear, Susan to William Guinn 4-25-1841
Odom, Eliza to John Lillis 11-26-1868
Odon, Keziah to Thomas Gillbreth 12-25-1848 (12-26-1848)
Oglesby, Miss J. A. to J. A. Reagin 5-19-1869 (5-20-1869)
Oldham, Elizabeth Ann to Daniel B. Stamps 8-19-1844 (8-22-1844)
Oliver, C. A. to Abner Wilkinson 8-11-1841 (no return)
Oliver, Eliza to Felix G. Sanders 11-?-1842 (11-?-1842)
Oliver, Frances A. to Pendleton F. Sandridge 7-26-1842 (8-2-1842)
Oliver, Jemima to Alexander S. Acklin 1-11-1849
Oliver, M. A. to Nathan Sims 2-15-1844
Oliver, M. E. to A. P. Moore 2-14-1840
Oliver, Mariah to Williamson R. Floyd 5-24-1856 (5-25-1856)
Oliver, Mary E. to R. J. Turner 12-9-1857 (12-10-1857)
Oliver, Mary to Atwood Clevins 1-13-1853 (1-18-1853)
Oliver, Mary to Daniel H. Taylor 11-12-1842 (11-13-1842)
Oliver, Rebecca to Orville Belle 12-21-1853 (12-22-1853)
Olliver, Melinda B. to William Bryant 3-18-1839 (no return)
Omings, Agnis to Zachariah R. Dotson 4-26-1848 (4-27-1848)
Orear, Allice to N. G. Freeman 11-19-1870 (11-20-1871)
Orear, E. M. to Benjamine H. Meadows 10-21-1874 (no return)
Orear, Eliza to John Finney 4-2-1847 (4-18-1847)
Orear, Margret to John Worn 9-12-1859
Orear, Martha to Wm. B. Hannah 12-3-1859
Orr, Josephene C. to G. A. Brown 12-10-1874 (no return)
Osborn, Elizabeth to William C. Lexton 11-2-1846 (11-5-1846)
Osborn, Isabella to L. D. Jones 3-6-1839 (no return)
Osborn, Lorena to Hezekiah Jiles 12-24-1841 (12-27-1841)
Osborn, M. J. to W. R. Limbaugh 10-3-1868 (no return)
Osborn, Mima to Meredith Hutton 2-8-1849 (2-9-1849)
Osborn, Nancy L. to William M. Wood 3-18-1873 (3-20-1873)
Osborn, Nannie C. to N. S. Anthony 3-10-1874 (3-12-1874)
Osborn, Sally to Martin C. Burkes 9-21-1838 (10-4-1838)
Osborn, Sarah E. to Jesse F. Stafford 10-25-1865 (10-26-1865)
Osborne, Mary to William Cole 11-2-1852
Overton, Mary to Jonas Barnes 5-19-1860 (5-20-1860)
Owens, Mary Ann to Thos. N. Fowler 8-5-1872 (no return)
Owins, Amelia Ann to John J. Scivally 1-25-1849 (2-2-1849)
Oyler, Sarah A. L. to V. E. Wallraven 5-20-1871 (5-21-1871)
Pace, Mary to Charley Barnes 9-1-1858
Pack, Canzada to John Collins 9-23-1867
Pack, Elizabeth to John Mason 8-14-1865 (8-20-1865)
Pack, Elizabeth to John Prince 6-6-1851
Pack, Jane to Thomas Terril 11-28-1873 (11-30-1873)
Pack, Mary Ann to Martin Simmons 9-25-1872 (9-26-1872)
Pack, Mary Jane to James Long 10-31-1860
Paden, N. J. to Elijah Sanders 4-7-1860 (4-8-1860)
Pane, Sarah to Bengamin Crownover 5-15-1857
Panter, Bettie to Jno. W. M. Kinsey 4-24-1874 (4-25-1874)
Parham, Lizzie to John Holder 8-11-1870 (no return)
Parker, Amelia to C. V. Higgins 2-10-1868
Parker, Margrett R. to Joseph W. Barley 1-31?-1860 (1-21?-1860)
Parker, Rachiel to Rodney Dotson 1-20-1843 (1-23-1843)
Parks, Cathrine H. to Ambros Shelton 9-8-1851
Parks, Clarrissa to James Davison 12-22-1852 (12-23-1852)
Parks, Creasy to Syler Acklin 11-12-1868 (no return)
Parks, Eliza Jane to Daniel Sills 2-14-1849

Parks, Elizabeth to James C. Grant 9-16-1851 (no return)
Parks, Esther to Hayston Gray 1-1-1875 (1-4-1875)
Parks, Febe P. to James M. Thomas 1-30-1849
Parks, Julia to Joseph Rodgers 1-7-1850
Parks, Julitty to George E. Whaley 1-2-1847 (1-3-1847)
Parks, Lavenia to John K. Bennette 9-24-1873 (9-25-1873)
Parks, Lucy T. to Samuel P. Ray 10-14-1852
Parks, M. G. to L. G. Wedington 12-9-1869 (no return)
Parks, Margret A. H. to J. C. Troxler 12-5-1866 (no return)
Parks, Martha J. to Daniel Thompson 3-7-1844
Parks, Mary A. to John Tipps 11-13-1854 (11-16-1854)
Parks, Mary F. to John R. Downum 12-8-1846 (12-22-1846)
Parks, Mary to Robert Newman 8-6-1866 (no return)
Parks, Nancy C. to Wm. B. Brandon 9-18-1855
Parks, Nancy to Calvin C. Burt 6-4-1854
Parks, P. E. to W. M. Davis 2-1-1871 (no return)
Parks, S. M. J. to D. K. Poe 12-11-1869 (12-16-1869)
Parks, Sally to J. W. Burress 6-24-1873
Parnell, Terressa to James Bramley 9-22-1847 (9-23-1847)
Parry, Sarah A. to Thomas Godby 2-8-1871 (no return)
Parsons, Elizabeth to A. J. Catchings 3-21-1859 (3-28-1859)
Parsons, Margret E. to William Law 5-23-1857 (no return)
Partin, A. J. to Joseph Connant 12-3-1873 (12-4-1873)
Partin, America to Jas. Long 10-25-1865 (10-29-1865)
Partin, Delitha to Armstead R. Oliver 6-1-1857
Partin, Elizabeth to Samuel Baker 2-12-1852
Partin, Malinda to John Wilder 3-12-1852
Partin, Martha to Albert Brannan 3-19-1846
Partin, Martha to George W. Wagner 11-6-1873 (11-11?-1873)
Partin, Polly to F. G. Bostick 12-15-1865 (no return)
Partin, Rebecca to Anderson A. Camp 10-3-1855 (10-4-1855)
Partin, Tennessee to John H. Hendley 3-21-1872
Partlow, Sarah to T. W. Culver 12-31-1872 (1-2-1873)
Patrick, Amelia H. to John M. Hyndes 11-21-1854
Patrick, Eliza A. to Jos. M. Burrough 11-9-1859 (11-10-1859)
Patrick, F. M. to P. S. Moseley 11-5-1867 (11-6-1867)
Patrick, Margret C. to Albert G. Handley 6-24-1850 (6-26-1850)
Patrick, Mollie H. to Sim West 2-16-1870 (2-17-1870)
Patterson, N. J. to C. L. Bolin 8-25-1868 (8-26-1868)
Pattie, Annie to Joseph M. Hawkins 6-26-1858 (6-27-1858)
Patton, Jerusha to Wm. Payne 8-1-1865 (8-5-1865)
Patton, M. J. to H. B. West 9-22-1859
Payne, Araminta M. to Gaston Burt 7-30-1855 (7-31-1855)
Payne, Elizabeth to Wm. Bishop 11-7-1865 (11-24-1865)
Payne, Louisa J. to John W. Booth 2-24-1872 (2-25-1872)
Payne, Mary J. to Robert Singleton 2-10-1870 (no return)
Payne, N. E. to M. C. Wells 9-5-1859 (9-6-1859)
Payne, Nancy J. to J. D. Young 5-17-1871 (no return)
Payne, Nancy to Levi Hofman 1-14-1874 (1-24-1874)
Peacock, Corsady E. to Sampson M. Malone 8-2-1859
Pearson, Ann to Robt. Syler 11-17-1853
Pearson, E. J. to Thornton Martin 6-17-1867
Pearson, Frances to Hilliard R. Shores 4-28-1852 (4-29-1852)
Pearson, Lizzie to William Gaines 7-1-1871 (7-27-1871)
Pearson, Lucinda to Joseph Winton 3-13-1872 (3-14-1872)
Pearson, Lurinda to Joseph Winters 3-13-1872 (3-14-1872)
Pearson, Margrett to George Garner 8-28-1871 (8-30-1871)
Pearson, Mary A. to Levi Leverton 8-7-1865 (8-10-1865)
Pearson, Mary to Josiah Collins 9-6-1844
Pearson, Mary to Richard Shepard 12-20-1864 (12-21-1864)
Pearson, Sarah to Stephen Rose 6-1-1843
Peery, Sarah to David Gipson 1-8-1844
Pelham, Iby to Arnold McBee 7-8-1867 (no return)
Pelham, Margret to George Barnes 5-23-1859
Pelham, Margret to Jefferson Pack 9-8-1866 (no return)
Pelham, Margret to Lewis Miller 8-15-1865 (8-16-1865)
Pelham, Nancy A. to Dennis Barnes 11-27-1865 (no return)
Pelham, Nancy to Pleasant Harrison 1-12-1871 (1-13-1871)
Pelham, Rena C. (Miss) to Albert Clensman 2-3-1874
Pelham, Sarah to George Hooser 2-28-1870 (3-2-1870)
Pelham, Sarah to R. B. Miller 3-23-1874 (3-25-1874)
Pelham, Serena to Joseph Pack 5-7-1854
Pellam, Rena to Daniel Singleton 11-23-1865 (11-28-1865)
Pellum, Elizabeth to Thos. Pearson 8-7-1865 (8-8-1865)
Pellum, Malinda to H. Cannon 8-1-1865 (8-5-1865)
Pellum, Margret to Thomas Rose 8-29-1865 (8-30-1865)
Pennington, Annie L. to John Simmons 12-18-1872
Pennington, Luticia A. to W. G. Pennington 11-26-1868
Peril, Sarah A. to John Jefferson 1-13-1853 (1-14-1853)
Perkins, M. E. to Richard L. Holland 11-29-1853 (no return)
Perkins, Margrett to William Rogers 4-14-1871
Perkins, Milly to Joseph Miller 9-28-1840 (no return)
Perkins, Nancy J. to Richmond T. Buckner 12-11-1843 (12-12-1843)
Perkins, Sarah A. to Richmond T. Buckner 4-7-1849
Perry, Barbary to Daniel Wells 2-2-1853
Perry, Elizabeth to Melledge Gambol 12-27-1849
Perry, Jane to George Ellis 4-15-1871
Perry, Jemima to John M. Haskins 3-26-1841
Perry, Jennie to Jonas A. Nelson 6-1-1874
Perry, Martha N. to Richard Hill 10-29-1866 (11-?-1866)
Perry, Matilda to Ferney Swearingame 3-14-1850 (3-17-1850)
Perry, Pegg to Samuel Norwood 10-6-1873
Perry, Sarah J. to John W. Adams 4-10-1852
Perry, Sarah to Bayly Hill 2-17-1842 (2-20-1842)
Perry, Sarah to Wm. Davis 8-24-1865 (9-15-1865)
Perryman, Artemecia to F. M. Nixon 9-24-1870 (9-28-1870)
Peters, Agness to Clay Buchanan 10-2-1873
Petty, Sarah F. to John R. Fagg 10-26-1870 (no return)
Peyton, Evy to Peter Mayes 10-23-1873
Phelin, Mary Harris to Robt. L. Watt 2-3-1872 (2-6-1872)
Phillips, Elizabeth to G. G. Banks 2-24-1859
Phillips, Fanny to T. B. Farris 12-4-1868 (no return)
Phillips, Louisa J. to Payton Darwin 7-19-1873 (7-23-1873)
Phillips, Lucy J. to A. J. Little 1-13-1870 (no return)
Phillips, Lucy to H. A. Shelton 11-25-1867 (11-26-1867)
Phillips, M. A. to P. B. Darwin 8-22-1868 (no return)
Phillips, Martha E. to William P. Taylor 2-6-1850 (2-13-1850)
Phillips, Nannie E. to Benj. B. Jones 7-12-1858
Phillips, Patsey to Henry Sanders 1-2-1844 (1-15-1844)
Pickeny, M. F. to A. Z. Campbell 11-22-1873
Pickett, Easter Ann to John Smith 4-23-1840 (no return)
Pickett, Pitor Ann to John Pulliam 7-30-1846
Pickle, Elizabeth to Samuel Hill 12-24-1867
Pierce, Jane to Henry Miles 7-1-1851 (no return)
Piggeon, Katy to John W. Miles 1-15-1873
Pippin, Nancy E. to James Grider 2-21-1861
Pitcock, Amanda M. to Joseph C. Parks 9-28-1852
Pitcock, Cassy A. to Ephraim Michiel 5-2-1852
Pitcock, Dana to Temple J. Cashion 11-25-1856 (no return)
Pitcock, Jane to Sampson Kennada 2-11-1855 (2-12-1855)
Pitcock, Nancy to Alford Williamson 9-23-1843 (no return)
Pitt, Mary E. to William Puryor 10-3-1838 (10-4-1838)
Pless, M. to H. H. Bramlett 2-10-1870 (no return)
Poats, Elizabeth M. to Joel J. Manier 6-20-1846 (6-?-1846)
Poe, E. H. to J. F. Black 12-23-1867 (12-26-1867)
Poe, Frances to John Poe 7-18-1840 (7-20-1840)
Poe, M. E. to Thos. B. Raney 12-31-1859 (11-22-1859?)
Pollock, F. D. to W. B. Smith 7-19-1869 (7-20-1869)
Pollock, Malinda to J. C. Reynolds 10-4-1858 (10-16-1858)
Pollock, N. C. to Martin Sansom 12-31-1867
Pollock, S. R. E. to Wm. M. Reynolds 9-14-1859 (9-15-1859)
Pope, Laura to J. C. Powell 9-22-1874 (8?-27-1874)
Porter, Allice to W. W. Garner 10-30-1867
Porter, Elizabeth M. to Hugh Thomas 12-30-1852 (1-3-1853)
Porter, Hannah E. to Marcus M. Henderson 6-20-1850
Porter, Pattie E. to A. J. Kiningham 2-5-1872 (no return)
Porter, Sarah Ann to William W. Petty 11-12-1844
Posey, Eliza A. to Samuel Dodson 9-25-1857
Posey, Martha to Isaac Gross 6-10-1856 (6-12-1856)
Poston, M. E. to R. J. Bridges 4-23-1867
Potes, Sarah A. to William P. Heiston 4-9-1846 (7-9-1846)
Potts, Frankey A. to Freeman Moore 7-27-1848
Powell, Arrina to Jessee Vann 7-8-1851
Powell, Manerva to James Mahan 1-14-1871 (1-16-1871)
Powell, Mary Jane to William Vaun 9-3-1855 (9-4-1855)
Powell, Nancy to William Keedy 8-27-1845 (8-28-1845)
Powell, Precilla Jane to George W. Hunt 3-21-1844
Powell, Telitha J. to H. H. Huffer 5-27-1874
Powell, Virginia A. to Geo. W.? Hall 11-6-1866 (no return)
Powels, Angeline to E. F. Tripp 9-2-1865 (9-5-1865)

Power, M. to George Ethridge 12-?-1858 (12-20-1858)
Power, Sallie A. to William L. Thompson 3-11-1873 (3-12-1873)
Powers, Mary E. to B. C. Starnes 10-25-1871 (no return)
Pratt, H. to Wm. Sutherland 10-17-1859 (no return)
Pratt, Martha to George Stephens 11-28-1874
Pratt, Martha to Joseph Bibbons 2-19-1853 (2-20-1853)
Pratt, Susanah to Robert Gifford 12-15-1851 (no return)
Presswood, Cathrine to David Buchanan 9-18-1858 (9-19-1858)
Preuet, Cathrine H. to John W. Blakley 4-17-1872 (no return)
Prewett, Mary (Miss) to William R. Tankersley 4-2-1874 (4-5-1874)
Prewit, Sarah to Laten Cooper 1-20-1843 (1-22-1843)
Price, E. to A. Thomas 10-8-1867 (10-10-1867)
Price, Jennie (Miss) to John Stewart 1-20-1874 (1-28-1874)
Price, Mary Ann to John Winford 10-27-1845
Price, Nancy Jane to Samuel Stone 11-28-1866 (no return)
Price, Sarah S. to Joseph M. Burrough 4-25-1850
Prince, Charity D. to John Lynch 12-4-1872 (no return)
Prince, F. E. to William Miller 3-21-1868 (3-22-1868)
Prince, Jennie to John B. Seargeant 10-21-1874 (no return)
Prince, Margrett to Shadrick Pellum 2-14-1842 (2-20-1842)
Prince, Mary to Thos. J. Jetton 8-17-1870 (no return)
Prince, Nancy Ann to Andrew J. Garner 1-29-1872 (2-3-1872)
Prior, Mary C. to J. C. Garner 3-20-1866
Provine, M. A. to James S. Colyar 8-28-1840
Prudee, Ann to John Dending 3-8-1859 (no return)
Pruit, Nancy J. to Wm. A. Marris 12-19-1851 (12-22-1851)
Pulliun, Sarah Ann to George W. Pickett 12-10-1846
Purvers, Martha R. to William N. Ragsdale 8-24-1841 (9-7-1841)
Purvis, Virginia A. to Peter Waldman 9-13-1848
Putnam, Rebecca to Thomas Daniel 2-2-1860 (no return)
Pyland, Frances C. to Williford Davis 12-2-1857 (12-3-1857)
Pyland, Margret A. to C. A. Booth 11-12-1870 (11-16-1870)
Pylant, Fannie E. to James W. Womack 9-11-1873 (9-12-1873)
Pylant, Marena to Peter Wensell 2-14-1870 (no return)
Pylant, Martha to Stephen Whitson 9-28-1870 (no return)
Qualls, Constance A. to Harrison Hall 8-19-1852
Qualls, Harriett to Wesley Sanders 12-6-1853
Qualls, Sarah to Wm. P. Sandridge 12-27-1853 (12-29-1853)
Radigins, Eliza to Wm. Brown 12-1-1858 (12-2-1858)
Raggins, Cathrine H. to Geo. S. McCutcheon 2-13-1843 (2-14-1843)
Ragsdale, M. E. to William Martin 1-5-1870 (no return)
Ragsdale, Mary P. T. to Joseph Newman 11-10-1842
Rail, Mahala to Francis Cavin 10-14-1843
Rainey (Mrs.), Ruth to Josiah W. Marshall 2-3-1864 (2-5-1864)
Rallston, Julia to W. J. Gillespie 1-18-1872 (no return)
Rane, Rosanah to Jacob Holt 10-31-1857 (11-1-1857)
Raney, Rebecca to A. J. Woodard 9-9-1871
Ransom, Nannie L. to Mark H. White 11-20-1873
Rask, Elizabeth to Wm. J. Mathews 6-30-1860 (7-1-1860)
Rate, Susan to J. A. Wingait 3-27-1872 (3-28-1872)
Rauney?, Phebe J. to Hezekiah Ray 9-29-1856 (no return)
Ray, Bettie to R. S. Atkins 1-12-1870
Ray, Jane to Benj. A. Buchanan 11-28-1872
Ray, Jane to Fredrick T. Dean 8-6-1853 (8-8-1853)
Ray, Margret to John Griffin 4-26-1872 (no return)
Ray, Mary C. to Henry Hendricks 8-18-1856 (8-19-1856)
Ray, Nancy to Jacob Church 7-5-1865 (7-7-1865)
Ray, Nancy to James Shropshire 9-29-1843
Ray, Ruhama E. to Jas. C. Gantt 8-8-1860 (8-9-1860)
Ray, Sarah M. to Robt. Dean 12-27-1859 (12-28-1859)
Ray, Susan J. to Thos. L. Poe 12-27-1871 (1-2-1872)
Ready, M. A. to J. A. Hasty 2-7-1860 (no return)
Reagin, Caroline to William M. Evans 7-6-1849
Reagin, Delphia J. to John Hockersmith 1-21-1856
Reagin, Douzella to E. M. Rawlins 8-1-1870 (8-4-1870)
Reagin, E. F. to John Anderson 1-7-1840
Reagin, N. P. to W. P. Nevill 8-28-1866 (no return)
Reagin, Patsy to E. J. Hockersmith 6-25-1859 (6-26-1859)
Reagus, Elizabeth to William Davis 8-2-1853 (no return)
Reasoner, Sarah to William Stewart 2-17-1851
Reed, Angeline to James H. Cook 3-5-1858 (3-7-1858)
Reed, Ann to Wm. Langan 4-16-1859
Reed, Barbary to Daniel Hendricks 12-27-1858 (1-1-1859)
Reed, Fanny to T. J. McBride 12-19-1871 (12-21-1871)
Reed, Harriett to William C. Richardson 10-16-1844

Reed, Mary Jane to Carter Mahaffey 8-16-1859 (8-18-1859)
Reed, Mary to John A. Hethcoat 12-14-1872 (12-15-1872)
Reed, Polly to Michiel Aikin 8-23-1849 (8-28-1849)
Reed, Sarah to James P. Rice 9-21-1853
Reed, Virginia Ellen to John Gipson 3-14-1872
Reed, Virginia to Balis Ladd 4-10-1865 (4-13-1865)
Reeves, Caroline W. to F. A. Laughmiller 9-9-1847
Reeves, Cornelia E. to Richard F. Sims 1-28-1853
Reeves, Martha A. to Atwood Hayde 11-29-1849
Reeves, Mary C. to William J. Bryant 9-25-1851
Reeves, Nancy R. to Henry P. S. Alspaugh 9-3-1853 (9-4-1853)
Reeves, Prudence A. to John F. Robertson 11-28-1855 (11-29-1855)
Reeves, Sarah E. to John B. Feemster 4-8-1851
Reid, Malinda J. to Joel Jetton 7-20-1859 (7-24-1859)
Renegar, Emily to J. N. Russell 9-15-1870 (no return)
Renfro, Caroline A. to Anderson J. Lee 2-7-1855 (2-8-1855)
Rengar, A. to Z. R. Murrell 2-11-1868 (2-13-1868)
Revis, Delila P. to Geo. W. Brown 2-15-1872
Reynolds, Adaline to Thomas Grant 7-25-1866 (no return)
Reynolds, Amanda M. to John Bishop 10-2-1873
Reynolds, Martha A. to Robt. S. Hampton 11-30-1858 (12-2-1858)
Reynolds, Mary to S. A. Catchings 12-11-1867 (12-12-1867)
Reynolds, S. R. E. to James Hime 12-14-1867
Reynols, W. C. to W. M. Kitchens 7-6-1871
Rhew, Elizabeth F. to John Chitwood 7-31-1871 (8-2-1871)
Rice, E. to William Money 4-7-1860 (no return)
Rice, Elizabeth J. to Andrew Hicks 9-5-1851 (9-7-1851)
Rice, Elizabeth to William G. Griffith 6-17-1841 (no return)
Rice, Lyddia J. to Mc. H. Davis 2-16-1872 (2-18-1872)
Rice, Margret A. to Green H. Byrom 10-7-1854 (10-15-1854)
Rich, Eliza Jane to John W. Brandon 4-10-1841 (4-11-1841)
Rich, M. (Miss) to B. T. Elliott 6-2-1874 (6-7-1874)
Rich, Mary Ann to Dink Jackson 11-3-1871 (11-5-1871)
Rich, Mary F. to William Newel 9-23-1871 (9-24-1871)
Rich, Sarah W. S. to A. J. Finney 2-20-1869 (2-22-1869)
Rich, Sarah to Newton Green 2-7-1870
Richards, Mary to Martin Crabtree 6-18-1874
Richardson, Elizabeth to John Howell 6-7-1855 (6-9-1855)
Richardson, Hannah to A. S. Jones 2-16-1865 (2-19-1865)
Richardson, Margaret to Calvin Richardson 5-19-1853
Richardson, Margrett to Wm. E. Brown 8-11-1874 (8-13-1874)
Richardson, Martha to Joseph Vaughan 6-24-1868
Richardson, Mary to J. C. Coker 3-5-1866
Riddicks, Nancy to James Sexton 7-19-1856 (7-20-1856)
Riddle, Caroline to Bayley Hays 6-7-1856 (no return)
Riddle, Elizabeth to Robinson Wagner 5-9-1839 (no return)
Riddle, Jane to Cowan Montgomery 3-17-1862?
Riddle, Lucinda to Chaney Smith 1-6-1857 (1-7-1857)
Riddle, M. C. to W. P. Cole 10-14-1869 (no return)
Riddle, Mary A. to Wm. McClain Kilpatrick 9-10-1855 (no return)
Riddle, Mary to Carroll E. Marshall 12-27-1855
Riddle, Nancy to A. J. Wagoner 10-22-1860
Riddle, Nancy to Reuben S. Faris 3-16-1861? (with 1851)
Riddle, Susan to James Damron 1-3-1868 (1-8-1868)
Rigeway, E. A. to James A. Taft 11-20-1860 (11-21-1860)
Riggins, Mary M. to Simpson Sewell 9-8-1849 (9-9-1849)
Ripps, Rachiel M. to Geo. L. Houston 10-13-1846 (10-14-1846)
Roan, Elizabeth to James C. Crownover 5-29-1856
Robbins, Elizabeth to Wm. J. Mason 5-26-1858 (no return)
Robbins, Unice L. to E. R. McDaniel 11-17-1840 (11-20-1840)
Robenson, A. P. to S. M. Robenson 8-12-1865 (no return)
Robenson, Rachiel A. to James R. Mankin 2-7-1854 (no return)
Roberson, Elizabeth to Joseph Cook 1-10-1845
Roberson, Martha to Eli Honey 7-17-1865 (no return)
Roberson, Martha to Joseph Brown 9-20-1850 (9-21-1850)
Roberson, Nancy to William Hinshaw 5-2-1844
Roberson, Rebecca to George Fox 12-23-1845
Roberson, Sarah T. to Andrew J. Taylor 8-18-1874 (8-20-1874)
Roberson, Susan to George W. Hopkins 9-11-1850 (9-12-1850)
Roberts, Ann to Daniel Cunningham 12-9-1865 (12-10-1865)
Roberts, Julia to James Brewer 5-29-1874 (5-31-1874)
Roberts, Mary F. to James F. Mayes 8-20-1869 (no return)
Robertson, Cathrine to Alford Bradford 5-15-1850 (no return)
Robertson, John F. to Prudence Reeves 11-28-1855 (11-19-1855)
Robertson, M. E. to John W. Denson 5-10-1860

Robertson, Martha to Henry Jones 12-9-1865
Robertson, Martha to James Hopkins 7-31-1858 (8-1-1858)
Robertson, Martha to James Robertson 7-1-1858 (no return)
Robertson, Mary to John Davis 9-12-1857 (9-13-1857)
Robertson, Nancy M. to Henderson Neal 12-26-1872
Robeson, Christiana to Solomon Limbaugh 3-19-1838 (no return)
Robinson, Elizabeth W. to J. M. Sturdevant 6-10-1855
Robinson, Emeline to Daniel M. Williams 12-10-1850
Robinson, Hellen to Joseph Nassamer 12-22-1860
Robinson, M. J. to M. H. Rich 2-25-1862 (2-26-1862)
Robinson, Margret to Thomas C. Whitesides 5-24-1838
Robinson, Nancy J. to Wm. Miller 12-6-1853
Robinson, Sarah to Elijah Bradford 9-12-1844 (9-15-1844)
Roda, Martha to John Brougham 6-2-1859
Rodgers, Julia to Wm. Woodard 10-17-1868
Rogers, Elizabeth to Isaac Parks 9-6-1848 (9-8-1848)
Rogers, Elizabeth to Willis Burt 2-4-1853 (2-8-1853)
Rogers, Frances P. to Benj. Shasteen 1-4-1859
Rogers, Henrietta to James Austin 2-3-1872 (2-5-1872)
Rogers, M. J. to Thomas Guthrie 4-16-1860 (no return)
Rogers, Margret to John Nelson 6-29-1845 (no return)
Rogers, Mariah to G. J. Miles 5-2-1851 (5-3-1851)
Rogers, Martha J. to Thos. M. Guthrie 4-14-1860 (4-15-1860)
Rogers, Martha to John S. Hill 6-11-1851 (6-12-1851)
Rogers, Mary A. to John M. Brannon 10-7-1839 (10-8-1839)
Rogers, N. A. to W. A. Coldwell 9-26-1867
Rogers, Nancy A. to Wm. Smith 2-18-1865 (2-19-1865)
Rogers, Nancy P. to James M. Nelson 3-9-1853 (3-10-1853)
Rogers, Terressa to A. J. Simpson 4-6-1846 (4-9-1846)
Rogers, Terrissa to Ezekiel F. Shasteen 9-15-1857
Roleman, Lucy A. to Wm. W. Webb 8-9-1855
Roleman, Lucy to William Gunn 4-25-1871 (4-26-1871)
Roleman, Martha to James S. Parks 8-3-1849 (no return)
Roleman, Rebecca to Wm. A. Parks 2-14-1849 (2-15-1849)
Rollins, Mary E. to G. G. M. Hockersmith 5-13-1871 (5-21-1871)
Rollins, Sarah to James V. Acklin 9-9-1839
Rone, Sarah A. to Jas. F. Bell 12-17-1867 (no return)
Rose, Denty to Wm. Pack 5-20-1851
Rose, Dinty to B. Odear 6-19-1869 (6-17?-1869)
Rose, Dolly to Henry Long 11-7-1865 (11-26-1865)
Rose, Elenor A. to Silas Thomas? 4-21-1850
Rose, Elizabeth to Charles Kelley 5-8-1867
Rose, Eveline to Wiley Dutton 1-17-1843
Rose, Lizzie to George King 1-30-1866 (1-31-1866)
Rose, Lucinda to Josiah C. Garner 11-19-1850
Rose, Malisa Ann to Benj. Catchings 8-12-1844
Rose, Mary A. to Harmon Bennett 9-12-1865 (no return)
Rose, Nancy to David Payne 1-28-1867 (no return)
Rose, Nicy to John M. Ake 10-12-1844
Rose, Sarah to William Williams 8-4-1870 (no return)
Rose, Virginia to J. A. Duncan 7-2-1866 (7-5-1867?)
Roseborough, Eliza M. to Clement Arledge 1-20-1853
Roseborough, Elizabeth J. to Joseph Frame 2-23-1852
Roseborough, Lucy A. to Rhalient Hunt 10-12-1853 (10-13-1853)
Roseborough, Marah? E. to Thomas J. Oakley 1-17-1859 (1-18-1859)
Roseborough, Mariel L. to John B. Lusk 12-27-1840
Roseman, Parmelia to William J. Grills 12-2-1843 (12-3-1843)
Roton, N. M. to T. A. Chapman 8-23-1865 (8-24-1865)
Roughton, Almira M. to Wm. M. McClure 12-28-1872 (no return)
Roughton, Hester A. to Isaac T. South 10-17-1874 (10-18-1874)
Rowe, Elizabeth O. to Elijah H. Ikard 1-25-1843 (1-26-1843)
Rowe, Fanny W. to J. L. W. Blair 3-1-1865 (3-2-1865)
Royalty, Mary to Nathaniel Parton 7-14-1838 (7-15-1838)
Royalty, Nancy A. to Patrick Harvy 7-21-1850
Ruder, Sarah to William Gipson 2-12-1847
Runnells, S. E. to Z. W. Webb 1-1-1866 (1-3-1866)
Runnels, Laura to John A. Adams 2-16-1856 (2-17-1856)
Runnels, Mary A. to Joseph Moses 4-29-1857 (no return)
Runnels, Matilda to Solomon Banks 7-31-1850 (8-4-1850)
Runnels, Nancy to Abram Bagget 7-19-1838
Runnels, Sarah to Wm. R. Finney 8-14-1851
Rusell, Mary to Joshua Sutherland 1-19-1842 (no return)
Russell, Adaline to J. C. McEnally 12-8-1859
Russell, Althenia to William F. Bass 10-27-1870
Russell, Althuna to Thomas H. Woods 1-20-1858 (1-21-1858)

Russell, Darcus to I. N. Brakefield 9-27-1847
Russell, Eliza E. to W. A. Bradshaw 12-31-1860 (1-1-1861)
Russell, Ellen to Thomas Linticum 10-7-1841
Russell, Margrett to John Guess 11-8-1842 (11-10-1842)
Russell, Nancy to Benjamin Vernor 9-2-1839 (9-3-1839)
Russey, Martha J. to William F. Henderson 11-17-1842 (11-16?-1842)
Russey, Mary E. to Edward J. Skyrme 6-6-1855 (6-7-1855)
Russey, Mary to John M. Hutchins 1-5-1869 (no return)
Russol, N. J. to Albert Foster 1-6-1868 (1-7-1868)
Rutledge, Lucy to Benza Raines 7-11-1859 (7-12-1859)
Rutledge, M. M. to J. T. Lipscomb 8-23-1869 (8-24-1869)
Rutledge, Mary E. A. to James A. Holder 7-17-1855
Rutledge, Ophelia E. to Thos. J. Larkin 8-20-1867 (no return)
Rutledge, Susan to Ivey Saunders 2-2-1852 (no return)
Sample, Martha to Michiel Parker 1-26-1867 (no return)
Sanders, A. M. to C. F. Tapscott 11-30-1870 (no return)
Sanders, Elizabeth to W. S. Partin 3-25-1868 (3-26-1868)
Sanders, Georgian to Levi Lawson 2-21-1866 (2-22-1866)
Sanders, Louisa to M. Madden 9-28-1866 (9-29-1866)
Sanders, Martha to C. C. Bean 6-7-1857
Sanders, Mary A. to H. P. Brooks 1-17-1872
Sanders, Mary to Wm. H. Neal 3-31-1859 (4-1-1859)
Sanders, Nancy Ann to Jessee G. Runnels 8-11-1856 (8-12-1856)
Sanders, Nancy C. to Wm. H. Neal 2-13-1850 (2-14-1850)
Sanders, Nancy to John Perry 12-3-1868
Sanders, Syntha to Jonathan M. Runnells 8-10-1839
Sandidge, Sarah to Joseph Sparks 12-7-1843 (12-19-1843)
Sandridge, M. M. to Jacob Langston 7-17-1865 (7-18-1865)
Sands, Louisa to Victor Vernier 1-15-1868 (1-21-1868)
Sansom, Martha M. to Wm. G. Hill 9-4-1865 (10-10-1865)
Sansom, Nancy C. to Jonas Barnes 10-4-1865 (10-6-1865)
Sargent, Mahala to Robt. Smith 5-30-1851 (6-1-1851)
Sartin, Clarra to Clarence Horn 9-25-1867
Sarton, Mary to John F. Black 1-14-1839 (1-17-1839)
Saxton, Elizabeth to William H. Phillips 1-12-1846 (1-13-1846)
Scivally, R. A. to James W. McLeroy 9-28-1872 (no return)
Scivily, Miss S. E. to W. L. R. Carson 4-17-1869 (no return)
Scoggins, Martha to John Brisco 8-27-1843
Scott, Adaline P. to James Lockhart 10-8-1844 (10-10-1844)
Scott, Jane H. to Geo. W. Waitt 12-24-1845 (12-20?-1845)
Scott, Louiza to Isaac Mason 7-2-1860
Scott, Nancy to George Hill 1-20-1840
Scott, Sarah A. to Reubin F. Henson 10-13-1850
Seargant, Elizabeth to John Bruce 1-14-1869
Seargeant, Ellen to C. B. Austell 12-11-1858 (1-1-1859)
Seargent, Elizabeth to John Sullivan 10-23-1854 (10-25-1854)
Seargent, Elizabeth to Michael Roberson 6-26-1854
Seargent, Ellen to R. A. Earndalo 1-5-1859 (no return)
Seargent, Jane to Peter Williams 6-28-1866 (no return)
Seargent, Julia A. to W. H. Cowan 3-31-1868 (?-?-1868)
Seargent, Martha Jane to William Swann 6-4-1844
Seargent, Martha to Lexington Asher 1-15-1853 (1-18-1853)
Seargent, Mary E. to Thos. F. Kuningham 4-4-1861
Seargent, Mary to Thomas Emerson 12-19-1839
Seargent, Sarah to Carrel Nevil 12-27-1866 (no return)
Seaton, Elizabeth J. to Henry J. Cardon 12-21-1855 (12-23-1855)
Seaton, Elizabeth to Howell Hally 11-14-1839
Seaton, Jane to Landon C. Jetton 11-19-1852 (no return)
Seaton, Sarah E. to Henry W. South 9-24-1856 (9-25-1856)
Seatyon, Julia to Wm. Seaton 1-21-1868 (no return)
Sells, Angeline to Wm. A. Stubblefield 7-6-1872
Sells, Elizabeth Hannah to William Sparks 9-30-1870
Sells, Elizabeth to Robert Morris 9-1-1869 (no return)
Sells, L. C. to J. P. Sells 8-26-1869 (no return)
Sells, Margret E. to James T. Skidmore 10-25-1855 (10-26-1855)
Sells, Martha J. to J. C. Summers 8-29-1865 (8-30-1865)
Sells, Mary F. to Benj. F. Holder 8-?-1870 (no return)
Sells, Mary Jane to Joseph Champion 11-17-1870 (11-20-1870)
Sells, Mary to George M. West 7-6-1871 (7-9-1871)
Sells, Nancy to John Wilkerson 3-13-1872 (3-14-1872)
Senter, Louisa to Warren Jackson 3-24-1844
Senter, Susan to John Hanley no date (with 1843)
Sentor, Mahala to William Paul 11-10-1848
Sewell, Cathrine to John H. Baxter 5-10-1854 (5-12-1854)
Sewell, Elendor to Squire B. Baxter 6-15-1850

Sewell, Margret A. to Daniel Champion 10-4-1856 (10-5-1856)
Sewell, Mary A. to J. T. Huddleston 12-31-1868 (no return)
Sewell, Rebecca to Joseph Norman 10-16-1855
Sewell, Rhoda Ann to Allen Christian 7-9-1855 (8-9-1855)
Sewell, S. M. to P. B. Hawkins 2-6-1871 (no return)
Sexton, Jane to W. C. Catchings 11-16-1858 (11-17-1858)
Sexton, Martha to Bradford G. Martin 11-15-1854 (11-16-1854)
Sexton, Mary J. to Newton J. Mitchell 3-24-1858
Sexton, Nancy to Nathaniel Osborn 1-15-1849 (1-17-1849)
Sexton, Pateena to Wm. Riley 7-29-1848 (7-30-1848)
Shaers?, Mary to Shelton Watson 2-15-1841 (no return)
Shaffitt, Levina to William Easley 1-20-1844
Sharp, Amelia Ann to James W. Sharp 6-11-1857
Sharp, Edney (Miss) to B. K. Duncan 11-25-1869
Sharp, Elizabeth J. to Napolian Cromwell 8-16-1843 (no return)
Sharp, Indiana C. M. to Eli Moss 8-20-1853
Sharp, Julia J. to Robert Hancock 4-16-1840
Sharp, Mary A. to Nicholas J. Ford 8-21-1842
Sharp, Mary Ann to Clifton R. Embrey 3-5-1846 (3-6-1846)
Sharp, Mary Ann to Green Brazelton 2-27-1845
Sharp, Virginia A. to O. H. B. Duncan 4-8-1843 (4-9-1843)
Shasteen, E. L. to Franklin Jarnegan 1-18-1867 (1-20-1867)
Shasteen, Elizabeth to Abram F. Poe 1-6-1851
Shasteen, Lauvisa to William R. Duvall 11-19-1874
Shasteen, Lethan to L. V. Holder 3-26-1867
Shasteen, Louisa J. to Thompson W. Graves 11-16-1852
Shasteen, Margrett to George Sisk 5-16-1846 (5-17-1846)
Shasteen, Martha E. to G. G. T. Ray 11-9-1874 (11-10-1874)
Shasteen, N. E. to W. J. Curle 11-14-1866 (no return)
Shasteen, Phebe to John H. Farris 9-15-1865 (9-17-1865)
Shasteen, Sarah E. to R. R. Grant 9-14-1867
Shasteen, Sarah to Joshua Brown 8-10-1870 (no return)
Shasteen, Sophia W. to Joab B. Muse 9-12-1856
Shasteen, T. E. to H. J. Byrom 12-22-1866
Shaver, Martha A. to Jessee M. Grubbs 9-4-1872 (no return)
Shavers, Elizabeth to John Parks 4-12-1855 (4-22-1855)
Shavers, M. A. to W. M. Anderson 7-23-1874 (no return)
Shaw, Elizabeth to Rice Collins 12-12-1870 (no return)
Shaw, Elizabeth to Samuel Partin 8-28-1851
Shaw, Martha to Robert Carson 3-12-1849
Shelby, Mollie to Fredrick Brooks 9-19-1870 (9-20-1870)
Shelton, Cathrine to William H. H. Bolin 5-10-1858
Shelton, Malinda J. to F. A. Snodgrass 9-7-1871
Shelton, Mary E. to D. W. Huffer 1-23-1874 (1-25-1874)
Shelton, Mary E. to Thomas Knight 11-13-1874 (11-21-1874)
Shelton, Stacy to W. G. Berry 9-30-1867
Sherell, Cathrine to Samuel Gunn 8-2-1841 (8-5-1841)
Sherman, Ida to William Comstock 1-29-1867
Shoo, Nancy to R. T. Bates 1-18-1868 (1-19-1868)
Shook, Jennie to Thos. J. Middleton 8-21-1871 (no return)
Shook, Mary to W. W. Jacoway 12-19-1871
Shook, Mollie to John B. Looney 12-18-1867 (12-19-1867)
Shores, Frances to William M. Pearson 10-11-1847 (10-13-1847)
Short, A. R. to John Butterworth 4-17-1872 (4-18-1872)
Short, Ledy to Joshua Muse 1-19-1843
Short, Margrett to James W. Fawner 2-5-1847
Short, Mary to W. C. Thomas 12-30-1865 (no return)
Short, Symantha to George Barnes 5-21-1867 (5-22-1867)
Shoup, Barbary Van Swearing to Andrew Jackson 7-30-1870 (8-2-1870)
Shultz, Mary A. to Geo. W. Henson 11-19-1847
Shutters, Nancy J. to James A. Simmons 3-20-1871 (no return)
Sides, Eliza J. to Marion Smith 9-29-1870
Sides, J. L. to Joshua Smith 10-16-1869 (no return)
Sides, Nancy to John Clark 7-12-1869 (no return)
Sigo, Cathrine to Charley Gilliam 1-21-1852
Sikes, Mary to Enoch Stephens 4-18-1848
Silvertooth, Mary F. to Henry D. Bevel 11-7-1874 (11-8-1874)
Silvertooth, Nancy C. to Moses C. Franklin 10-20-1851 (10-23-1851)
Simmons, A. V. H. to Thomas F. Mosely 12-10-1839
Simmons, Cacy to William H. Roseborough 11-12-1844
Simmons, Levina to John H. Duncan 1-18-1838
Simmons, Louisa to Thomas C. Murrell 5-13-1856
Simmons, Mary to T. D. Gregory 1-22-1868
Simmons, Samyra to Sherrod Lipscomb 11-23-1868 (no return)

Simmons, Sarah to Jacob D. Dial 7-17-1850 (7-18-1850)
Simmons, Susan A. to George G. Matlock 2-13-1866 (2-14-1866)
Simms, Sarah J. to James N. Pennington 7-8-1867 (7-10-1867)
Simpson, Ardema to Wm. Davis 12-18-1859 (no return)
Simpson, Arena to Charles H. Stewart 9-10-1867 (9-13-1867)
Simpson, Elizabeth to W. M. Trussel 11-2-1844 (no return)
Simpson, Emeline to James Cooper 8-17-1849
Simpson, Lucinda to A. Davis 5-4-1866 (5-7-1866)
Simpson, Margret to Alford Guest 11-26-1867 (11-28-1867)
Simpson, Marila to Thos. Royton 1-23-1860 (no return)
Simpson, Mary to John W. Smith 12-31-1838 (1-1-1839)
Simpson, N. E. (Miss) to W. B. Hilton 1-18-1869 (no return)
Simpson, Nancy P. to Jno. P. Koger 4-1-1871
Simpson, S. A. (Miss) to F. M. Stewart 12-29-1868
Simpson, Sallena to William Cooper 12-11-1848 (12-13-1848)
Simpson, Sarah to Seborn Holt 1-10-1840
Simpson, Zilpha M. to James Wells 7-3-1846 (7-5-1846)
Sims, Charlott P. to William W. Brazelton 12-16-1841 (no return)
Sims, Ellen to N. H. Coulson 4-29-1839 (4-30-1839)
Sims, Hesther Ann to John Thos. Slatter 12-15-1846
Sims, J. F. to Littleton Green 7-24-1865 (7-20?-1865)
Sims, Julia Ann to A. J. B. Foster 8-14-1848 (8-15-1848)
Sims, Margret E. to Littleton Farris 7-30-1856 (no return)
Sims, Margret to James M. Shed 12-2-1839 (12-3-1839)
Sims, Mary A. to Milton D. Farris 7-27-1840 (7-30-1840)
Sims, Mary E. to John Clark 1-10-1844 (1-11-1844)
Sims, Rebbeca D. to Thomas Short 7-25-1843
Sims, Sarah E. to Kindred P. Muse 8-23-1855
Singleton, Mary to Wm. Wagner 6-21-1840 (6-28-1840)
Singleton, Nancy to Francis M. Darivin 2-11-1846 (2-12-1846)
Singleton, Nancy to Thomas Pack 8-10-1843
Singleton, Nancy to Thos. Pack 8-14-1865 (8-15-1865)
Singleton, Patsey to Ambrose Wheeler 4-27-1838
Singleton, Sallie to Thomas Pack 11-19-1858 (11-21-1858)
Singleton, Tempy to Meredith Catchings 11-21-1843
Sisk, Eliza A. to Madison Miller 12-11-1856
Sisk, Eliza Jane to Aron Mahu 3-31-1847 (3-4?-1847)
Sisk, Elizabeth to J. E. Brown 5-31-1860 (6-3-1860)
Sisk, Elizabeth to James C. Malone 4-29-1841
Sisk, J. B. to Anderson Franklin 12-8-1873 (12-9-1873)
Sisk, Louisa Jane to W. A. Branch 7-13-1840 (7-?-1840)
Sisk, Martha to Robt. T. McBride 10-3-1855
Sisk, Mary E. to Benj. Clark 12-18-1858 (12-22-1858)
Sisk, Ritta to Isaac Stephens 8-6-1847 (8-?-1847)
Sisk, Sarah C. to Elijah Bice 8-31-1865 (9-15-1865)
Sisk, Sarah to Alfred Turley 1-8-1842 (1-9-1842)
Sitze, Angeline to N. Hill 12-22-1870
Sitze, Emma to H. F. Tulley 10-30-1873
Skidmore, Martha E. to Shadrick Taylor 12-13-1866
Skidmore, Mary J. to Isaac G. Stewart 3-5-1857
Slator, Emaline to E. C. Womack 7-26-1858
Slatter, Lillie B. (Miss) to Frank D. Whitesides 4-22-1874
Slot, M. M. to E. F. Smart ?-26-1870 (with Sept.)
Smith, Ann E. to Elijah Baker 2-10-1844 (no return)
Smith, Ann Eliza to J. A. Revis 11-19-1866 (no return)
Smith, Arrenia to Wm. Mitchell 1-10-1856 (1-13-1856)
Smith, Betsy to Charles Wood 4-16-1839
Smith, Bettie to A. C. Stewart 7-19-1871
Smith, Caroline to R. A. Daniel 12-24-1845
Smith, Cathrine to Samuel K. Farris 10-24-1843 (10-25-1843)
Smith, Christa E. to Wm. C. Ray 1-7-1850 (1-9-1850)
Smith, Daly to Ebenezer Martin 2-28-1842 (no return)
Smith, Elizabeth to Joseph McKelvey 11-1-1844 (11-6-1844)
Smith, Elizabeth to Nimrod Sandridge 8-26-1858 (8-29-1858)
Smith, Elizabeth to William S. Frame 10-26-1850 (no return)
Smith, F. A. to E. A. Majors 3-21-1866 (3-22-1866)
Smith, Frances L. to Joseph Ellis 12-15-1855 (12-18-1855)
Smith, Hannah T. to Martin V. Millsaps 2-10-1866 (no return)
Smith, Hannah to John W. Fox 10-9-1851 (10-14-1851)
Smith, Jane to John Garner 10-17-1857 (10-18-1857)
Smith, Josia to Jos. W. Power 1-15-1867 (no return)
Smith, Judith to Peter Limbaugh 7-17-1845 (7-18-1845)
Smith, L. E. to D. B. Corning 3-10-1866
Smith, Lucinda C. to L. N. Simpson 9-18-1855
Smith, M. E. to Saml. Jernegan 12-7-1867 (12-9-1867)

Smith, M. J. to Isaac Bridges 2-18-1839
Smith, M. L. to J. F. Brown 4-19-1867 (4-21-1867)
Smith, M. P. to Geo. W. Sanders 11-19-1866 (no return)
Smith, Mahala to H. C. Bass 2-18-1840 (no return)
Smith, Margret J. to Thomas H. Baggett 10-6-1856 (10-10-1856)
Smith, Margrett to Joel Dodd 3-17-1850
Smith, Martha C. to Andrew J. Wiseman 6-6-1842 (no return)
Smith, Martha to Robert Mashburn 12-27-1860 (12-31-1860)
Smith, Mary A. E. to Wm. Shasteen 11-20-1856
Smith, Mary A. to John Cobble 1-10-1857 (1-11-1857)
Smith, Mary E. to James M. Whitlock 1-4-1858 (1-7-1858)
Smith, Mary E. to R. C. Wiseman 1-18-1859 (no return)
Smith, Mary to James C. Smith 3-16-1871 (no return)
Smith, Mary to Joseph Bolin 1-11-1858 (1-16-1858)
Smith, Mary to Minyard Gilliam 7-27-1857 (8-2-1857)
Smith, Mary to William R. Bass 6-20-1849
Smith, N. M. to G. W. Adkins 2-10-1840 (no return)
Smith, Nancy Ann to W. E. Bohanan 2-25-1867 (3-4-1867)
Smith, Nancy C. to H. C. Fulmore 1-30-1865 (2-1-1865)
Smith, Nancy D. to Richard Lyans 8-18-1838 (8-23-1838)
Smith, Nancy M. to Ambors Parks 5-3-1851 (5-4-1851)
Smith, Nancy to J. J. Burt 10-29-1845 (11-19-1845)
Smith, Nancy to Wm. H. Leach 10-17-1867 (no return)
Smith, Paralee to William Stewman 1-31-1857
Smith, Polly to Giles Hill 1-27-1846 (1-29-1846)
Smith, Rachiel E. to Wm. Burt 9-6-1858 (9-8-1858)
Smith, Rebecca (Miss) to William Gossage 12-21-1842 (12-22-1842)
Smith, Rebecca to Joseph McKelvey 7-5-1849
Smith, Rebecca to Mathew W. Watson 11-27-1838 (no return)
Smith, Rilda to William Morris 12-29-1870
Smith, Rutha to Martin Hoke 9-20-1870 (9-23-1870)
Smith, Samantha to George Anderson 7-15-1853 (7-18-1853)
Smith, Sarah C. to I. Kemp 10-9-1867
Smith, Sarah Jane to Jonathan Sims 2-19-1867 (2-23-1867)
Smith, Sarah to Benjamin F. Jones 8-1-1839
Smith, Sarah to Hardin Williams 2-25-1845 (2-26-1845)
Smith, Susan E. to Thos. G. Rucker 5-11-1865 (no return)
Smith, Susan to John Marsh 11-13-1841 (11-14-1841)
Smith, Susanah to Josh Dyer 7-3-1858 (7-4-1858)
Smith, Viney to H. C. Bolin 2-12-1866 (no return)
Smith, Winney to Henry L. Byrom 10-24-1843 (10-25-1843)
Smyth, Sarah Jane to Dempsey Holder 12-22-1847
Sneede, Nancy P. to Pleasant B. Wood 12-5-1842 (12-15-1842)
Sofey, Cathrine to William Durn 4-5-1872
Souder, Mary A. to John G. Schrom 8-26-1869
Southerland, Louisa to J. N. T. Stephens 12-10-1866 (no return)
Southerland, Martha A. to David Vaughn 3-7-1850 (3-10-1850)
Southerland, S. K. to Richard Moore 8-29-1872 (9-1-1872)
Spain, Indiana C. M. to Richard Sharp 5-16-1839
Spann, Ann E. to Alexander G. Key 8-1-1839 (no return)
Sparks, Charity to Lawson Sparks 7-29-1845
Sparks, Elizabeth to Abner Sisk 4-8-1850
Sparks, Fanny to Francis M. Elliott 7-28-1873 (7-12-1873)
Sparks, Frances to George W. Deaton 4-10-1848
Sparks, Issabella to Henry L. Sills 9-26-1852
Spaun, Susan C. to Jessee McKelvey 7-15-1846 (7-16-1846)
Spears, Amanda to William T. Anderton 5-3-1873 (no return)
Spears, S. D. to W. B. Kitchens 7-26-1869 (no return)
Speck, Mary F. to G. W. Smith 12-23-1867 (12-20-1867)
Speck, Samntha E. to George W. D. Davis 9-5-1856 (9-9-1856)
Spence, Pheba to Daniel McCarter 3-4-1844 (no return)
Spindle, Mary Jane to Charles L. Turner 1-10-1842 (1-12-1842)
Spray, Elizabeth to Wm. Chavors 2-2-1852 (2-5-1852)
Spray, Sarah to James W. Barnett 10-25-1856 (10-26-1856)
Spyker, V. S. to B. S. Henderson 10-25-1859
Stalder, Emma to John F. Meicher 12-23-1874 (12-24-1874)
Stamper, Emma H. to Nathan Frizzell 2-19-1857
Stamper, Mary Jane to Preston B. Stroud 7-27-1847 (7-28-1847)
Stamper, Sarah to Lewis Metcalf 11-6-1843 (11-9-1843)
Stamps, Jane to Willis S. Embrey 12-22-1847 (12-23-1847)
Stamps, M. J. to Zack Smith 10-5-1859
Stamps, Mary to Joseph Banks 6-24-1858 (no return)
Stamps, R. H. to S. D. Mather 10-11-1865 (10-12-1865)
Stamps, Sarah D. to Isaac R. Warren 3-31-1851 (no return)
Stamps, Susan H. to Ruben P. Stephens 2-5-1849

Stanfield, M. E. to W. B. Malcom 3-28-1868 (no return)
Stanphiel, Julia A. E. to George H. Lefeber 9-3-1853 (9-4-1853)
Staples, Elizabeth J. to Allen F. Robertson 12-14-1847 (12-16-1847)
Staples, Ellen to Jack Keith 5-4-1870 (no return)
Staples, Frances to Jefferson Estill 1-17-1843
Staples, Laura to W. T. Martin 7-26-1872 (7-28-1872)
Starnes, Elizabeth A. to Joseph M. Smith 8-4-1860 (8-9-1860)
Starnes, Lucind L. to Thos. E. Jones 7-15-1858 (7-22-1858)
Statom, Frances to Lemuel Easley 12-1-1865 (no return)
Staton, Mary M. to W. H. Gillaspie 1-28-1865 (1-29-1865)
Statum, Elizabeth to A. J. Roddy 12-24-1870 (no return)
Statum, Martha to Amos Ladd 8-6-1855 (8-7-1855)
Statum, Willie to John Messick 5-5-1859 (no return)
Steel, Elizabeth to Mark Pellann 9-29-1860 (9-31-1860)
Steel, Lucinda to James M. Ashley 9-9-1871 (no return)
Steel, Nancy to George Steel 1-27-1866 (no return)
Stephens, Bethany to John M. Ake 6-30-1847
Stephens, Ethalinda A. to Thomas J. Goodloe 12-18-1856
Stephens, Frances L. to Thomas A. Sublett 8-25-1856
Stephens, Hannah to Dennis Gambol 9-21-1865 (9-24-1865)
Stephens, Jane F. to Harris Gilliam 8-26-1852 (8-23?-1852)
Stephens, Jane to James Wells 8-5-1871 (8-16-1871)
Stephens, Levina to George Gainer 1-8-1843
Stephens, Martha L. to H. B. Leverton 6-22-1867 (7-1-1867)
Stephens, Mary to John F. Anderson 8-27-1854
Stephens, Millie to J. K. P. Baxter 1-19-1859
Stephens, Nancy to A. J. Sells 9-24-1866 (no return)
Stephens, Nancy to James P. Cowan 3-4-1861 (3-5-1861)
Stephens, Nancy to Joseph Carter 10-19-1865 (no return)
Stephens, Sarah A. to A. A. Willcoxen 12-10-1867 (no return)
Stephens, Sarah to Dora Wilcox 4-12-1872
Stevens, Mary A. to Wm. Pack 8-7-1865 (8-10-1865)
Stevenson, Sarah A. to James Statum 4-30-1856 (5-1-1856)
Stewart, Ann to A. Williams 10-15-1868 (no return)
Stewart, Annie to R. F. Sloan 8-12-1869 (no return)
Stewart, Charity to Hamilton Stewart 11-28-1853 (11-29-1853)
Stewart, Elizabeth A. to L. S. Mathews 2-13-1870 (2-14-1870)
Stewart, Elizabeth to Jasper Guinn 10-24-1865 (10-26-1865)
Stewart, Margrett to William Pack 2-9-1843
Stewart, Martha B. to Jessee Lilley 8-13-1818 (no return)
Stewart, Martha Jane to Richard D. Spence 5-3-1844
Stewart, Mary A. to Benj. Sells 8-9-1838
Stewart, Mary Ann to George Boesman 2-15-1846
Stewart, Mary Ann to George Kelley 2-15-1846 (no return)
Stewart, Mary G. to William M. Ford 2-2-1874 (no return)
Stewart, Mary J. to L. S. Mathews 9-20-1859
Stewart, Nancy to John B. Rogers 7-30-1850
Stewart, Olevia J. to Albert Jackson 11-4-1856
Stewart, Peggy J. to John L. B. Williams 8-6-1856 (8-7-1856)
Stewart, Percie to Robt. Vaughn 12-26-1860
Stewart, Rebecca to Richard F. Little 12-15-1853
Stewart, Sally to Richard Green 12-30-1870 (no return)
Stewart, Samantha J. to James S. Nichols 12-27-1856
Stewart, Sarah B. to Allen B. Jones 7-15-1857
Stewart, Sarah E. to Charles King 5-28-1872 (6-2-1872)
Stewart, Sarah E. to Wm. M. Hammons 8-17-1870 (no return)
Stewart, Sarah to Isaac A. Hannah 7-18-1851
Stewart, Sarah to James C. Looney 11-9-1842
Stiles, Drucilla to Eli P. Cooper 6-8-1850
Stiles, Martha to John D. Smith 1-6-1857 (1-11-1857)
Stiles, Mary to Benj. R. Stovall 6-30-1854 (7-2-1854)
Stiles, Nancy to James Counts 4-22-1856
Stiles, Sivillia to Simeone Deaton 12-22-1854 (12-24-1854)
Stokes, Susan to William Simmons 9-29-1853 (10-4-1853)
Stoval, Ann to Edley Damron 9-17-1872 (9-19-1872)
Stovall, Ann to Levi Trigg 1-1-1866 (no return)
Stovall, Caroline to Nathan Bostick 7-17-1841 (7-18-1841)
Stovall, Cynthia to Lindsey May 7-20-1872 (no return)
Stovall, Darcas O. to Josiah Mason 1-9-1851
Stovall, Emeline to Rufus K. McCollum 3-11-1848 (3-16-1848)
Stovall, Frances A. to John H. Larkin 8-6-1853 (8-11-1853)
Stovall, Lutitia to Robt. Hester 7-2-1866 (no return)
Stovall, Martha to James E. Travis 11-23-1840
Stovall, Mary D. to James C. Tipps 8-30-1858 (9-2-1858)
Stovall, Mary J. to Geo. McClure 10-16-1866 (10-?-1866)

Stovall, Narcissa J. to Newton A. Hamilton 5-2-1851 (5-4-1851)
Stovall, Penina E. to Wm. E. McClure 11-27-1865 (11-28-1865)
Stovall, Susan S. to Chesley B. Bostick 5-7-1852 (5-9-1852)
Strambler, Martha F. to William C. Franklin 11-19-1841
Strambler, Mary to James Taylor 12-2-1845 (no return)
Strawn, H. A. to George Heathcoat 5-29-1871
Stringer, Lou to D. H. Mooney 11-6-1869 (11-7-1869)
Stringer, Margret to Henry Protter 3-19-1872
Stroud, Kate to Thomas T. Hines 10-10-1874 (10-11-1874)
Stroud, M. H. to Wm. B. Farmer 12-24-1870 (12-25-1870)
Stroud, Rebecca A. to John P. Darwin 1-6-1851
Stroud, Sallie B. to A. T. Hassey 9-7-1867
Stubblefield, Elizabeth A. to William I. Williams 6-1-1838 (no return)
Stubblefield, Elizabeth to Jeremiah Arnold 1-31-1839
Stubblefield, Mary J. to George W. Wilkerson 1-31-1874 (2-5-1874)
Stubblefield, Nancy to W. L. Wilkinson 8-4-1841 (8-6-1841)
Stubblefield, Sally to Thomas P. Wilkinson 2-28-1849
Sublett, Eleanor to James P. Griffin 8-28-1845
Sublett, Elizabeth G. to Wm. A. Darnaby 3-10-1855 (3-11-1855)
Sublett, Martha to William B. Fagg 7-27-1843 (7-30-1843)
Sublett, Susan to Geo. W. Warren 1-1-1849 (1-2-1849)
Suddarth, Harriett to Francis m. Oakley 11-25-1851
Suddarth, Margret E. to George N. Francis 7-29-1851
Sugg, nna to Riley Tankesley 5-1-1871
Suiter, Deliah to Constantine O. Odonnel 3-2-1851
Suiter, Sarah to Samuel M. Taylor 3-10-1850
Suiter, Susanah J. to George Crabtree 8-12-1849
Sullivan, Mary J. to Fountain King 10-5-1869
Sumbruen, Mary to Fredrick Wanger 11-6-1871 (11-8-1871)
Sumers, Cathrine to William Holder 10-1-1848
Summerell, S. E. to J. M. Hughes 5-11-1872 (5-15-1872)
Summerford, N. P. to L. E. Metts 3-2-1861 (3-3-1861)
Summers, Annie to Robert Gamble 1-12-1866 (1-14-1866)
Summers, Lizzie to James H. Sells 1-5-1873? (6-11-1874)
Summers, Nancy to James L. Cambrel 4-6-1861
Suthard, Nancy to Elijah Sisk 11-23-1843
Suthard, Polly to Daniel Ashley 4-16-1844 (4-25-1844)
Sutton, Frances W. to James Morris 10-4-1853
Sutton, Susan to Jessee Rogers 1-15-1839
Swain, Amanda to James M. Johnson 10-14-1867 (no return)
Swain, Ann to Noah Cook 8-12-1857
Swain, Jane T. to Michael Fitzgeralds 2-23-1857
Swain, Mary E. to Joseph B. Watts 5-21-1858 (no return)
Swain, Sidney to Fred Johnson 3-4-1871 (no return)
Swan, Eliza to G. W. Swan 9-24-1859 (no return)
Swann, Elizabeth to George T. Baker 7-1-1848 (7-2-1848)
Swann, Elizabeth to Robert Brannan 8-11-1852 (8-12-1852)
Swann, Fereby E. to William Baker 11-7-1857 (no return)
Swann, Mary A. to William Covey 1-12-1857 (1-13-1857)
Swann, Mary to James Bennett 1-8-1852
Swann, Piety A. E. to William Morris 9-14-1842 (no return)
Swann, Piety A. to Cyrus Barnes 2-28-1843
Swearengame, Sarah J. S. to Thos. Green 4-9-1868 (no return)
Swearengin, Mollie to Wm. Guthry 5-24-1871 (5-29-1871)
Swearingame, Nancy M. to Wm. H. Bishop 12-2-1874 (12-6-1874)
Swords, Elizabeth to William Orear 7-7-1853 (7-8-1853)
Syler, Barsheba to Rufus Speck 3-7-1869
Syler, E. A. to F. A. Leel 5-29-1866 (no return)
Syler, Julia to W. B. Jennings 9-23-1858 (no return)
Syler, Julia to W. B. Jennings 9-23-1859 (no return)
Syler, Louisa to Wm. A. Parks 12-19-1855 (no return)
Syler, Martha E. to James S. Oakley 1-27-1857
Syler, Mary A. to John B. Franklin 11-15-1860
Syler, Mary E. to George W. Stovall 7-4-1855 (7-5-1855)
Syler, Nancy C. to H. A. Trigg 10-4-1866 (no return)
Syler, Rebecca J. to James H. McClure 5-3-1852
Syler, Sarah A. to John Damron 10-27-1859 (no return)
Syler, Sarah A. to Samuel C. Smith 11-18-1852
Syler, Sarah to John Damron 10-27-1866 (10-28-1859?)
Syrrat, Jane to Peter Weaver 2-26-1845 (no return)
Tabbith, Partina to William R. Hill 1-8-1845 (1-9-1845)
Taft, Azubah M. to John J. Angel 9-20-1847 (9-21-1847)
Taft, E. A. to W. J. Rogers 12-13-1865 (12-18-1865)
Taft, Judith E. to Amos Taft 3-30-1857 (4-1-1857)
Talifarro, Frances M. to Thomas P. Sneed 8-14-1842

Talleferro, Mollie E. to Thomas J. McKelby 11-13-1873
Talley, Jane to Isaac R. Higginbotham 8-6-1856 (8-7-1856)
Talley, Louisa to Benjamin Franklin 12-29-1851 (no return)
Tankersley, Elizabeth to James W. Jackson 12-20-1852
Tankersley, Mary A. to A. J. Finney 12-24-1853 (12-25-1853)
Tankesley, Manerva to William Miller 6-22-1867 (6-19?-1867)
Tankesley, Melvina (Miss) to A. J. Southerland 12-3-1869
Tanner, Adelphia A. to Wm. D. Fletcher 8-6-1852 (8-8-1852)
Tanner, Sarah to Anderson A. Ivey 10-26-1854 (10-29-1854)
Tarbor, Elizabeth to Levi Reed 2-11-1854 (2-12-1854)
Tarbor, Julia E. to William Heathcoat 12-22-1852
Tarbor, Lydia A. to Isham R. Wamack 6-19-1852 (6-20-1852)
Tarpley, Sarah A. R. to Robt. R. Janes 1-4-1858 (1-5-1858)
Tarpley, Sarah A. R. to Robt. R. Jones 1-4-1858 (no return)
Tarwater, Darcas to William Garrett 10-10-1850 (10-12-1850)
Tarwaters, Martha J. to A. J. Andrews 11-3-1858 (no return)
Tarwaters, Martha J. to A. J. S. Anderson 11-31-1858
Tate, Dulana to Wm. H. Ayres 8-28-1852 (9-10-1852)
Tate, Lucretia to J. M. sr. Elkins 1-8-1866 (no return)
Tate, Mahala to John A. Reagin 10-29-1853 (11-1-1853)
Tate, Margrett to J. E. Horton 1-20-1870
Tate, Nancy to W. M. McAfee 9-7-1865 (no return)
Tate, Sarah to Newton Thompson 5-2-1854 (5-5-1854)
Taylor, Amanda M. to Samuel Russell 2-26-1848 (3-2-1848)
Taylor, Amanda M. to Wm. M. Farris 10-19-1867 (10-17?-1867)
Taylor, Amanda to Columbus Templeton 3-23-1854
Taylor, Bell to George L. Gray 12-4-1860
Taylor, Cathrine to Patrick Sullivan 10-23-1854 (10-24-1854)
Taylor, Eliza E. to W. F. Winford 1-21-1859 (1-27-1859)
Taylor, Elizabeth to Jason Addington 11-13-1842
Taylor, Elizabeth to Shipman Reed 7-12-1869 (7-13-1870?)
Taylor, Feby to Jonathan Crownover 1-?-1842 (1-10-1842)
Taylor, Frances to W. C. Fanning 2-15-1867 (no return)
Taylor, Jane to Cornelius Cooper 3-27-1841 (no return)
Taylor, Jane to George W. Warren 3-7-1846 (3-15-1846)
Taylor, Lucy to Solomon Sells 12-26-1839
Taylor, Martha to John S. Lambert 1-20-1848
Taylor, Marthy to Pleasant Lovelady 2-16-1850 (2-17-1850)
Taylor, Mary A. to William Russell 8-26-1848
Taylor, N. C. to W. M. Wiseman 9-5-1859 (
Taylor, Nancy C. to John A. Gilbert 11-4-1846 (11-5-1846)
Taylor, Rebecca A. to Edward F. Lee 1-21-1845
Taylor, Sarah to H. L. Lambert 8-8-1840 (8-10-1840)
Taylor, Sarah to Wm. B. Swann 11-29-1850
Taylor, Susan A. to James M. Lindsley 8-21-1868
Teasdel, M. A. to J. P. Stevenson 4-15-1869 (4-23-1869)
Temple, Dicey A. to John F. Sublett 1-7-1843 (1-8-1843)
Temple, M. E. to M. B. Russey 7-18-1868 (7-19-1868)
Templeton, Simonie? to Jon Roton 2-12-1866 (no return)
Terrell, Ellen to W. M. Tankesley 2-9-1866
Teters, Elizabeth to Samuel Stephens 9-26-1855 (9-27-1855)
Thomas, Amanda L. to Jos.? B. Jones 12-29-1849 (12-30-1849)
Thomas, Delia to William Hutton 5-31-1850
Thomas, Martha Jane to James Williamson 6-6-1849
Thomas, Niagra Ann to John R. Payne 2-25-1874 (2-27-1874)
Thomas, P. P. to James D. Morgan 11-28-1853 (12-1-1853)
Thomas, Sarah J. to Jessee E. Jones 10-17-1855
Thomas, Sarah to Jessee Collins 2-8-1851 (2-9-1851)
Thomison, N. C. (Miss) to John M. Pack 12-12-1868 (12-13-1868)
Thompson, Amanda to Jacob W. Hise 12-8-1840 (no return)
Thompson, Amanda to Milton Speck 2-28-1871
Thompson, Eliza B. to Samuel Caldwell 1-10-1839 (1-11-1839)
Thompson, Eliza to Joseph Allison 9-5-1854 (9-10-1854)
Thompson, Elizabeth to Richard Barnes 12-28-1847
Thompson, Emma J. to Rufus Baker 11-23-1867 (11-25-1867)
Thompson, F. J. to Thos. L. Reedy 8-7-1865 (8-10-1865)
Thompson, Harriett to Jessee Rogers 8-3-1865 (12-11-1864?)
Thompson, Mary J. to Wm. N. Mickles 10-8-1855 (10-10-1855)
Thompson, Sarah A. to David McGowan 3-29-1839 (no return)
Thurman, Cordelia to Francis M. Williams 11-29-1849
Thurman, Cyntha to John McKhenen? 1-8-1850
Thurman, Martha to Isaac R. Huddleston 12-4-1845 (12-5-1845)
Thurman, Samira to Jacob H. Brazelton 1-7-1842
Thurman, Sarah A. to Michael N. Mathews 11-27-1854 (11-30-1854)
Thurman?, Hannah to Robt. H. Cowan 12-19-1872 (no return)

Thurman?, Susan J. to James B. Foster 5-6-1840
Tickel, Mary E. to George Simmons 11-28-1871
Tillitt, Sarah E. to J. G. Gilbert 11-14-1866 (no return)
Tims, Martha to Daniel Miles 2-5-1855 (2-8-1855)
Tinsley, Ruthy to Isham H. Beard 9-20-1846 (9-21-1846)
Tipps, Adaline to John C. Reagin 1-30-1867 (4-23-1867)
Tipps, Cynthia A. to William Ballard 8-29-1860 (8-30-1860)
Tipps, M. J. to J. F. Tipps 11-20-1866 (no return)
Tipps, M. J. to John W. Partin 9-1-1859 (no return)
Tipps, M. L. to J. M. Mathews 10-28-1867 (10-29-1867)
Tipps, Mary A. to John Smith 6-23-1851 (no return)
Tipps, Mary A. to William Hendricks 10-20-1870
Tipps, Mary C. to Wm. C. Styles 12-29-1865 (12-31-1865)
Tipps, Mary to William Statum 3-30-1854
Tipps, R. E. (Miss) to E. Pulliam 5-8-1869 (5-9-1869)
Tipps, R. E. (Miss) to J. E. Pulliam 5-8-1869 (no return)
Tipps, R. M. to J. F. Neal 1-5-1874
Tipps, Rebecca to John E. Hise 11-19-1842 (11-20-1842)
Tipps, Rutha A. to Geo. W. Stewman 7-14-1869 (no return)
Tipps, Sarah A to Joel Limbaugh 12-5-1870 (no return)
Tipps, Susan to Michiel Limbaugh 10-15-1866 (no return)
Tipton, Elizabeth to Gilliam Hilliard 8-30-1871 (no return)
Todd, S. J. to J. F. Wright 1-4-1870 (no return)
Travis, Mary C. to Washington P. Simpson 9-9-1858 (9-10-1858)
Travis, Mary J. to C. H. Bean 10-18-1856 (10-19-1856)
Travis, Nancy C. to C. C. Knott 3-3-1870 (no return)
Trevis?, Rutha A. to Charley Shivers 4-18-1866 (4-19-1866)
Tribble, Caroline to J. V. Scivily 12-21-1868 (12-23-1868)
Trigg, Dosha Ann to James M. Donaldson 9-2-1846 (?-?-1846)
Trigg, Elizabeth to John L. Keith 1-9-1847 (1-12-1847)
Trigg, Esther Ann to W. H. Hitch 1-14-1846 (1-15-1846)
Trigg, Mary A. to Thomas Rivers 11-12-1843 (11-13-1843)
Trigg, Mary to James J. Sisk 7-22-1873 (no return)
Trigg, Nancy C. to Newton A. Hamilton 3-28-1873 (9-24-1873)
Trimble, Ada A. to Charles A. Johnson 7-23-1873 (7-24-1873)
Tripp, Angeline to W. N. Weaver 11-26-1873 (11-27-1873)
Tripp, Mariah E. to Isham Teters 12-18-1852 (12-23-1852)
Tripp, Mary A. R. to John Brimage 11-9-1852
Tripp, Mattie to Jas. H. Miller 4-8-1872 (4-13-1872)
Tripp, Susan D. to James M. Frame 4-6-1856 (no return)
Troop, Eliza E. to Bazil Stewart 10-14-1853 (no return)
Trussel, Nancy J. to Thos. S. Wells 6-7-1847 (6-12-1847)
Tucker, Caldonia to James Dial 3-21-1874
Tucker, E. J. to Benj. Roberts 4-14-1841
Tucker, Eliza Ann to George W. Faris 4-14-1853
Tucker, Elizabeth to William Stewman? 8-17-1849
Tucker, Jane to C. L. Hatfield 12-25-1865 (12-27-1865)
Tucker, Mary Ann to Solomon J. Hopkins 8-13-1849
Tucker, Mollie N. to Nathan W. Garner 10-1-1873 (10-2-1873)
Tucker, Olly to James Evans 10-4-1856 (10-5-1856)
Turley, Caroline to Dennis Stephens 7-4-1856 (7-8-1856)
Turley, Sarah L. to Jos. W. Gifford 7-21-1871
Turley, Sarah to Robert Horon 10-12-1844 (10-13-1844)
Turman, Lizzie to J. Wiley Grizard 4-5-1870 (no return)
Turman, Martha A. to H. H. Dulin 5-30-1860
Turman, Sarah to Joseph J. Lambertson 1-14-1858
Turner, Euphria S. to Alfred H. Travis 8-18-1845
Turner, Mary C. to I. A. Oldwell 12-12-1867
Turner, Mary J. to W. L. Bickley 4-24-1860
Turner, Mollie to George W. Montgomery 3-26-1874
Turner, Nancy C. to Newton C. McIntosh 12-23-1844 (12-24-1844)
Turner, Willie K. to C. B. Russey 12-2-1874 (12-3-1874)
Turney, Catharine to Thos. McTorrick 3-25-1859 (no return)
Turney, E. E. to Henry R. Estill 3-2-1848
Turney, Malinda J. to WM. E. Taylor 7-24-1855
Turney, Nannie to Alford Henderson 11-14-1870
Turney, Virginia C. to Temple Harris 3-24-1874 (no return)
Tuttle, Ida C. to Charles Oppell 10-11-1870 (no return)
Underwood, Annie to Wm. T. Garner 11-6-1873
Underwood, Mary A. to Pinkney G. Homes 9-29-1857 (no return)
Upton, Ann J. to Geo. W. Faris 9-17-1854 (9-18-1854)
Usleton, Martha to James Sandford 9-27-1838
Vace, Susan to J. W. Martin 11-24-1869 (11-25-1869)
Vandergriff, Nancy to Stephen Fergerson 3-2-1851
Vann, M. J. to Robert Winford 5-12-1869

Vanzant, Cornelius E. to Henson G. Blanton 9-16-1844 (9-17-1844)
Vanzant, H. C. to W. T. Patton 7-5-1866 (7-12-1866)
Vanzant, Jane S. to Charles L. Blanton 11-25-1842
Vanzant, M. E. to A. J. Travis 11-8-1866
Vanzant, Matilda to Calloway Daniel 6-26-1851 (no return)
Vanzant, Nancy to S. J. Moore 12-20-1871 (1-2-1872)
Vanzant, Sallie A. to William Payne 3-17-1870 (?-?-1870)
Vanzant, Sally to C. E. McCroy 6-13-1865 (no return)
Vanzant, Sena to Elisha Bridges 12-12-1844
Vanzant, Susan to Wm. H. Willis 11-25-1851
Vanzant, Vinece J. to Jasper N. Seivally 7-17-1856
Vaughan, Dicy to Jordan Driver 2-12-1840 (2-13-1840)
Vaughan, Elizabeth E. to James McDaniel 8-8-1857 (no return)
Vaughan, Julian C. to Thomas J. Lockhart 11-6-1851
Vaughan, Mariah to James H. Kiningham 1-23-1852
Vaughan, Mattie to Wm. M. McClure 7-31-1865 (8-1-1865)
Vaughan, Susan to James H. Amond 12-27-1856 (12-28-1856)
Vaughn, A. E. (Miss) to Georg Gowry 12-29-1869 (12-31-1869)
Vaughn, Bety to Elmore Burk 9-29-1870
Vaughn, Nancy S. to John Putman 12-24-1859 (12-29-1859)
Vaughn, Sally to F. B. Wade 7-24-1865
Vaughn, Zerilda E. to Mathew N. Perry 10-4-1849
Venable, Lota to Robt. W. Officer 12-20-1871 (12-25-1871)
Vibbert, Nancy to James Ladd 2-15-1855
Vibbet, Elizabeth G. to G. W. Blackman 1-12-1861 (1-13-1861)
Vincent, Lucinda to James L. Downum 3-17-1847 (3-21-1847)
Vinson, Margrett to Josiah Miller 4-10-1848 (4-12-1848)
Wade, Elenor J. to Polk Hill 7-12-1871 (7-13-1871)
Wade, L. J. to T. W. Farris 10-3-1867
Wade, Martha to Bernard Richardson 12-11-1845 (no return)
Wade, Mary to James Cashon 1-3-1852 (1-4-1852)
Wade, R. P. to A. D. Tate 9-28-1868
Wade, Sarah A. to John A. Winfro 7-13-1866
Wadlington, Elizabeth A. to Wm. McMurray 5-3-1861 (5-30-1861)
Wagner, Adaline A. to Charles A. Gadsey 9-7-1853
Wagner, Betsy to Geo. Walker 2-18-1840 (no return)
Wagner, Bettie to S. P. Rogers 10-13-1870
Wagner, Cathrine to H. G. Gibson 5-27-1873 (5-29-1873)
Wagner, Dicy A. to Wm. S. Lynch 6-1-1872 (no return)
Wagner, Eliza to A. J. Willis 11-28-1870 (no return)
Wagner, Ellen to William Church 5-14-1870 (5-16-1870)
Wagner, Julia A. to Joseph C. Taylor 10-4-1853
Wagner, Mary E. to Daniel S. Montgomery 2-23-1874 (2-6?-1874)
Wagner, Nancy J. to William Hill 3-5-1866
Wagner, Nancy to G. R. Keel 12-16-1868 (no return)
Wagner, Rachel to G. W. Teters 8-1-1859 (8-11-1859)
Wagner, Sarah J. to F. B. Jones 8-25-1868 (no return)
Waisen?, Louisa to Mordent Young 5-18-1839
Wakefield, Christiana E. to Davis McElroy 4-27-1840
Wakefield, Eliza J. to Charles M. Wiseman 10-5-1850 (no return)
Wakefield, Lucy C. to John S. Blanton 6-19-1852 (6-24-1852)
Wakefield, Lucy to W. N. Taylor 7-24-1854 (7-27-1854)
Wakefield, Margret to Joshua jr. Smith 9-4-1839 (no return)
Wakefield, Mary A. to Martin V. Wiseman 9-1-1856 (9-9-1856)
Wakefield, Mary L. to James W. Noe 1-17-1859 (no return)
Wakefield, Nancy L. to Charles B. McDaniel 1-1-1844 (1-4-1844)
Wakefield, Nancy L. to James W. Bowling 1-17-1859 (1-18-1859)
Walker, Isabella C. to Richard H. McLaughlin 1-16-1840
Walker, Mollie to Wesley Edmonson 10-8-1869
Walker, Nancy to Mansel Garner 2-25-1847
Walker, Peggy to George Taylor 9-12-1841
Walker, Sarah to John Sells 2-3-1842
Wallace, Amanda J. to Charles H. Bohannan 8-28-1874 (8-29-1874)
Wallace, Margrett L. to Jesse Sharp 3-30-1844
Walls, Elizabeth to George Wagner 2-23-1847
Walls, M. J. to James H. Adams 8-6-1872 (8-8-1872)
Walraven, Julia to Warren Jackson 3-3-1868 (no return)
Walsh, Mary to Thomas Sullidin 7-26-1853
Ward, Louisa to A. P. Darell 8-6-1839
Warren, E. to J. M. Howell 8-8-1868 (8-4?-1868)
Warren, Eliza to James H. Moore 9-16-1847
Warren, Jane to William Wildman 9-7-1854
Warren, M. A. to John C. Landenberger 9-7-1868 (no return)
Warren, Mahala to John F. Morris 5-9-1845 (5-13-1845)
Warren, Martha to B. D. Gipson 12-9-1868

Warren, Martha to Robt. Dermott 8-11-1866 (no return)
Warren, Mary J. to James Will Corcson 6-17-1866 (no return)
Warren, Mary to Richard C. Holt 12-22-1841 (12-23-1841)
Warren, Nancy C. to James Roberts 10-19-1866 (no return)
Warren, Nancy H. to George R. Lawson 12-21-1855 (12-23-1855)
Warren, Nancy to Zachriah Smith 1-2-1872 (1-3-1872)
Warren, Sarah J. to Edwin J. Talleferro 1-30-1851
Warren, Susan to John B. Corn 11-17-1853 (11-19-1853)
Watson, M. C. (Miss) to C. B. Brewer 4-29-1869
Weaver, Ann to Williams Evans 11-19-1860 (11-21-1860)
Weaver, Annie to William Bean 1-28-1843 (1-29-1843)
Weaver, Caroline to John A. Brown 7-2-1870 (7-4-1870)
Weaver, Cinda to James M. Pyland 11-20-1866 (no return)
Weaver, Delilah to John Grant 3-31-1866 (4-1-1866)
Weaver, Elizabeth to Alex Smith 12-15-1858 (12-16-1858)
Weaver, Elizabeth to Noble Ladd 12-9-1850
Weaver, Eve to Samuel Church 1-6-1848 (1-9-1848)
Weaver, Lucy to W. H. Weaver 12-8-1860 (12-11-1860)
Weaver, Luraney to Henry Rolman 7-23-1846
Weaver, Manerva E. to Thomas Malone 9-19-1854 (no return)
Weaver, Martha to Wm. Davis 8-6-1873
Weaver, Mary E. to Thos. J. Humphrey 4-23-1859 (4-24-1859)
Weaver, Mary to John E. Welch 12-3-1851
Weaver, Mary to Saml. J. Shasteen 12-20-1853
Weaver, Nancy E. to J. A. Walker 12-23-1867 (12-24-1867)
Weaver, Nancy to John Pollock 1-22-1847 (1-24-1847)
Weaver, Polly to Joshua F. Tipps 10-29-1846
Weaver, Rachiel C. to John S. Brooks 1-29-1866 (1-30-1866)
Weaver, Sarah E. to B. A. Osbourn 2-5-1855
Weaver, Sarah to William Shelton 2-11-1851
Webb, Cynthia A. to George W. Sors 12-26-1849
Webb, Elizabeth to Ryon Caperton 12-21-1846
Webb, Elizabeth to William Grant 12-5-1838
Webb, Mary E. to Wm. L. Baker 10-7-1873 (no return)
Webb, Mary to William Magors 5-12-1857 (no return)
Webb, Nancy to William Cobble 7-19-1854 (7-23-1854)
Webb, Pheba Emaline to George W. Tipps 8-20-1860 (8-23-1860)
Webb, S. E. to J. E. Wiseman 9-23-1870
Webb, Sarah to Marion Winkler 1-30-1854
Weddington, Jane to Wm. Smith 6-5-1856 (no return)
Wedington, Eliza to John Snoddy 9-24-1857 (9-25-1857)
Wedington, Fanny to A. B. Garner 9-20-1870 (no return)
Wedington, Susan M. to John W. Young 3-4-1873
Welb, Eve to Francis M. McCoy 1-10-1856 (1-16-1856)
Welch, Cathrine to James Golden 8-22-1853 (8-23-1853)
Welch, Julia to Patrick Rogers 7-16-1853 (7-18-1853)
Wells, Anna to James Taylor 11-22-1845
Wells, Elizabeth to M. D. Embrey 8-16-1869 (no return)
Wells, Margret to Martin Woodson 6-4-1844 (6-11-1844)
Wells, Milethia to John Arnold 9-?-1855
Wells, Nancy to Matthew Trussell 6-12-1846
Wells, Sally to Thomas Summers 1-26-1846
West, Josephine to Mc? Wells 7-31-1865 (8-2-1865)
West, Lucy to Dennis Gambol 10-24-1855
West, Margret E. to Jas. Wells 12-21-1871 (12-23-1871)
West, Margrett to William Guthrie 8-8-1850
West, Martha J. to Thos. Stephens 9-21-1865 (9-26-1865)
West, Mollie J. to J. W. Bragg 11-30-1871 (no return)
West, Pelina Jane to William Rogers 4-11-1874 (4-12-1874)
West, R. E. to W. W. Brakefield 7-13-1872 (7-14-1872)
West, S. M. to F. W. Moore 8-16-1871 (no return)
West, Sarah to A. J. McCoy 9-7-1865 (no return)
Westmer, Mary to A. J. Anderson 7-20-1867 (7-21-1867)
Westmoreland, Jennie to Wm. Thomas 6-14-1866 (no return)
White, Georgia A. to Henry T. Case 2-10-1870 (no return)
White, Lutitia to Thomas P. Howard 12-29-1855
Whitlock, M. A. to G. W. Williams 3-26-1868 (3-28-1868)
Whitson, Eliza C. to Samuel Pearson 7-8-1838 (7-12-1838)
Wicks, Louisa C. to Barbee Collins 1-22-1850 (1-24-1850)
Widener, Sarah R. to Robt. V. Butner? 1-2-1872 (1-3-1872)
Wiggin, Elizabeth R. to Wesley W. Chilton 11-18-1857 (11-26-1857)
Wiggin, Rebecca F. to Jessee Megee 12-16-1841 (12-19-1841)
Wiggin, Sarah to D. J. Davis 2-24-1859 (3-8-1859)
Wiggin, Susan to Henry Gillaspie 1-11-1854 (not executed)
Wiggin, Susan to Wm. Hendon 5-3-1854 (5-4-1854)

Wiggs, Mary C. to James S. Vaughn 12-22-1858 (no return)
Wilcher, Rebecca to Wesley Davis 8-13-1845 (no return)
Wileman, C. C. to George W. Winn 2-15-1844 (2-21-1844)
Wileman, Nancy to Daniel Finch 11-24-1845 (no return)
Wileman, Rebeca to John W. Finch 2-16-1857 (no return)
Wileman, Sarah to Charles Garner 2-10-1858 (no return)
Wiley, Fannie to J. M. Castleberry 6-29-1872 (7-4-1872)
Wiley, Jane to Lewis H. Shearl 11-17-1860 (11-18-1860)
Wilhite, Betsy to Samuel King 8-8-1855 (no return)
Wilhite, Jemima to Spencer Hunt 11-26-1844
Wilhite, Sumira to David A. Little 11-13-1852 (no return)
Wilhoite, Margrett to E. D. Swann 9-20-1870
Wilkenson, Nancy S. to Samuel McBee 3-12-1857
Wilkerson, Anna J. to Wm. H. Jenkins 9-30-1868 (10-1-1868)
Wilkerson, Darcas to Elisha Garner 1-4-1870 (no return)
Wilkerson, Elizabeth E. to C. T. Morris 11-29-1865 (12-3-1865)
Wilkerson, Martha S. to James Hughes 2-23-1874 (2-26-1874)
Wilkerson, Mary E. to P. R. Curtis 10-22-1873
Wilkins, Emeline to John C. Jones 10-19-1842 (10-20-1842)
Wilkins, Peggy (Mrs.) to Samuel Butler 2-28-1861 (3-4-1861)
Wilkins, Permintha A. to John Kimsey 5-5-1858 (no return)
Wilkinson, Harriet to John Stubblefield 1-15-1849 (1-16-1849)
Wilkinson, Martha to George Henson 12-21-1845
Wilks, Mary A. to Linsfield Berryhill 1-17-1854
Willerford, Sally to Charles V. Goolsby 7-7-1838 (7-8-1838)
Willhite, Elizabeth to Captain McKelvey 8-16-1840
Willhite, Martha to George L. Camp 7-14-1842
Williams, Angeror A. to Josiah Pike 3-4-1843 (3-5-1843)
Williams, Eliza to Thomas Perry 2-16-1855 (2-18-1855)
Williams, Elizabeth to Elijah Lynch 6-2-1838
Williams, Elizabeth to Isaac Jetton 8-10-1848
Williams, Elizabeth to John King 12-4-1856 (12-5-1856)
Williams, Elvira J. to Alford W. Russey 1-15-1854
Williams, Indianna to Wm. Cowan 11-6-1867 (11-7-1867)
Williams, Jane to Norman Cates 7-27-1841
Williams, Jennie M. to James W. Cowan 2-14-1872 (no return)
Williams, Jennie to Jacob H. Vanzant 10-10-1867 (no return)
Williams, L. J. to R. H. Shepard 3-5-1861 (3-11-1861)
Williams, Louisa J. to John W. Neal 1-3-1853 (1-6-1853)
Williams, Louisa to C. G. Holder 12-23-1867 (no return)
Williams, Lucinda to Hardy Prince 9-6-1844
Williams, Lucinda to Richard Cates 2-9-1848 (2-11-1848)
Williams, M. E. to James Lewis 1-10-1874 (1-11-1874)
Williams, Maggie to J. P. Newberry 10-15-1874 (no return)
Williams, Margaret to Robt. McBee 4-29-1851
Williams, Margret J. to Thomas Grant 4-13-1871 (4-15-1871)
Williams, Martha J. to G. W. Bowers 5-9-1865 (5-11-1865)
Williams, Mary A. to Edward Ashley 8-1-1842
Williams, Mary A. to Wm. Bennett 8-9-1852 (8-11-1852)
Williams, Mary J. to Stephen B. Carter 12-31-1872
Williams, Milden to Samuel Golden 12-27-1866 (no return)
Williams, Mollie F. to J. J. Martin 7-29-1868
Williams, Nancy A. to Ruben Z. Sanders 12-31-1871 (no return)
Williams, Nancy Ann to Henry L. Smith 11-26-1872
Williams, Nancy J. to William F. Reed 1-20-1873 (1-23-1873)
Williams, Pelitha A. to Jonathan H. Davis 5-21-1840
Williams, Priscilla to Green B. Whitby 2-5-1855 (3-15-1855)
Williams, R. S. to J. L. Knight 10-24-1870 (no return)
Williams, Rebecca A. to John B. Ligret 2-2-1850 (2-6-1850)
Williams, Rebecca to Richard F. Price 1-3-1856 (no return)
Williams, Sally Ann to Stephen Lowe 4-7-1838 (4-17-1838)
Williams, Sarah A. to W. B. Mason 10-13-1869
Williams, Sarah E. to James Miller 1-10-1858 (1-13-1858)
Williams, Sarah E. to John G. Barber 1-9-1856 (1-10-1856)
Williams, Sarah E. to Leonidas Vanzant 3-18-1846
Williams, Sarah J. to Wm. M. Jetton 2-22-1849 (2-?-1849)
Williams, Sarah M. to Calvin C. Payne 2-28-1853 (3-3-1853)
Williams, Sarah to William M. Beck 9-7-1855 (9-9-1855)
Williams, Susan to Joseph Austell 3-20-1873
Williams, Susan to Joseph jr. Holder 9-27-1840 (2-27-1840?)
Williams, Susan to Ryan Caperton 2-15-1840 (no return)
Williams, Temperance P. to Stanton J. Green 10-10-1855 (10-11-1855)
Williams, Tranquilla to James Pitcock 10-11-1842 (10-13-1842)
Williamson, Cathrine to John Luck 11-8-1838
Williamson, Martha Ann to Wallace E. Walker 12-3-1846

Williamson, Sarah N. to William Jett 8-5-1846 (8-6-1846)
Williason, Elizabeth to George Swords 10-6-1846
Willis, Elizabeth to John Janes 12-14-1840 (12-?-1840)
Willis, Mary to George Litle 6-13-1868 (6-14-1868)
Willis, Susanah to William Armstrong 3-16-1842
Wilson, Bethana to Joseph Hambrick 10-22-1840 (no return)
Wilson, Charlina to Jasper Money 4-18-1868 (no return)
Wilson, Eliza to J. P. Hindman 5-31-1866 (no return)
Wilson, Elizabeth to James McDanal 6-29-1838
Wilson, Hiron to Edward Duffer 12-24-1849 (12-25-1849)
Wilson, Jennette N. to George H. Nelson 2-28-1850
Wilson, Lidia to Moses Y. Brooks 2-18-1858 (no return)
Wilson, Louisa M. to John Bradford 3-2-1850 (no return)
Wilson, Mary J. to E. P. Baker 9-2-1868 (9-3-1868)
Wilson, Mary to John Mason 11-24-1851 (11-27-1851)
Wilson, R. B. to J. S. Claborn 6-29-1874 (6-30-1874)
Wilson, Rebecca Ann to William Colton Bryant 12-30-1845
Wilson, Sallie P. to Samuel B. Rather 6-29-1874 (6-30-1874)
Wilson, Susan to James Cox 4-1-1844 (no return)
Wilson, Susan to Jas. Pitman 1-15-1866 (no return)
Wilson, Virginia to A. C. Bennett 3-2-1868 (3-3-1868)
Windsor, Margrett to William Cooper 3-19-1840 (3-18?-1840)
Winford, Elizabeth to John Anderson 1-7-1869 (no return)
Winfro, Jane E. to Jno. H.R. Bostick 9-25-1848 (9-26-1848)
Winkler, Cathrine to James Hall 6-2-1841
Winkler, Charity to Alexander Bromage 9-1-1852
Winkler, Elizabeth to Geo. W. Shelton 8-16-1846 (8-17-1846)
Winkler, Evaline to A. M. Sims 11-28-1841 (12-2-1841)
Winkler, Jane to A. M.? Tims 11-21-1855 (no return)
Winkler, Lucinda to Michael Ashley 12-7-1852 (12-8-1852)
Winn, Frances to Cammel Hill 4-16-1851 (no return)
Wiseman, Adeline to Wm. B. Parks 12-22-1852 (12-23-1852)
Wiseman, Joe to J. T. Bickley 9-28-1870
Wiseman, L. N. to R. A. Gray 5-7-1866 (5-10-1866)
Wiseman, Martha J. to Wm. D. Young 1-4-1858
Wiseman, Mary E. to Franklin Johnston 3-9-1857 (3-10-1857)
Wiseman, Mollie P. to J. L. Bruce 9-30-1868 (no return)
Wiseman, N. L. to T. E. Spencer 10-2-1865 (10-5-1865)
Wiseman, Sarah C. to Wm. A. Cashion 12-23-1871 (no return)
Wiseman, Susan to Layfayette Cone 6-13-1865 (6-15-1865)
Witt, Mary to Wm. Nuckles 3-21-1872 (3-24-1872)
Womack, Fannie to J. A. Battle 4-21-1871 (no return)
Womack, Mary to George Bennett 5-3-1851
Womack, Rebecca E. to John A. Buchanan 12-5-1872 (12-6-1872)
Wood, Elizabeth A. to Robt. Hannah 3-25-1858
Wood, Elizabeth to James Shelton 8-11-1865 (8-25-1865)
Wood, Jennie E. to Jessee E. Brown 11-5-1873
Wood, R. A. (Miss) to F. B. Wade 8-31-1867
Wood, S. A. to H. K. Posey 3-2-1868 (no return)
Wood, Sarah C. to Jessee B. Corn 11-1-1853 (11-3-1853)
Woods, Mary (Mrs.) to Jesse McDonald 1-9-1868 (1-12-1868)
Woods, Mary Ann to Edam Holder 10-28-1844
Woods, Mary E. to David L. Anderson 9-16-1867
Woods, Ruth H. to Plesant G. Turner 2-3-1845 (2-4-1845)
Woods, Susie S. to Robt. L. Hagin 10-17-1872
Woodson, Margret to Henry Linville 9-26-1848 (9-30-1848)
Woodward, Martha J. to James Kitchens 8-11-1850
Worth, Mary E. to Lorenzo Beshier 9-16-1873 (9-18-1873)
Wright, Anna B. to Lee Colton 8-6-1872 (no return)
Wright, Artemetia T. to William Holladay 2-28-1856 (no return)
Yarber, Margret to George Martin 7-23-1874 (7-26-1874)
Yarber, Matilda to Jacob Hammers 2-10-1861
Yarborough, Elizabeth to J. T. Arnold 9-22-1866 (no return)
Yarborough, Martha to John M. Robinson 9-12-1866 (no return)
Yarborough, Mary to Julius Pickeny 7-15-1871 (7-16-1871)
Yates, Delila to William Smith 12-18-1838
Yates, Jane to Hardin Williams 6-6-1842
Yates, M. J. to C. Morris 9-19-1859 (9-20-1859)
Young, America H. to Benj. W. Higginbotham 11-10-1856 (no return)
Young, Cathrine to Anthony Stuart 2-2-1871 (no return)
Young, Elizabeth A. to David A. Franklin 11-8-1849 (11-9-1849)
Young, Elizabeth to C. M. Clark 12-24-1873 (12-25-1873)
Young, Louisa A. to Daniel, jr. Champion 7-18-1842 (7-20-1842)
Young, Margret A. to Albert Price 6-23-1853
Young, Margrett to John Hill 3-5-1847 (3-7-1847)
Young, Martha E. to Benj. W. Franklin 7-2-1852 (7-4-1852)
Young, Mary J. to G. W. Faris 12-28-1864 (12-29-1864)
Young, Mary M. to Wm. E. Wedington 9-27-1860
Young, Polly A. to Isaac Cook 7-21-1842
Young, Rachiel to Jacob Head 8-11-1865 (8-22-1865)
Young, Sarah A. to B. W. Higginbotham 2-6-1858 (2-7-1858)
Young, Sarah to Benj. W. Horton 11-22-1852
Young, Susan A. to Hardy H. Smith 10-25-1841 (10-17?-1841)
Zerbee, Rebecca to H. J. Krotzer 10-14-1871 (10-15-1871)

www.ingramcontent.com/pod-product-compliance
Lightning Source LLC
Chambersburg PA
CBHW081259170426
43198CB00017B/2853